The Big Steal

The Big Steal

Ideology, Interest, and the Undoing of Intellectual Property

JONATHAN M. BARNETT

OXFORD
UNIVERSITY PRESS

Oxford University Press is a department of the University of Oxford. It furthers
the University's objective of excellence in research, scholarship, and education
by publishing worldwide. Oxford is a registered trade mark of Oxford University
Press in the UK and certain other countries.

Published in the United States of America by Oxford University Press
198 Madison Avenue, New York, NY 10016, United States of America.

CIP data is on file at the Library of Congress

ISBN 978–0–19–762952–9

DOI: 10.1093/oso/9780197629529.001.0001

Printed by Marquis Book Printing, Canada

*For my father, Alan Barnett, who taught me the
value of commitment, truth, and integrity.*

Mercantilism is a process through which rent seeking alters property rights systems in socially inefficient manners, reducing exchange, efficiency, and economic welfare. Mercantilism flowers when political institutions, formed from constitutions, permit rent-seeking redistributions of property rights.

—Robert B. Ekelund and Robert D. Tollison, Jr. (1997, 235)

Intellectuals . . . cultivate those of their ideas which find a market. Ideas without demands are simply as hard to sell as other products without demands.

—George J. Stigler (1980, 185)

Contents

Figures and Tables

Figures

Tables

Acknowledgments

This book, together with my previous book, *Innovators, Firms, and Markets: The Organizational Logic of Intellectual Property*, represents the culmination of almost two decades of research and teaching relating to intellectual property, antitrust, and innovation law and policy issues that stand at the heart of today's knowledge economy. Throughout this intellectual journey, I have benefited greatly from comments on my scholarship from colleagues at several institutions and research centers in law, economics, and business management, including (among others) the University of Southern California Gould School of Law, the Intellectual Property, Innovation, and Prosperity Working Group at the Hoover Institution at Stanford University, the Center for Innovation x Intellectual Property (formerly known as the Center for the Protection of Intellectual Property) at the Antonin Scalia Law School at George Mason University School of Law, the Dynamic Competition Initiative at the Berkeley Research Group Institute, the Classical Liberal Institute at New York University School of Law, and the International Center for Law and Economics.

I would like to thank in particular Profs. Richard Epstein, Bowman Heiden, and Adam Mossoff, who organized a workshop in spring 2023 dedicated to the book manuscript, as part of the Technology, Innovation, and Intellectual Property Program at the Classical Liberal Institute at New York University School of Law.

I am extremely grateful for comments received from several anonymous referees and support from the editorial team at Oxford University Press. I am especially indebted for assistance provided by Paul Moorman and Karen Skinner, reference librarians at the USC Gould School of Law. I also would like to thank Alina Aghakhani, Lia Barnett, Eli Levinson, Burke Peterson, Mira Pranav, Melissa Schneider, and Sophia Zahn, who were research assistants on various stages of this project.

Portions of Chapter 11 originally appeared in Jonathan M. Barnett, "Antitrust Mercantilism: The Strategic Devaluation of Intellectual Property

Rights in Wireless Markets," *Berkeley Technology Law Journal* 38 (Special Issue): 259–312 (2023).

I periodically act as a consultant and expert to various organizations and companies concerning antitrust and intellectual property law and policy. The views expressed in this book are solely my own.

Organizational Note

This book is divided into five parts. To facilitate reading, each part is preceded by an Introduction that provides an overview and each chapter ends with a "Concluding Thoughts" section that summarizes the content of the chapter.

For readers who are primarily interested in antitrust and patent law and policy in technology markets, Part II (which focuses on copyright law and policy) can be omitted. For readers who are primarily interested in antitrust and copyright policy in content markets, Part III (which focuses on patent law and policy) can be omitted. Other parts integrate legal, economic, and political-economic issues that are common to intellectual property, antitrust, and innovation policy across technology and content environments.

Note that acronyms are defined when first used in each chapter, unless widely understood. References to the "2000s" refer to the first decade of the 21st century.

Introduction

The Price of Free

Suppose billions of dollars in wealth were involuntarily transferred from one group of individuals, corporations, and other entities to another group of individuals, corporations, and other entities. In a market economy grounded in the rule of law and respect for property rights, it would be expected that this form of generalized expropriation would attract the attention of the press, arouse the ire of government authorities, and trigger dismay among the general public. This book is about just such a monumental wealth transfer that has taken place since the late 1990s and continues apace today. Yet the expected has not occurred. Rather, this mass expropriation has either not been recognized as such or, if it has been noticed, has been praised and welcomed. In fact, it would now generally be deemed primitive or uninformed to call this "theft"; rather, it is called "sharing" or, in a recent fashionable variation, "efficient infringement." Academics and activists mostly laud this involuntary transfer, and judges (including many of those who sit on the U.S. Supreme Court) and regulators widely exonerate, bless, or facilitate it.

Since the launch of the internet, some of the largest firms in the digital economy have developed business models that earn billions of dollars each year through the use of content, technology, and other informational assets that have been developed by others, sometimes at great cost and risk. Much of the time, those firms pay exactly nothing for the use of those valuable assets. It might be objected that this practice is not obviously bad for consumers. In fact, it seems obviously good. Digital aggregators obtain access to large and rich pools of content at no out-of-pocket cost, and content is then passed on to consumers at that same price of absolutely nothing. In the latest version of this content giveaway, "large language models" such as ChatGPT "vacuum" masses of online content, which are then used to generate new literary, visual, and musical works—all of which typically takes place without securing consent from the original artist or current rights holder. As these examples illustrate, the digital economy is inextricably entangled with the practice of

The Big Steal. Jonathan M. Barnett, Oxford University Press. © Oxford University Press 2024.
DOI: 10.1093/oso/9780197629529.003.0001

appropriating content and technology developed by others without negotiation, payment, or authorization. While this practice stands at odds with the fundamentals of a market economy grounded in the consensual exchange of goods and services at negotiated prices and other terms of exchange, it has become so normalized or even lauded that using the once-prevalent term "piracy" now connotes intellectual backwardness, lack of business savvy, or sheer greed.

In 2002, David Bowie (of 1980s pop star fame) astutely observed: "Music itself is going to become like running water or electricity" and added: "I'm fully confident that copyright . . . will no longer exist in 10 years, and authorship and intellectual property is [sic] in for such a bashing."[1] To a substantial extent, Bowie has been proved right on both counts. In today's digital environment, "free" has become the dominant pricing strategy for a wide variety of digital services, including general-purpose search engines, video and music file-sharing sites such as YouTube, job-search services such as Glassdoor and LinkedIn (free for job seekers), real estate search services such as Zillow and Redfin (free for buyers), and a substantial (but declining) portion of news sites. In some cases, these giveaways are voluntary: Zillow and Redfin choose to provide information on real estate properties at no fee. The same is true of Waze, a GPS-enabled traffic-navigation service offered by Google. In other cases, however, these giveaways are involuntary. When a new music video or movie trailer is uploaded and "shared" by users through YouTube, it is not the case that the record label or movie studio agreed ahead of time with YouTube on that distribution strategy. (Subsequently I discuss YouTube's more recent shift toward licensed, and other forms of consensual, content distribution.)

Yet, contrary to what Bowie may have envisioned in a utopian moment, sites such as Zillow and YouTube are not run as a public service. So if it *seems* like everything is free, then *something* must not be free somewhere else. Zillow and YouTube have to meet payroll and deliver returns to shareholders, and Waze management must report to higher-up managers at Alphabet, Google's parent company, which must ultimately report back to the capital markets.

The solution to this puzzle is neither difficult nor a secret. The answer is what economists call *cross-subsidization*. Digital platforms that rely on giveaway models almost always operate two-sided platforms in which the "free" side of the platform is indirectly funded by revenues from the "pay" side. Advertisers are willing to make payments to the platform owner in exchange for access to users of the Google search engine, the TikTok social network, or Instagram's video-sharing service. In all these cases, the giveaway firm develops the technology (or acquires it), often at great expense, and then gives it away to users, who attract paying advertisers. In a variant on this cross-subsidization model, vertically integrated information technology firms "give away" valuable services at no separate charge—for example, Microsoft's Internet Explorer browser that is integrated into its Windows operating system, or the Siri voice recognition application integrated into an Apple iPhone—by embedding it within a complex product and services system that is difficult for other firms to replicate.

Academic and policy discussion has long been dominated by what I will call loosely the "information wants to be free" school of thought. With few exceptions, a worldwide echo chamber occupied by scholars, judges, regulators, and legislators holds that intellectual property (IP) rights are often or typically a monopoly franchise that confers undeserved windfalls on overcompensated pharmaceutical firms and legacy entertainment companies. In much of the academy, it is hardly considered out of the mainstream to call for the abolition or substantial curtailment of IP rights.[2] More moderate commentators concede that IP rights may sometimes be necessary in certain industries to support innovation (usually, the exception is made for pharmaceuticals, with significant qualifications), but in all cases should be strictly circumscribed to minimize the risk of outsized gains for IP owners who can presumably set prices at will for their "essential" technology or "must have" content.

Following this perspective, "intellectual property" is a misnomer for what sophisticated observers understand to be nothing more than a regulatory dispensation that should be adjusted and, when necessary, revoked through the exercise of judges' and regulators' expert discretion. Concerning patents, seven out of the nine Justices of the Supreme Court came close to saying so in the *Oil States Energy Services v. Greene's Energy Group* decision in 2018, stating that "[p]atents convey only a specific form of property right—a public franchise" that Congress can choose to rescind by statutory provision (or by authorizing the U.S. Patent & Trademark Office to do so).[3] With a stroke of a pen, the Justices placed tens of millions of in-force patents under a cloud of insecurity, marking the culmination of a process of patent erosion the Court had set in motion with its 2006 decision in *eBay Inc. v. MercExchange LLC* to remove the nearly automatic presumption of injunctive relief for infringed patents.[4]

The "information wants to be free" school is sometimes attributed to an essay posted on the internet in 1994 by John Perry Barlow bearing that phrase[5] (which he in turn attributed to technology commentator Stewart Brand[6]). Barlow had argued that the standard assumptions behind property rights do not translate to the digital environment. Many academics and other commentators have pursued a similar line of argument that conventional copyright is a relic of the "analog" content economy that does not fit the unique characteristics of the digital environment in which informational assets can be produced, copied, and distributed at low cost and high quality. The proposed modifications to the copyright regime invariably involve substantial reductions in the protections provided to content owners against unauthorized use. This proposition that "digital is different" has been widely adopted and promoted by academics, think tanks, legislators, and other policymakers.

The "digital is different" claim (and the policy implications that IP rights have widely been rendered defunct in a wide range of circumstances) is hardly novel. It has long been argued that the standard assumptions behind property rights in tangible goods markets do not apply to intangible goods markets. In the late 19th century, large portions of European industry supported a "free trade" movement that advocated for the abolition of the patent system (or resisted the extension of the patent system) and even achieved that goal for extended periods in Switzerland (which delayed adopting a patent system until 1888) and the Netherlands (which abolished its patent system in 1869 and only revived it in 1912).[7] In 1934, economist Arnold Plant cast doubt on the necessity for copyright protection, illustrating the point by observing the apparent commercial success of British authors in the United States in the late 19th century even though they were then denied copyright protection as foreign authors.[8] That position (and the same example) was reiterated in 1970 by Stephen Breyer (then a Harvard law professor and later a Supreme Court Justice) in one of the most widely cited articles on copyright, in which he concluded that the case for copyright was "uneasy."[9] As shown by Zorina Khan, both Plant and Breyer overlooked a crucial fact in this historical episode: U.S. publishers were only able to earn profits from sales of books by British authors by entering into a cartel-like agreement in which each publisher agreed not to poach British authors from each other.[10]

But there is something else that *is* new about the 21st-century version of IP skepticism. Unlike their 19th-century forebears that sought to abolish patents entirely, IP skeptics have been exceptionally successful in achieving their policy objectives through changes to U.S. patent and copyright law, whether implemented through judicial, administrative, or legislative action. A critical factor that stands behind the success of modern IP skeptics is what I call an "accidental alliance" composed of a well-resourced business constituency that shares an interest in weakening IP rights with academics and advocacy groups that have ideological or other intellectual commitments to a strong presumption against robust forms (or, in some cases, any form) of IP protection. This unlikely convergence of interests can be illustrated by a brief history of the open-source model of software development.

In its pure form, open-source software is developed by a community of volunteers, who distribute the software code at no charge, subject only to the contractual restriction, enforced by an open-source license, that the licensed software (including modifications by subsequent users) continues to be distributed on those same terms. The model was adopted by ideologically motivated programmers who sought to develop a non-commercial alternative to for-profit software firms' "closed-source" models in which use is conditioned on payment of a fee and is governed by IP licenses that closely regulate modification, distribution, and other uses. The open-source community sought to create an alternative to the proprietary model and to preserve an open-access environment for software development as it migrated to the market from the sheltered labs of universities, government departments, and government-subsidized corporations that had dominated the post–World War II defense-oriented tech economy.

While this is well-known, what is less widely appreciated is that some of the most successful open-source programs have been extensively sponsored by leading technology firms and then incorporated by those firms into profit-seeking business models. IBM, a leading sponsor of Linux (an open-source operating system [OS] that is the basis for Google's Android OS for mobile devices), sought to promote Linux as a "free" alternative to Microsoft's Windows OS in the industrial server market. IBM's strategy rested on a cogent business strategy. Specifically, it sought to "commoditize" Microsoft's core IP asset and, by doing so, shift the locus of competition in the server market to the hardware segment in which IBM enjoyed a comparative advantage. This commoditization strategy, which is a critical component of giveaway business models in much of the digital economy, can explain why most leading platform-based technology companies have advocated for weaker IP rights in patent and copyright law. This is simply a business strategy to achieve commoditization by the force of law.

The public debate over IP policy, which has translated into decisions by courts and policy actions by regulators and legislators, has largely fallen prey to an intellectual illusion in which the private interests of companies that rely on a particular business model and the normative positions expressed by certain scholars, commentators, and advocacy organizations *appear* to converge with the amorphously defined "public interest." The rhetoric deployed by these constituencies is directed toward conveying this message. It has worked. For end-users, it must have seemed intuitively appealing to support tech companies' and advocacy organizations' calls to "save the internet" in response to proposed congressional legislation in 2012 that would have bolstered protections for copyright owners and therefore potentially increased users' costs of accessing content online. In response to the resulting public outcry, the legislation was hastily withdrawn. The content industry argued that it lacked any effective legal deterrent against the mass uncompensated usage facilitated by leading digital platforms. This line of argument was widely dismissed by many scholars and thought leaders as nothing but a ruse to recover the purported monopoly franchise that the record labels and studio moguls had lost once the internet "democratized" access to content.[11]

What many observers did not seem to appreciate is that a weak-IP environment may simply advantage leading platforms that specialize in the organization and distribution of the otherwise unstructured mass of informational assets that proliferate in digital environments.[12] For Google's search engine, YouTube's video streaming site, and Facebook's newsfeed, content is an input that is required to attract users and, in turn, advertisers. The platform intermediary rationally seeks to minimize its input costs and pursues that objective by adopting an advocacy strategy designed to weaken IP protections, which lowers the price (often to zero) of acquiring the content that is necessary to attract platform users and advertisers. Policymakers and like-minded academics and advocacy entities pursue this same objective on the publicly interested grounds of expanding access to content and other informational assets—hence the close alignment of interests between privately and (ostensibly) publicly motivated proponents of weak IP regimes.

The same commoditization-by-law strategy in content markets—including the same confluence of business and ideological interests—can account for the campaign mounted by some of the country's leading information technology firms, and large financial services firms, against the robust enforcement of patents in technology markets. While companies such as Google, Apple, Intel, and others are innovation leaders, it is often not appreciated that they tend to occupy "mid-stream" positions in the technology supply chain and, as such, are often intermediate users that assemble and integrate technological inputs supplied by more narrowly specialized and R&D-intensive firms.

This point can be illustrated by looking at differences in R&D intensity, which is the percentage of a firm's revenues that it spends on R&D activities, among firms in the smartphone ecosystem. In general, during 2000–2020 (or starting in the earliest and ending in the latest year for which data were available during that period), firms that were principally situated further down the smartphone supply chain exhibited lower average R&D intensity as compared to firms that principally operated in the upstream portions of the supply chain. Arm, which designs and licenses the chip architecture used by almost all chip-design firms in the smartphone industry, invested on average 27.5% of its annual revenues in R&D. Qualcomm, an upstream firm that focuses on developing chip designs for use in smartphones and other electronic devices, invested on average 20% of its annual revenues in R&D. By contrast, during the same period, hardware producers such as Samsung, LG, and Xiaomi invested on average 6.1%, 4.5%, and 3.1%, respectively, of annual revenues in R&D activities. Diversified providers of hardware and software products, such as Intel, Alphabet, and Apple, invested on average 16.9%, 14.6% and 4.5%, respectively, of annual revenues in R&D during this same period.[13]

This division of labor among innovators and implementers along the technology supply chain dictates a firm's bargaining objectives in negotiations over the terms of use of IP-protected assets. Apple, Samsung, Xiaomi, and other customer-facing device producers naturally have an interest in minimizing the patent royalties that they must pay to R&D suppliers that stand at the top of the technology supply chain. This objective can be pursued both through "business-level" negotiation of the terms of the patent license—as in any supplier-producer relationship—and "policy-level" advocacy and litigation efforts to limit the strength of patents and other forms of IP protection. These two efforts are interrelated. As actual and prospective licensees' policy-level advocacy weakens IP protections, they gain leverage in business-level negotiations over licensing terms, effectively resulting in a transfer of wealth from upstream R&D-focused firms to downstream customer-facing firms. Just as Google's YouTube subsidiary has an interest in commoditizing content to reduce its input costs, so too Apple has an interest in commoditizing the building blocks of wireless communications, which it integrates into the iPhone while making a limited contribution to the development of those building blocks. In both cases, a successful commoditization strategy implemented by a leading platform lowers the platform's input costs and shifts the locus of competition to a point on the supply chain in which it enjoys a comparative advantage.

Now it could be the case that "what is good for Google, Apple, and Intel is good for America" (to paraphrase a slogan about General Electric in a pre-digital world). I take this possibility seriously but find that, at least concerning these companies' approach toward IP policy, it rests on a less than compelling basis. In the short term, it is true that weakening IP protections reduces the commoditizing firm's input costs, an effect that may redound in part to the benefit of the consumer in the form of lower prices (depending on competitive conditions in the end-user market). However, the consumer may be (and, I argue, is likely to be) worse off over the medium to long term. Over that more relevant policy horizon, the IP policy objectives pursued by midstream and downstream technology firms and, in the creative markets, content aggregators, search engines and similar distribution platforms, are likely to depart from the public interest (and even the platforms' *own* long-term interest) in maintaining a robust creative and technology ecosystem.

Any well-functioning innovation economy must achieve a reasonable balance between, on the one hand, the interests of intermediate and end-users in minimizing the costs of accessing content, technology, or other informational assets, and on the other hand, the interests of innovators and other upstream firms in earning a positive return on the costs and risks incurred to originate and commercialize new content or technology assets. Widespread commoditization of IP assets is not consistent with the public interest in a robust innovation economy that maximizes the size of the "economic pie" over time through continuous investments in high-risk innovation (which must be protected against low-risk imitators who can "cherry pick" from the minority of innovation projects that succeed), rather than simply reducing the costs of consuming a "slice" from the pie in its current size. The current policy consensus has put a heavy weight on the scale in favor of the immediate interest in reducing the cost of accessing *currently available* technology and content over the future interest in sustaining a continuous stream of *new* technologies and content. While this is a politically attractive position for policymakers, who can appeal to individuals' and business users' short-term interest in "free stuff," it may—and in some industries almost certainly— disserves the long-term interest of any constituency other than aggregator firms that thrive under weak-IP conditions in which technology and content input costs are reduced to a bare minimum. Even the aggregator is likely to lose out over the long term once incentives to support investment in the production of new technology or content assets wither under a legal regime that facilitates unauthorized usage.

In a famous contribution, Robert Solow estimated that 87.5% of U.S. economic growth between 1909 and 1949 could not be explained by capital and labor inputs and therefore represented advances in technological and scientific knowledge as implemented through the development of new products and services.[14] The social gains from incentivizing the production of new content and technologies almost certainly outweigh by a considerable measure the social gains from reducing the price of accessing existing content and technologies. Over anything other than the immediate short term, the world is better off by having replaced the kerosene lamp with electric lighting, rather than simply reducing the price of kerosene lamps. The current IP policy trajectory toward increasingly weaker IP rights risks giving us a cheaper kerosene lamp, but no electric lighting. That may be a good deal for the lamp maker and its existing customers, but it will be a bad deal for just about everyone else.

PART I

CONCEPTS AND BACKGROUND

Intellectual property law has been the subject of an intensive debate among scholars and policymakers concerning the appropriate level of protection that the state should provide for new technologies (principally, through patent law) and original content (principally, through copyright law). Both sides of that debate have principally engaged in what might be called an "idealized" analysis concerning the level of protection that best advances the public interest. As set forth in this Part I, this book adopts a different methodology. Rather than inquiring in the abstract concerning the preferred level of IP protection, this book assesses the confluence of ideological and economic interests that can account for policy actions by courts, regulators, and legislators that impact the strength of IP protection. This political-economy approach ultimately can yield normative insights into whether those policy actions promote the public interest in a robust innovation ecosystem.

1

Making and Unmaking Intellectual Property Rights

This book is about how intellectual property (IP) law has changed dramatically in a relatively short period of time and how it has changed in a manner that has specifically advantaged the interests of firms that operate under a particular business model. This argument requires a conceptual framework for analyzing how a given body of law can change over time in response to the interests of private constituencies. Relying primarily on the tools and concepts of public choice economics,[1] I assemble this framework in two steps. First, I present a general theory of legal change in which privately interested constituencies make investments to influence the actions undertaken by policymakers. I then apply this general theory to the specific institutional context in which IP law is continuously being "made," "unmade," and "re-made."

1.1. A Theory of Legal Change

Generally speaking, any particular change in a relevant body of law is most likely to occur when the following conditions are satisfied: (1) interested parties make substantial investments in influencing policymakers to make the change, and (2) the change tracks what policymakers perceive to be what I will call the "dominant preference"[2] of their constituencies. I will assume for the moment that the policymaker determines the dominant preference by assessing the majoritarian preference of the policymaker's constituencies, reflecting preferences as communicated through verbal advocacy and financial contributions, and weighted roughly by the popularity and intensity of those preferences. I will also assume that a policymaker has no ideological or other personal preference concerning a particular legal change, but rather seeks to accrue political goodwill by tracking the perceived dominant policy preference. Even if policymakers do have an ideological or other policy

The Big Steal. Jonathan M. Barnett, Oxford University Press. © Oxford University Press 2024.
DOI: 10.1093/oso/9780197629529.003.0002

preference in certain cases (which I address subsequently when relevant), it is likely that they would still take into account information concerning the perceived dominant policy preference, which may bolster, attenuate, or, if sufficiently intense, override the policymaker's personal policy preference.

Figure 1.1 depicts this framework for understanding legal change. The vertical axis reflects the monetary and non-monetary "influence expenditures" by interested constituencies to express policy preferences and influence the policymaker's actions concerning a particular legal change. The horizontal axis reflects the "intellectual distance" between that particular legal change and the perceived dominant policy preference. As shown in Figure 1.1, line *a* indicates a high likelihood of legal change because the interested constituency is making large influence expenditures and the legal change is close to the dominant policy preference. By contrast, line *c* indicates a low likelihood of legal change because the interested party is making meager influence expenditures and the legal change is distant from the dominant policy preference. Line *b* denotes a legal change with a moderate likelihood of being realized.

Specific examples can make this framework more concrete. Consider a particular constituency that feels strongly about, and therefore invests substantial resources in advocating for, the revival of mandatory military service for male U.S. citizens at age 18. This potential legal change most likely has little chance of succeeding. Even if the interested constituency makes a large investment in political influence, it is unlikely that this legal change would be consistent with the dominant policy preference of a policymaker's relevant constituencies. This scenario corresponds to the region located somewhere between lines *a* and *b* in Figure 1.1: while the interested constituency makes substantial expenditures, the distance between the proposed legal

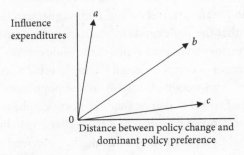

Figure 1.1 Likelihood of legal change.

change and the dominant policy preference is large, yielding a low likelihood of success. Conversely, consider a particular constituency that feels strongly about, and therefore invests substantial resources in advocating for, a tax reduction for middle-income households. This potential legal change has a reasonable chance of succeeding. The interested constituency has made a large investment in political influence and, given that the beneficiaries of this change most likely reflect a significant if not predominant portion of the policymaker's constituency, the proposed change is likely consistent with what the policymaker perceives to be the dominant policy preference of the constituency taken as a whole. This scenario lies somewhere in the region between lines *b* and *c* in Figure 1.1: the interested constituency has made a large influence investment and there may not be a significant distance between the proposed policy change and the dominant policy preference.

1.2. The Consensus: The Imbalance of Power in IP Politics

To enrich this basic model of legal change, we can consider a more complex scenario in which the policymaker does not ascertain a clearly dominant policy preference among the policymaker's constituency taken as a whole.

This may arise because the policymaker's constituency, or large portions of the policymaker's constituency, is indifferent, only holds a weak policy preference (or holds multiple weak policy preferences), or suffers from a collective action problem in which no single individual, firm, or other entity has a sufficient incentive to invest the time and resources required to effectively communicate a particular policy preference. When there is no clearly dominant policy preference, the policymaker is likely to be swayed by influence expenditures made by discrete constituencies that have especially strong preferences concerning a particular policy change. In a well-known result, political scientists have observed that a small and concentrated group with strongly held preferences can exert a powerful influence over political outcomes, as compared to larger but dispersed groups.[3] Smaller groups have a higher expectation of being able to internalize the gains from making influence investments and therefore are more willing to invest time and resources to secure a particular legal change. Moreover, all other constituencies may be uninformed or indifferent, or only have weak policy preferences, and, as a result, the policymaker observes few other opposing views. In the game for political influence, small size, when combined with sufficient resources and strong preferences, can be a potent force for implementing a particular policy change (especially if the policymaker has no ideological predisposition concerning any such change or has an ideological predisposition that is sympathetic to it).

This well-known insight from political science is consistent with a mainstay of legal academic scholarship, and much popular commentary, on IP policy. Following that conventional view, it is believed that the IP system is captured by "Big Business," which satisfies the small-number, strong-preferences, and sufficient-resource conditions that political science anticipates would enhance a small constituency's ability to exert disproportionate influence over policy outcomes. As a result, it is commonly argued that IP systems are predisposed to provide excessively strong levels of IP protection that operate against the interests of the more numerous pool of individual users.

This line of argument is predicated on the intuitive assumption that large firms generally seek stronger IP rights to acquire or preserve pricing power by erecting entry barriers against imitative competitors. By contrast, it is assumed that individual users favor weaker IP rights to minimize consumption costs but have little political influence because they do not satisfy the small-numbers and sufficient-resource conditions that can mitigate the collective-action problem, although they may sometimes have strong policy preferences (especially concerning copyright protections over content and patent protections over pharmaceuticals). If those assumptions about the inherent imbalance of political influence over IP policy between large corporations and individual users are correct, then it naturally follows that the IP system, and in particular the policymakers that "make" IP law through legislative, judicial, and regulatory actions, are predisposed to deliver an excessive level of IP protection that confers advantages on content and technology firms beyond what is required to sustain those firms' innovation incentives.

1.3. Revisiting the Imbalance of Power in IP Politics

Given these widely held assumptions concerning the imbalance of political influence over IP policymaking, it is unsurprising that arguments in favor of robust IP rights are often characterized as merely advancing the profit-seeking objectives of large media and technology firms (in the copy-right context) or large pharmaceutical firms (in the patent context). Yet those assumptions often tend to be incorrect when examining real-world innovation markets. The balance of political influence is often skewed to deliver a *weak* level of IP protection that favors the business interests of firms that specialize in aggregating and assembling content and technology inputs, at the expense of firms that specialize in producing and supplying those inputs. Relatedly, other firms principally monetize innovation through an integrated product and services ecosystem that is difficult to imitate and, as a result, have little demand for patent protection and may oppose it to reduce their litigation exposure or to disadvantage stand-alone innovators that often rely on patent protection to secure positive returns. Aggregation intermediaries in digital-content markets and large integrated firms in information-technology markets can therefore acquire a competitive advantage by weakening IP rights and, as will be discussed in detail, often have the incentives and resources to make influence investments that can increase significantly the likelihood of that policy outcome. This preference for weak IP protection exhibited by some of the largest firms in the digital economy casts doubt on the widely held view that strong IP rights necessarily shield incumbents from competitive entry; rather, it suggests that precisely the opposite is sometimes the case.

1.3.1. Technology Markets: Large Firms Usually Like Weak Patents

In technology markets, it is not the case that incumbents, or businesses in general, have uniformly lobbied for strong levels of patent protection. In the patent system, roughly the opposite is the case for industries other than pharmaceuticals. The history of U.S. technology markets provides repeated examples in which large firms have lobbied against strong patent protection or against the extension of patent protection to new technologies. For example, railroad companies in the late 19th century lobbied for a change in the judicial calculation of damages in patent infringement suits to reduce exposure to suits brought by individual inventors and other entities that were disparaged as patent "speculators" (akin to today's claims made by many large technology firms that broadly characterize entire categories of patent owners as "patent trolls").[4] Similarly, in the 1960s and 1970s, IBM, then the world's leading computing company, along with other computer hardware manufacturers, advocated against the extension of any form of IP protection (patent, copyright or *sui generis* forms) to software.[5]

The same pattern is apparent in today's ongoing process of "patent reform" in Congress and the courts, which resulted in the America Invents Act in 2011 and an almost uninterrupted string of patentee-unfriendly Supreme Court decisions since approximately 2006. Among other steps, those decisions have limited significantly the range of patentable subject matter and the circumstances in which injunctive relief is available even in the case of valid and infringed patents.[6] Most large information-technology firms (with the exception of certain segments of the hardware and semiconductor industries) and almost all large financial services firms have generally advocated (directly or, more commonly, through trade associations) for changes by Congress and the Supreme Court that have weakened patent protections. By contrast, the biopharmaceutical industry, venture capital funds (which back start-ups and other emerging firms), and research universities (which rely on patents to monetize research through licensing and sale transactions) almost always back the patent owner's interest in a secure form of legal exclusivity.

The prevailing preferences among large technology platforms for weak patent protections derive logically from the business strategies they use to acquire or develop technology inputs. As a general matter, IP-skeptical firms tend to use business models in which technology inputs are mostly obtained through transactions with outside suppliers or are developed internally but monetized through a capital-intensive production and distribution infrastructure. Under either model, the firm is indifferent to, or has a strategic interest against, strong IP protections. For example, the 19th-century railroads embedded technological innovations in integrated and capital-intensive transportation systems and then monetized those innovations indirectly by offering improved services to passenger and freight customers. Whether acquired unilaterally by imitation or through a negotiated license, strong patent protection inflated the price (either the market-negotiated royalty or judicially determined damages) that the railroad, as a net technology consumer, would expect to pay external innovators, while exposing it to the prospect of nuisance litigation. Similarly, IBM in the 1950s and 1960s sold end-to-end bundled computing packages in which internally developed software was bundled with hardware components, rather than being priced as a separate stand-alone product. Like the railroads, a combination of technical and capital entry requirements protected IBM and other integrated hardware manufacturers against competitive threats posed by firms that specialized solely in the software components of the computing systems bundle. By contrast, the smaller population of technology firms that tend to prefer stronger patent protections often operate under vertically disintegrated models in which the firm invests heavily in research and development (R&D) and extracts value through licensing arrangements with hardware manufacturers or, in the case of independent software developers, through direct sales to business or home users.

The exception to this inverse relationship between organizational integration and the "demand for IP" is the biopharmaceutical industry, which almost universally supports strong forms of patent protection. This can be explained by the fact that a biopharmaceutical firm faces an exceptionally large gap between innovation, testing, and commercialization costs on the one hand (estimated to exceed $2.5 billion on average in the case of a new drug, taking into account the costs of failed projects[7]), and imitation costs borne by competitors on the other hand. As a result, even large, vertically integrated incumbents generally cannot adequately monetize R&D investments without secure IP protection against imitation by second-movers. However, even in that case, it should be noted that patents are especially critical for smaller biotechnology firms that often partner with a large "Big Pharma" firm to execute the capital-intensive testing, production, and distribution functions required to reach market. A classic example is the partnership between BioNTech, a small firm founded by two academic scientists and backed by venture-capital investors, and Pfizer, a large pharmaceutical firm, which together succeeded in testing, producing, and distributing a COVID-19 vaccine on a mass scale and in an accelerated time frame. Without patents, a biotech startup such as BioNTech would likely have been unable to attract venture-capital investors, could not have comfortably shared information with its large-firm partners, and its scientist-founders may have elected to remain in academia or to pursue careers as salaried researchers at a large pharmaceutical firm. (In Chapter 14, this example will be discussed in further detail.)

1.3.2. Content Markets: A Shift in the IP Balance of Power

Conventional assumptions concerning the imbalance of political influence in IP-intensive markets have historically been realized to a substantial extent in content markets. Media and entertainment companies have a self-evident interest in maximizing the ability to use legal tools to preclude unauthorized imitation and, in that respect, are in the same position as a pharmaceutical firm that requires a secure barrier against unauthorized imitation. This explains why content producers have consistently and (mostly) successfully lobbied for legislative or judicial extensions of the copyright laws in response to each new technological medium for copying and transmitting content. In 1865, copyright was extended to photographs; in 1897, it was extended to the public performance of musical compositions (approximately coinciding with the emergence of the radio industry); in 1909, it was extended to "mechanical" reproductions of musical compositions (in response to the invention of "piano rolls" for player pianos); and in 1912, it was extended to motion pictures.[8] The belated extension of federal copyright protection to sound recordings in 1972[9] was likely due to the natural technological barrier created by the high costs of copying physical records on a mass scale prior to the invention of the cassette tape.

This consistent preference for strong IP protection reflects the business models that have predominated in the content and entertainment industries. Production and distribution entities in these markets almost always rely on the direct delivery of content to consumers or, in the case of independent production companies, to movie studios or television networks (and now licensed streaming services) that specialize in the financing and distribution of content. Additionally, most content assets are stand-alone products that can often be copied at a relatively low cost, as distinguished from technological assets that are sometimes difficult to reverse-engineer and may lack utility unless integrated into a larger product system.

Consistent with standard expectations in political science, the content industry has been well situated to secure extensions of copyright because the largest firms have been relatively few in number and can therefore internalize much of the gains from investments in political influence. Hence the extension by Congress in 1998 of the copyright term[10] is often derided as the "Mickey Mouse Term Extension Act" (a play on the actual title, the "Sonny Bono Copyright Term Extension Act"), purportedly reflecting the lobbying power of the Disney corporate group and other large media companies. (This popular account is incomplete since there was a concurrent interest in matching the length of the term in foreign copyright laws.) In contrast, viewers, readers, and listeners of creative content have at least a short-term interest in weaker or no IP protections but, as a large and dispersed group, each individual member lacks sufficient incentives to contribute resources toward securing that legal outcome and therefore is likely to exert little influence over the policymaking process. In this context, there is credible support for the conventional view that the lawmaking process may push IP rights (specifically, copyright) toward a level of protection that is "too strong" relative to the socially efficient level that would be set by a benevolent and perfectly informed policymaker.

Standard scholarly and other commentary has assumed that this historical imbalance of power over the strength and direction of IP rights has persisted in the digital environment. Hence, with few exceptions,[11] academic and other commentary on copyright policy in the digital context has tended to characterize any extension of copyright protections, whether through legislative or judicial action, as evidence of the continued disproportionate political influence wielded by content owners, often known in this context as "Big Media"[12] (although the term seems to have fallen into disuse since "Big Media" is not especially big compared to the "Big Tech" platforms that now predominate in digital-content distribution). This position reflects the view that copyright protection is at best a tolerated evil that is necessary to provide the minimal reward required to elicit artistic production (as distinguished from the view that copyright is a legal tool that enables the market pricing of creative assets, which then efficiently directs the allocation of resources to creative projects). From this perspective, it follows that any form of advocacy to bolster copyright protections in the face of mass infringement is presumptively characterized as a thinly disguised rent-seeking effort to perpetuate the dominant position that had been enjoyed by large motion picture studios, television networks, and record labels in the pre-digital creative economy.

As I will discuss in greater detail in Chapter 3, assertions that the balance of political influence over IP (and, in particular, copyright) laws strongly favors content producers is a grossly inaccurate characterization of the political economy of content markets since the adoption of digital file-sharing technologies in the late 1990s and certainly by the following decade. By that time, major search engines and digital-content aggregators had established large global businesses and had acquired the resources to exert influence over the process of "remaking" copyright law, largely pushing aside the views expressed by the content industries.

This shift in the balance of political influence over copyright law from "Content" to "Tech" arose for two reasons.

First, although individual users continued to lack individually rational incentives to contribute toward advocacy efforts (and therefore suffered from the collective-action problem that afflicts large but dispersed groups in the competition for political influence), they could effectively "vote with their feet" (or more exactly, with their "clicks") by declining to respect the IP rights of content producers and owners. Even novice users can easily access, copy, and distribute proprietary content in a digital environment and, given the low likelihood of detection and enforcement, the expected legal penalty for doing so is nominal. Technological changes in copying and transmitting content assets, which enabled individual users to infringe at little cost and with almost complete impunity, reduced dramatically the practically effective level of IP protections. The devaluation of legal protections against unauthorized usage in turn depressed the value of IP-protected content by forcing content owners to compete against a shadow zero price in the unlicensed (or "pirate") content market.

Second, digital markets rely on aggregation intermediaries that deploy business models in which content assets represent an input that must be secured to attract users, which in turn enables the aggregator to earn revenue through the sale of advertising services to businesses. Aggregators and similar entities do not generally invest in content origination (although, as will be discussed in Chapter 16, some aggregation entities have more recently invested in content production or acquisition to replenish the creative "pipeline") and earn revenues by distributing all or portions of others' content to users (or enabling users to do so through "sharing" technologies) at a zero fee and then monetizing the user base through ad sales to businesses. Critically, this means that aggregator firms, unlike traditional media and entertainment companies, are net content users that have an interest in reducing content-acquisition costs.

This objective can be pursued through two avenues: (1) negotiating with content owners to secure a license on acceptable terms, or (2) forgoing a license, encouraging users to distribute content irrespective of content protection, and investing in advocacy and litigation efforts to minimize legal exclusivity for content assets. To the extent strategy (2) is successful, IP protections for content assets decline in force, content owners' litigation threats lose credibility, and the aggregator can act as if IP protections had been effectively waived or curtailed substantially. For a content aggregator, reducing or destroying the value of IP assets makes good business sense (at least in the short term): the aggregator reduces its content-acquisition costs to zero and maximizes its expected profit margin on revenues from advertisers.

The emergence of commercially viable "IP giveaway" business models in digitized content markets, combined with the enforcement challenges inherent to online environments, fundamentally altered the balance of political influence in copyright-governed markets. Content aggregators meet both conditions for a high level of influence over policy outcomes: they are relatively small in number (at least the handful that lead in digital-content-distribution markets) and are endowed with abundant resources to support advocacy efforts, sustain protracted litigation, and promote policy actions to weaken copyright protections. Critically, content aggregators pursued a policy objective that was almost certainly preferred by a majority of policymakers' constituents, who naturally welcomed paying nothing for content assets that had formerly only been accessible at a significant price. This is a powerful political coalition given that either measure of the perceived dominant policy preference (the majoritarian preference of the policymaker's constituencies or, if that dominant preference is not sufficiently clear, the preference expressed by an intensively interested discrete constituency) directs the policymaker to accrue political goodwill by favoring weaker IP rights.

Content owners have fewer advocacy and litigation resources as compared to the largest digital-aggregation platforms and pursue an objective that probably diverges from the preferred policy outcome of most of the policymaker's constituents. As a result, content owners' efforts to influence the trajectory of copyright law have been outmatched by the lobbying and advocacy efforts of content aggregators, the thought leadership of similarly minded scholars and other commentators, and the close alignment of aggregators' policy preferences with those of individual users (at least in the short term). Absent a strong ideological preference to the contrary, a rational policymaker has little incentive to support (and every reason to resist) the copyright policy preferences of content firms that operate under conventional content-delivery models.

This shift in the balance of political influence over IP policy in content markets was most vividly illustrated by content owners' attempt in late 2011 and early 2012 to lobby Congress to pass legislation to bolster copyright protections against online infringement. The legislation was known by the acronyms SOPA (Stop Online Piracy Act), for the bill in the House of Representatives,[13] and PIPA (PROTECT IP Act), for the companion bill in the Senate.[14] These bills would have provided prosecutors and content owners with expanded legal remedies to shut down "pirate" websites by securing court orders prohibiting search engines, payment networks, and advertising services from engaging with those sites. Nonetheless, as I discuss subsequently in Chapter 3, the bills were soundly defeated by a combination of lobbying by digital intermediaries, trade associations representing various segments of the technology industry, IP policy organizations, and grassroots users' protests. On January 20, 2012, Senate Majority Leader Harry Reid announced that the vote on PIPA was being postponed, and Chairman Lamar Smith of the House Judiciary Committee made a similar announcement concerning the SOPA bill.[15]

The rapid defeat of the PIPA and SOPA bills, supported by industry lobbying and vigorous expressions of popular support, illustrates the shift in the balance of influence over IP policy in digital-content markets, where the advocacy efforts of content aggregators have mostly prevailed over the advocacy efforts of content originators and owners. In general, individual users (who either naturally like "free stuff" or are ideologically sympathetic to the "information wants to be free" school of thought) appear to have largely supported this outcome, along with the scholars, policy commentators, and advocacy organizations that advocated for the now-consensus position favoring weak copyright protections in digital-content markets.

1.3.3. Technology Markets (Again): The Imbalance of Power Re-Emerges

The enactment of the Bayh-Dole Act in 1980,[16] the establishment of the Court of Appeals for the Federal Circuit in 1982,[17] and the case law developed by the Federal Circuit in the years after its establishment together put in place a regime of historically strong patent protection. This stood in contrast to a largely overlooked period, from the late 1930s through the 1970s, characterized by several decades of weak patent protection.[18] This reinvigorated foundation of patent protection has supported innovation and commercialization activities undertaken through various business models in different industries. This group includes large integrated firms in the pharmaceutical industry that maintain end-to-end innovation, production, and distribution pipelines, as well as smaller firms in biotechnology and information-technology markets that specialize in R&D and then monetize that investment through licensing, joint ventures, or other transactions with downstream firms. Similarly, the technology transfer divisions of academic research universities have relied on this increase in the strength of patent protection and almost certainly would not be commercially viable without it.

In contrast, most large firms in the information technology and financial services industries have supported a long-running advocacy campaign, targeted at the Supreme Court and Congress, to roll back some or all of the changes that had bolstered patent protections. Here, too, policy preferences reflect business models. With some exceptions, large information-technology firms and, in particular, online platforms are typically net users of technology inputs or invest significantly in R&D but monetize that investment through a vertically integrated production and distribution infrastructure or a horizontally integrated "systems" infrastructure. This group encompasses firms such as Sony, which invests a relatively moderate amount in R&D (6.13% mean annual R&D intensity during 2000–2020), Intel, which invests significantly in R&D (16.9% mean annual R&D intensity during 2000–2020) and maintains a vertically integrated organizational structure, and Alphabet, which similarly invests substantially in R&D (14.6% mean annual R&D intensity during 2004–2020) and maintains a systems-integrated organizational structure.[19] (R&D intensity is calculated by dividing total sales by total R&D expenditures in any given year.) All these firms operate under business models in which robust IP protection is not a necessary condition for economic success and, to the extent robust IP rights facilitate entry by potential competitors, may detract from it.

When a firm is sufficiently large, or a group of firms is sufficiently large, it then becomes rational to invest resources in changing the "rules of the game" that govern the relevant market. Consistent with these expectations, IP-skeptical firms in the information-technology markets—which include some of the world's largest companies by market capitalization—invested considerable efforts in seeking to weaken patent protections. Acting individually or through trade associations or other collective entities, various members of the information-technology industry have undertaken or supported lobbying, advocacy, and litigation efforts to undo the changes that followed the establishment of the Federal Circuit and to shift the patent system toward a weaker level of protection along several key parameters.

These IP-skeptical firms in the information-technology sector typically exhibit at least two of the three characteristics that support a high likelihood of securing a preferred policy objective. They are relatively small in number and have ample resources to fund advocacy efforts. It is not immediately obvious, however, how a policymaker would assess whether the preference for weak patent protections among large integrated-technology firms aligns with the dominant policy preference of the policymaker's constituencies. This uncertainty derives from the fact that, outside pharmaceuticals, patent protection is most likely not an especially salient policy issue for most individual constituents. Under this state of uncertainty, the policymaker can still accrue political goodwill by satisfying the policy preferences for weaker patent protection intensely expressed by a discrete constituency. Firms and other entities that prefer stronger patent protection—typically, entities that invest heavily in R&D, have few or no production and distribution capacities, and monetize R&D investments principally through licensing relationships with external partners—are often smaller in size and cannot match the advocacy resources of large digital intermediaries and other tech firms that operate under vertically or systems-integrated business models in which IP assets are monetized within a difficult-to-replicate production and distribution infrastructure.

Table 1.1 shows the market capitalization and lobbying expenditures of some of the largest firms in the information-technology sector that consistently exhibit strong-patent or weak-patent policy preferences, respectively. Patent policy preferences are based on firms' revealed preferences in amicus briefs before the Supreme Court (discussed in Chapter 2 in more detail), petitions to challenge patents through the Patent Trial & Appeals Board (PTAB), and other relevant information. The weak-patent group comprises firms that tend to have larger market capitalizations, use vertically or systems-integrated business models, and make greater lobbying expenditures, as compared to the strong-patent group, which comprises information-technology firms that tend to have lower market capitalizations, use an innovation-focused and licensing-based business model, and make smaller lobbying expenditures.

As can also be observed in Table 1.1, the biopharmaceutical industry (which encompasses both large integrated and smaller unintegrated firms) does have substantial resources to mount a significant advocacy campaign and is sufficiently concentrated to mitigate collective-action obstacles to investments in group advocacy efforts. However, the industry still has fewer resources as compared to the largest information-technology firms that favor weaker IP protections and, most importantly, advocates a policy position that is almost certainly distant from the majoritarian preferences of policymakers' constituencies. While a policymaker's individual constituents

Table 1.1 Lobbying Expenditures and Patent Policy Preferences of Selected Technology Firms

Firm; Market Capitalization	Industry	Principal Business Model	Dominant Patent Policy Preference	Ranking among PTAB Petitioners (2021)	General Lobbying Expenditures (2022, Federal Only)
Apple ($2.39T)	ICT	Integrated (systems)	Weak	2	$9.4M
Microsoft ($1.9T)	ICT	Integrated (systems)	Weak	6	$10.5M
Alphabet ($1.18T)	ICT	Integrated (systems)	Weak	3	$13.2M
Samsung ($263.9B)	ICT	Integrated (vertical)	Weak	1	$5.8M
Cisco ($199.9B)	ICT	Integrated (vertical)	Weak	17	$2.9M
Intel ($109.4B)	ICT	Integrated (vertical)	Weak	4	$7.1M
Qualcomm ($130.9B)	ICT	Innovation/ licensing	Strong	n/a	$9.3M
Nokia ($25.5B)	ICT	Innovation/ licensing	Strong	n/a	$.9M
Ericsson ($18.9B)	ICT	Innovation/ licensing	Strong	n/a	$1.5M
Eli Lilly ($300.9B)	Pharma	Integrated (vertical)	Strong	n/a	$7.5M
Novo Nordisk ($250B)	Pharma	Integrated (vertical)	Strong	n/a	$5.2M
Pfizer ($220.4B)	Pharma	Integrated (vertical)	Strong	n/a	$14.8M

ICT = information and communications technology.

Notes: Market capitalization represents average of market capitalization for each firm on all trading days during 2022. Patent policy preferences based on preferences expressed through Supreme Court amicus briefs, ranking among PTAB petitioners, and other information.

Sources: Information on lobbying expenditures: Open Secrets, https://www.opensecrets.org. Information on PTAB petitions: Wingrove 2022.

may not have strongly held views concerning the patent system in general, they are likely to have views that disfavor strong patent protections for pharmaceuticals, given the anticipated effect on drug prices, and that same view would be shared and conveyed by insurers, hospitals, and government entities that are large-volume purchasers and satisfy the small-numbers and sufficient-resource characteristics that translate into political influence.[20] Outside the case of a policymaker who holds a strong personal policy preference concerning the value of patents for biopharmaceutical innovation over the longer term or who represents a geographic region with a strong pharmaceutical industry, most policymakers are unlikely to be willing to deplete political goodwill by supporting a policy position for which there is little popular support.

1.4. Closing Thoughts

The shift in political influence in both the technology and content markets has resulted in a systematic weakening of IP protections for the owners of technology and content assets. These legal changes imply an across-the-board devaluation of IP-protected assets in industries impacted by these changes. Among a large portion of the scholarly and advocacy communities, this outcome has been widely portrayed as a laudable change that has protected the interests of individual users in lower access costs while restraining the pricing power attributed to IP owners. For the most part, policymakers—including legislators, regulators, and judges—have embraced this view. This is unsurprising. At least in the case of policymakers who occupy elected positions, there are likely few policymakers who would be willing to risk political goodwill by arguing against weakening IP protections over pharmaceuticals to preserve the integrity of the patent system or campaigning to shut down Google Books to protect the viability of the copyright system. In either case, the policymaker would sacrifice political goodwill by adopting these positions (although certain policymakers may nonetheless do so when they have strong ideological or policy preferences).

As I will discuss in the next chapter, it is not clear that the private interests of integrated-technology firms in weakening IP rights align with the public's interest in preserving an institutional environment that sustains innovation over the long term, whether in the content or technology markets. In particular, it has not been widely appreciated that the legal devaluation of IP assets tends to favor platform-based firms that specialize in the assembly, organization, and dissemination of existing technology and content assets, while disadvantaging innovation-intensive firms and individuals that specialize in generating new technology and content assets, without which a knowledge-based ecosystem cannot thrive. Ultimately, "free stuff" may turn out not to be very free at all.

2

The Accidental Alliance

The advocacy and lobbying campaign successfully pursued by certain large information technology firms has deployed the rhetoric of public interest to make the case for weaker IP rights. In particular, it has been asserted that relaxing IP protections advances the public interest in reducing the costs of accessing informational and technological assets and avoiding the transactional and litigation costs associated with stronger forms of IP protection. A coalition of like-minded scholars and advocacy groups, often with ideological orientations that disfavor property rights in informational assets as a matter of principle, have made these same arguments. These types of publicly interested arguments, and the overlapping views expressed by scholars and policy advocates, have credibly signaled to policymakers that there is little distance between the weak-IP policy preferences of certain large information technology firms and the dominant preferences of policymakers' constituencies. This "accidental" convergence between, on the one hand, the business interests of large technology platforms in weaker IP protections, and, on the other hand, the ideological and intellectual preferences of influential scholars and policy advocates has been the driving force behind the commoditization through law of patent and copyright-protected assets in the U.S. innovation economy over approximately the past three decades. To the extent that large integrated technology firms' interest in weak IP rights is inconsistent with the public interest in sustaining a robust innovation economy that is open to a broad range of business models for cultivating knowledge assets, these efforts to weaken IP rights present an unconventional case in which firms have pursued market rents through the erosion of state-issued property rights.

2.1. Commoditization Logic

A well-known episode from the U.S. technology industry can illustrate the powerful logic of commoditization.[1]

The Big Steal. Jonathan M. Barnett, Oxford University Press. © Oxford University Press 2024.
DOI: 10.1093/oso/9780197629529.003.0003

In 1994, Netscape introduced Netscape Navigator, the first widely available internet browser that was accessible to average users. Microsoft feared that Netscape's browser could become the new platform layer in the "computing stack" for PCs and other devices, which would in turn threaten Microsoft by inducing developers to write applications for the Navigator browser rather than the Windows operating system (OS) and Microsoft Office applications suite. Even though Navigator was a nascent product, it achieved rapid adoption and offered developers a potentially larger target market because the browser could communicate with both Windows and non-Windows OSs. Microsoft responded with full force. At an estimated cost of several hundreds of millions of dollars, Microsoft developed a competing browser (Internet Explorer) to Netscape Navigator and, in 1995, Microsoft included Internet Explorer as part of the Windows OS at no incremental charge to users.[2] This posed a stiff challenge to Netscape, which offered its browser product at no charge for non-commercial use but sold the browser at a positive price to business users.[3]

Microsoft's commoditization strategy was highly potent, as browser market share shifted from Navigator to Internet Explorer in just a few years. As of August 1995, Netscape Navigator held 90% of the internet browser market; by August 1999, Microsoft held 76%.[4] The mechanism behind this dramatic turn of events is straightforward. Without a sufficiently attractive complementary asset like the Windows OS to generate revenues, Netscape had no effective means to cross-subsidize a giveaway of its core product, the internet browser. To meet the competitive threat posed by Microsoft's bundling strategy, Netscape responded by cutting the price of the browser to zero and releasing the browser source code to elicit interest from developers to write applications compatible with the Netscape browser.[5] In 1998, Netscape was acquired by America Online (AOL),[6] a transaction that may have reflected in part the expectation that the free browser product could be monetized through AOL's suite of complementary goods and services. Under AOL's ownership, however, Navigator continued to lose market share, ultimately exiting the browser market in 2008 (although the Netscape browser source code was the basis for the Firefox browser, which was released in 2004 on an open-source basis through the Mozilla Foundation).[7]

The use of IP giveaways to commoditize a competitor's "crown jewel" product, exemplified by Microsoft's response to Netscape, has mixed welfare effects from an economic point of view. It is obviously beneficial in the short term for users: the price of the internet browser fell from approximately $49 to $0 for business users and the "OS plus browser" bundle may have offered integrated functionalities that could not be replicated through the former Windows plus Navigator combination. Whether this represents a net positive outcome as a matter of competition policy is a closer call. While users enjoyed reduced prices for internet browsers, they may have been harmed in the longer term to the extent that Microsoft's commoditization strategy increased entry costs for future providers of internet browsers. Given the inability to extract revenues from the browser directly, any entrant would be compelled to offer another complementary product from which to earn returns. This effect can still be observed in the market today, where all general-purpose internet browsers are distributed at no charge and are used to "drive traffic" to other services from which the browser's owner can extract revenues.

Microsoft's commoditization strategy to compel exit by Netscape is neither anomalous nor nefarious. This is simply part of the business toolbox in technology markets, which are replete with commoditization strategies through which firms with a rich suite of complementary products and services seek to induce exit by a rival firm that has a single product or service from which it extracts revenue directly. Google can provide two illustrations of the potency of a commoditization strategy.

2.1.1. Android Operating System

Consider Google's Android OS for mobile computing and communications devices. Relying on the open-source Linux kernel, Google (and the startup that Google acquired in 2005) reportedly developed the Android OS at a cost of several hundreds of millions of dollars.[8] As of 2004, Nokia was the global leader in the cellphone device market and its Symbian OS enjoyed a 65% share of the mobile OS market.[9] Starting in 2009, Google then licensed the Android OS at no charge to telecom carriers and handset producers, subject to certain contractual conditions (which I will discuss subsequently). Android immediately made inroads on Symbian's market share. As of 2010, the dominant OSs for mobile devices held the following market shares: Symbian OS, 37.6%; Google Android, 22.7%; Blackberry RIM, 16%; Apple iOS, 15.7%; and Microsoft Windows, 4.2%. Aside from Microsoft Windows, these OSs were developed internally by handset manufacturers and generally were not licensed to others (with the limited exception of

Symbian, which Nokia licensed on an open-source basis in 2010 in response to the competitive challenge posed by Android).

Figure 2.1 illustrates the remarkable speed with which Google secured a dominant market share from incumbents that had hundreds of millions of users and seemed to be unbeatable. By 2013, Android had captured over 80% of the global market, with the remainder being occupied principally by Apple iOS.[10] The resulting market structure enabled Google to earn exceptional returns on its investment in developing Android through promotion of an Android-based ecosystem that attracts device producers and end-users on the "free" side of the platform, which in turn can be used to support the sale of advertising services to businesses on the "pay" side of the platform.

Like Microsoft's commoditization strategy in the browser market, Google's commoditization strategy in the mobile OS market gives rise to ambiguous welfare effects. On the one hand, the entry of Android into the market benefited consumers by lowering the price of a key input into handset devices, which may have lowered prices offered by device manufacturers or telecom carriers. The availability of a zero-price OS may have also lowered entry costs for producers into the handset market, which again promotes

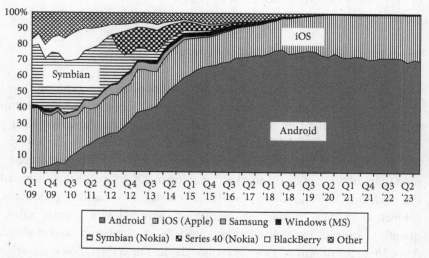

Figure 2.1 Global market share in mobile phone operating systems (2009–2023).

Note: Market share based on sales to end-users.

Source: Statista, Market share of mobile operating systems worldwide, 2009 to 2023 (based on data from StatCounter).

competitive conditions at least in the short term. On the other hand, the overwhelming market share secured by Android through its royalty-free, open-source licensing strategy may have harmed the competitive intensity of the market over the longer term by precluding entry by any stand-alone provider of a mobile OS. Any future entrant would be compelled to develop both an OS product and a complementary (and excludable) hardware or software product from which it could extract positive revenues. This effect can be observed in the general search market where Google's only significant competition (until the recent entry of AI-enabled search services) has been offered by Microsoft, which could maintain the Bing search service by cross-subsidizing it through its proprietary Microsoft Office applications. Hence, over the longer term, Android increased entry costs into at least one segment of the smartphone ecosystem, although it expanded access and improved user convenience by integrating Android with a larger ecosystem of computing and communications services.

2.1.2. Google Maps

The Google Maps service is provided at no charge and is integrated with the Google search engine, which in turn supports the broader Google ad-based ecosystem. This ad-supported giveaway business model contrasted with the incumbent digital mapping services that Google Maps challenged. Those services were pioneered by stand-alone suppliers such as Garmin, Tom Tom, and Magellan, which offered mapping software as part of a portable GPS-enabled navigation device, primarily for use in cars.[11] To develop a competing digital mapping technology that could be integrated into its search service, Google acquired three start-ups in 2004 and 2005 (Where 2 Technologies, Keyhole, and Zipdash).[12]

The launch in 2005 of Google Maps and its release as a free GPS-enabled navigation service for smartphones in 2009 rendered physical GPS-enabled navigation products obsolete. The capital markets appreciated immediately the severity of this competitive threat: on the date Google launched the Google Maps service for smartphone users, Garmin shares fell 16% and Tom Tom shares fell 21%.[13] Both companies subsequently lost market share and unsuccessfully attempted to provide alternative navigation products.[14] At any positive price, however, consumers preferred the free Google Maps application that was integrated into users' smartphone devices, which has since faced no meaningful competition other than Waze (which launched in 2006 and was acquired by Google in 2013) and Apple Maps (which, unlike Google Maps, is specific to the iPhone devices). Two competing free ad-based digital mapping services, MapQuest (acquired by Verizon in 2000) and Yahoo! Maps (launched in 2004), failed to pose significant competition to Google Maps.

The consumer welfare effects are again ambiguous. In the short term, consumers clearly gained by the emergence of a zero-price mapping service with no apparent reduction (or perhaps even an increase) in quality. In the longer term, entry may be discouraged since any new navigation systems developer must enter the market with another excludable complementary asset (as Garmin did when it successfully shifted to the market for wearable fitness devices) or, as in the case of the Waze traffic-informed navigation application (acquired by Google in 2013), must be acquired by a large platform or other systems-integrated entity that can cross-subsidize the "free" asset through the revenues generated by an excludable and complementary service or product. Under a more secure IP environment, Waze may have remained an independent company and licensed its technology to all interested search engines and providers of other complementary software applications, rather than selling its technology to a single firm, which would have been a more attractive outcome as a matter of competition policy.

2.2. A Commoditization Shortcut

As illustrated by Microsoft's and Google's strategies in the browser and mobile OS markets, respectively, commoditization strategies can be powerful tools to capture market leadership. Nonetheless, commoditization strategies have two key limitations.

First, commoditization can be exceptionally costly and therefore highly risky since it involves incurring development costs and then relying on revenue from complementary goods to cover those costs and generate a positive net return. Microsoft reportedly expended more than $100 million per year during 1995–1997 to develop and launch Internet Explorer by August 1995, followed by updated versions, to rival the functionality of the pioneering Netscape Navigator product, which had been launched in April 1994 (and apparently took Microsoft by surprise).[15] By August 1999, Internet Explorer had captured the majority of the market as measured by usage and continued to grow thereafter, even after Netscape was acquired by AOL in 1998.[16] While Microsoft's gamble paid off, there was no assurance up front that this would be the case. Netscape's acquisition by AOL (then the leading internet services provider in the U.S. market) might have resulted in an integrated suite of services in which Navigator was not separately priced but regained market share and drove sales of complementary goods and services. In that case, Microsoft's wager may have failed.

Second, commoditization sometimes may not be feasible as a legal or technological matter. Microsoft was only able to commoditize the browser because presumably Netscape lacked a sufficiently robust IP portfolio to preclude competing products that could achieve comparable functionalities. In fact, Microsoft was apparently able to release a competing browser within slightly more than 12 months after the launch of Netscape Navigator because it licensed the Mosaic browser technology from Spyglass, a smaller firm in the nascent browser market that concurrently entered into licensing deals with 82 other firms.[17] Copyright protections over Netscape's source code could only have deterred literal replications of the code, but had no legal force against other software that implemented comparable functionalities. But suppose that Netscape had owned a patent portfolio that covered at least some of the browser's key functionalities or, even in the absence of patent protection, Netscape's engineers had developed functionalities that could not be easily reverse engineered. Microsoft would then have been either legally or technologically precluded from releasing a browser with comparable functionalities, and Netscape could have continued selling its browser as a stand-alone product and at a positive price.

In this hypothetical scenario, Microsoft would have had three remaining competitive options. First, it could have made an acquisition offer for Netscape, which would likely have been barred by antitrust enforcers given that these were the two principal competitors in the relevant market. (In fact, Microsoft made an offer for Netscape when it first entered the market but was rebuffed.[18]) Second, it could have sought a license from Netscape. Microsoft tried this option as well but was rebuffed—an unsurprising response since Netscape was understandably reluctant to license a direct competitor with unequaled financial and technical resources. Third, Microsoft could have developed and released a browser product that potentially infringed upon Netscape's patent portfolio and then, once sued by Netscape for infringement, sought to challenge the validity of the underlying patent and/or attempt to enter into a settlement. Given the enormous costs invested in developing a new browser, that would have been a high-risk investment in light of the uncertainty concerning judicial outcomes (compounded by the fact that, at the time, it was easier to secure injunctions against adjudicated patent infringers).

But there is a lower-cost and potentially more effective alternative to achieve commoditization. A firm threatened by an entrant's innovation can undertake advocacy efforts to secure a legal change that devalues the competitor's IP asset and ultimately leaves the asset legally unprotected (or subject to tenuous forms of legal protection) and therefore free to be imitated, subject only to reverse-engineering obstacles. Without incurring the costs of replicating Netscape's technology, Microsoft could have invested resources in lobbying legislators, or allying with similarly minded public-interest organizations or trade associations, to put forward arguments why awarding patents to cover browser technology is inconsistent with the policy objectives of the IP system and confers monopoly rents on incumbents who prevent challengers from distributing a comparable browser for free. If this advocacy strategy had been successful, Netscape's patent portfolio would have been legally vulnerable, and imitators (including Microsoft) could have contemplated entering the market by offering similar browser technology at a lower price, taking advantage of the fact that imitation costs would be significantly lower than the originator's R&D costs. To complete this hypothetical, Netscape may then have undertaken counter-advocacy efforts to preserve patent protection for browser technology but would likely have elicited little interest among policymakers, who would perceive that Microsoft's policy preferences closely aligned with constituents' dominant preferences for reducing the price to access browser software. In the market for political influence, it's hard to beat arguments for more "free stuff."

2.3. Commoditization by Law

A firm that seeks to commoditize a competitor's content or technology assets can do so through business or legal strategies. Assuming the absence of IP-related or technological barriers, a business strategy requires that the firm develop a comparable product and then give it away, while earning positive revenues on a complementary good. A legal strategy requires that the firm persuade policymakers to take an action that commoditizes its competitor's knowledge asset by exposing that competitor to legal imitation or rendering ineffective any potential legal threat it could wield against imitators. The theory of legal change presented in Chapter 1 anticipates that successfully implementing a legal commoditization strategy requires identifying an "overlap zone" between, on the one hand, a firm's (or group of firms') preferred legal action, and on the other hand, the dominant policy preference of the policymaker's constituencies (or, when a salient majoritarian policy preference is not observed, the dominant policy preference of a discrete constituency with intensively expressed preferences).

The legal commoditization strategy that has transformed patent and copyright law has been so effective because it has operated within an overlap zone that captures the policy preferences of three relevant constituencies:

1. *Tech firms*: A well-organized and well-resourced business constituency consisting of technology firms that monetize R&D internally through integrated production and distribution infrastructures, rely on "IP giveaway" mechanisms in which a zero-price content or technology asset drives sales of complementary goods and services, or are otherwise net users of IP-protected assets;
2. *Thought leaders*: A small population of influential thought leaders in academia, think tanks, and advocacy organizations that are skeptical of the social value of robust IP rights (or, in some cases, any IP rights at all);
3. *End-users*: A large but dispersed and poorly organized pool of individual users that benefit from reduced prices of IP-intensive goods and services or are intrinsically sympathetic to an "information wants to be free" ideology.

The convergence of interests among these three groups has enabled platform-based and other integrated technology firms to enjoy the intellectual leadership and reputational capital supplied by thought leaders, while motivating policymakers to pursue a trajectory that is likely to prove popular among end-users. This is a difficult coalition to overcome for firms that rely on robust IP rights since those firms are advocating for legal changes that would limit access to "free stuff" and hence are unlikely to secure support from end-users or thought leaders that prioritize maximizing access to existing intellectual assets above all other policy considerations. Put differently: even if IP-dependent constituencies satisfy the small-numbers and sufficient-resource conditions to exert political influence, they are advocating for a policy position that stands at a significant distance from the perceived dominant policy preference of a policymaker's constituency as a whole. It is therefore unsurprising that the campaign to weaken patent and copyright protections, which originates in a powerful confluence of business interests, thought leaders, and individual users, has found a ready audience in policymakers who rationally seek to accrue goodwill among the constituencies that determine their political survival.

2.4. Software Utopians: The Curious Origins of the Accidental Alliance

The weakening of IP protection that has been successfully advocated by large integrated technology firms cannot be found in a secret blueprint in the digital archives of any one of those firms or the trade associations that represent those firms. Most of the firms that have benefited from the unraveling of IP rights in the content and technology markets were only start-ups or not even in existence at the onset of the digital economy in the late 1990s and were not in a position to dedicate substantial resources to influence public policy. Rather, the intellectual and philosophical origins of the technology community's IP skepticism (and its practical result, commoditization by law) can be found, at least partly, in the "anti-property" and "anti-market" ideology that characterized important segments of the software community that predated the launch of the personal computer and the commercialization of the internet. Ironically, this communitarian ideology has provided the rhetorical and ideological umbrella for the commoditization strategies pursued so profitably by many of the companies that have become the leaders of today's technology markets.

This ideology is often summarized by the phrase "information wants to be free" (which, as discussed previously, appears to have originated in remarks by Stewart Brand, a well-known technology commentator). This phrase is sometimes understood as a less technical explanation of the economic concept that informational goods are "non-rivalrous"—that is, unlike physical goods, two or more users can use an informational good without depleting its value. Two or more people can simultaneously make use of the Pythagorean theorem and it is not exhausted in any respect. The same is true of the Microsoft Windows OS: I can download one copy, but (especially in a digital environment) an infinite number of copies are still available for others. However, the same would not be true if someone drove away in my car or ate the pizza I just ordered. The non-rivalrous characteristic implies that charging any positive price for an informational good inefficiently precludes access to a good for which the cost of delivering an additional unit is zero.[19] Setting aside for the moment the economic gains that can arise from the innovation and commercialization incentives attributable to IP protection (which Brand recognized in an often-omitted phrase that "information [also] wants to be expensive"[20]), this outcome appears to be inefficient.

The "information wants to be free" approach to IP policy is not a merely theoretical proposition. It is the motivating principle behind the open-source model of software production, which I described briefly in the Introduction. This model relies on the unpaid contributions of volunteer programmers to develop a software program, which is then released subject to an open-source copyright license. While there are many varieties of licenses that fall into this category, an open-source license in its purest form provides for a zero royalty and authorizes distribution of the code without restrictions on subsequent usage, distribution, or modifications, except that the licensee agrees that the code, and any modifications of the code, will be distributed on the same open-source terms. This proviso is sometimes known as a "viral" clause because it can cause the open-source license to "propagate" itself as the licensed code is incorporated into other programs, which may have been developed within a proprietary closed-source model. In practice, many widely used open-source licenses offer more permissive terms to encourage adoption of open-source code by firms that already rely on closed-source code or wish to incorporate open-source code into a commercial model that relies on fees from users.[21]

The open-source model has been widely described as an illustration that the "information wants to be free" principle is a workable basis for a robust innovation ecosystem that is free or largely free of IP rights.[22] More specifically, these commentators have argued that the open-source software model shows that we can often ignore the second part of Brand's statement ("information wants to be expensive"), which recognizes the costs involved in producing and distributing commercially valuable informational assets (and therefore implies the necessity of some form of legal or functional exclusivity). If that is the case, it may sometimes (or, for these commentators, will often or even usually) be possible to have "IP without IP." That is: robust IP rights, or even any IP rights, are unnecessary to sustain incentives for individuals and entities to invest in the production and distribution of significant categories of informational assets. A cottage industry of academic scholarship has emerged that seeks to identify creative or other innovative activities that appear to function well without robust, or any, form of IP protection. However, these examples involve low-cost endeavors such as fine cuisine, adult entertainment, stand-up comedy routines, magic tricks, and fashion design,[23] which casts some doubt on whether "IP without IP" is a workable model in more costly and commercially significant innovation environments. The success of the open-source model in software markets has attracted interest precisely because it appears to demonstrate the possibility of "IP without IP" in commercially significant undertakings that are purportedly sustained by the contributions of hundreds of volunteer developers.

If this interpretation of the open-source software market were accurate, it would cast substantial doubt on the standard assumptions concerning the "selfish" incentives of profit-seeking inventors that drive conventional reward-based justifications for IP rights. Yet closer scrutiny of the most widely adopted open-source software application reveals a more complex picture that casts doubt on this widely adopted interpretation.[24]

2.4.1. Linux OS Project: Origins and Development

The Linux OS project, founded and led by Linus Torvalds, is based on the GNU project, founded and led by famed developer, Richard Stallman, and distributed under an open-source license. Since its launch in 1991, the Linux OS is generally described as the most widely used open-source application and therefore might appear to illustrate the feasibility of a non-proprietary model of intellectual production. But there is an inconvenient fact. The Linux project only achieved widespread market adoption once it received significant infusions of funding and other support from commercial sponsors. In 2000, IBM committed to contribute over $1 billion in funding to the Linux Foundation and concurrently dedicated teams of engineers to the project through the IBM Linux Technology Center.[25] During 2008–2009, technology firms, including IBM, Red Hat, Oracle, Novell, and Intel, contributed almost 80% of the code contributions to the project and over 85% of the "sign-offs" on code changes.[26] This suggests that paid contributors were not only a clear majority of all contributors, but were especially prominent in leading the project. An IBM publication was straightforward on this point: "[T]he often quoted notion that such [open source] software is written primarily by people working *gratis* for the general good is false."[27]

Given that the Linux OS only achieved meaningful adoption in the global server market following the infusion of financial and personnel contributions from IBM and other corporate sponsors, this sequence of events casts doubt on widespread assertions that the success of the Linux project demonstrates the feasibility of non-profit-based, volunteer-driven models of informational asset production (at least in the absence of public or philanthropic funding). To the contrary, it shows that most Linux contributors are not volunteers and suggests that extensive contributions of personnel, capital, and expertise from for-profit sponsors was essential to enable the project to achieve widespread adoption.

This is not to say that the altruistic and ideological motivations behind the Linux project are immaterial or a mere charade. These sincerely held views played a critical role in the initial launch of the Linux project by enlisting contributions from individuals with an ideological affinity for a sharing-based model of software production. Moreover, these motivations may continue to play a role in promoting adoption of the OS by developers and other users who feel that they can rely on the open-source commitments under which Linux is distributed. Without such trust, developers may be wary of contributing to, or investing in the adoption of, an open-source application. There are several scenarios in which an entity that administers an open-source application could adversely change the terms of access, ranging from restricting participation in the code sign-off process, limiting or delaying access to future code releases, or transferring project control to an external entity with commercial motivations. The remarkable success of Linux, which has achieved broad adoption in the server market and provides the kernel for the most widely used OS (Google's Android) in the smartphone market, has relied on the convergence between the ideological motivations behind the developers who launched Linux and the profit-seeking motivations of the firms that assisted in its development for commercial purposes.

2.4.2. Linux OS Project: Rationales and Implications

It is straightforward to understand the attraction of the Linux open-source OS project to programmers driven by an ideological commitment to a voluntaristic IP-free model of software development (or more precisely, "IP-lite," since even an open-source model relies on copyright to enforce the contractual terms that govern subsequent adaptations and distributions of the licensed code). However, the profit motivation behind corporate sponsorship of this project may not be as obvious, especially since it generates economic gains that sponsors cannot fully capture due to the absence of an exclusive ownership right over the software produced by the project.

There are three factors that can reconcile this apparently altruistic action with business rationality. First, sponsoring firms may wish to seed adoption of the open-source platform to promote sales of complementary goods and services that those firms offer or expect to offer. This can be illustrated by a firm such as Red Hat (acquired in 2019 by IBM for $34 billion[28]), which earns revenues by providing the user support, customization, and upgrading features that are absent in the Linux program. Second, some of those firms may produce hardware or other software products that rely in part on Linux code, in which case commoditizing the OS can yield long-term advantages insofar as it reduces the firm's costs of obtaining a required technology input for its combined suite of hardware and software products. Third, some of those firms may wish to commoditize the OS segment of the market to drive value toward other segments in which those firms have a competitive advantage. For example, IBM may have sought to commoditize the OS segment to drive value away from Microsoft, the provider of the Windows OS (distributed at a positive price), and toward the hardware segment of the market in which IBM was a leading provider. Reducing the price of the OS segment in the server technology "stack" to zero could increase market demand for server hardware, a market in which IBM was (and is) a leader. Ironically, IBM sought to deploy against Microsoft in the server OS market the same strategy that Microsoft had successfully deployed against Netscape in the PC browser market: that is, redirect the point of value-capture in the technology stack by commoditizing a rival's crown jewel asset.

The successful Linux-IBM alliance provides the model for the accidental alliance between ideologically motivated adherents of the "information wants to be free" school and for-profit firms that deploy "IP giveaway" and related systems-based business strategies that thrive by commoditizing informational assets and then extracting value from a suite of complementary goods and services. To extend the commoditization strategy from the realm of business to the realm of politics requires, however, an additional step. It requires persuading policymakers that commoditization-by-law is consistent with the dominant preferences of the policymakers' constituents taken as a whole and will therefore result in an accretion of political goodwill. So long as individual users in the aggregate, or discrete and well-organized constituencies, recognize that open-source software may translate into favorable pricing effects (or identify with IP-skeptical views more generally), this is likely to be an easy case to make. Policymakers would then be inclined to accrue political goodwill by taking steps to favor a weaker level of IP protection, the same policy objective advocated, either on ideological or economic grounds, by policy activists and technology firms that rely on business models that thrive under weak-IP conditions.

Here, too, the Linux-IBM alliance provides a template for the commoditization of informational assets through the political process. Even though it had provided significant funding for the Linux Foundation and had supplied a large number of the programmers who contributed code to the project, IBM and other corporate sponsors took care not to intrude unduly upon the governance of the Linux Foundation, which might have cast doubt on the "commons" ideology that had motivated its launch and impeded subsequent adoption of the Linux OS in the server market. In the case of the Linux Foundation, Linus Torvalds, the founder, continues to lead the Foundation and maintains ownership of the Linux trademark. Critically, the Foundation's executive director may not be an employee of any sponsoring member, and governance authority is diffused across multiple "councils" so that no individual sponsor can unilaterally dictate the direction of the Linux project.[29] Consistent with this approach, the Linux Foundation has stated: "The Linux Foundation serves as a neutral spokesperson for Linux. . . . It's vitally important that Linux creator Linus Torvalds and other key kernel developers remain independent."[30] This form of self-restraint on the part of its corporate sponsors—that is, a willingness to exercise governance power that is less than proportionate to the sponsors' financial contribution to the project—enabled the Foundation to continue making a credible case that developers and other users could expect that the terms of the open-source license would remain unaltered. The result: Linux was able to secure broad adoption in the server market, both thanks to and despite the substantial support provided by commercial sponsors.

2.5. Putting the Accidental Alliance into Action

The two key constituencies in the IP-skeptical alliance independently converged on a common policy position, motivated either by ideological resistance or principled skepticism toward IP rights, or by economic interests in minimizing the costs of securing IP inputs that can drive sales of complementary goods or that can be embedded in products or services in which the firm has a competitive advantage. The activities undertaken by advocacy groups, complemented by a like-minded body of scholarly commentary, have been critical to the success of large integrated technology firms in securing legal changes that have substantially weakened IP rights in content and technology markets. The converging efforts made by the two members of this "accidental" alliance to impact the trajectory of IP rights, and the less successful efforts made by entities and individuals with opposing policy preferences, can be observed in data on amicus briefs, lobbying, and other forms of influence investments concerning IP policy.

2.5.1. Lobbying

The extent to which firms or industries place a value on IP policy issues can be assessed by examining the efforts these firms and industries invest in lobbying Congress on those issues. Under federal law, registered lobbyists in Congress must submit quarterly reports of their activities with the U.S. House of Representatives and the U.S. Senate.[31] These quarterly reports specify the firm or other entity on behalf of which the lobbyist acted and describe generally the policy matters on which the lobbyist was engaged. Figure 2.2 shows the number of such reports that were filed annually during 1998–2019 and that mentioned patents, copyright, or trademark. The sharply increasing

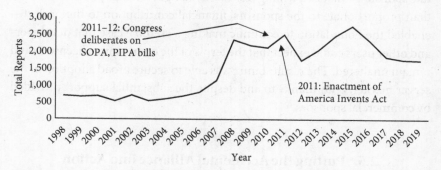

Figure 2.2 Annual number of lobbying reports mentioning copyright, patent, or trademark (1998–2019).

Source: Data extracted from OpenSecrets (https://www.opensecrets.org), which provides information from disclosure reports filed by lobbyists as required by law with the U.S. Senate and the U.S. House of Representatives.

Table 2.1 Lobbying Reports Filed by Selected Entities with the U.S. House of Representatives (2005–2018)

Filer	Patent Mentioned (percentage of lobbying reports filed by each entity)	Copyright Mentioned (percentage of lobbying reports filed by each entity)
Amazon	23%	17%
Apple	45%	25%
Facebook	20%	5%
Google	39%	40%
Microsoft	21%	5%

Source: vpnMentor, https://www.vpnmentor.com/research/us-lobbying-report/ (based on "lobbying reports submitted to the House of Representatives" by the above-named companies).

volume of reports since 2008 that mention these issues reflects the increasing value that businesses or other entities placed on IP policy during the years preceding and following deliberations on major legislative initiatives concerning patent and copyright law.

Table 2.1 presents data on the percentage of lobbying reports that were submitted by registered lobbyists acting on behalf of each of the five largest technology firms during 2005–2018 and in which copyright or patents were mentioned. The large percentages of lobbying reports in which these issues were referenced provide some indication of the value that these firms placed on these issues during this period. As shown, Google and Apple accounted for the highest percentages of reports that mentioned patent or copyright law, suggesting that these two firms viewed these policy areas as being of special importance.

Data concerning lobbying expenditures in connection with the America Invents Act of 2011, a major amendment to the patent statute, provide further insight into the extent to which certain industries place a value on influencing the strength of IP rights and, in this case, the patent system. Table 2.2 presents data on the estimated lobbying expenditures reported by registered lobbyists acting on behalf of firms or other entities, which were then aggregated on an industry-specific basis, in connection with the House and Senate versions of the bill. The total estimated amounts spent are significant: $125 million in connection with the House bill and $358 million in connection with the Senate bill, amounting to over $483 million in total. The academic research, biopharmaceuticals, financial services, medical device,

Table 2.2 Estimated Lobbying Expenditures on the America Invents Act of 2011 ($M)

Industry	Tends to Favor Stronger Patents?	HR1249 (House Bill)	S1145 (Senate Bill)
Academic research	Yes	$3.96	$14.98
Agricultural	Yes	$0.03	$2.27
Automotive	No	$3.68	n/a
Biopharmaceuticals	Yes	$13.06	$65.69
Chemicals	Yes	$0.18	$6.79
Consumer goods	No	$0.47	$10.57
Financial services	No	$33.5	$76.83
ICT (general)	No (not uniform but larger portion disfavors)	$14.57	$6.58
ICT (hardware)	Mixed	$1.13	$19.37
ICT (platform)	No	$15.1	$4.9
ICT (software)	No	$1.85	$9.43
ICT (semiconductors)	Mixed	$7.14	$8.09
ICT (telecom)	No	$3.4	$5.09
IP licensing	Yes	$13.96	$2.0
Media/entertainment	No	$0.71	n/a
Medical device	Yes	$0.31	$9.81
Manufacturing	No	$5.91	$24.21
Energy (oil/gas)	Yes	$1.35	$17.71
Total (favors stronger patents)		$32.83	$109.89
Total (favors weaker patents)		$79.41	$172.02
Total (mixed preferences)		$7.46	$26.32
Total (unassigned entities)		$5.52	$49.98
Grand Total		$125.22	$358.21

ICT = information and communications technology.

Notes: Each filer (or entity on behalf of which a report was filed) was assigned to a unique industry category based on information available through the entity's website or other relevant sources. "Unassigned" refers to entities that were not clearly associated with a single industry category. Whether a particular industry tends to favor stronger or weaker patents is based on general understandings in the scholarly literature, including survey evidence and amicus briefs filings (see Table 2.3). Note that lobbying expenditures are estimates and may be overstated in cases where a filer aggregates expenditures in a single report relating to multiple bills.

Sources: Data were extracted from lobbying reports filed with the House of Representatives and the Senate by lobbyists acting on behalf of clients in connection with the aforementioned bills. Reports were accessed through the "Open Secrets" database, as follows. For the House bill: https://www.open secrets.org/federal-lobbying/bills/summary?id=hr1249-112. For the Senate bill: https://www.open secrets.org/federal-lobbying/bills/summary?id=s23-112.

and information and communications technology (ICT) sectors, in particular, expended significant amounts. These data also provide insight into the balance of power between industries that tend to value stronger or weaker levels of IP protection, which can explain in part why the enacted statute conformed closely to the policy preferences of firms and industries that tend to favor weaker patent protection. Specifically, the data show that patent-dependent industries, such as biopharmaceuticals, medical devices, and academic research (which encompasses technology-transfer entities), were outmatched monetarily by industries that generally do not rely on patents (such as manufacturing and financial services), are net IP users (such as consumer goods), or derive a competitive advantage in a weak-patent environment (such as digital platforms). Industries that tend to favor weaker patents were able to make substantially greater lobbying expenditures as compared to industries that tend to favor stronger patents.

2.5.2. Amicus Briefs

Tables 2.3 and 2.4 present data on amicus briefs filed in patent-related litigation before the Supreme Court and copyright-related litigation before the Supreme Court, Second Circuit, and Ninth Circuit during 2006–2016. There are only a small number of copyright-related cases at the Supreme Court during this period, so copyright-related decisions by the Second and Ninth Circuits (generally considered to be the two most prominent appellate courts in copyright law) were added to the sample to provide insight into firms' copyright-related advocacy activity.

In both patent-related and copyright-related litigation, telecommunications, search, and platform firms favored the alleged infringer almost all the time. In the ICT industry, there was a greater range of views expressed in briefs filed in patent-related litigation by semiconductor firms and briefs filed in copyright-related litigation by software firms. The briefs filed by advocacy organizations and, to a lesser but still significant extent, by individual academics largely adopted policy positions favoring weak IP rights. In both patent-related and copyright-related litigation, a substantial majority of the briefs filed by advocacy organizations favored the alleged infringer (81% of the time in patent-related litigation and 67% of the time in copyright-related litigation). Similarly, consumer organizations tended to favor the alleged infringer in both categories of litigation (65% of the time in patent-related

Table 2.3 Amicus Briefs Filed by Selected Industries in Patent-Related Supreme Court Cases (2006–2016)

Entity/Industry Type	Number of Briefs Filed	Percentage Favoring Patent Owner	Percentage Favoring Alleged Infringer	Percentage Favoring Neither
Venture capital	26	100%	0%	0%
Research institutions (incl. tech transfer)	82	96%	1%	2%
IP licensing entities	55	80%	6%	15%
Biopharmaceutical	89	75%	19%	6%
Academia (individuals)	85	34%	47%	19%
ICT (semiconductors)	39	21%	72%	8%
Advocacy organizations	118	13%	81%	6%
ICT	388	10%	75%	15%
Consumer organizations	88	10%	65%	25%
ICT (telecom)	21	5%	62%	34%
ICT (platform/ search)	77	1%	78%	11%

ICT = information and communications technology.

Notes: Percentages may not always sum to 100% due to rounding. Each brief filer is assigned to a unique entity category, except for subcategories of ICT firms.

Source: Data sourced from amicus briefs filed in relevant litigation. Some data originally appeared in Barnett 2021a, 147, Table 7.2.

litigation and 82% of the time in copyright-related litigation). A plurality of the briefs filed by individual academics favored the alleged infringer in patent-related litigation (47% of the time), and a majority of briefs filed by individual academics in copyright-related litigation (52% of the time) favored the alleged infringer. In copyright-related litigation, library associations have been especially active filers of amicus briefs and mostly adopt copyright-skeptical views, favoring the alleged infringer 88% of the time.

Table 2.5 presents data showing only the positions expressed by ICT firms, ICT trade associations, and advocacy groups that filed at least 10 briefs in patent litigation before the Supreme Court during 2006–2016. There is an almost complete overlap in policy preferences among these members of

Table 2.4 Amicus Briefs Filed by Selected Groups in Copyright-Related Cases in the Supreme Court, Second Circuit, and Ninth Circuit (1998–2021)

Entity/ Industry Type	Number of Briefs Filed	Percentage Favoring Copyright Owner	Percentage Favoring Alleged Infringer	Percentage Favoring Neither
IP licensing entities	39	79%	13%	8%
Entertainment (incl. sports) and media	678	76%	23%	1%
Academia (individuals)	211	42%	52%	6%
ICT (software)	59	40%	48%	12%
Advocacy organizations	216	31%	67%	2%
Consumer organizations	73	18%	82%	0%
ICT (telecom)	74	17%	82%	1%
Library associations	98	11%	89%	0%
ICT (incl. search)	50	6%	88%	6%
Research institutions	22	5%	95%	0%

ICT = information and communications technology.

Notes: Percentages may not always sum to 100% due to rounding. Each brief filer is assigned to a unique entity category, except for subcategories of ICT firms.

Source: Data sourced from amicus briefs filed in relevant litigation.

the "accidental alliance." None of these entities filed a single brief in patent-related litigation during this 10-year period favoring the patent owner. Moreover, many of these ICT firms are members of trade associations, such as the Computing and Communications Industry Association (CCIA) and Software Information and Industry Association (SIIA), which have been active filers of amicus briefs in patent-related litigation before the Supreme Court. For example, Amazon, Facebook, Apple, Google, Intel, and Samsung are members of the CCIA, while Apple, Google, Red Hat, and several large financial services companies are members of the SIIA,[32] both of which have filed briefs in Supreme Court patent litigation favoring the alleged infringer in all cases.

Table 2.5 Amicus Briefs Filed by Most Active ICT Firms, ICT Trade Associations, and Advocacy Organizations in Patent-Related Supreme Court Cases (2006–2016)

Filer	Entity Type	Number of Briefs	Entity Supported
Google	Firm	16	81% AI; 19% N
Intel	Firm	15	79% AI; 21% N
Electronic Frontier Foundation	Advocacy	13	92% AI; 8% N
Computing and Communications Industry Association	Trade assoc.	12	100% AI
Cisco	Firm	12	83% AI; 17% N
Yahoo!	Firm	12	83% AI; 8.5% P; 8.5% N
Public Knowledge	Advocacy	11	100% AI
Hewlett Packard	Firm	10	90% AI; 10% N
Facebook	Firm	10	80% AI; 20% N
Microsoft	Firm	10	80% AI; 20% N

AI = alleged infringer; P = patentee; N = neither party.
Source: Data sourced from amicus briefs.

The concurrence of views in the briefs filed by technology companies and the briefs filed by trade organizations and advocacy groups have most likely signaled to policymakers that taking actions to weaken IP rights stood at a close distance to the dominant policy preference of policymakers' constituencies (in particular, individual end-users) and would therefore result in the accretion of political goodwill. In particular, policymakers might have reasonably concluded that the views advanced by IP-skeptical portions of the ICT sector likely track individual users' preferences for "free stuff," whether motivated by ideological commitments to an "information wants to be free" philosophy or an interest in minimizing consumption costs involving ICT-related products and services. By contrast, biopharmaceutical firms (who favored the patent owner 75% of the time in patent-related litigation) and entertainment and media firms (who favored the copyright owner 76% of the time in copyright-related litigation) took positions that would raise individual users' consumption costs involving goods (drugs and media) that individuals use on a regular basis. The natural compatibility between the IP policy preferences of certain technology firms and individual end-users was illustrated most vividly by the mass protests against the SOPA and PIPA bills in late 2011 and early 2012, both of which were widely opposed by the tech community. As will be discussed in more detail in Chapter 3, those protests were actively encouraged by leading internet firms and conveyed to policymakers that taking actions to bolster copyright would not be welcomed by end-users and would likely result in a significant depletion of political capital. Legislators responded accordingly and the bills were withdrawn.

2.5.3. Advocacy Organizations

It is widely known that large corporations fund think tanks, industry associations, or other organizations that engage in various forms of policy advocacy and thought leadership on policy issues that are of importance to the corporate sponsors. The same is true of IP policy issues, although the resources available to the large platforms and other ICT firms that have a business interest in weaker IP rights tend to be greater than the resources available to the technology innovators and content producers that have an interest in bolstering those rights. Table 2.6 lists advocacy organizations and trade associations that are involved with IP policy issues and received funding from Alphabet/Google, Amazon, Apple, or Meta/Facebook during 2010–2022. These organizations generally advocate for weaker IP protections, whether in the content or technology industries, before Congress, the Supreme Court (through amicus briefs), or federal regulatory agencies. Among these organizations, Public Knowledge and the Electronic Frontier Foundation have been among the most consistent and effective advocates and thought leaders for weakening IP protections, both through patent and copyright law.

2.5.4. Coup at the Copyright Office?

In 2016, Maria Pallante, the Register of Copyrights, was removed from her position by the Librarian of Congress.[33] This was the only time a Register of Copyright—typically, a politically uncontroversial position—has ever been removed from office, and it elicited a formal letter of protest to Congress from the two preceding Registers of Copyright.[34] There are reasons to believe that

Table 2.6 Advocacy and Trade Organizations Funded by Leading Technology Platforms (2010–2022)

Organization	Google/ Alphabet	Facebook/Meta	Apple	Amazon
American Library Association	2012–2019	—	—	—
Coalition for Patent Fairness	2010–2016	—	—	—
Computer & Communications Industry Association	2010–2022	2015–2019	2021	2015–2022
Computing Technology Industry Association	2016–2022	2016	2015, 2017–2019	2019–2022
Consumer Technology Association	2010–2022	2015–2017	2015, 2017–2021	2016–2017, 2019, 2021–2022
Electronic Frontier Foundation	2012–2017, 2019	2015–2019	—	—
Engine Advocacy	2012–2022	2022	—	2019, 2021–2022
Public Knowledge	2010–2022	2015–2021	—	2018–2022
Software & Information Industry Association	2010–2022	—	2015, 2017–2019	—
United for Patent Reform	2017–2020	—	—	2015–2016

Notes: Membership in an organization is deemed to represent funding through membership fees. Consumer Technology Industry Association was formerly known as the Consumer Electronics Association. Different sources may use different reporting methodologies or may be incomplete in certain respects. Information presented does not purport to be comprehensive of all funding provided by the selected technology firms to these organizations.

Sources: Amazon.com Inc. 2017–2021, 2022; Apple Inc. 2020, n.d.; Electronic Frontier Foundation 2017; Google 2010–2021; Meta n.d.; Public Knowledge 2021, 2022; Tech Transparency Project, Tech Funding Database, https://django.techtransparencyproject.org/techfundingdb; Tech Transparency Project n.d.

Pallante's removal reflected to some extent a policy and intellectual climate influenced by the "information wants to be free" principles promoted by the "accidental alliance" of advocacy organizations, academic commentators, and technology platforms that have sought to establish a weak-copyright regime, either on ideological or business grounds.

Some of Pallante's views on copyright were clearly unwelcome among portions of the tech community that rely on content giveaway models as a business matter and constituencies that resist robust copyright protections as an ideological matter. In particular, Pallante emphasized the importance of copyright for individual artists, a consideration that is often dismissed by the copyright-skeptical alliance across much of the tech, advocacy, and academic communities. In a speech given in 2011, Pallante had emphasized this theme.[35] To promote this policy objective, she later suggested establishing a small-claims adjudicative mechanism that would avoid the legal costs of a full-blown litigation that is beyond the means of many individual artists[36] (a proposal that was adopted by Congress when it enacted the Copyright Alternative to Small-Claims Enforcement Act of 2020[37]). In 2014, she stated: "I am aware that many kinds of creators, including book authors, songwriters, photographers, and performers, feel underserved if not marginalized by the copyright law, and I share their concern about long-term implications."[38] This statement likely elicited displeasure among the ideological, scholarly, and business communities that promoted the prevailing weak-copyright consensus.

Perhaps most controversially, Pallante had raised concerns in an August 2016 letter on behalf of the Copyright Office to the Federal Communications Commission (FCC)[39] about the FCC's "AllVid" proposal (which had been supported by Google[40]) that would have ordered pay-TV service providers to enable outside companies to supply the set-top boxes for home pay-TV installation, rather than requiring customers to lease them from the pay-TV provider.[41] Specifically, she expressed reservations that the proposal could facilitate the transmission of pirated content or enable the use of content in a manner that would violate the terms of existing licensing agreements between content providers and pay-TV distributors. While advocates (including Public Knowledge)[42] argued that the proposal would expand choice for consumers, others observed that the AllVid system contemplated requiring pay-TV distributors to provide device manufacturers with access to distributors' digital transmissions so that manufacturers could index the content through the set-top box, provide users with a search function, and then monitor users' viewing habits to support targeted advertising.[43] If implemented, this proposal would have enabled platforms or other set-top box providers (such as Google, which had been identified as a potential provider[44]) to extract value from content for which they had provided no financial support, either directly as a content producer or indirectly as a licensed distributor. In the guise of reducing the costs borne by consumers to acquire a set-top box, the proposal would have transferred economic value from content producers to third parties that had never incurred any of the costs to produce that content.

The advocacy community responded vigorously to Pallante's copyright-friendly statements and actions. On September 8, 2016, Public Knowledge released a document titled, "Captured: Systemic Bias at the U.S. Copyright Office." Among other claims, the Public Knowledge report asserted that the Copyright Office had been "captured" by the content industry, a view that was largely predicated on the view that certain individuals at the Copyright Office had worked for companies in that industry and the Office had taken certain positions that tended to favor copyright owners.[45] Of course, this assertion overlooks the possibility that policy positions that favor copyright owners may be consistent with the public interest in preserving incentives for the production and distribution of creative works. Moreover, it overlooks the fact that, as shown in Table 2.6, Public Knowledge had received funding from Google and Facebook since 2010 and 2015, respectively, two platform-based companies with a business interest in weakening copyright protections (and one of which had apparently planned to enter the market for third-party-supplied set-top boxes contemplated by the AllVid proposal).

On October 21, 2016, Pallante was reassigned without notice by the Librarian of Congress to the status of "senior advisor," a position that Pallante unsurprisingly declined. After Pallante's resignation, Public Knowledge reportedly tweeted that the change "represents a great opportunity to bring balance to the Office's policy work."[46] The opposite would appear to be the case. A regulator who had dared to challenge the prevailing weak-copyright consensus was apparently compelled to leave government service in a policy climate dominated by a coalition of business entities, thought leaders, and advocacy entities with a common economic or ideological interest in limiting copyright protections for the individuals and entities that fuel the creative ecosystem.

2.6. Closing Thoughts

The extensive investments made by substantial portions of the technology industry to influence the trajectory of IP law are unsurprising. Like any business, technology platforms that have a business interest in devaluing IP rights deploy resources not just to "win the game" as it is currently played, but to change the rules of the game so that they can keep winning, or win more often, in the future. In subsequent chapters, I describe the great success achieved by leading technology firms in transforming substantial elements of the patent and copyright system to advance a business model that thrives under a weak-IP environment, while disadvantaging innovation and commercialization models that rely on robust IP protections. This success has relied to a great extent on the convergence of views among technology firms that have an economic interest in weakening IP rights and policy advocates and academics who have ideological or other principled commitments that disfavor robust IP protections or, in some cases, reject such protections altogether. While the origins of this alliance may have been accidental, large platform-based technology companies have invested significant efforts in building upon this convergence to signal to policymakers that weakening IP rights is consistent with the public interest and tracks the preferences of policymakers' constituencies. In the following chapters, I will show how policymakers across all branches of government have largely adopted this IP-skeptical view and have undertaken policy actions that have resulted in a sweeping devaluation of the IP rights that underlie the U.S. innovation economy.

PART II
UNMAKING COPYRIGHT LAW

In Chapter 1, I provided a general framework for understanding how firms can make investments in advocacy efforts to pursue preferred changes in the law and, specifically, in the IP rights arrangements that govern creative or technology markets. In Chapter 2, I made that model more concrete by showing how technology firms and digital intermediaries that operate under "IP giveaway," systems-integrated or vertically integrated business models, have entered into a marriage of convenience with constituencies that have ideological or other principled commitments that favor weakening IP rights. In Part II of the book (encompassing Chapters 3–6), I apply this framework to account for the significant reductions in the force of copyright protections since the advent of the "digital revolution" in the late 1990s. These changes reflect both technological innovations that increased dramatically the costs of enforcing IP rights over creative assets in digital environments and advocacy and lobbying strategies undertaken by digital intermediaries that have a rational interest in weakening IP protections over content assets. The reason is straightforward. Content aggregators are net users of content assets, so any reduction in IP protection reduces those firms' input costs, or host content assets that are circulated by users, so any reduction in IP protections limits both users' and firms' liability exposure to infringement claims. This strategic devaluation of property rights has been supported by sympathetic academics and advocacy organizations and has attracted widespread support among individual users who have a rational interest in procuring content for as little cost as possible. These short-term-focused efforts to minimize consumption costs have eroded the property-rights infrastructure that supports the substantial investments of capital, talent, and other resources that sustain a robust creative ecosystem over the longer term.

3

The Political Economy of Copyright Law

In this chapter, I discuss how the dramatic reordering of property-rights arrangements in content markets emerged within a short time due to advocacy, lobbying, and litigation activities by the two key components of the accidental alliance. Those components are technology firms that operate giveaway business models that thrive under weak or zero copyright protections, and thought leaders (including academics, commentators, and advocacy organizations) who have an intellectual or ideological commitment to weaker (or, in some variants, no) protections for copyright owners. This alliance of ideological and economic interests promoted a policy package that was inherently attractive to consumers and, as a result, was an "easy sell" to legislators, regulators, and judges since it aligned with the perceived dominant preferences of policymakers' constituencies. The result has been a wealth transfer from content owners and originators to content users, favoring the interests of digital intermediaries and other aggregators that capture a significant portion of the economic value generated through the unauthorized distribution of content assets in online environments.

3.1. The Digital Shock

Legal protections against the unauthorized copying and distribution of content assets only have meaningful incremental effect in environments where there are no technological means available to deter and regulate unauthorized usage effectively and at a comparable or lower cost. This explains why, as noted previously, Congress only included sound recordings under the protection of the copyright statute in 1972.[1] Prior to that time, it was too costly for unauthorized producers to make large volumes of bootleg copies of vinyl records at a comparable quality that could feasibly compete with the original. Technology, not law, provided a natural barrier against unauthorized copying.

The Big Steal. Jonathan M. Barnett, Oxford University Press. © Oxford University Press 2024.
DOI: 10.1093/oso/9780197629529.003.0004

The advent of the internet, and digital technologies for copying and distributing audio, video, and textual content in digital form, is something like the sound-recording episode in reverse. Like cassette tape technology in the 1970s, but operating at a far larger scale and with far greater potency, the launch of the commercial internet in the mid- to late 1990s constituted a technological shock that dramatically lowered the costs of copying and distributing audio and other content assets, effectively devaluing the practical force and economic value of a content owner's copyright portfolio. In this case, technological changes overwhelmed existing legal barriers to unauthorized copying. For the 20-year period extending from 1990 through 2010, Figure 3.1 shows the dramatic effect on sales of sound recordings in all formats at the onset of, and in the years following, the digital revolution in content distribution. For this purpose, I treat the launch in 1999 of the Napster service, the first widely adopted online technology for peer-to-peer distribution of digitally stored music, as the starting point of this process of digital transformation.

To restore legal security for copyright owners in response to the increased ease of copying and distribution in a digital environment, it would seem to be necessary to bolster copyright protections and increase penalties for unauthorized usage. Mass unauthorized usage of proprietary content (known in some normative quarters as "piracy" and in other normative quarters as "sharing") poses an enforcement challenge for content owners given the high costs of detection and enforcement in an environment where there are tens to hundreds of millions of potentially infringing individual users. U.S. copyright law does provide stiff statutory damages (that is, damages available without having to prove lost profits), which, subject to judicial discretion, can go as high as $150,000 per work if the infringement is shown to be

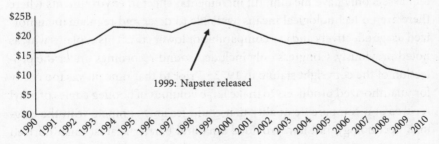

Figure 3.1 U.S. sales of recorded music, all formats (1990–2010, $B).
Source: Recording Industry Association of America.

willful.[2] However, the *expected* damages for infringement by an individual user who rationally discounts maximal damages by the extremely low probability of detection and enforcement are nominal. This reasoning (together with the fact that record labels now seldom pursue individual infringing users) explains why infringement widely persists: the costs are low and deferred, and the benefits are high and immediate. As a result, content owners' only meaningful litigation target—that is, the only target that could meaningfully curb the distribution of infringing content—has always been the much smaller group of digital intermediaries that either copy or distribute proprietary content or, more commonly, facilitate the ability of individual users to do so. As we will see, infringement-friendly judicial decisions have largely impeded content owners from deploying meaningful legal remedies against intermediaries that specialize in the aggregation and distribution of content assets.

At the onset of the internet, it might have seemed that content owners would likely prevail in the game of political influence over the enforcement of copyright laws against unauthorized use of proprietary content. For reference, Table 3.1 lists the primary commercial and legal developments in the years during the emergence and spread of mass file-sharing, which are all consistent with strict enforcement of the copyright laws.

In May 1999, Shawn Fanning and Sean Parker launched Napster, an online peer-to-peer file-sharing service, which immediately attracted millions of users. In December 1999, the Recording Industry Association of America filed a lawsuit seeking an injunction to shut down the Napster site.[3] A preliminary injunction was issued in July 2000 and then stayed by the appeals court, which upheld the lower court's ruling in April 2001, with instructions to modify the injunctive remedy.[4] As ultimately crafted, the injunction required Napster to remove from its site, within 72 hours, all infringing material identified by the record labels. Reportedly, the district court judge acknowledged the difficulties Napster would face in complying with this order, but stated that "[t]his difficulty ... does not relieve Napster of its duty."[5] In January 2002, the district court issued the final order that effectively shut down Napster, and the appellate court upheld the order in March 2002.[6] The district court judge reportedly stated in the proceedings that "Napster wrote the software; it's up to them to write software that will remove from users the ability to copy copyrighted materials. . . . They created a monster."[7] In a case decided in 2000 against mp3.com, a site that enabled users to store digital copies of CDs on a central server, the judge who rejected the infringer's

Table 3.1 Major Legal and Other Developments at the Emergence of Mass Digital File-Sharing (1999–2007)

May 1999	Launch of Napster
December 1999	Recording Industry Association of America files suit against Napster.
July 2000	Preliminary injunction issued against Napster but stayed on appeal.
April 2001	Appeals court affirms district court ruling in part, with instructions to modify certain terms of the injunction.
January 2002	Bertelsmann, German media conglomerate, enters into a partnership with Napster to launch a subscription site. Napster continues settlement talks with major record labels.
March 2002	Appeals court upholds injunction to shut down Napster site.
June 2005	Supreme Court issues *Grokster* decision, establishing a broad definition of secondary infringement liability under "inducement" theory.
May 2007	Ninth Circuit issues decision in *Perfect 10 v. Amazon.com et al.*, applying *Grokster* and clarifying that failure to take reasonable measures to stop user infringement can support secondary liability.

Sources: Hu 2002; *A&M Records Inc. et al. v. Napster, Inc.*, 114 F.Supp.2d 896 (N.D. Cal. 2000); *A&M Records Inc. et al. v. Napster, Inc.*, 239 F.3d 1004 (9th Cir. 2001); *Metro-Goldwyn-Mayer Studios Inc. et al. v. Grokster, Ltd., et al.*, 545 U.S. 913 (2005); *Perfect 10, Inc. v. Amazon.com, Inc. et al.*, 508 F.3d 1146 (9th Cir. 2007).

fair use defense employed similarly condemnatory language: "[S]tripped to its essence, defendant's . . . argument amounts to nothing more than a bald claim that defendant should be able to misappropriate plaintiff's property simply because there is a consumer demand for it. This hardly appeals to the conscience of equity."[8] This type of language would soon virtually disappear from judicial opinions issued in copyright litigation.

While Napster's peer-to-peer file-sharing service was soon replicated with some modification by other sites, such as Grokster, Kazaa, and Limewire, it was nonetheless clear that the courts had adopted an understanding of copyright law that prioritized meaningful protections for copyright owners. This impression was confirmed by the Supreme Court's 2005 ruling in *MGM et al. v. Grokster*.[9] In that case, the Court adopted two holdings that generally lowered the bar for copyright owners who sought to hold an online intermediary liable for mass user infringement on its site. Both holdings operated to the advantage of the originators and owners of content assets.

First, the Court effectively eliminated what had been known as the "Sony safe harbor," a generously defined exemption to indirect infringement liability that the Court had established in a 1984 case, *Sony Corporation of America v. Universal City Studios, Inc., et al.*[10] Under that safe harbor, a firm could avoid liability for indirect infringement so long as its technology enabled at least one type of non-infringing use (subject to the condition that the firm did not have "specific knowledge" of particular cases of infringing activity). Hence, Sony avoided indirect infringement liability for having distributed the Betamax video cassette recorder since it had no knowledge of specific infringing activities by individual users, and the device was capable of being used to record public-domain content that was not protected by copyright. Under the Sony safe harbor, Grokster might have similarly avoided liability because, unlike Napster, it did not use a central server (rather, users were directly connected to each other through a peer-to-peer network) and therefore could arguably claim it had no direct knowledge of specific cases of infringing activity.

Second, the court adopted an "inducement" theory under which an intermediary could be liable for indirect infringement if it either facilitated user infringement or failed to take reasonable measures to deter and stop infringement. This owner-friendly holding—especially the possibility of liability by omission—was reiterated in 2007 by the Court of Appeals for the Ninth Circuit in *Perfect 10, Inc. v. Amazon.com et al.*[11] In that case, Google (among other defendants) was sued for facilitating infringement of the plaintiff's copyright-protected images to which the plaintiff sold access through a subscription site. While the court found that Google was not liable for displaying "thumbnail" versions of the images, it did find that Google's search function enabled users to locate third-party sites that displayed full-size versions of the images and were offering access at no fee. Google was therefore exposed to potential liability for contributory infringement for failing to take reasonable measures to stop infringement. Given that liability for "crimes of omission" can never be fully eliminated (since there is always doubt about what additional "reasonable" measures could have been undertaken), the *Grokster* and *Perfect 10* decisions bolstered content owners' bargaining position in any prospective litigation or settlement negotiation with digital intermediaries engaged in facilitating the copying and distribution of copyright-protected content. Yet this victory for content owners would be short-lived. While the Grokster site was shut down in connection with a settlement following the Supreme Court's decision,[12] any credible threat of injunctive relief against similar sites would soon evaporate.

3.2. The Anti-Copyright Movement

Decisions such as *Napster* and *Grokster*, coupled with the music industry's occasional suits against individual users during the early days of the internet, elicited something close to a rebellion among key constituencies in the then-emerging anti-copyright coalition. These constituencies included individual users (especially, college-age users of file-sharing networks), advocacy organizations, legal academics, and legal clinics at law schools around the country. While a dispersed large-numbers group such as individual users would not typically be expected to have a strong voice in the political process, end-users in this case could exercise some influence at a low cost by simply continuing to engage in the type of mass infringement that had given rise to the *Napster* and *Grokster* litigations. Unlike other forms of political expression, this was not a costly exercise. To the contrary: listening to music on free file-sharing services is an enjoyable activity and saves money compared to the transaction costs and out-of-pocket expenses involved in purchasing a physical CD. Combined with the nominal level of expected infringement penalties, it is therefore unsurprising that neither the judiciary's copyright-friendly decisions nor the music industry's infringement suits against individual users had a meaningful deterrent effect. Unauthorized consumption of digitally distributed music continued to grow in tandem with the free fall in the sales of CDs at retailers such as Tower Records and Virgin Records. Effectively, uncoordinated individual acts of user infringement continuously reduced the effective strength of copyright protections and, as a result, the commercial value of the underlying pool of creative assets in the face of a zero-price alternative (coupled with a low chance of legal liability).

Concurrently with the user-led rebellion against the enforcement of copyright over musical works, an influential group of commentators, legal academics, think tanks, and advocacy organizations provided intellectual leadership that promoted a critique of the existing copyright regime and its initially forceful response to digital copying and transmission technologies. According to this critique, copyright law, and in particular the courts that elected to enforce it strictly, had been captured by the profit-seeking interests of "Big Media," which purportedly sought to protect its "monopoly franchise" against the competitive forces unleashed by the digital revolution.[13] These commentators argued that much of copyright law reflects a useful "romantic" fiction that creative production would decline dramatically absent the ability to earn returns through the legal exclusivity provided by copyright. Pointing to the apparent success of open-source software even though developers had largely waived copyright protections, these commentators rejected or heavily qualified the incentive-based justification of IP rights, which in turn supported proposals that copyright could be weakened considerably at little risk of harming content production.[14] Taking this argument a step further, some commentators questioned the system of authorial copyright in place since enactment of the Statute of Anne in 1709 and the U.S. Copyright Act in 1790.[15] William Patry, copyright counsel at Google since 2006 (and the author of the second most widely cited treatise on copyright law[16]), wrote in 2009 that "[a]ll works of authorship are to some extent communal works; it is therefore inappropriate to vest one person with rights that have the ability to impede the birth of future generations of works."[17] It is hard to articulate a more explicit rejection of the intellectual basis for the copyright system.

To be clear, commentators' proposals to curtail copyright protections differed in scope and intensity, and some sought to preserve meaningful levels of protection for originators and owners of creative assets. However, they shared in common the underlying view that, from the perspective of copyright policy, "digital is different" and merited a significant curtailment of copyright protections. This view rested on the observation that the digital revolution had dramatically lowered the costs of production, copying, and transmission of audio, video, and textual content. A YouTube music video could be produced and uploaded from a suburban garage, rather than renting expensive space in a professional studio and hiring the services of a professional sound engineer. If costs had fallen dramatically, then it followed that the economic returns necessary to motivate an investment in content production had been correspondingly reduced and copyright protections could be safely relaxed with little risk of causing harm to artists' production incentives. This argument applied the accepted utilitarian logic behind U.S. copyright law and, in light of changes in the cost structure of content production and distribution, deployed it to argue that copyright should be substantially curtailed (and, for some commentators, even potentially abolished in digital environments[18]). The result would be a policy "win-win" in which content production would remain robust and distribution would be enhanced while consumers would continue to enjoy the same or even greater amount or variety of content at a lower price. If that line of argument is correct, then any counterarguments made in favor of maintaining—or, even worse, enhancing—copyright protection could be safely dismissed as nothing but strategic rent-seeking by private interests or the intellectual confusion of misguided or uninformed commentators. In the remainder of this chapter, I will explore whether this widely held view withstands scrutiny in light of subsequent research in the empirical literature and subsequent developments in digital content markets.

3.3. The Making of the "Piracy Is Harmless" Myth

Between 1999 (when Napster launched) and 2008, the U.S. music industry experienced a steep decline in the sales of physical recorded music, falling from $12.8 billion to $5.5 billion in annual revenue.[19] Naturally, the music industry viewed the concurrent rise of file-sharing services as the cause of this exceptional decline in sales. As a matter of analytical rigor, this interpretation cannot be assessed without considering the potential influence of other factors. In academic and policy commentary (and in the Napster litigation itself), the industry's interpretation was challenged by those who argued that file-sharing either had no appreciable effect, or even promoted, sales of recorded music. The economic and legal academic literature produced several theoretical models in which the unauthorized consumption of creative goods either has little effect on sales of proprietary content or confers gains on copyright owners, usually due to hypothesized "sampling" and other "positive spillover" effects.[20] If demonstrated empirically, these arguments would challenge not only the conventional business model in the content industry, which had relied on the ability to preserve exclusivity over content assets, but the incentive justification for copyright itself.

To be clear, some of these arguments appropriately corrected for the exaggerated estimates of economic harm from piracy that had sometimes been claimed by the music industry, which reflected the implausible assumption that every illegally downloaded or shared album represented a lost sale on a one-for-one basis. This is not defensible since it is implausible that all file-sharers who "paid" a price of $0 for a particular album on Napster would otherwise have been willing to pay the full retail price of approximately $15 for that album at Tower Records. Yet it must also be the case that some of those users might have purchased the album absent the free option. In particular, it seems unlikely that the once-in-a-generation decline in record sales starting in the early 2000s was not attributable in substantial part to the roughly concurrent launch of Napster and other file-sharing sites, and the ensuing explosion in file-sharing activities by individual users. Attributing this sudden plunge in sales principally to other factors seems unlikely since no other contemporary development had taken place that could account for this development. To use social science terminology, the relationship between these two events seemed to be "highly suggestive" of a causal relationship, pending confirmation through formal empirical methods.

Researchers undertook this task by testing whether piracy has an adverse, positive, or neutral effect on purchases of recorded music (principally, in the form of CDs). Initial studies supported the expected adverse effect hypothesis, while recognizing that a material portion of file-sharing did not represent lost sales.[21] However, a working paper posted by economists Felix Oberholzer-Gee and Koleman Strumpf in 2004 and published in 2007 in the prestigious *Journal of Political Economy*[22] (the "OGS study") claimed to have demonstrated the opposite result and had a powerful impact on policy discussions and actions.

The authors presented statistical analysis purporting to show that file-sharing had an insignificant adverse impact on sales of recorded music. If correct, this would imply that almost all the unprecedented decline in recorded music sales following the launch of Napster was attributable to other causes. It is important to appreciate the narrow context in which the OGS study reached this result. To test whether file-sharing discourages recorded music purchases, the OGS study sought to test the causal effect on album purchases by U.S. consumers, during the last third of 2022, of an assumed increase in file-sharing usage by German high-school-age users during Christmas school holidays. This research strategy relied on three assumptions: (1) German high-school students have more leisure time during school holidays; (2) German high-school students use that leisure time to upload more albums than usual to file-sharing services; and (3) the increased music uploaded by German students to file-sharing services increases the supply of downloadable music to U.S. users of file-sharing services. If *all* those assumptions are true, then researchers could potentially test whether this assumed increase in file-sharing by German high-school students during school holidays in the last third of 2002 had an adverse impact on U.S. album purchases. Within this particular analytical framework, the study found that the purportedly increased availability of downloadable digital music for U.S. consumers during this period had no statistically significant impact on album purchases by those consumers.

This finding attracted considerable attention in the press and was sometimes referenced in copyright-skeptical policy commentary as almost definitive evidence for the far broader claim that the record industry's claims of substantial economic losses due to file-sharing were false or grossly exaggerated. The OGS study was covered in the *New York Times*, which called attention to a "heretical view of file sharing" when the study was posted online in 2004, and again in 2007 when it was published.[23] The generalized interpretation of the paper was typically made without reference to the narrow time period analyzed in the study and the fragile chain of assumptions on which its findings rested. The study's authors engaged in similar generalizations by suggesting that the results cast doubt on the loss in sales and other economic harms attributed to file-sharing.[24] In the Supreme Court's 2005 case, *Metro-Goldwyn-Mayer v. Grokster*, the authors filed an amicus brief, in which they asserted that the steep decline in recorded music sales since the advent of file-sharing was likely due to causes other than the sudden availability of free music.[25] The study was cited for that proposition in the dissenting opinion by three Supreme Court Justices who had supported finding in favor of the defendant file-sharing site.[26]

Today the OGS study is an outlier in the empirical literature on file-sharing and has been reviewed closely by other researchers, who have identified logical inconsistencies, undemonstrated assumptions, and imprecise data sources (especially, data on file-sharing activity) in various parts of the paper.[27] With the exception of only one other study (which itself has been rebutted by subsequent researchers who sought to replicate its results and discovered significant omitted data[28]), all other peer-reviewed economic studies have found support for the mundane but unsurprising proposition that file-sharing at a zero price causes a material reduction in purchases of recorded music at a positive price. While the state of the literature is still sometimes described as "mixed," this is only true concerning the *size* of the adverse effect of piracy on sales of recorded music. Moreover, there is general agreement in the empirical literature that the size of the adverse effect is significant, and a substantial portion of the literature takes the view that piracy can explain most of the decline in sales of recorded music.[29] A 2014 review of the literature observes: "[O]ne may wish to view their [OGS's] result relative to the large number of more recent papers, and more recent data sets, finding a strong and significant impact of piracy on music sales."[30] More broadly, the review states: "[T]aken as a whole we see a very consistent story across the academic literature: the vast majority of papers that have been published in peer-review journals—papers spanning a variety of methods, time periods, and contexts—find that piracy causes a statistically significant decrease in sales."[31] Even the authors of the

OGS study have recognized in two more recent papers that the empirical literature observes that piracy "displaces" a material percentage of recorded music sales (although they still point to other factors as playing a more predominant causal role in the decline of recorded music sales).[32]

Figure 3.2 presents all relevant published empirical studies in the peer-reviewed literature (to my knowledge, as of March 2022) on the effect of unauthorized consumption on sales of recorded music and other forms of content, such as motion pictures, television, and video streaming. With one limited exception (concerning movies shown on broadcast television[33]), the same result is found: free content displaces paid content to some significant extent. Additionally, Figure 3.2 includes three studies that show significant

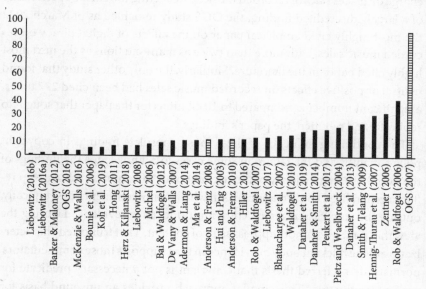

Figure 3.2 Citations per year to peer-reviewed empirical studies on effect of unauthorized consumption on content sales (recorded music, motion pictures, and streaming video).

Legend: Solid bars denote papers that find no significant adverse effects of piracy on sales of original content. Bars with a stripe pattern denote papers that find significant adverse effects. OGS = Oberholzer-Gee & Strumpf.

Notes: All citations located through Google Scholar, as of March 2022 (various dates), and presented on a per-year basis since year of publication. For this purpose, the year of publication is counted in full and three months of 2022 are counted. Citations include self-citations and acknowledgements. Anderson and Frenz (2010) is a modified version of Anderson and Frenz (2008). Barker and Maloney (2012) is a replication study of Anderson and Frenz (2010) and Liebowitz (2017) is a replication study of Oberholzer-Gee and Strumpf (2007), which are both unable to replicate the findings of the original study.

Sources: For full citations to sources, see References.

increases in paid music consumption in jurisdictions that adopted anti-piracy penalties or requirements to block piracy websites,[34] which supports by negative implication the finding that piracy suppresses paid consumption of musical or video content.

Despite the abundance and consistency of evidence in the empirical literature, some commentary and scholarship on copyright policy continue to focus on two published studies (and in particular, the OGS study) out of over 30 studies in total that have failed to find significant adverse effects from file-sharing on sales of recorded music. Hence, it is still sometimes stated (usually by policy advocates and academics outside the economics literature) that there is no clear factual case that unauthorized distribution of music at no charge displaces sales of recorded music.[35] Reflecting the curious persistence of a largely discredited finding, the OGS study remained as of March 2022 the most highly cited empirical paper on the effects of digital piracy on recorded music sales, with more than twice as many citations as the next most highly cited paper in the literature. Similarly, the only other study that found neutral or positive effects on recorded music sales had been cited 277 times, a significant number as compared to 10 citations for the paper that sought to replicate, and rebutted, the paper's findings.[36]

The continuing influence of these mostly obsolete findings in copyright policy analysis and the failure in some cases to acknowledge the findings of the overwhelming majority of the relevant body of empirical scholarship reflect a generalized confirmation bias in which many commentators (typically, outside the empirical research community) focus on evidence favoring the view that piracy does not suppress sales of content. That truncated characterization of the relevant body of evidence in turn supports those commentators' normatively preferred thesis that copyright is not a necessary predicate for content production. This circular approach provides an unsound basis for policy analysis. While there remain difficult-to-resolve empirical questions concerning the precise impact of file-sharing on the quantity and quality of content production (quality being an especially complex parameter to assess objectively), and the net welfare effects of file-sharing (to which I will return), it *is* settled that making available content at a zero price displaces a substantial volume of sales of that same content at a positive price.

It is almost bewildering that so much effort had been necessary to establish this common-sense proposition. It is especially puzzling since, if it were really true that file-sharing does not threaten, and may even promote, sales of recorded music (as some legal academics have asserted, referring to a "flattery effect"[37]), then the music industry should have *welcomed* Napster, put its founder Shawn Fanning on a generous retainer and national speaking tour, and subsidized the site's launch and expansion, rather than "foolishly" seeking to shut it down. Since that is not the case, it must then follow that scholars who argued (and sometimes still argue) that file-sharing does not discourage (and may even promote) recorded music sales know more about the music business than individuals who depend on it for their livelihood.

This type of "experts know better" argument is typically supported by reference to the example of the video cassette recorder (or VCR), which the motion picture industry apparently resisted in *Sony Corporation of America v. Universal City Studios, Inc.*, decided by the Supreme Court in 1984.[38] Following the standard account, the industry was foolish to bring the litigation (or was lucky to have lost it) since the VCR spawned the home video market, which generated lucrative revenue streams for the motion picture industry through VHS and DVD sales and rentals. This common interpretation overlooks two key points.

First, the motion picture industry never sought to suppress the VCR; rather, it sought legislative intervention to assess a levy on VCR sales to secure some compensation for the infringing uses for which the device inevitably would be used.[39] Second, the economic success of the market for VHS tapes, and subsequently DVDs, arose in part from the fact that the industry had technological and legal means to deter piracy for each medium. In the case of VHS tapes, copies could not easily be made on a mass scale and had inferior quality relative to the original. In the case of DVDs, the motion picture industry adopted an encryption standard that blocked copying by most home users[40] and secured court rulings that the anti-circumvention clause in the Digital Millennium Copyright Act (DMCA) barred the sale of software and hardware that would enable users to copy DVDs easily.[41] Absent these barriers to copying, the motion picture industry may well have been correct in viewing the VCR (and its subsequent iteration, the DVD player) as a serious threat. This possibility is supported by the fact that CDs, unlike DVDs, were sold without effective copy protection, which, combined with the availability of CD "burners," MP3 digital files, and file-sharing services starting in the late 1990s, contributed to the dramatic decline in sales of recorded music.

3.4. From Open Source to "Free" Search

The analytical efforts by some IP scholars, and the practical efforts of open-source developers, to develop a non-profit-motivated model of software production that mostly waives copyright protections might have fallen into the crowded graveyard of failed experiments to sustain economic activity based on altruistic arrangements in lieu of property rights. However, a not-so-accidental development resulted in the adoption by federal courts of the "IP-lite" policy approach preferred by copyright-skeptical advocates and commentators. While these thought leaders and policy activists were advocating a weaker copyright regime to preserve access for users against purported overreaching by "Big Media," and small groups of open-source developers were experimenting with volunteer-based models of software production as an alternative to the profit-making model then epitomized by Microsoft, start-ups in Silicon Valley were engineering a business strategy that thrives on the uncompensated use and distribution of informational assets generated by others. Unlike the "hacker culture" programmers who had originated open-source software projects in the 1970s,[42] or the academics who endorsed this model and proposed applying it more broadly as a copyright-free template for intellectual production, these tech start-ups were profit-seeking enterprises backed by profit-seeking investors and, in that respect, indistinguishable from the incumbent software companies and media and entertainment companies that defended the necessity of copyright protection.

Unlike those established companies, however, the tech start-ups had developed a business model for which IP protections were a *hindrance*. That model relies on a giveaway strategy that unilaterally makes use of others' content assets, delivering an abundance of audio, video, and textual content at a zero out-of-pocket cost for end-users. Conventional enterprises in content markets operate under a business model that invests in the production of original content and other informational assets, which are then sold at a positive price to users. By contrast, the tech start-ups developed business models in which informational assets are appropriated from content producers and "shared" among end-users, who in turn support the sale of advertising or complementary services to business users.

3.4.1. The Dilemma of Commercial Search

This two-sided strategy (free content for users, paid ads from businesses) arose in part as a solution to a fundamental business dilemma to which there was no clear solution at the inception of the commercial internet. Specifically, it was not clear how to extract value from the search engines that enabled users to feasibly navigate the wealth of information available through the internet. To appreciate this point, it is necessary to review briefly the historical development of the search-engine market, both in terms of its technology and leading business models.

The genesis of Google can be dated from Sergey Brin and Larry Page's citation-based PageRank algorithm,[43] which arose out of their research as doctoral students in computer science at Stanford. Existing search services then relied on keyword methodologies that rank and display webpages based on the pages' relevance to the user's search terms (as measured by the number of times a search term appears on a particular page or other criteria). Inspired by the citation-based criteria used to rank academic researchers and papers, Brin and Page's search technology ranked web pages based not only on a page's relevance to the user's search terms, but on how many other relevant web pages linked to that page. This modification improved considerably the relevance of search results to a user's search words. The PageRank algorithm was described by Brin and Page in an academic paper in 1998, "The Anatomy of a Large-Scale Hypertextual Web Search Engine," and in a subsequent technical paper released (with additional coauthors) in 1999, "The PageRank Citation Ranking: Bringing Order to the Web."[44] The papers followed Page's submission in 1997 of a provisional patent application, which resulted in a patent being issued in 2001 (U.S. Patent No. 6285999B1, "Scoring documents in a linked database"). The patent was "first assigned" to Stanford University (meaning that the individual inventors listed Stanford as the assignee on the issued patent), which then licensed it back to Google on an exclusive basis for the duration of the patent term. In 1998, the Google search service was launched.

For Google's founders and investors, the search-engine method for organizing and enabling access to information on the internet posed not only a technical but an economic challenge. While the search engine required significant and ongoing development and maintenance costs, it lacked a business model for funding these activities and earning a positive return on investment. This question required an answer if Google would be economically viable and could retain and elicit investor interest. Google's founders were initially wary of advertising on the grounds that it might compromise the search results and contemplated licensing the search service to internet service portals and selling customized search services to businesses.[45] In a 1998 paper, they wrote: "[A]dvertising income often provides an incentive to provide poor quality search results. . . . In general, it could be argued from the consumer point of view that the better the search engine is, the fewer advertisements will be needed for the consumer to find what they want. This of course erodes the advertising supported business model of the existing search engines."[46]

Google's founders ultimately rethought this position. Google adopted a hybrid search model comprising organic search results, which reflect relevance to the user's query as determined by the search algorithm, and "sponsored" search results, which reflect a combination of the bid fee offered by an advertiser for a particular keyword through the "AdWords" program and the relevance of the bidder's website to that keyword. In sponsored search results, the advertiser pays its bid price whenever a user clicks on the advertiser's ad, reflecting a "pay per click" model pioneered by a rival search engine, GoTo.com.[47] As a result of this shift in strategy, advertising became Google's dominant revenue stream. Subsequently, Google introduced the "AdSense" program in which website owners can sell display space on their websites to Google's network of advertisers, which are selected based on a combination of bid price and search relevance. In both the AdWords and AdSense programs, payments by advertisers subsidize the search services used by individuals at no charge and enable Google to provide organic search results that are uninfluenced by advertiser bid payments.

3.4.2. How Commercial Search Commoditized Content

Google's search engine solved the founders' business dilemma by providing a matching technology that enables mutually beneficial relationships between users, websites, and advertisers, which in turn generate a revenue stream that can fund continued operation and maintenance of the search service. While this two-sided business model proved to be a successful mechanism for indirectly extracting returns on investments in developing, updating, and delivering search-engine services, it inherently posed a threat to the one-sided business model of content owners who invest in the production of audio, video, and textual works and then deliver those works to consumers in exchange for direct payment.

To illustrate this risk, suppose a user searches for "Madonna's Greatest Hits." Excluding for simplicity sponsored search results, the search engine would display a list of sites with the most relevant information as determined by the search algorithm. While some of those sites would be a licensed source of the queried content and may charge a fee for access, other sites may offer at no charge content that was copied without authorization. Alternatively, a user might search for "free new movie releases," which would direct the user primarily to sites offering pirated versions of newly released movies while enabling Google to earn revenues when it auctions the keywords (the AdWords program) and sells ad display space on pirate websites (the AdSense program).[48] Magnified many times over, the Google search engine could link millions of users to millions of items of infringing material, rendering it virtually impossible for a content owner to detect and take action against any meaningful portion of these infringing sites. At the same time, Google earns revenues from content to which it contributed nothing to produce.

The value that can be generated through a "take and give away" model is most vividly illustrated by YouTube, which was founded in 2005 and was acquired by Google in 2006 for $1.65 billion.[49] All content on YouTube, which is now the world's leading video-sharing website, is uploaded by users and then is searchable by other users, who can choose to view selected content. According to internal surveys reportedly conducted by YouTube in the early years of the site (and referenced by the plaintiffs in the *Viacom v. YouTube* litigation), 75%–80% of all streams available on YouTube during this period contained copyright-protected material.[50] This abundance of free content likely explains in part why YouTube rapidly became the leading online site for accessing music, rather than paid-download alternatives that had been established by various music industry consortia. In 2001, Pressplay, a paid-download music website, was launched by Vivendi Universal and Sony, two of the largest record labels, and MusicNet was launched by RealNetworks (in cooperation with BMG and EMI, another two of the largest record labels, and AOL Time Warner), in both cases as legal alternatives to unlicensed sites such as Napster.[51] Both sites failed to secure user adoption.

Various reasons are reported for these sites' failure: subscription-only offerings (as distinguished from MP3 downloads), limited inventories (because the sites only offered music from the sponsoring labels), intrusive anti-copy protections, antitrust concerns raised by a cooperative venture among direct competitors, and managerial incompetence.[52] Yet the simplest explanation is price. Napster (and, after it was shutdown, substitutes such as Kazaa, Limewire, and Grokster) was free, while Pressplay and MusicNet were not. Unless there are significant differences in product coverage, user convenience, or site safety, or a substantial portion of users have an exaggerated expectation of liability exposure for copyright infringement, it is difficult to compete with a free version of the same product, just as Netscape was defeated by Microsoft's free internet browser and Garmin and Tom-Tom were defeated by Google's Google Maps application. (I will subsequently discuss why Apple's iTunes music subscription service was nonetheless able to secure significant user adoption in a weak-copyright environment.) The same consideration may account in part for YouTube's success over MySpace, a free music file-sharing site that had enjoyed a dominant market share prior to YouTube's entry. In contrast to YouTube's merely reactive (if not dismissive) policy toward copyright infringement, MySpace made affirmative efforts to detect and remove infringing material from its site.[53] That posed a liability in its competition with YouTube, which did not make similar efforts and therefore offered users a richer inventory of musical content.

There is one obstacle that stood in the way of YouTube's success. A giveaway business model that relies on content or other intellectual assets originated by others requires a conducive legal environment—specifically, relaxed or no protection of IP rights over that content. For a site like YouTube that directly hosts infringing content uploaded by users, and to a lesser but still significant extent for a site like Google Search that links to infringing material, robust enforcement of the copyright laws is not conducive to eliminating content acquisition costs, minimizing infringement liability exposure, and maximizing net returns. Put more simply: strong copyright is bad for business. There are three reasons.

First, when enforcement of IP rights over content is robust, content owners can credibly threaten to withhold a valuable content asset absent a license, and the site operator may be compelled to pay fees to acquire a content inventory that is sufficient to attract a user base to support advertising sales. Second, the threat of copyright liability may lead users, or at least more risk-averse users, to avoid using the site—for example, users faced with a meaningful threat of copyright liability might decline to upload content to the YouTube site, which would then fail to attract other users, which would in turn harm the site's ability to attract advertisers. Third, the threat of *indirect* liability for facilitating copyright infringement could expose a site like YouTube to the threat of a shutdown injunction and billions of dollars in statutory damages. This was precisely the predicament YouTube faced in the infringement litigation brought against it by Viacom and other content owners, who claimed approximately one billion dollars in damages. Since YouTube did not produce original content, it was a net content consumer and therefore preferred a regime of weak copyright protection that would keep the platform's content-acquisition costs to a minimum, reduce users' and the platform's liability exposure in connection with using the site, and increase the platform's profit on the advertising services offered to paying firms. (As I discuss in Chapter 16, YouTube may now adopt a more nuanced view on copyright protection given that it operates the paid-subscription YouTube Premium and YouTube Music services, although these services' approximately 80 million paying subscribers still represent a small portion of YouTube's approximately 1.1 billion users, as of 2022.[54])

It is sometimes argued that content aggregators are simply following the long-standing monetization model developed by terrestrial radio, which distributes content at no cost while extracting revenues through paid advertisements. The analogy fails, however, in one critical respect. Under the public performance right in U.S. copyright law,[55] all terrestrial radio stations must pay a royalty to the owners of the composition copyrights (typically represented by a collective licensing entity) in the music that is being played on the air. By contrast, YouTube's founders chose to pay nothing to content owners and, at least initially, apparently took no meaningful efforts to deter users from distributing content through the YouTube site. In some cases, YouTube management even facilitated these activities. This is clear from the factual record developed in the *Viacom v. YouTube* litigation, which shows that YouTube management selected specific TV shows and other high-value content to remain on the site, did not regularly monitor the site for infringing material, and sometimes chose to leave infringing material on the site to attract users and advertising revenue.[56] Internal emails obtained through discovery in the *Viacom v. YouTube* litigation show that YouTube management was aware that copyright-protected content accounted for three-quarters or more of the views on the site in its early years.[57]

This behavior may seem morally unremarkable today—for some commentators and a significant portion of the tech industry, this is just a different strategy of earning returns on content. But that was not the case when Napster, YouTube, and similar services were launched. In the litigation involving Napster, the district court judge reportedly called the website a "monster" (as noted previously) and then issued an injunction to shut down the site.[58] Similarly, the Supreme Court's majority opinion in the *Grokster* case observed in 1996 with apparent dismay that the "probable scope of copyright infringement is staggering."[59] When Google purchased YouTube in 2006 for $1.65 billion, the famous entrepreneur Mark Cuban wrote a short piece called "I think Google is crazy," writing: "I still think Google Lawyers will be a busy, busy bunch. I don't think you can sue Google into oblivion, but as others have mentioned, if Google gets nailed one single time for copyright violation, there are going to be more shareholder lawsuits than Doans [a pill manufacturer] has pills to go with the pile on copyright suits that follow."[60] In more diplomatic language, the *Financial Times* observed that "[in] spite of YouTube's popularity there have been questions about the sustainability of the company in light of the large amount of illegally copied material on the site and limited advertising revenues to date."[61]

Twenty-five years after the launch of Napster and almost 20 years after the *Grokster* decision, few contemporary judges would use such condemnatory language to describe the activities of a content aggregator, and no one doubts the business wisdom of Google's acquisition of YouTube. In its 2012 decision in favor of YouTube in the *Viacom v. YouTube* litigation, the district court took an entirely different view of the legal obligations of an online intermediary in a mass-piracy environment: "Plaintiffs often suggest that YouTube can readily locate the infringements by using its own identification tools. It had no duty to do so."[62] While Cuban was right that Google's lawyers were busy, its lawyers secured legal precedents that almost entirely neutralized concerns about "pile on copyright lawsuits." As I will discuss subsequently, changes in case law concerning indirect copyright infringement (which in turn reflect changes in judicial attitudes toward copyright infringement) mean that YouTube today has virtually no practical exposure to legal liability (provided it meets certain easy-to-satisfy requirements) even though it operates a website that is still heavily populated by proprietary content that has been copied and distributed without consent. The legal landscape and the accompanying norms concerning the unauthorized consumption of copyright-protected content have changed considerably since the shutdown of Napster in 2002.

3.5. Closing Thoughts

This chapter has described the genesis of the accidental alliance between ideological opponents of copyright and profit-motivated technology companies that relied on appropriating and giving away content to attract a large user base, which could then be used to generate ad revenues. The concurrence of ideological and profit-driven constituencies with a mutual interest in weakening copyright protections emerged as a powerful force in shifting copyright law away from courts' issuance of shutdown injunctions against file-sharing sites that facilitated mass piracy. Those decisions elicited a vigorous response by the key members of the accidental alliance, which was in turn broadly supported by individual users who had an economic interest in securing access to "free stuff." This response took multiple forms. First, the academic and policy advocacy communities widely advanced the view that robust copyright protections posed a grave risk to user access and content production in the creative and software markets. Some members of those communities also asserted that piracy posed little risk of economic harm to copyright owners (a view that has since been rebutted empirically) and contended that exclusivity was not necessary to sustain content and software production. Second, search engines, file-sharing, and social networking platforms (likely inspired in some cases by the institutional precedent set by open-source software communities) developed business models that thrived in a legal environment in which copyright protections were weakly interpreted and enforced. As will be discussed in the following chapters, the convergence of these two forces—one ideological, one commercial—produced a perfect storm that led to a dramatic shift in the trajectory of copyright law.

4

The Rise of Unfair Use

The doctrine of fair use as it is currently applied by the federal courts bears little resemblance to the understanding of the doctrine when it first entered the case law, when it was codified in the copyright statute in 1976, or as it was generally interpreted by courts through approximately the mid-2000s. In this chapter, I explore how courts have significantly expanded the scope of the fair use doctrine in a manner that departs from historical understandings of the doctrine's narrow purpose and that suits the business model of search engines, content aggregators, and other intermediaries that rely on using content produced by others. In particular, I illustrate how one of the world's largest digital content aggregators, together with intellectually convergent views expressed by thought leaders in the academic and advocacy communities, changed the "rules of the game" in content and information markets by securing decisions that expanded the scope of the fair use exemption in landmark infringement litigations triggered by three Google projects: Google Books, Google Images, and Google's Android operating system.

4.1. Judicial Expansion of the Fair Use Doctrine

The currently expansive understanding of the fair use doctrine—and in particular, the concept of "transformative use"—is usually attributed to the Supreme Court's 1994 decision in *Campbell v. Acuff-Rose Inc.* As I discuss, it is not clear that the Court intended in this decision to make any substantial departure from historically narrow applications of the fair use doctrine. Rather, it appears that the view that the *Campbell* decision had endorsed a newly expansive understanding of the fair use doctrine arose primarily due to lower-court decisions starting about a decade after the decision had been issued. Some of those decisions have understood fair use so expansively that it is hard to reconcile with other protections—in particular, the derivative right—expressly granted to copyright owners under the copyright statute. As

The Big Steal. Jonathan M. Barnett, Oxford University Press. © Oxford University Press 2024.
DOI: 10.1093/oso/9780197629529.003.0005

will be discussed, the Supreme Court's 2023 decision in *Warhol Foundation for the Visual Arts v. Goldsmith*[1] has placed limits on the fair use exemption in an apparent effort to address this tension.

4.1.1. The Back Story

The origins of the fair use doctrine in U.S. copyright law are usually attributed to *Folsom v. Marsh*, an 1841 decision in which Supreme Court Justice Joseph Story carved out an exemption to copyright infringement for copying limited portions of an existing work for "the purposes of fair and reasonable criticism."[2] (Ironically, the actual result in the case was a finding that there had been *no* fair use under that standard.) In this opinion, Story drew a key distinction between uses that "criticize" and uses that "supersede" the original work:

> A reviewer may fairly cite largely from the original work, so long as his design be really and truly to use the passages for the purposes of fair and reasonable criticism. On the other hand, it is as clear, that if thus cites the most important parts of the work, with a view, not to criticize, but to supersede the use of the original work, and substitute the review for it, such a use will be deemed in law a piracy.[3]

Based on the language codifying the fair use doctrine in the Copyright Act of 1976, the doctrine applies most clearly to certain specified forms of commentary and criticism, such as "criticism, comment, news reporting, teaching . . . scholarship, or research."[4] Fair use does not automatically encompass these activities and may extend to other unspecified activities, in each case subject to a four-factor test set forth in the statute. Specifically, the statute instructs courts to consider the purpose and character of the infringing use, the "substantiality" of the infringing use, the nature of the original work (creative or factual), and the extent to which the infringing use substantially impacts the actual or potential market for the original work.[5]

Harper & Row v. Nation Enterprises, a case decided by the Supreme Court in 1985,[6] set forth a relatively narrow understanding of the fair use exemption and arguably reflected the general understanding of the fair use doctrine at that time and for much of its history. The facts involved a brazen act of expropriation. The *Nation* magazine had obtained access to a copy of the unpublished manuscript of former President Gerald Ford's memoirs and published an excerpt from the book. The excerpt only consisted of about 400 words but was substantively significant and led *Time* magazine (at the time, one of the country's most widely read news publications) to withdraw its prior commitment to publish selected portions from the book. While the infringing use was for news reporting purposes, a statutorily recognized category of fair use,[7] the Court rejected the *Nation*'s fair use defense on the ground that it had copied a critical portion of the original work, resulting in direct financial harm to the copyright owner, as shown by the loss of the *Time* contract. Additionally, the infringing use was made for commercial purposes, which the Court held "tends to weigh against a finding of fair use."[8] Using the terminology from *Folsom v. Marsh*, the publisher's use had therefore "superseded" the original work, in which case the fair use defense must fail. Emphasizing this point, the *Harper & Row* decision clarified that the market effect factor "is undoubtedly the single most important element of fair use,"[9] a view that flows naturally from the understanding that copyright supports the incentives of artists and other participants in the creative ecosystem to make investments in the development and cultivation of new creative works.

4.1.2. The *Campbell* Decision

If a lawyer familiar with the *Harper & Row* decision and subsequent case law had been told that federal courts would apply the fair use doctrine to exempt from liability entities that engaged in mass unauthorized reproduction of copyright-protected works, that lawyer might well have been incredulous. Case law during the two decades following the *Harper & Row* decision exhibited a tendency to apply the fair use doctrine fairly narrowly under what Neil Netanel has called a "market-centered" paradigm, which treats fair use "as an anomalous exception to the copyright owner's exclusive rights."[10] In 1994, the Second Circuit ruled that fair use did not extend to photocopying by a corporation's employees of articles from a scientific journal solely for internal use within the corporation's laboratories, even though the corporation had legitimately purchased multiple copies of the original journal (but fewer than the number of copies the corporation required).[11] In 1995, the Southern District of Texas held that the reproduction of warning labels used in computer hard drives did not constitute fair use, even though it found

THE RISE OF UNFAIR USE   83

that the infringing use could not cause any market harm to the copyright owner.[12] In 1996, the Northern District of California held that the reproduction of a "trailer" from a motion picture for purposes of demonstrating the defendant's 3D-viewing technology did not qualify for fair use, again in the absence of evidence of market harm.[13] In 1997, the Second Circuit held that a *four-and-a-half second* appearance of a quilt in a television show did not clearly qualify for fair use (due to the absence of any commentary on the original work and potential lost licensing revenue) and therefore reversed a district court's dismissal of the claim on summary judgment.[14] These are just a few examples of a prevailing tendency during this period to read the fair use exemption narrowly.

The genesis of the dramatic shift in the scope of the fair use exemption finds its somewhat accidental origins in the Supreme Court's decision in the 1994 case, *Campbell v. Acuff-Rose Inc.*[15] The case involved the deliberate use of a portion of the music and lyrics (including the distinctive opening bass "riff") in Roy Orbison's hit song, "Oh, Pretty Woman," by the rap group 2 Live Crew in its song bearing almost the same title, "Pretty Woman." The Court held that 2 Live Crew's song qualified as "parodic use" and was therefore the type of "critical commentary" that the fair use doctrine was designed to protect. Prior case law in the lower courts had repeatedly found fair use in the case of parodic uses so this determination was not especially remarkable.[16] In light of the Court's conclusion that it was at least reasonable to conclude that 2 Live Crew's use of the original work was a parodic commentary on the original work, it remanded the fair use defense for factual inquiry concerning the potential for economic harm to the copyright owner. The Court also held that the burden of proof on economic harm in a fair use claim rests with the defendant,[17] a ruling that made it *harder* to prevail on a fair use claim. The Court's determinations would not necessarily have suggested any significant shift in the scope of the fair use exemption and might have been interpreted as a special case of parodic infringing use—an entirely uncontroversial result since criticism had always been understood to be a classic case of fair use. In fact, some commentary following the case adopted this narrow understanding, effectively treating the *Campbell* case as a minor clarification of existing case law.[18]

Two elements of the opinion, however, provided the basis for the lower courts' subsequent expansion of the fair use exemption beyond the bounds that had been set forth in *Harper & Row* and *Folsom v. Marsh* (and arguably in the *Campbell* decision itself).

First, the Court held in *Campbell* that a commercial purpose should not categorically bar a fair use defense.[19] This statement arguably only clarified existing case law, rather than modifying it, given that the Court in *Harper & Row* had already stated that commercial character was merely a factor that "tends to weigh against a finding of fair use."[20] Second, and more importantly, the Court expanded fair use to encompass not only the types of commentary, criticism, and news reporting specifically contemplated by the statute and existing case law as fair use–eligible categories, but a potentially wider category of what the Court called "transformative" uses that add a "new expression, meaning, or message to the original work."[21] The Court's cited source for this principle was not found in prior case law or legislative history, but rather in a law review article published in 1990[22] by Judge Pierre Leval of the Southern District of New York. Claiming a historical pedigree dating to an 1802 British case,[23] Leval argued that "transformative use" encompassed both existing recognized categories of fair use, such as "criticizing the quoted work," and more loosely defined categories, such as "symbolism, aesthetic declarations, and innumerable other uses."[24] At the same time, Leval emphasized that "[t]he existence of any identifiable transformative objective does not . . . guarantee success in claiming fair use" and "[t]he transformative justification must overcome factors favoring the copyright owner."[25] The Court referenced Leval's transformative use concept in supporting its treatment of parody as fair use (a type of use explicitly referenced by Leval[26]), although it could have reached the same conclusion based on existing case law and statutory language specifically applying the fair use exemption to criticism. Hence, it is plausible to argue that the reference to "transformative use" in the *Campbell* opinion was merely an effort to clarify existing case law but without any intention to expand (or expand significantly) the boundaries of the fair use exemption.

4.1.3. *Campbell* in the Lower Courts

Lower courts might have plausibly read the *Campbell* decision narrowly and confined it to cases involving parodic use. This is arguably the most natural interpretation since the specific question for which the Court had heard the case was "to determine whether 2 Live Crew's commercial parody could be a fair use."[27] Some contemporary commentators, who advocated expanding the fair use exemption, even criticized the decision on the ground that the "transformative use" concept, which demands a showing of new meaning, message, or purpose for purposes of the first factor of a fair use analysis, had *raised* the bar for making a successful fair use defense.[28] This view had some foundation. Leval's article, which was referenced by *Campbell* as the source of the transformative use concept, had applied the concept to criticize what the author felt to be certain *overly generous* applications of fair use, which were described as "takings of protected expression without sufficient trans- formative justification."[29] Two legal scholars writing three years after the *Campbell* decision observed that lower courts generally continued to deny fair use whenever a plaintiff could show market harm under the fourth factor of a fair use analysis.[30] This suggests that courts had adhered to the Court's instruction in *Harper & Row* that the market harm factor should be given preeminence in a fair use analysis.[31] This also suggests that courts did not initially view *Campbell* as having broken new ground in fair use doctrine (except possibly in the special case of parody).

These qualitative discussions are consistent with the results reached by scholars who have surveyed fair use case law comprehensively. Prior to ap- proximately 2005, these studies find that post-*Campbell* decisions in the lower courts generally did not signal that any significant change in the case law had taken place. In a comprehensive study of fair use decisions from 1978 to 2005, Barton Beebe found that, even after *Campbell,* a statistically significant number of decisions continued to cite to *Harper & Row* for the principle that commercial use and market harm generally bar a finding of fair use.[32] However, there appears to have been a shift in the case law after this period. In an empirical study of fair use cases from 2006 to 2010, Neil Netanel concluded that "the transformative use paradigm . . . overwhelm- ingly drives fair use analysis in the courts" and that use of this concept in an opinion almost always was accompanied by a positive finding of fair use.[33] Additionally, courts that found transformative use almost always tended to find no market harm, suggesting that courts were placing more emphasis on the first factor (transformative use) than the fourth factor (market harm).[34] These jurisprudential tendencies departed sharply from pre-*Campbell* and even pre-2005 case law, which had generally treated market harm as a deter- minant factor in fair use analysis. That is just as the *Harper & Row* decision had instructed,[35] and the *Campbell* opinion had not suggested that the Court had changed its position on this point.

The substance of a Supreme Court ruling is often a function of the manner in which it is interpreted by the lower courts, who have the latitude to adopt a broader or weaker reading of the opinion's literal language. In the case of *Campbell*, the lower courts initially adopted a narrow reading and then shifted to the broad reading that prevails today. As a result, *Campbell* is now commonly understood as having extended fair use to a broad category of "transformative uses," rather than simply setting forth a special treatment of parodic expression within the framework of the fair use exemption. Concurrently, courts have tended to apply a relaxed level of scrutiny to defendants' claims that the allegedly transformative use did not cause material economic harm to the copyright holder and, with some exceptions, have largely ceased to view commercial use as an adverse factor for purposes of fair use analysis. Without explicit instruction from the Court, *Campbell* has been interpreted in a manner that heavily qualifies *Harper & Row* by making it easier to show that a challenged use is transformative and harder to show that any such use causes significant market harm. The end result is a significant increase in the ease with which an infringing defendant can escape liability.

These tendencies can be illustrated by a controversial 2013 decision by the Second Circuit, *Cariou v. Prince*.[36] In that case, the Second Circuit applied the fair use doctrine to exempt from infringement liability a celebrity artist, Richard Prince, who had copied the photographs of Patrick Cariou, an artist who had spent six years living among and photographing Rastafarians in Jamaica. Cariou had published the photographs in a book that only sold several thousand copies. Prince copied (or "appropriated") some of the images in the book, both partially and fully, and then modified them with line drawings or used portions of the images in a collage. The resulting artworks were exhibited at a prominent New York gallery, achieving more than $10 million in sales, far greater than the $8,000 earned by Cariou from royalties on his book.

The court found that 25 of Prince's 30 infringing artworks constituted transformative uses that fell within the scope of the fair use exemption. Although Prince stated in his deposition that he was not "trying to create anything with a new meaning or a new message," the appellate court nonetheless determined that "Prince's images . . . have a different character, give Cariou's photographs a new expression, and employ new aesthetics with creative and communicative results distinct from Cariou's."[37] The court also dismissed any market harm attributable to Prince's infringing action on the ground that Cariou had not "aggressively marketed" his work and the fact that "Prince's audience is very different from Cariou's."[38] Yet it appears that the original artist did suffer economic harm as a result of the infringing action: a gallery that had agreed to exhibit Cariou's work withdrew its commitment once it learned of Prince's exhibit.[39] The court's reluctance to infer market harm is hard to reconcile with the Supreme Court's statement in *Harper & Row* that fair use can be negated merely by showing that the infringing use "would adversely affect the *potential* market for the copyrighted work."[40] If a court can exercise discretion to set such a low bar for showing transformative use and such a high bar for showing market harm, then the legal security provided by copyright law is largely reduced to a judicial lottery skewed in favor of infringers.

4.1.4. Going International: Exporting Fair Use

Copyright laws in jurisdictions outside the United States generally do not have a fair use exemption. Rather, these jurisdictions rely on statutory provisions that provide for exemptions from copyright infringement liability in specified uses relating to news reporting, education, and research. In the United Kingdom and other countries that follow British law, this is known as the "fair dealing" exception. Historically, the exceptions under fair dealing and equivalent statutes have been narrowly construed.[41] As U.S. courts have expanded the fair use exemption to encompass a greater range of uses under the influence of the transformative use doctrine, the gap between fair use and fair dealing has also expanded. In particular, the fair dealing doctrine (or other so-called closed exception statutes) does not endow courts with comparable discretion—or, more precisely, with comparable discretion as understood by post-*Campbell* case law—to grant exemptions from infringement liability for uses that fall outside the categories enumerated by statute.

Given that digital intermediaries operate globally, this discrepancy between the expanded version of fair use adopted by U.S. courts and the fair dealing principle that applies elsewhere is undesirable from a business perspective. To close this discrepancy, Google has invested efforts in persuading jurisdictions outside the United States that substituting fair use for fair dealing would be a wise policy choice.[42] In these advocacy efforts, Google could rely on the well-developed body of scholarly commentary, especially among U.S. legal academics, that extols the virtues of expanded fair use in general and the transformative use concept in particular.

These efforts apparently achieved results. During 2000–2020, 10 countries adopted the fair use exemption, either explicitly or implicitly by reconstruing the fair dealing principle in an open-ended fashion that approximates U.S.-style fair use principles. Additionally, formal commissions or similar entities were established to study reform proposals to adopt the fair use exemption in Australia, Canada, the European Union, Hong Kong, Ireland, Japan, New Zealand, and the United Kingdom.[43] In 2017, Google's senior copyright counsel made a statement to a local newspaper supporting this proposal: "The Australian government should amend the Copyright Act 1968 to replace the current fair dealing exceptions with a broad exception for fair use. The new exception should contain a clause outlining that the objective of the exception is to ensure Australia's copyright system targets only those circumstances where infringement would undermine the ordinary exploitation of a work at the time of the infringement."[44] Google and advocacy organizations such as the Electronic Frontier Foundation also lobbied the U.S. government to negotiate for a mandatory fair use exemption in the Trans-Pacific Partnership Agreement, a proposed trade agreement that would have extended fair use to an additional 10 countries, and in bilateral fair trade agreements with specific countries.[45] Complementing this effort, a group of copyright scholars issued in 2008 the "Max Planck Institute Declaration,"[46] a statement calling for expansion of the exceptions to copyright infringement understood to be permitted under the "three-step" test (which permits exemptions from copyright infringement in "certain special cases" that do not "unreasonably prejudice the legitimate interests of the author") in the Berne Convention, an international copyright treaty.[47]

This global advocacy campaign to export fair use principles promotes the interests of search engines, content aggregators, and digital intermediaries that seek to replicate on a worldwide basis their success in transforming U.S. copyright law into an instrument that enables the acquisition of content at the lowest price possible (and, when the fair use exemption applies, at a price of zero). Yet there is no reason to assume, as much scholarly and policy commentary assumes, that the public interest would necessarily be promoted by adopting the broadly defined fair use principles developed by U.S. courts.

Evidence from Canada, which expanded its fair dealing exceptions by statute in 2012[48] to include "education," provides reason for caution. Prior to the amendment, Canadian schools had paid licensing fees to content owners through a copyright collecting society, which indicates that there was no transactional obstacle faced by users to acquire access to the distributed material on a licensed basis. After the amendment, some Canadian primary and secondary schools and universities adopted interpretations of the amended fair dealing exception under which up to 10% of a work can be copied and distributed for a single course without seeking a license.[49] The result, according to PwC (a major accounting firm), was an estimated loss of over $30 million a year in copyright royalties for Canadian content owners.[50] Notwithstanding these losses, the schools' interpretation was largely upheld by the Supreme Court of Canada in 2021, placing substantial legal and practical obstacles in the path of publishers (and especially small and medium-sized publishers) who seek to secure payment for the use of copyright-protected materials by Canadian educational institutions.[51] This form of expropriation-by-law is incompatible with copyright law's mission to provide a secure property-rights infrastructure to support private investment in content production and distribution.

4.2. The Political Economy of Fair Use

Law reviews and policy publications can supply an abundance of doctrinal and conceptual discussions of whether the judicially directed expansion of the fair use defense is correct as a matter of law, policy, or both. Among legal academics and copyright policy advocates, these discussions are usually characterized by agreement that fair use should be understood expansively, based on the rationale that fair use protects the "rights" of individual artists and consumers against the interests of large content owners. (As the *Cariou v. Prince* litigation illustrates, this assumed correspondence between the fair use defense and the interests of the individual artist is not always or even typically valid.) Discussion is then typically confined to marginal adjustments to the broad scope of the fair use exemption in particular circumstances.

Yet this large body of commentary has paid little attention to the broader constellation of economic forces that can account in large part for why the fair use doctrine happened to expand starting in the mid-2000s—that is, why courts overwhelmingly shifted from a narrow to a broad reading of the *Campbell* decision only about a decade after the decision had been issued.

In the following discussion, I provide an economic explanation for this doctrinal shift by identifying the business constituencies that stood to benefit from weakening copyright through the vehicle of the fair use doctrine. This explanation casts considerable doubt as to whether the current consensus, which reflexively assumes that every fair use claim "protects" the public interest against purportedly overreaching copyright owners, has it right. Just the opposite is sometimes the case: that is, expanding fair use runs counter to the public interest by protecting the interests of large aggregators and other firms that thrive under a legal regime in which copyright is difficult to enforce, if at all.

4.2.1. Fair Use as a Business Strategy

To appreciate why fair use, and especially broad understandings of fair use, would be welcomed by entities that operate under certain business models, it is helpful to return to the two-sided market structures that thrive in a weak-IP environment. Content aggregators and other entities that operate under similar business models have an economic interest in expanding the fair use exemption to reduce two sources of liability under the copyright laws.

First, users are exposed to infringement liability when engaging in the unauthorized copying and distribution of proprietary content that is widespread on content-sharing sites. Any material level of legal risk concerns the operators of these sites because it may discourage usage, which in turn would limit the pool of user data that can be used to offer targeted advertising to paying advertisers. Additionally, the intermediary may be deemed to infringe directly if it makes and displays copies of copyright-protected content as part of the process of storing and displaying audio, video, and other content that is hosted on the site. Second, the intermediary is exposed to liability for indirect infringement, under common law doctrines of vicarious and contributory infringement, to the extent it is deemed to facilitate infringement by users. Under the closely related "inducement" theory of indirect copyright infringement, a digital intermediary may be liable if it fails to undertake reasonably available measures to detect and deter users' infringing activities.[52]

As a matter of business strategy, the fair use doctrine can mitigate these liability risks for the operators and users of websites that host infringing content. If infringing activities by individual users qualify for the fair use exemption, then two welcome consequences follow for the site operator: users are exempt from liability for direct infringement, and, as a result, the intermediary cannot be held liable for facilitating infringement that is deemed to have never occurred as a legal matter. This reduction of the legal risk associated with operating certain content aggregation sites has an important practical consequence. If copyright owners cannot credibly threaten to bring suit for direct or indirect infringement, then content aggregators either have no incentive to pay license fees to those owners or, if there is still some residual risk of liability, would exert considerable leverage in "bargaining down" the license fee. In either scenario, the aggregator's cost of doing business has been reduced and, everything else being equal, its profit margins have increased. In economic terms, any application of the fair use doctrine therefore shifts wealth from content producers to intermediaries that are principally content users.

The same logic applies in the case of search engines that are exposed to secondary liability for directing users toward sites that copy, display, and distribute copyright-protected material without consent (which is one of the theories of liability under which Google was sued in the *Perfect 10* litigation discussed previously). Expansive use of the fair use doctrine to cover the copying and display functions inherent to a search engine, as illustrated by the *Perfect 10* litigation, minimizes the search engine's liability exposure and maximizes its freedom of operation in designing search tools. The importance of fair use to the search-engine business model was emphasized by Google's senior copyright counsel, who stated: "Our search function, which is the basis of the entire company, is authorized in the U.S. by fair use."[53]

Contrary to what this statement might imply, internet search engines would remain viable even without a broad understanding of fair use. As Justin Hughes has shown, there is no indication that the development or operation of search engines was impeded prior to U.S. court decisions that applied fair use specifically to protect search-engine activities (the first appellate decision to do so was a Ninth Circuit decision in 2003,[54] five years after Google launched its search engine in 1998). Moreover, Hughes did not find any significant impediments to search-engine operations in the vast majority of non-U.S. jurisdictions that do not recognize the fair use exemption but rather, as described previously, operate under the narrower fair dealing exception.[55] This suggests that fair use reduces a search engine's input costs and limits its liability exposure; however, it is not the case that search engines would have to cease activity if the fair use exemption did not exist in its current expansive form.

4.2.2. Fair Use as a Political Strategy

This line of argument is not intended to imply that the federal judiciary has been explicitly captured by content aggregation sites, search engines, and other technology firms with a business interest in raising obstacles to copyright enforcement. A federal judge with the security of a lifetime appointment is largely immune to such pressures. Rather, my contention is that certain constituencies within the tech business community, and similarly minded academics and advocacy organizations, have been successful in persuading courts that a broad application of the fair use doctrine in digital content environments coincides with a certain understanding of the public interest. Under that understanding, the public interest lies in maximizing access to existing information and other content, a policy position that is likely to be popular among the general public that has a natural preference for reducing the costs of accessing content that it consumes on a day-to-day basis. Even if an unelected federal judiciary is largely immune to capture by private interests, it is plausible to assume that, in the case of controversial legal issues as to which there is a perceived range of reasonable views based on existing law, much of the federal judiciary would prefer to select a point within that range that most closely aligns with what is perceived to be the dominant policy preference. (Again, I define "dominant policy preference" as being equivalent to either the majoritarian policy preference of the policymaker's constituencies or, in the absence of any sufficiently clear majoritarian policy preference, the preference expressed by an especially vocal discrete constituency.)

In a landmark work, Lee Epstein, William Landes, and Richard Posner explored a variety of "external" factors that can explain judicial decision-making, in addition to "internal" analysis of governing statutory, regulatory, or case law. Among those external factors, Epstein and her coauthors posited that a judge, subject to any ideological predisposition on a particular issue, will prefer to take positions that minimize conflict with other judges, the broader public (including the press), or the legal profession (including lawyers and law professors). That is: judicial decision-making exhibits a strong preference for conformity to the perceived consensus (subject to a judge's ideological predisposition to the contrary). Doing so can reduce a judge's costs of interacting with colleagues, the press, and the public, while conferring gains in the form of reputational capital. Additionally, judges who seek promotion within the judicial hierarchy or seek to minimize the chance of a decision being overturned on appeal may favor views that comport most closely with what is perceived to be the consensus on a particular issue.[56] Assuming that judges generally do not have a strong ideological predisposition on copyright-related matters, it follows that judicial decision-making will be principally governed by a mix of legal analysis and the judge's interest in minimizing these "interaction costs" and accruing reputational capital by tracking the perceived dominant policy preference. When the law is sufficiently ambiguous, then the dominant policy preference will be the predominant source of influence. As I will discuss, even when applicable law is not sufficiently ambiguous but the dominant policy preference is especially intense, some judges may be willing to adopt legal interpretations that would be difficult to justify through "objective" interpretations of applicable law.

Courts' sensitivity to the perceived dominant policy preference favoring a weak-copyright trajectory can explain why, as previously discussed, the fair use doctrine only shifted, and the transformative use concept was only expansively interpreted, starting around the mid-2000s, rather than immediately following the *Campbell* decision in 1994. The use of online file-sharing sites only became a widespread development starting with the launch of Napster in 1999, which raised an enforcement challenge for content owners in the music industry and, at the same time, led to the rise of a vocal constituency consisting of tens of millions of individual users with a strong interest in preserving access to "free music." File-sharing sites used MP3, a digital audio compression technology that was launched in 1994 and dramatically reduced the costs of transmitting audio content without significant loss of quality. MP3-enabled sites provided consumers with access to large selections of music through a home computer, which avoided the transaction costs and out-of-pocket expenditures when purchasing physical media. As of the late 1990s, users faced a stark option between listening on a file-sharing service to a single song at no cost, as compared to purchasing an album in the form of a physical CD at approximately $15.[57] Given the emergence of this large constituency with a strong interest in "free stuff," and a small but vocal group of ideologically motivated commentators and advocacy groups that opposed robust forms of IP protection, some judges— especially judges that valued accruing reputational capital and lacked any ideological predisposition to the contrary—might have been reluctant to make decisions that would limit access and therefore placed less weight on the potentially adverse economic effects of mass piracy on content producers and owners.

4.2.3. The Undeclared Revival of the *Sony* Safe Harbor

The Court had previously adopted this type of politically sensitive approach when faced with a case that raised tensions between technological innovation, consumer preferences, and copyright protections. In *Sony Corporation of America v. Universal City Studios, Inc.*, decided in 1984, the Court applied the fair use doctrine to shield home recording of television broadcasts by use of a video cassette recorder (VCR) for "time-shifting" purposes (as distinguished from so-called space-shifting for archival purposes).[58] The application of the fair use exemption to this practice was doctrinally implausible given the absence of any commentary or criticism on the original, which would mean fair use would be deemed inapplicable under the first factor of the fair use test. That is the position the Ninth Circuit had taken.[59] At oral argument in the Supreme Court, counsel for Sony pointed out to the Justices the practical implications: a ruling against Sony would expose millions of consumers—at the time of the decision, almost 10 million VCRs had been sold—to liability for statutory damages under copyright law.[60] Research by Jessica Litman shows that private communications among the Justices expressed concern about the "staggering" liability for individuals who had no commercial intent while acknowledging that it would be doctrinally awkward to apply fair use in this context.[61] While the studios had disclaimed any intention of suing individual users (they instead advocated for legislation that would entitle copyright owners to a royalty on each VCR sold[62]), the prospect of mass infringement liability may have led the five Justices in the majority to support a strained application of the fair use exemption. Litman finds that the decision was well received in the popular press,[63] suggesting that the Court had accrued reputational capital through its decision.

Similarly, in post-*Campbell* case law (or more precisely, post-2005 post-*Campbell* case law), sensitivity to public opinion concerning the prospect of mass infringement liability for online file-sharing may have led some judges to adopt a broad understanding of the fair use doctrine, as reflected by the adoption of a low bar for showing transformative use and a high bar for showing market harm for purposes of the fair use test. This is notwithstanding the fact that this approach would be difficult to reconcile on purely "objective" grounds with *Harper & Row*, a governing precedent identifying market harm as the most important factor in fair use analysis.[64] As I discuss in the following section, a sequence of landmark appellate cases involving major Google projects developed the expansive interpretation of the fair use doctrine with which *Campbell* is now associated. The end result has been an especially pliable safe harbor that conforms to the ideological predilections of open-access advocates, the business model of digital content aggregators, and the economic (and in some cases, ideological) interests of digital users—and, as a result, the interests of the judiciary in accruing goodwill through decisions that conform to dominant policy preferences.

4.3. Google's Three Big Wins: The Normalization of Infringement

To illustrate the practical effects of the convergence between profit-motivated and ideologically motivated supporters of copyright erosion, I describe in this section the response of copyright law to three major projects undertaken by Google: Google Images, Google Books, and Google's Android operating system (OS).[65] Each of these projects necessitated (or at least was facilitated by) a significant change to existing copyright law and, since Google developed and launched each project prior to securing those changes, represented a significant gamble that Google could be exposed to infringement liability that could shut down the project or require substantial alterations that would limit the project's economic value. In each case, Google's gamble paid off. Together, these three landmark litigations altered substantially the balance of interests reflected in U.S. copyright law.

4.3.1. (Mostly) Big Win I: Google Images

The convergence between the policy preferences of copyright skeptics and the business preferences of digital content intermediaries has resulted in legal outcomes that suit both constituencies. This interest-group perspective on the evolution of fair use law can be illustrated by two decisions by the Ninth Circuit: *Kelly v. Arriba Soft Corp.*,[66] decided in 2003; and *Perfect 10, Inc. v. Amazon.com, Inc. et al.*, decided in 2007.[67] Both decisions delineated a legal "safe zone" for certain activities by digital intermediaries that replicate, display, or otherwise facilitate access to visual images that were originated or are owned by other individuals or firms.

The *Kelly v. Arriba Soft Corp.* decision involved an infringement suit filed by a commercial photographer against the Arriba search engine that reproduced and displayed the photographer's works (along with millions of other photographic works) in the form of "thumbnail images." The thumbnail images involved direct infringement of the copyright owner's exclusive rights over the reproduction, display, and distribution of the images. Relying on the fair use doctrine, the court held that the search engine's activities qualified as transformative uses under the *Campbell* decision, principally on the ground that the copied images served a new function in the search engine as compared to the original work. As part of its fair use analysis, the court held that the thumbnail reproductions did not cause material economic harm to the copyright owner because the reduced-size images could not substitute for the copyright owner's full-size images and may have had positive effects by encouraging consumers to view the full-size images on the copyright owner's website.[68] Fair use case law in this opinion departed substantially from the cautious approach reflected in *Harper & Row* (which had emphasized the importance of economic harm in fair use analysis), the arguably parody-specific ruling of the *Campbell* opinion, and the literal language of the fair use exemption in the copyright statute.

Four years later, the same court addressed a similar fact pattern in *Perfect 10, Inc. v. Amazon.com, Inc. et al.*, which involved a copyright infringement litigation brought by the owner of a subscription-based adult images site against Google's online images search engine. In that case, the court adopted the same approach to fair use concerning alleged infringement by a search engine, holding that the infringing actions taken by the search engine for purposes of generating a thumbnail display constituted transformative uses. Concerning market harm, the court reached the same conclusion as the court in *Kelly v. Arriba Soft Corp.*, finding that the reduced-size images could not substitute for the full-size images to which the content owner offered subscription-based access and therefore had not caused economic harm.

The Infringer-friendly holdings in *Arriba Soft Corp.* and *Perfect 10* still left image search engines potentially exposed to liability for enabling "linking" by users from the thumbnail images to third-party sites that had copied and displayed the full-size images. The point was addressed in the *Perfect 10* opinion, which held that the website operator would be contributorily liable if it had "induced" infringement by users through the linking mechanism.[69] Relying on the Supreme Court's ruling on this point in its 2005 decision in *Grokster*,[70] the appellate court held that inducement could be shown either by affirmative actions, such as actively encouraging infringement or providing assistance that facilitates user infringement, or by a "knowing failure to prevent infringing actions."[71] While the appellate court did not make a factual determination on this point (which was remanded to the lower court), its guidance implied an expansive understanding of the scope of indirect liability that captured failures by an intermediary to take sufficient actions against user infringement on its site. While this holding (and the *Grokster* opinion on which it relied) favored content owners by lowering the bar for showing contributory liability, it turned out to have little practical consequence for reasons that I discuss subsequently.

4.3.2. Big Win II: Google Books

The judicial remaking of copyright law in the accidental service of the search-engine industry is perhaps best illustrated by a series of widely publicized decisions in 2014 and 2015 by the Second Circuit in connection with the Google Books projects.[72] These cases address copyright owners' reproduction rights in literary works, the historical core of the copyright statute, in connection with the "Hathi Trust" and "Google Books" projects.

Both projects originated from a partnership launched in 2004 between Google and four university libraries through which Google digitized over 20 million books. For this purpose, Google developed new digital compression technologies for executing high-quality textual scans in high volume and new viewing applications to enhance user accessibility.[73] In 2006, a larger group of university libraries and other nonprofit institutions formed the HathiTrust Digital Library (HDL), a "digital repository" that stores digitized materials from the Google Books project and member institutions, all of which is made available to the public on a non-commercial basis.[74] The Google Books project is operated separately by Google and offers users different search functionalities and, at the time of the events described in the litigation, had provided access to a greater portion of the digitized books, in all cases free of charge. Some books made available through the HDL and Google Books websites were in the public domain, but others were within copyright's statutory term.

It is insightful to compare the Google Books projects with the Open Content Alliance (the OCA), which had been formed in 2005 in cooperation with Microsoft and Yahoo! and was similarly designed to digitize members' book collections for purposes of facilitating public access through an online site. Unlike the Google partnership, the OCA only digitized texts that were either in the public domain or from which consent had been secured from the copyright owner. This more cautious approach to copyright compliance mattered. As of 2008, the Google Books project had reportedly scanned 7 million books; as of 2006, the OCA had reportedly scanned only 100,000 books.[75]

By discarding the distinction between in-copyright and out-of-copyright texts, the Google Books and HDL projects achieved greater scanning volumes but engaged in two clear acts of copyright infringement. First, the mass digitization activities undertaken by Google and its academic partners constituted infringement of the copyright owners' reproduction rights, except for older works that were in the public domain. Second, the display choices concerning the digitized results in the Google Books site constituted infringement of the owners' reproduction rights, display rights, and distribution rights. On the HDL site (at the time of the events addressed in the litigation), a user could only view information concerning the pages on which the user's search word or phrase appeared and the number of times the word or phrase appeared on each page. Displaying this limited information was unlikely to raise liability issues as a matter of copyright law. However, on the Google Books site (at the time of the events addressed in the litigation), public-domain works were shown in full view while in-copyright works were shown in the form of a limited number of "snippets" (equivalent to approximately one-eighth of a page) in which the user's search terms appeared. This practice supported a more robust claim for copyright infringement.

Both digitization projects prompted copyright infringement litigations against HDL by the Authors' Guild (the largest organization of professional writers in the United States) and certain foreign authors' associations, and against Google by the Authors' Guild and certain individual authors acting as representatives of a class of authors for purposes of the litigation. Google and HDL prevailed in both cases and the authors' organizations walked away without any remedy on behalf of their members. This total loss should have been unexpected in light of applicable law at the time, which may explain why Google had initially agreed to a settlement that would have entitled copyright owners to royalties based on the number of times a work was viewed on the site. After the settlement was rejected by the district court (on the ground that it was unfair to copyright owners who bore the burden of electing to opt out of the settlement),[76] the subsequent litigation led to a finding of no liability in both the district and appellate courts,[77] leaving the authors with no remedy at all.

In reaching a finding of no liability, both courts relied on the expansive understanding of fair use that had been developed in the search-engine context in the *Arriba Soft Corp.* and *Perfect 10* opinions, reasoning that the "digital catalog" provided by the HDL and Google Books sites constituted a transformative use since the sites used the original works for a different purpose, even though they lacked the criticism or commentary that courts had traditionally required to satisfy the first factor of a fair use analysis. The courts noted in particular that the Google Books site only showed snippets[78] and the HDL site only showed information relating to the number of times and the pages on which a particular word appeared in a particular work.[79] This supported a finding in both cases that the infringing but transformative use could not substitute for the original works and therefore did not cause material economic harm for purposes of the last factor in a fair use analysis.[80]

This application of the fair use doctrine (and specifically, the transformative use concept) effectively meant that the largest single act of copyright infringement resulted in no compensation being paid to the copyright owners from the entity that had engaged in, and benefited financially from, this undertaking. In contrast to terrestrial radio or broadcast television, this ruling enabled Google to secure user traffic and ad revenue through the Google Books site without paying any royalty to the copyright owners whose works populated its site. As Google and others argued, some copyright owners may have benefited to the extent that users subsequently purchased elsewhere the full version of books appearing on the Google Books site. Both the district court and appellate court rulings were widely lauded as a creative use of judicial discretion to preserve a publicly interested service that had greatly expanded access to literary works.[81] The Google Books litigations resulted in the accrual of reputational capital for the judiciary as an institution, which applied fair use doctrine to reach an outcome that tracked the dominant policy preference of individual users who naturally valued reducing the access costs to literary content, as emphasized by advocacy organizations. Additionally, a predominant portion of the academic community sided strongly with the outcome preferred by digital intermediaries, as reflected in an amicus brief signed by more than 150 humanities and legal scholars in the *HathiTrust* litigation.[82] It would be hard for a policymaker to miss these signals and the opportunity to accrue political goodwill through an expansive application of the fair use exemption.

The Google Books decisions rest heavily on the assumption that, but for the fair use defense, the HDL and Google Books projects would have been infeasible due to the costs of identifying and securing consent from tens of thousands of copyright owners. Yet it is not clear that this is true. First, the fact that Google entered into a settlement agreement with the Authors' Guild to provide for a fund out of which authors would have been compensated shows that it was possible to undertake these projects through a mechanism that preserved some remuneration for copyright owners. Second, the evolution of the Google Books site after the court's decision shows the feasibility of negotiating and implementing licensing arrangements involving a large pool of copyright owners. Today the HDL and Google Books sites often display substantially larger portions of published books, which reflects the fact that these sites have entered into licensing agreements with copyright owners to permit levels of usage well beyond the snippets that courts deem to be fair use. Given the apparent ability of the market to negotiate over the uses of even millions of copyright-protected books, it seems at least plausible that Google could have assembled a site similar to Google Books by including the full text of public-domain works and declining to digitize, display, or distribute in-copyright works without obtaining a license from the owner.

4.3.3. Big Win III: Android Operating System

In markets for visual and literary content, Google has successfully taken the risk of using the litigation process to secure legal precedents that have lowered its costs of acquiring the content that it requires to elicit user traffic, which can then be used to promote sales to advertisers. This strategy exploits the fact that Google's competitive advantage lies in search services, rather than content production, which therefore leads it to take actions to commoditize content and extract value from the search market in which it is the established leader. As mentioned previously, Google has pursued this commoditization strategy—devalue the competitor's core asset and shift value-extraction to complementary-asset markets—with great success in the OS market for mobile communications devices. In the following discussion, I provide an expanded analysis of this strategy and show how it relied on appropriating a competitor's asset and then securing a legal ruling to extinguish liability for infringement.

4.3.3.1. Google's Qualified Giveaway Strategy
Google reportedly invested hundreds of millions of dollars in the development of the Android OS (after acquiring a start-up that had initiated the

project),[83] which is based on a modified version of the open-source Linux kernel. Unlike existing operating systems at the time of its launch, which were either licensed for a royalty or, as in the case of the Apple iOS, only used internally, Android was (and is) distributed at no charge to device makers and other original equipment manufacturers (OEMs) under an open-source license. The "power of free" was irresistible. Within two years of its launch in 2008, Android had established itself as the world's most widely used OS for smartphones and other mobile communications devices. Within four years, it had secured almost 70% market share, leaving Apple's iOS as the only significant remaining competitor and defeating the well-resourced effort by Microsoft to seed adoption of its mobile Windows OS.[84]

However, the "free" distribution of the Android OS through an open-source license comes with several important strings attached, as implemented through a set of interlinked agreements between Google and various OEMs (estimated to cover 200–300 OEMs during 2009–2017[85]).

First, under a contract known as a Mobile Application Distribution Agreement (MADA), the OEM must agree to load a required suite of Google applications, to set Google Search as the default search engine, to display certain Google applications (for example, the Google Play Store) prominently on the user interface, and to include a "client ID" that enables Google to track usage of its applications on the device.[86] In exchange for undertaking these obligations, the OEM has the right to use the Android trademark for certain purposes and gains access to the most popular Google applications. (This is a general description of principal MADA terms, which have changed from time to time.) Without the MADA agreement, the OEM would not have access to the latest version of Android or Google's popular proprietary applications such as Gmail, Google Play Store, and YouTube.

Second, the MADA agreement is conditioned on the OEM entering into an "anti-fragmentation agreement" (AFA), which prohibits the OEM from undertaking efforts to "fork" (i.e., develop customized versions of) the Android code or to distribute devices that are not compatible with Android code.[87] Lastly, use of the Android trademark by an OEM is conditioned on the OEM's device passing a "compatibility test, which discourages the OEM from distributing any product that is not compatible with Android.[88]

Google's giveaway strategy (qualified by the limitations imposed by the MADA and AFA contracts) is perfectly rational in light of the expected revenue streams resulting from device makers' integration into the Android-based ecosystem, which expands the user base that can be used to deliver targeted. advertising for paying advertisers. The development of Google's Android OS follows the same strategy that was deployed in connection with Google Books and Google Images: take now, give away to users, attract a dedicated user base, and, if necessary, litigate later to resolve infringement claims.

4.3.3.2. *Oracle v. Google*: Closed-Source v. Open-Source

In undertaking the Android project, Google exposed itself to an infringement claim from Oracle, which leads the enterprise software market and, unlike Google, relies on a closed-source subscription-based business model. Google made use of portions of the source code in the Java programming language that had been developed and released in 1996 by Sun Microsystems, which Oracle had acquired in 2010. Java is a widely used cross-platform language designed to enable programmers to write applications for devices that use different operating systems and would otherwise be incompatible. This concept is captured by the slogan, "write once, run everywhere." Oracle made Java available to all interested parties, who could select from a menu of licensing options offered at different price points. The most expansive license, which permitted licensees to use Java to launch their own commercial products, required payment of a royalty and an obligation "to pass certain tests to ensure compatibility with the Java platform" and to maintain the platform's interoperability.[89]

After extensive licensing negotiations between Google and Oracle reached an impasse due to Google's refusal to commit to Java interoperability,[90] Google copied 7,000 lines of "declaring" (as distinguished from "implementing") source code[91] from 37 packages of application programming interfaces (APIs) in Java and incorporated those elements into the Android OS that was then in development. Oracle responded by suing for infringement. Google mostly prevailed in the district court based on a finding of non-copyrightability of most of the replicated code elements, while Oracle prevailed in the appellate court, which upheld the copyrightability of those elements and remanded Google's fair use defense to the district court.[92] In April 2021, the Supreme Court ruled in Google's favor. The Court upheld Google's fair use defense, principally on the ground that the disputed use of the replicated code elements constituted a qualifying "transformative" use.[93]

Even accepting this application of the transformative use concept, it remains the case that Google had turned down a licensing offer from Oracle and it would therefore seem that the fair use defense should necessarily fail since Google had directly deprived the copyright owner of licensing income. In *Harper & Row*, the Court had held that the market harm factor "is undoubtedly the single most important element of fair use,"[94] which implies that a fair use defense fails if the plaintiff can demonstrate that the infringing use causes or will cause significant harm to the copyright holder in actual or potential markets. In *Google v. Oracle*, however, the Court re-characterized "market harm" analysis as "market effects" analysis, a novel concept that reflects the view that the fourth factor of a fair use analysis requires that the court "take into account the public benefits the copying will produce."[95] This modified standard for assessing market harm—or more precisely, under its redefinition, *net* market harm—makes it easier for infringers to escape liability under a fair use defense, possibly even including cases in which such harm is significant but offset by more significant (and loosely defined) "public benefits."

Even within this novel cost-benefit framework for assessing fair use claims, it is not certain the Court got it right. In granting Google's fair use defense, the Court emphasized the constructive role that fair use can play by removing the burdens of litigation risk and licensing overhead from the software development process.[96] However, that observation would be true of virtually any environment in which IP rights are used to protect informational assets. A complete cost-benefit analysis must consider the extent to which any such cost-savings are offset by the adverse effects on innovation attributable to weakening copyright protections through the fair use doctrine. In the software industry, a broad definition of fair use, and a resulting weak-copyright regime, is unlikely to bring software innovation to a halt given the mix of IP-dependent and non-IP-dependent business models observed in the industry. However, a weakened copyright regime may skew organizational choices toward business models in which software development is monetized by integrating original code into a larger product ecosystem in which "free" services (such as the distribution of code under an open-source license) are cross-subsidized by revenue streams on complementary "pay" services to which access can be regulated and therefore priced. While this giveaway business model may be viable for certain firms, or certain segments of the software market, that is unlikely to be true for all firms or all parts of the software market—who will effectively be compelled to exit or will decline to enter in the first place.

This risk of organizational distortion is illustrated by the facts of the case. The infringer, Google, deployed a giveaway business model that relied on ad revenues that were indirectly promoted through use of its zero-price OS (with the contractual strings attached by the MADA and AFA agreements). The originator, Oracle, used a subscription model that relied on licensing fees paid by users of its software. Expanding the fair use doctrine threatens the economic viability of the licensing-based monetization model used by a firm such as Oracle, which relies on the ability to extract revenue from users for access to its intellectual assets on a stand-alone basis. At the same time, the Court's decision induces firms to favor a giveaway-based business model since expanded application of the fair use doctrine reduces the input costs borne by the giveaway firm, enabling it to extract larger profit margins on the portions of the technology bundle in which it enjoys a competitive advantage. That was Google's strategy in the mobile communications OS market. By seeding adoption of the Android OS through a giveaway strategy, Google rapidly attracted a user base that could be monetized through the complementary advertising service market in which it enjoyed a leading position. When contextualized within these strategic business considerations, it appears that the Court's application of the fair use doctrine in *Oracle v. Google* arbitrarily favors one party's business model for monetizing software innovation over another.

This point was overlooked by the Court, which appeared to assume that Google's private interest in what it calls "software reuse" necessarily tracks the public interest. The Court stated: "To the extent that Google used parts of the Sun Java API to create a new platform that could be readily used by programmers, its use was consistent with that creative 'progress' that is the basic constitutional objective of copyright itself."[97] Taking Google's arguments at face value, the Court's reasoning fails to consider the strategic motivations behind Google's legal arguments in favor of a broad application of fair use to encompass its use of the Java APIs or Google's business decision to decline a license to use the Java APIs, which had precipitated the litigation in the first place. When explaining Google's refusal to take a license due to Oracle's required interoperability commitment, the Court almost sounds like it is part of Google's litigation team, stating that "Google envisioned an Android platform that was free and open" and adopting the required interoperability commitment "would have undermined [the] free and open business model."[98]

This assertion might seem to be supported by the fact that the Android OS is released through a zero-royalty, open-source license, while Sun (and later Oracle) charged a royalty to licensees who sought to develop a commercial application based on Java. Yet this assertion overlooks the complication that, as described previously, Google contractually conditions OEMs' access to popular *closed-source* Google applications (such as Gmail and Google Play Store) on those firms' agreement to treat Google as the default search engine and to provide preferential display to certain Google applications.[99] These contractual restrictions challenge the simple assertion that Google seeks to maintain a "free and open" environment. Rather, it is more precise to say that Google rationally seeks to maintain a mixed property-rights environment that promotes adoption of a (mostly) open-source operating system through a giveaway strategy and then drives users toward complementary closed-source applications, which in turn generates ad revenue that sustains the Android ecosystem as a whole. From this perspective, the Court's decision in *Oracle v. Google* effectively "opened up" and "closed down" property rights across different elements of the mobile communications ecosystem in a manner that corresponded to Google's competitive strengths and weaknesses within that ecosystem. For Oracle (or any other software provider that relies on a subscription-based delivery model), the outcome was precisely the opposite.

4.3.3.3. Why "Free and Open" Can Never Really Be Free and Open

Google's *qualified* open-source distribution strategy is illustrated by the Open Handset Alliance (OHA), an 84-member organization led by Google and founded in 2007, concurrently with the launch of Android. Consistent with the OHA's commitment to "greater openness in the mobile ecosystem," all members are contractually bound not to make any devices based on a "fork"—that is, an alternative version—of the Android system.[100] Since Android is distributed under an open-source license, an anti-forking commitment was deemed necessary to enable Google to establish a uniform version of Android among its licensee base of device manufacturers, which in turn promotes the laudable objective of achieving interoperability. The OHA's anti-forking commitment has been mirrored by the terms of the AFA to which each Android licensee is a party. Hence, while it is true that Android is distributed on an open-source basis and therefore any OEM or other entity can distribute its own modified version of Android, the large group of device producers encompassed by OHA members and Android licensees is contractually bound not to do so. OHA founding members include many, if not most, of the leading manufacturers of handsets and electronic devices, such as Acer, Asus, Dell, Foxconn, Fujitsu, Huawei, HTC, Kyocera, Lenovo,

LG, Motorola, Oppo, Samsung, Sharp, Sony, Toshiba, and ZTE.[101] The anti-forking commitments implemented through the OHA and the AFA likely explain why Amazon appears to be the only company to have launched successfully a device (the Kindle Fire tablet, manufactured by Quanta) in the U.S. market that is based on a "fork" of the Android OS known as Amazon Fire OS.[102]

Taking into account the contractual structure in which the Android OS is embedded yields a more complex transactional landscape than the "free and open" environment described by the Court in its decision in *Oracle v. Google*. While Android OS may be an "open" software environment, it is situated within (and might not be viable economically without) a richer transactional bundle that comprises "closed" elements such as Google's most popular (and proprietary) applications, the MADA, the AFA, and the OHA commitment. While this bundle may have legitimate technological and business justifications (in particular, fragmentation risk), it raises entry barriers to any firm that seeks to build a commercially competitive device that is not compliant with Google's Android OS. This more complex understanding of the Android ecosystem casts doubt on Google's argument, and the Court's view, that the refusal to take the Java license was simply based on a commitment to a "free and open" ecosystem. Properly understood, that commitment reflects the rational business objective of establishing a Google-specific ecosystem of complementary applications that is difficult for competitors to replicate, aside from the largest tech platforms.

This interpretation more plausibly explains why Google declined to take a license to Java (as Samsung and Amazon did) or to develop the Android OS without using any Java code (as Apple and Microsoft did).[103] Google's behavior appears to reflect a business strategy in which it made unilateral use of portions of the Java code, which reduced its input costs (since it avoided a license fee or independent development costs) and, by avoiding the interoperability commitment, enabled it to establish a platform that could compete with the Java platform in the wireless ecosystem. Unlike Apple and Microsoft, which built operating systems "from scratch," Google chose to lower its development costs and to accelerate adoption among the Java programming community that had already been cultivated by Sun, subject to the risk that its practices would result in infringement liability in future litigation.

Google's gamble again paid off, both at the Court and in the metaphorical court of public opinion. The Court's decision was widely lauded as having protected developers' "reuse practices" in the software community, signaling that the decision had generated goodwill for the judiciary among an important constituency.[104] Yet the facts of *Oracle v. Google* do not present a compelling case that a decision in favor of Oracle would have blocked development of the Android OS. Google never faced any obstacle to accessing the Java APIs; rather, Sun (and later Oracle) simply conditioned access on payment of a license fee, and an interoperability commitment that was the fundamental feature of the Java platform. This is not a case in which the denial of fair use would have resulted in denial of access; rather, it would have compelled the parties to set a price to that input, enabling the originator to earn some return on its investment. Alternatively, Google had the financial and technical resources to develop a new OS independently (rather than reaping the rewards from Sun's investment in building the Java developer community), which was the choice made by two other large technology companies. Contrary to the Court's view, the decision in *Oracle v. Google* does not necessarily track the public interest in a robust innovation ecosystem, which requires preserving expectations that a successful innovator can expect to earn a market-determined reward for the costs and risks of technological development. Rather, the Court's decision rewards entities that "take without asking," gambling on a favorable judicial ruling that extinguishes any liability for the infringer while eliminating any reward for the innovator.

4.4. Closing Thoughts

It is not accidental that courts expanded the fair use doctrine substantially starting in the mid-2000s, about a full decade after the Court's *Campbell* decision. Like other policymakers, judges seek to accrue reputational goodwill by taking actions that conform to perceived dominant policy preferences. As the deployment of the internet substantially lowered the costs of copying, modifying, and distributing digital content, courts faced powerful pressures from content aggregators, thought leaders, advocacy groups, and individual users to apply copyright law in a manner that did not disrupt these novel opportunities to consume content at little or no cost. Absent strong ideological preferences for protecting the property rights of content originators and owners, it would be expected that judges would reach legal determinations that preserved individual users' newly expanded opportunities to access an immense pool of creative content. The existing fair use doctrine, coupled with the *Campbell* decision's apparently novel concept of transformative use, provided lower courts with the vehicle to do so. While expanding fair use preserved low-cost or zero-cost access for individual users, it has eroded the property-rights structure that enables markets to price creative assets and to deliver market-determined returns to individuals and entities who invest in the production and cultivation of those assets. It is difficult to reconcile that result with the historical and substantive purposes of copyright law.

5

How Courts Rewrote the DMCA

It is often stated that "Big Media" did not anticipate the digital revolution and was caught flat-footed, left with few options other than bringing counter-productive infringement suits against individual users and legally dubious suits against content aggregation sites, all to preserve its "monopoly" franchise against technological disruption. Certainly, suing one's own customers is not a great public relations strategy, even if the underlying legal argument is sound. However, it is not the case that the industry failed to anticipate the unique opportunities and risks posed by the advent of low-cost, high-quality technologies for producing, reproducing, and distributing content through online media. Anticipating those opportunities, the music industry took steps at the onset of the commercial internet to manage the transition to a digital environment through the PressPlay and MusicNet initiatives, which, as discussed previously in Chapter 3, attempted to assemble a fully licensed digital service for downloading music.

These efforts largely failed. A big reason: mass user infringement significantly limited the industry's ability to extract revenues from recorded music in a digital environment. This result, however, was not inevitable. Rather, it was due in part to a successful litigation and advocacy strategy undertaken by digital platforms, and applauded by scholarly commentators and advocacy organizations, that largely precluded record labels from seeking effective legal recourse against digital platforms, the only entities that could feasibly take action to restore a meaningful property-rights regime in digital content markets. Critically, the success of this strategy relied on the ability of digital platforms to make a credible case that its business-motivated preference for weak copyright enforcement coincided with the public interest in a robust creative ecosystem. If digital platforms could make a publicly interested argument for "free stuff," then policymakers and judges seeking to accrue political goodwill would be inclined to agree. As we will see, they were enormously successful in achieving this objective.

The Big Steal. Jonathan M. Barnett, Oxford University Press. © Oxford University Press 2024.
DOI: 10.1093/oso/9780197629529.003.0006

5.1. Political Signals: The SOPA Rebellion

It has been commonly lamented among scholars and commentators that copyright law is "dangerously" expanding to promote the interests of entrenched media and entertainment companies. The language used is often dramatic, using motifs of a captured legislative and judicial apparatus that seeks to suppress free expression for the sake of a small group of large media and entertainment conglomerates. This is a straw man proposition that substitutes rhetoric for fact and analysis. Since the emergence and adoption of digital technologies for copying and distributing audio, video, and other content, the economic strength of "Big Media" has declined to such an extent that the term is now antiquated. There can be no comparison between Alphabet/Google (annual revenues in 2023 of $307.3 billion) and Meta Platforms/Facebook (annual revenues in 2023 of $134.9 billion), on the one hand, and even the largest entertainment companies like Netflix (annual revenues in 2023 of $33.7 billion), Walt Disney (annual revenues in 2023 of $88.9 billion), and Universal Music (annual revenues in 2023 of $12 billion), on the other hand. As the practical force of copyright law has shrunk in the face of widespread infringement, content owners have struggled to maintain revenues through a business model predicated on maintaining exclusivity over creative properties that are costly to produce, market, and distribute. Yet large digital platforms have thrived in a weak-IP environment in which content inputs can be aggregated without payment to originators and owners and then converted into a vehicle for attracting users, which in turn attracts payments from advertisers.

In 2011 and 2012, the entertainment, media, and other content industries—which encompass not only well-compensated production executives but a much larger group of creative, technical, and administrative personnel who are not comparably compensated—sought legislative intervention. This took the form of a proposed statute, known as SOPA (Stop Online Piracy Act) in the version considered in the House of Representatives and PIPA (Protect IP Act) in the version considered by the Senate, which would have enhanced content owners' enforcement capacities against sites that facilitate user infringement. SOPA was proposed by the House Judiciary Committee in September 2011, and PIPA was approved by the Senate Judiciary Committee and proceeded to the floor of the Senate in October 2011. Both statutes would have enabled courts to issue orders requiring search engines to cease linking to websites "primarily" operated for the purpose of enabling infringement (in the SOPA draft) or "dedicated to infringing activities" (in the PIPA draft), requiring payment-processing companies to stop servicing such sites, and requiring internet service providers (ISPs) to block access to such sites. At the time, the statutes were almost universally vilified as a desperate attempt by "Big Media" to preserve its endangered "monopoly" against disruption by a new technological paradigm that would somehow deliver unlimited content without undermining the investment incentives of content producers. This line of argument was put forward not only by technology companies but, with equal vigor, by individual users, advocacy organizations, the press, and much of the legal academy.

Today it is hard to imagine that the country's largest tech companies could enlist millions of individual users in a mass protest against proposed legislation that clearly operates to the advantage of those very same companies. Yet that is precisely what occurred when Congress deliberated over the SOPA and PIPA statutes. On January 18, 2012, Google and other websites engaged in a coordinated "blackout" in which a black screen appeared with a single banner protesting the bills.[1] A petition against the bills at Google's website collected over 4.5 million signatures.[2] Visitors to Wikipedia's website were greeted with the following message: "Imagine a World Without Free Knowledge. For over a decade, we have spent millions of hours building the largest encyclopedia in human history. Right now, the U.S. Congress is considering legislation that could fatally damage the free and open internet." The public protest worked. A short time after the blackout date, several legislators who had formerly supported the bill expressed serious concerns, and ultimately it did not proceed forward in Congress.[3]

This is a vivid illustration of the three-way convergence of interests among digital intermediaries that rely on content giveaway models, ideologically motivated commentators and advocates opposed to robust (or any) copyright protection, and policymakers who sought to satisfy the perceived dominant policy preference. In the case of the SOPA and PIPA bills, policymakers could observe what appeared to be their constituents' policy preferences and therefore endorsed the policy position communicated by profit-motivated and ideologically motivated opponents of the bills. It is hard for an elected legislator to go wrong by resisting legislation that would allow consumers to continue to enjoy creative content at a zero price. For the same reason, it was easy for digital intermediaries to make publicly interested arguments against legislation that posed a threat to a business model predicated on using, without payment, content produced by others.

Table 5.1 U.S. Copyright Law and the Digital Transformation (2001–2015)

Year	Litigation or Other Policy Action	Outcome	Content or Tech "Win"
2001	*A&M Records v. Napster* (9th Cir.)	Napster shut down	Content
2005	*MGM et al. v. Grokster* (S. Ct.)	Expansive definition of indirect infringement	Content
2011–2012	SOPA/PIPA bills (Congress)	Anti-piracy bills targeting intermediaries proposed and withdrawn	Tech
2012	*Viacom et al. v. YouTube* (2nd Cir.)	YouTube wins under broad definition of DMCA safe harbor	Tech
2014	*Authors Guild et al. v. HathiTrust* (2nd Cir.)	HathiTrust wins on fair use defense	Tech
2015	*Authors Guild et al. v. Google* (2nd Cir.)	Google wins on fair use defense	Tech

The "SOPA rebellion" sent a clear signal to policymakers that weakening copyright (or at least, taking no actions to bolster copyright) was a pathway to accrue reputational capital among users in digital content markets. These events may have played a role in the policy calculus that drove subsequent judicial decisions that substantially reduced copyright protections, including most notably, as discussed subsequently, YouTube's litigation victory over Viacom in 2012[4] and, as discussed previously in Chapter 4, Google's litigation victories concerning the Google Books project in 2014 and 2015.[5] These developments are summarized in Table 5.1, which provides a timeline of major copyright developments since the shutdown of Napster through the landmark Google Books decisions. The practical result: a legally engineered windfall enjoyed by everyone in the creative ecosystem except the vast majority of the artists and other personnel that fuel the ecosystem with new content—that is, the "Authors" for whom the Constitution empowered Congress to provide legal exclusivity through the vehicle of copyright law.

5.2. The Judicial Remaking of the DMCA

Even prior to the launch of Napster in 1999, the content industry took proactive action through the negotiation and drafting of the Digital Millennium

Copyright Act (DMCA), a statute specifically enacted in 1998 to address copyright enforcement in a digital environment.[6] The DMCA is often described as an attempt to balance the interests of content owners in maintaining legal exclusivity against the interests of digital intermediaries and online sites in mitigating litigation risks and transaction costs that might impede the free flow of information in a digital environment. In the hands of the courts, however, the DMCA has largely been converted into a generously defined safe harbor that largely exempts content aggregators from copyright liability, absent the most explicit cases of encouraging, and providing assistance to, infringing users. The practical result is that content owners bear the overwhelming portion of the burden of policing the unauthorized consumption of copyright-protected creative works. However, content owners cannot achieve deterrence effects through suits against individual users and, given the judicial remaking of the DMCA safe harbor, usually have no credible cause of action against leading digital intermediaries that are often in the best position to mitigate unauthorized usage. As a result, the practical effect of copyright in the digital economy has been substantially limited.

5.2.1. The DMCA and the Content/Tech Bargain

Based on the groundbreaking work on regulatory capture by George Stigler and Sam Peltzman[7] and theoretical and historical work on rent-seeking by James Buchanan and Gordon Tullock,[8] social scientists widely understand statutes, regulations, and other forms of government lawmaking as an indirect form of bargaining by constituencies that have an interest in promoting or blocking a proposed legal change. Without always using this terminology, legal academics have often implicitly understood copyright law (especially copyright law since the advent of the internet) in these same terms by widely characterizing it as a form of industry capture in which corporate lobbyists acting on behalf of large media and entertainment firms have purportedly secured excessive IP protections to the detriment of the public interest. This view of the copyright law-making process appropriately recognizes that the outcome of that process—like other law-making processes—reflects to some extent the influence of interested (and sufficiently motivated and resourced) constituencies. However, for purposes of understanding fully the political economy of copyright law, this view is also substantially incomplete. Specifically, it fails to contemplate that constituencies that advocate *weakening* copyright may have privately interested objectives that deviate from the public interest. As I will argue, this is precisely what has occurred in the courts' application of the DMCA.

5.2.1.1. The Clash of Business Models

The bargaining framework developed by political scientists and economists for understanding the process of drafting and enacting statutes can be usefully applied to the DMCA, which was the result of negotiations between two well-organized and well-resourced interest groups, mediated through the statute-drafting process in congressional committees. One group, which I will call "Content," comprised traditional media and entertainment industries, while the other group, which I will call "Tech," encompassed a wider range of industries, including hardware and device manufacturers, telecom carriers, ISPs, search engines, and websites that host and distribute user-uploaded content.[9] While the precise composition of these camps (especially Tech) has changed to some extent during the period following enactment of the DMCA, it remains the case that, broadly speaking, Content comprises firms and individuals who are net producers of creative assets, while Tech comprises firms and individuals who are net consumers of creative assets. While individual artists and users were not well-represented directly in the legislative process (an outcome consistent with the standard expectation that constituencies consisting of numerous but dispersed members do not have strong political influence), each of these constituencies were indirectly represented by the Content and Tech industries, respectively. As would be expected, Content pursued strong-copyright outcomes that are generally preferred by individual artists (as net producers of creative assets), while Tech pursued weak-copyright outcomes that are generally preferred by individual users (as net consumers of creative assets).

The list of organizations that testified at the hearings held by the U.S. Senate and House of Representatives committees on the proposed legislation illustrate the range of interests represented in the policymaking process behind the drafting and enactment of the DMCA (Table 5.2). Search engines and social networking sites, which play a central role in today's online ecosystem, were not well-represented because they were at a nascent stage of development (Yahoo! was only founded in 1995, and Google was only founded in 1998) or were not yet in existence (Facebook was only founded in 2004).

In negotiating the substance of the DMCA, each constituency's preferred point on the range of potential legislative outcomes stood at a considerable

Table 5.2 Speakers (Selected) at U.S. Senate and House of Representatives Committee Hearings on the DMCA (February 7–8, 1996; September 4 and 16–17, 1997)

Content and Other Net Copyright Producers	Tech and Other Net Copyright Users
Motion Picture Assn. of America	Computer & Communications Industry Assn.
Broadcast Music, Inc.	Home Recording Rights Coalition
Business Software Alliance	Consumer Electronics Manufacturers Assn.
National Music Publishers Assn.	Institute for Electrical and Electronics Engineers
Association of American Publishers	U.S. National Commission on Libraries and Information Science
American Society of Composers, Authors, and Publishers	Information Technology Industry Council
Recording Industry Assn. of America	America Online
McGraw Hill Co.	CompuServe, Inc.
Universal Music Group	Prodigy Services, Inc.

Source: U.S. Congress, Senate 1998, 3–4, 6.

distance from each other, reflecting the divergence in the business models used by each constituency to extract value from creative assets and, in some cases, the extent to which each constituency was a net producer or consumer of creative assets. Members of the Content constituency operated under a conventional model in which revenues are extracted through the production of original content, which is then distributed to consumers in various media: books, records, cassettes, CDs, DVDs, and so forth. Under this stand-alone monetization model, it is critical that the content owner have an effective suite of technological and legal tools to deter unauthorized usage by copiers who incur none of the originator's production and distribution costs. At the time of the enactment of the DMCA, the principal members of the Tech constituency comprised ISPs such as America Online (AOL), CompuServe, and Prodigy, internet browser providers such as Netscape and Microsoft, telecom carriers, computer hardware manufacturers, and web directories or search engines such as Yahoo!, Alta Vista, Lycos, and Excite. While the business models on which those Tech entities relied were more diverse as compared to Content entities, each Tech entity operated at least partially through a business model in which revenues are extracted indirectly from content that is produced by others.

AOL, which was probably the most prominent representative of Tech in the deliberations relating to the DMCA, relied on a mixed business model that sourced revenues from subscribers to its dial-up internet service (coupled with email and instant messaging services provided at no charge). That service offered subscribers the opportunity to access proprietary content through AOL's "walled garden," user-generated content through instant messaging and other digital communications services, or, less conveniently given the undeveloped state of contemporary search technologies, through the "external" internet. While AOL's proprietary content assets were sourced through licensing arrangements and therefore posed no liability risk, certain contemporary court rulings indicated that AOL was potentially subject to indirect infringement liability in connection with copyright-protected content posted by users through AOL's instant messaging, electronic bulletin boards, and similar services.[10] Hardware manufacturers such as Apple extracted revenue from technological innovations through the sale of personal computers, which increased in value the lower the expected costs (including the costs associated with infringement liability risks) to use the device to access content through ISPs. Internet directories, digital bulletin boards, and search engines benefited even more directly from the availability of third-party content since users would be more likely to use those services to the extent they provided access to a large pool of online content at a low (and preferably, zero) price. In turn, more users enhanced the ability of the directory, bulletin board, or search engine to source revenue from paying advertisers. In short, there existed significant constituencies on the Tech side that had an economic interest in the devaluation of property rights over creative assets for purposes of removing litigation risk, lowering input costs, and maximizing the potential user base from which subscription or ad revenues could be extracted.

5.2.1.2. Content v. Tech: Bargaining over the DMCA

The fundamental discrepancy between the direct and indirect monetization models of Content and Tech, coupled with the fact that only Content bore the costs of content production and promotion, set the boundaries of each constituency's bargaining range in the negotiation and drafting of the DMCA. By "bargaining range," I refer to the set of terms to which each party could agree in "negotiating" the DMCA and still be better off as compared to having no deal at all. Figure 5.1 provides a visual rendition of this concept.

If Content were the legislative dictator, then the DMCA would have provided Tech with no exemptions from indirect infringement liability in order

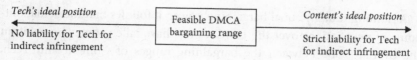

Figure 5.1 DMCA bargaining range.

to maximize Tech's incentives to incur the costs required to deter copyright infringement in a digital environment. In fact, an initial set of proposed amendments to the copyright statute, set forth in a document known as the "White Paper" (issued by the Information Infrastructure Task Force established by the Clinton administration in 1995), had expressed the view that "the best policy is to hold the service provider liable" for infringement activities facilitated through its website or other services since it is "in a better position to prevent or stop infringement than the copyright owner."[11] Going further, the White Paper specifically rejected any broad immunity for ISPs and other intermediaries on the ground that "[i]t would be unfair ... to allow one class of distributors to self-determine their liability by refusing to take responsibility. This would encourage intentional and willful ignorance."[12] Those words proved to be unusually prescient.

Legislation modeled on this approach (known as the National Information Infrastructure Copyright Protection Act) failed to secure passage in Congress in 1996 after having elicited opposition from telecom carriers and hardware manufacturers.[13] It is clear that insisting on the approach reflected in this failed legislation would have resulted in no statute being enacted since at least some members of the Tech constituency (in particular, ISPs such as AOL) would have anticipated that the resulting liability risk may have challenged the economic viability of their business model.

If Tech were the legislative dictator, the DMCA would have provided a complete, or at least broadly defined, exemption from indirect infringement liability for its constituency's members, effectively preserving the broad exemption that Tech had enjoyed under the Sony safe harbor since the mid-1980s. Given that at least some members of the Tech constituency had little or no economic incentive to detect and deter infringement, preservation of this safe harbor in the digital environment would have compelled content owners to rely entirely on technological means to preserve legal exclusivity and to extract a return from their investments in content production. This policy outcome would have fallen outside Content's bargaining range.

Assuming roughly equal bargaining power, it follows that the actual out-come of negotiations over the DMCA must have fallen somewhere within the overlap zone between the bargaining ranges of Content and Tech, constrained by policymakers' ideological preferences (if any). This assumption is consistent with an extensive account of the negotiations that led to the DMCA. Robert Levine describes significant lobbying efforts by tel-ecom carriers and hardware manufacturers, on the one hand, and media and entertainment companies, on the other hand.[14] This assumption is also consistent with the Senate Committee's characterization of the legisla-tive outcome: "[T]he DMCA enjoys widespread support from the motion picture, recording, software, and publishing industries, as well as the tele-phone companies, long distance carriers, and other OSPs [(online service providers)] and ISPs." Similarly, the House report states that the legislative committee "believe[d] it [had] appropriately balanced the interests of con-tent owners, on-line and other service providers, and information users in a way that will foster the continued development of electronic commerce and the growth of the internet."[15]

As I will discuss, many courts have adopted the view that the DMCA was drafted to provide a broadly defined exemption for Tech that places almost all of the copyright enforcement burden on Content. This view cannot be reconciled with the view that Content and Tech exerted roughly equal bar-gaining power in the negotiation of the terms of the DMCA, or the alter-native view that the balance of power favored Content. At the time of the statute's enactment, there is no commentary to my knowledge arguing that Tech enjoyed a decisive advantage in political influence and had secured a "great deal" in negotiating the terms of the DMCA. This is not surprising given the fact that "Big Tech" did not exist at the time: Google was a startup, Yahoo! had only been founded five years earlier, and Facebook did not even exist. Even if it were accepted that Content rather than Tech had the upper hand in the drafting of the DMCA, then it is implausible to assert for purposes of legislative construction that the DMCA had been drafted with the intention of placing on Content the bulk of the copyright enforcement burden. Under the assumption that Tech and Content enjoyed a roughly equal split of bargaining power concerning the scope of the DMCA safe harbors, or that Content enjoyed the upper hand, it is implausible that the negotiation process would have produced a statute that instituted a drasti-cally unequal allocation of enforcement responsibilities in Tech's favor. The fact that leading courts have interpreted the DMCA as having implemented such an unequal allocation of enforcement responsibilities suggests that the statute has effectively been renegotiated through litigation, reflecting the shift in the balance of economic leverage and political influence in digital content markets in the years following enactment of the statute.

5.2.2. How the Courts Amended the DMCA

An understanding of the DMCA as reflecting a "fair deal" between Content and Tech is consistent with the view that the statute's safe harbors were designed to allocate enforcement burdens among Content and Tech to reflect a split that lies somewhere in the overlap region on the bargaining range bounded by each constituency's ideal but unrealizable statute. This intermediate approach is consistent with the tailored architecture of the Section 512 safe harbors, which set forth limited circumstances under which four types of online service providers (OSPs) are shielded from indirect liability for user infringement. The mere existence of the DMCA safe harbors tracks the expectation that Content would be forced to cede some ground in the legislative bargaining process so that Tech would not be subject to unqualified liability for user infringement. Yet it is also the case that the safe harbors have significant qualifying criteria, which is consistent with the expectation that Tech would be forced to make some concessions so that a meaningful level of copyright protection persists in digital markets and preserves Content's ability to extract a return on its investments in creative production.

This view of the Section 512 safe harbor as a negotiated compromise is reflected in the Copyright Office's understanding of the intent behind the statute, which observes that the safe harbor was "intended for copyright owners and internet service providers to cooperate to detect and deal with copyright infringements that take place in the digital networked environment."[16] The Copyright Office has reiterated this understanding, stating that the DMCA was designed to achieve a balance between, on the one hand, the interest in "providing important legal certainty for OSPs, so that the internet ecosystem can flourish without the threat of the potentially devastating economic impact of liability for copyright infringement" and, on the other hand, "the legitimate interests of authors and other rightsholders against the threat of rampant, low-barrier online infringement . . . through a system where OSPs can enjoy limitations on copyright liability . . . in exchange for meeting certain conditions. . . ."[17]

The most commonly discussed and applied DMCA safe harbor is set forth in Section 512(c), which applies to OSPs that are potentially liable for infringement of copyright "by reason of the storage at the direction of a user" of infringing material.[18] It is clear that the 512(c) safe harbor, which shields a qualifying "hosting" OSP from monetary liability and injunctive relief that would result in a shutdown of the OSP's site (as distinguished from injunctive relief targeted at specific content on the site), was not intended to provide an unconditional license to facilitate, or turn a blind eye to, user infringement.

This is reflected by the fact that the 512(c) safe harbor predicates the OSP's immunity on multiple requirements. For ease of reference, these requirements are set forth in Table 5.3. First, the OSP must designate an agent to receive "takedown" notices from owners of allegedly infringed copyright-protected material and to respond to such notices expeditiously by removing the infringing material from the OSP's network. Second, the OSP must maintain and implement a policy to terminate users who are repeat infringers. Third, the OSP must not receive "a financial benefit directly attributable to the infringing activity" (provided the OSP has the right and ability to

Table 5.3 Statutory Requirements for DMCA Section 512(c) Safe Harbor

Requirement	Description
No actual knowledge	No actual knowledge of infringing activity on system or network or, if the intermediary acquires such knowledge, takes action expeditiously to remove or disable access to infringing material
No "red flag" knowledge	Not aware of facts or circumstances from which infringing activity on the system or network is apparent or, if aware, takes action expeditiously to remove or disable access to infringing material
No financial benefit	No financial benefit directly attributable to infringing activity on system or network, provided it has the right and ability to control infringing activity
Takedown agent	Designates agent to receive takedown notices and responds expeditiously to such notices by removing infringing material
Repeat-infringer policy	Adopts and reasonably implements a repeat-infringer termination policy
No interference with anti-copying measures	Accommodates and does not interfere with standard technical measures to prevent unauthorized copying

Source: 17 U.S.C. §§ 512(c)(1)(A)-(C), 512(i).

control such activity). Fourth, the OSP must not have "actual knowledge" of infringing material on its network (or, if it has such knowledge, acts expeditiously to remove such material). Fifth, in what has become known as the "red flag" test, the OSP must not be aware of "facts or circumstances from which infringing activity is apparent" or, upon obtaining such awareness, must take action "expeditiously to remove . . . the material." Sixth, the OSP must reasonably accommodate technological measures taken by copyright holders to prevent unauthorized copying.

The highly conditional application of the Section 512(c) safe harbor reflects an effort to provide Tech with some protection from indirect liability for user infringement while avoiding the moral hazard problem that would arise if Tech were entirely immune from liability, in which case the interests of telecom carriers, ISPs, hardware manufacturers, and search engines would most likely lead them to facilitate user infringement or to take no action to stop it. It can be reasonably disputed whether the split of enforcement responsibility between Content and Tech is intended to be an equal split. However, it is unreasonable to argue that the tailored construction of the safe harbor reflects a legislative deal in which copyright holders would bear an overwhelming share of the enforcement burden. This one-sided interpretation is inconsistent with the statutory language of the DMCA safe harbors, the bargaining positions occupied by Content and Tech at the time of the drafting of the DMCA, and the legislative history of the DMCA that refers repeatedly to the compromise reached between Content and Tech to achieve an equitable split of copyright enforcement burdens in digital environments.[19]

Even in the face of these historical facts, an implausibly Tech-sided interpretation has prevailed in much of the case law interpreting the DMCA safe harbors and in particular Section 512(c). With some exceptions, courts have mostly adopted relatively loose interpretations of each of the predicate conditions, which makes it difficult for copyright owners to show that an intermediary fails to qualify for the safe harbor outside cases in which it is blatantly encouraging user infringement or fails to maintain a notice-and-takedown mechanism and repeat infringer policy.[20] The result is a split of enforcement responsibility that heavily favors Tech at the expense of Content, which in turn leaves Content largely powerless to impede or deter widespread infringement through legal action. The legislative history does not support this one-sided interpretation of the statute and it is difficult to reconcile that interpretation with the plain language of the statute.

5.3. The Coevolution of Technology and Business Models in Online Environments

To fully appreciate the interaction between the DMCA's statutory construction, its post-enactment judicial reinterpretation, and the political-economic influences that have driven those developments, it is necessary to review the technological advancements in digital communications, and associated changes in online business models, that have taken place following enactment of the DMCA. For ease of reference, Figure 5.2 shows, during 1997–2010, the rate of internet usage among U.S. households and concurrent business and legal developments in the digital economy.

As of 1997, just prior to the enactment of the DMCA, less than one-quarter of all U.S. households accessed the internet,[21] and downloading a four-minute song took 80 minutes.[22] This was in part due to the fact that the internet could only be accessed through dial-up access, which had slow download and transmission speeds, and content available through the internet could only be searched through "Yellow Pages"–style directories or relatively inaccurate search engines. Use of the internet, and the purposes for which the internet could be used, expanded dramatically with the introduction of high-speed broadband service starting about 2005, reflected by the fact that, as of 2010, over 70% of U.S. households accessed the internet regularly, a dramatic increase compared to only about a decade previously.[23] These technological changes greatly expanded the pool of content that users could access digitally and were accompanied by the development of more sophisticated search technologies to enable users to access efficiently a

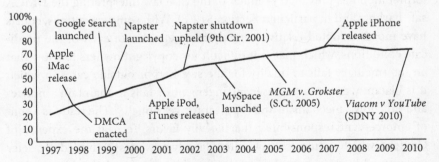

Figure 5.2 Internet usage among U.S. households; concurrent developments (1997–2010).

Source: For data on internet usage, U.S. Department of Commerce 2013, 3.

dramatically increased volume of online content. The combination of broadband and sophisticated search technologies enabled the online experience that is familiar to users today, consisting of rapidly delivered streams of textual, visual, audio, and video content, accessible through desktops, laptops, smartphones, and other devices equipped with refined search technologies.

These advances in transmission and search technologies were accompanied by changes in the dominant business model in the digital content ecosystem. At the time of the enactment of the DMCA, the prevailing business model consisted of ISPs such as AOL, which primarily offered curated (and licensed) content for paying subscribers, complemented by revenue streams from advertisers.[24] A subscription-based model relies on the ability to maintain exclusivity over creative content, an assumption that drove the merger of AOL, the leading ISP, and Time-Warner, a leading content company, in 2000, for $182 billion. By the mid-2000s, however, the walled-garden model was already becoming obsolete since users could access the internet directly (and more rapidly) through DSL, cable, and broadband services, and locate uncurated (and mostly unlicensed) content through more sophisticated search engines provided at no charge by companies such as Google (launched in 1999), rather than being confined to an ISP's curated environment of selected proprietary content. Critically, users could not only search the web directly and efficiently but, with the widespread adoption of MP3 audio compression technology in the late 1990s, could easily transmit and listen to musical content through online media.[25] The launch of MP3 players, which enabled users to download music from the internet to portable devices, accelerated the erosion of meaningful technological obstacles to the unauthorized consumption of digitally transmitted music. The ease with which users could access a virtually unlimited inventory of content on the open internet rendered obsolete not only the subscription-based services provided by ISPs such as AOL but, by enabling users to copy and transmit content at no cost, placed at risk users' willingness to pay for proprietary content in brick-and-mortar stores.

The late 1990s and the early years of the following decade witnessed the rapid emergence of a digital ecosystem through which users could independently transmit and receive content that was formerly only available through in-person purchases of physical media. This period encompassed the launch of music-sharing sites such as Napster (1999) and video-sharing sites such as MySpace (2003) and YouTube (2005), among others. These content-sharing intermediaries exacerbated the copyright enforcement challenge that Congress had identified at the time of the enactment of the DMCA. While Content naturally lamented content-sharing services that posed a high infringement risk and therefore endangered its stand-alone content monetization model, Tech welcomed this development since it increased users' interest in making use of the internet, which could then support an ad-based business model that relied on revenues from paying advertisers. This follows the logic of commoditization: devalue the market segment in which a rival has a competitive advantage and shift the point of value-extraction to another market segment in which the commoditizing firm has a competitive advantage. Based on this rationale, search services such as Google and file-sharing sites such as YouTube therefore welcomed, whether explicitly or implicitly, technologies that facilitated user copying and distribution of content since it increased the value that users could extract through those services. This could occur directly, in the case of a file-sharing service such as YouTube, or indirectly, in the case of a search service such as Google (since a search could lead to proprietary content on third-party websites where a user could access that content).

Hardware manufacturers such as Apple similarly welcomed digital copying and transmission technologies since this development expanded the uses to which its new personal computer (the iMac, launched in 1998) and portable media player (the iPod, launched in 2001) could be applied and reduced the costs that users would incur to take advantage of those devices' various functionalities. Apple's marketing strategies in the earlier years of the internet are consistent with the objective of minimizing the risks and costs that users might incur in connection with potential allegations of copyright infringement. In 2001, Apple launched the iMac with a memorable "Rip, Mix, Burn" advertising campaign that effectively encouraged users to engage in copyright infringement. The ad campaign reflected Apple's rational interest in eliciting consumer demand for its device by maximizing the pool of content that users could access and minimizing the costs that users would incur in doing so. Technology had lowered the cost of accessing, copying, and distributing content, and weakening the strength of copyright protection would reduce those costs further, which in turn increased the price that a user would be willing to pay for the hardware that was necessary to access and transmit that content.

Technology intermediaries, encompassing search engines, file-sharing sites, and hardware manufacturers, welcomed the ability of users to access content at a zero cost and therefore took no actions to stop such activity and, in certain cases, encouraged it. Ad-supported intermediaries welcomed this development since it enabled them to build a user base from which advertising revenues could be extracted. Hardware manufacturers welcomed this development since it increased the value of devices that enabled the copying and transmission of digital content.

However, the economic gains enjoyed by intermediaries through user infringement, whether directly or indirectly, required a change in the law (or at least, a clarification of the law) to remain viable. Specifically, intermediaries required that the courts interpret the DMCA in a manner that minimized their exposure to indirect liability for facilitating user infringement. Complete immunity was an implausible policy goal given the conditions to eligibility set forth in the DMCA safe harbor. However, digital intermediaries' business strategy would remain viable so long as the courts read the DMCA safe harbor sufficiently broadly so that intermediaries could qualify for it with relative ease, in which case they could operate without any significant risk of liability for indirect copyright infringement. As I will now describe, that is exactly the outcome those intermediaries have pursued, with great success.

5.3.1. How Technology, Economics, and Politics Drove Courts to Distort the DMCA

In the years around and following enactment of the DMCA, most of the major types of intermediaries in the digital content supply chain—hardware manufacturers, search providers, and file-sharing sites—used some form of a giveaway-based business model that thrives on zero-cost access to creative content produced at a positive cost by other firms and individuals. As a result, these intermediaries shared a rational interest in minimizing the strength of copyright protections, thereby limiting both users' and intermediaries' cost of accessing content and exposure to potential infringement liability for engaging in, or facilitating, unauthorized copying and distribution activities. The rise of the content giveaway business model and the decline of the walled-garden model drove the stark opposition between Content and Tech concerning copyright enforcement in general and the interpretation of the DMCA safe harbor in particular.

In the walled-garden model, the digital intermediary acts as the principal gatekeeper to an exclusive and mostly licensed content inventory, derives substantial revenues from paying subscribers, and therefore shares a mutual interest with Content in preserving exclusivity over creative assets (since subscribers would otherwise have no reason to pay for a subscription). This is qualified by the fact, as previously noted, that the intermediary could bear some liability for copyright-protected content distributed by users through messaging or other content-sharing functions on the provider's site. Under the giveaway model, the online intermediary acts as the principal gatekeeper to a non-exclusive content pool and, since users pay no access fee, derives almost all revenues from paying advertisers. The intermediary therefore shares with users an interest in minimizing copyright protections, which attracts users by expanding access to online content, which in turn attracts advertisers and maximizes gains for the intermediary. This runs directly contrary to Content's policy preferences and stand-alone monetization strategy.

To promote a broad interpretation of the DMCA safe harbor, and a weaker copyright regime more generally, Tech adopted the "information wants to be free" rhetoric favored by scholarly commentators and advocacy entities that had similar views on copyright policy. Tech's accidental allies argued that a narrow interpretation of the DMCA safe harbors was both inconsistent with the intent of the statute and merely advanced the private interests of media and entertainment companies that were seeking to preserve a proprietary content business model that purportedly had become outdated in a digital environment. This signaled to policymakers—in this case, courts—that a broad interpretation of the DMCA safe harbors would track the perceived dominant policy preference. For example, the Electronic Frontier Foundation argued that "[w]ithout the DMCA's safe harbors from crippling copyright liability, many of the [online] services on which we rely . . . would not exist" and "the safe harbors, while imperfect, have been essential to the growth of the Internet as an engine for innovation and free expression."[26] A significant body of academic literature and policy commentary has repeatedly called attention to the "chilling effect" that purportedly excessive application of Section 512 (specifically, automatic removals of infringing content in response to takedown notices) poses to fair use and free speech.[27] These types of publicly interested arguments have been widely asserted in the scholarly literature, advanced by advocacy organizations, and adopted by courts in construing the scope of the Section 512 safe harbors. The result has been a consistent devaluation of copyright protections in digital environments and an implicit transfer of wealth from individuals and entities who create content to individuals and entities who consume it.

5.3.2. The Turning Point: *Viacom v. YouTube* (2010–2013)

The post-enactment interpretation of the DMCA, and the relationship between that interpretation and concurrent technological and economic
developments, can be illustrated by the 2010 decision of the Southern
District of New York, in the landmark case *Viacom International Inc.
v. YouTube, Inc.*[28], and ensuing decisions in the litigation.

The court's decision, which relieved YouTube of liability for indirect infringement, was later mostly upheld in 2012 on appeal[29] and then largely
reaffirmed on remand by the district court in 2013.[30] The case involved a
copyright infringement litigation brought by Viacom and other major
content producers and distributors against YouTube, on the grounds that
YouTube had facilitated copyright infringement by users through the site.
Evidence of infringing activity was not hard to find. Viacom claimed that
"tens of thousands of videos on YouTube, resulting in hundreds of millions
of views, were taken unlawfully from Viacom's copyrighted works without
authorization."[31] The district court held that YouTube nonetheless qualified
for the safe harbor even though it conceded that a jury could find, based on
the factual record, that "the defendants not only were generally aware of, but
welcomed, copyright-infringing material being placed on their website."[32]
An email exchange among YouTube management observed: "As of today
episodes and clips of the following well-known shows can still be found on
YouTube: *Family Guy, South Park, MTV Cribs, Daily Show, Reno 911, Dave
Chapelle....*" A YouTube executive also wrote that "[a]lthough YouTube is not
legally required to monitor content ... and complies with DMCA takedown
requests, we would benefit from preemptively removing content that is blatantly illegal and likely to attract criticism," and then nonetheless proceeded
to recommend "a more thorough analysis" until any further action was
taken.[33]

This dismissive approach to the IP rights of content owners, combined
with rampant distribution of infringing content on the site, did not spell
legal doom for YouTube. To the contrary. YouTube was able to secure a dismissal in the district court—on summary judgment—of the copyright infringement claims filed against it by the copyright owners-plaintiffs. In
federal civil litigation, summary judgment requires that the court find that
"there is no genuine dispute as to any material fact" and the party seeking
summary judgment "is entitled to judgment as a matter of law."[34] While
the appellate court overturned the lower court's dismissal of the claim as a

matter of summary judgment, it upheld much of the substance of the lower court's opinion. On remand, the district court did not qualify its one-sided understanding of the DMCA, stating that "knowledge of the prevalence of infringing activity, and welcoming it, does not itself forfeit the safe harbor" and that YouTube could place "much of the burden on Viacom . . . to search YouTube 24/7 for infringing clips."[35] Both the subsequent settlement and YouTube's initial success in securing summary judgment against some of the largest media companies undoubtedly had an important signaling effect for other copyright owners who might contemplate embarking on legal action against intermediaries with the resources to fund protracted litigations.

To appreciate these implications fully, it is necessary to consider the principal elements of the district court's analysis of the copyright owners' infringement claims against YouTube. In the case of each of these elements, it is difficult to reconcile the court's ruling with the plain language and legislative history of the statute.

5.3.2.1. Actual and Red-Flag Knowledge

In the part of its opinion with the most significant implications, the district court determined that mere knowledge that infringing activity is rampant on the YouTube site did not provide sufficient support to infer that YouTube had either "actual or constructive knowledge of specific and identifiable infringements"[36] or "red flag" knowledge of infringing activity. If either form of knowledge had been found, YouTube would have been ineligible for the safe harbor. The court flatly stated that "awareness of pervasive copyright-infringing, however flagrant and blatant, does not impose liability on the service provider," without actual knowledge of specific cases of infringement.[37] This narrow construction of red-flag knowledge would appear to depart from any plausible understanding of the statutory language, which specifically provides that a service provider cannot qualify for the 512(c) safe harbor if, "in the absence of *actual* knowledge," an intermediary is "aware of facts or circumstances from which infringing activity is apparent."[38]

The court defended its narrow construction on the ground that it was mandated by another provision in the DMCA (Section 512(i)) stating that safe harbors in the statute are not conditional on "a service provider monitoring its service or affirmatively seeking facts indicating infringing activity."[39] This reasoning misunderstands the function of this provision. As observed by the Copyright Office,[40] the no-monitoring provision was designed to protect users' privacy expectations against monitoring by service providers, not to limit a service provider's obligations to take action once it is aware of piracy on its site. This interpretation is supported by a simple observation: Section 512(i) (the no-monitoring provision) is entitled "Protection of Privacy." Moreover, the no-monitoring provision is qualified by reference to the service provider's obligations to implement a repeat-infringer policy and not to interfere with "standard technical measures" used by copyright owners to prevent unauthorized usage.[41] The legislative history suggests how to reconcile any apparent conflict between the no-monitoring provision and the red-flag knowledge test, stating that the test "shall not be construed to condition the limitation [on liability] on monitoring a network for infringement" but also stating that "[o]nce one becomes aware of . . . information [concerning infringing activity] . . . one may have an obligation to check further."[42] Elsewhere, the legislative history similarly states that a "service provider would have no obligation to seek out copyright infringement, *but it would not qualify for the safe harbor if it had turned a blind eye to 'red flags' of obvious infringement.*"[43]

These important nuances were overlooked in the *Viacom v. YouTube* court's legal acrobatics to reduce red-flag knowledge to a threshold that is barely distinguishable from specific knowledge. The court's implausibly narrow understanding of red-flag knowledge translates into an implausibly broad understanding of the safe harbor that effectively places almost the entire enforcement burden on copyright owners. That interpretation cannot be reconciled with well-established norms of statutory construction against adopting interpretations that render any part of a statute redundant. Recall that the safe harbor provision already conditions eligibility on the absence of specific knowledge of infringing material on the intermediary's site. If the absence of red-flag knowledge is largely conflated with the absence of specific knowledge of infringing activity, then the other eligibility requirement is made redundant—a clear violation of the legal principle that strongly disfavors interpretations that render moot any part of a statute. Nonetheless, the appellate court upheld the district court's interpretation by adopting yet another tenuous distinction between "actual knowledge," understood to reflect subjective knowledge of specific infringing activity, and "red flag knowledge," understood to reflect subjective awareness of "facts that would have made the specific infringement 'objectively' obvious to a reasonable person."[44] As observed by the influential Nimmer treatise on copyright, this exercise in judicial fiat finds no support in the plain language or legislative history of the statute.[45]

While the appellate court remanded the case to determine whether YouTube executives had specific knowledge of infringing material and did not act expeditiously to remove it, the district court and appellate court decisions in the case (together with similarly narrow understandings of "red flag" knowledge in previous rulings by courts in the Ninth Circuit[46]) delivered a precedent that significantly increased the burdens faced by copyright owners who bring litigation against platform intermediaries. The result can be seen in the YouTube litigation itself. On remand, YouTube was able to avoid a finding of actual or red-flag knowledge despite evidence that, as noted previously, senior management was aware of specific infringing material on the site and delayed or declined to remove it.[47] It is therefore unsurprising that the Nimmer treatise has observed that the court's application of the DMCA safe harbor "reduces red flags almost to the vanishing point."[48]

The appellate court in the *Viacom v. YouTube* litigation did make one minor concession to copyright owners' interests by adopting the common-law principle that willful blindness could in some cases be deemed tantamount to actual knowledge of infringing activity for purposes of the DMCA safe harbor.[49] The concession has little practical effect, however, since the court limited application of the doctrine to the "deliberate avoidance of specific incidences of infringement, rather than avoidance of acts of infringement generally."[50] As the Copyright Office later observed, this understanding of willful blindness is not only higher than the standard used historically in copyright cases, but also higher than the standard used in *criminal law*.[51] The perverse result is that intermediaries have an incentive to avoid acquiring knowledge of specific acts of infringement, which would be the very type of behavior that the willful blindness principle is designed to deter.

5.3.2.2. Financial Benefit

The district court in the YouTube litigation addressed whether YouTube had satisfied the condition under the Section 512 safe harbor that an intermediary may not derive any financial benefit "directly attributable" to the infringing activity, *in the event* the intermediary exercises the "right and ability to control such activity."[52] Echoing its narrow understanding of red-flag knowledge, the district court found that the "right and ability to control such activity" requires evidence that the intermediary had specific knowledge of actual infringement.[53] Since YouTube lacked such knowledge, the no-financial-benefit condition could not bar its eligibility for the safe harbor even though it derived significant financial benefit from the unauthorized distribution of content produced and owned by others.

This narrow construction of "right and ability to control" again departs from legislative history, which had contemplated that courts would adopt the understanding of this concept as found in existing case law on vicarious liability for indirect infringement. As that history reflects, the case law on vicarious infringement contemplates that, for purposes of assessing "right and ability to control," a court adopts a broad perspective that "examines all relevant aspects of the relationship between the primary and secondary infringer."[54] If the court had adopted this perspective, then YouTube would likely have been deemed to have the ability to control user infringement and, since YouTube receives advertising revenue from videos posted on its site, it may then have been deemed to enjoy a financial benefit directly attributable to the infringing activity on its site. In that case, YouTube would no longer have been eligible for the safe harbor.

The appellate court initially rejected the district court's narrow understanding of "right and ability to control" on statutory construction grounds, finding that it would effectively conflate the no-financial-benefit condition with the no-specific-knowledge condition to the Section 512(c) harbor. Nonetheless, the court ultimately upheld the district court's rejection of the common-law understanding that the mere ability to exercise control would be sufficient, concluding that the no-financial-benefit condition for the safe harbor "requires something more than the ability to remove or block access to materials posted on a service provider's website."[55] A concurrent ruling by the Ninth Circuit held more specifically that control for purposes of the no-financial-benefit condition requires that the intermediary exert "substantial influence" over users' activities or take actions to induce users to infringe[56]—actions that any well-advised intermediary can easily avoid.

The practical result of these decisions is that it is now difficult to establish that an intermediary has the right and ability to control infringing activity on its site for purposes of the no-financial-benefit condition. Illustrating this effect, YouTube was able, on remand in the district court, to show that it had no right or ability to control infringing activity, in which case any financial benefit it may have derived from infringing uses on its site could not bar eligibility for the safe harbor.[57] This result defies common sense. YouTube has the ability to monitor and control user activity whenever it removes infringing material in response to takedown notices from copyright owners, blocks or limits access to user-generated content that violates the site's terms of use, and, as noted in the district court opinion, sometimes did take preemptive action to identify copyright-infringing material.[58] If the court's ruling on this point was an outlier in the case law, it might be treated as an aberrant case; remarkably, an implausible statutory construction has become the judicial standard.

5.4. The Legacy of *Viacom v. YouTube*

The *Viacom v. YouTube* litigation involved a head-to-head matchup between, on the one hand, the largest single repository of infringing content, and, on the other hand, the owners of some of the most valuable creative properties in the media and entertainment market. In short, a perfect embodiment of the dichotomous policy preferences of Tech and Content in a single litigation. The court's decision illustrates the federal judiciary's prevailing understanding of the DMCA safe harbors since approximately the early 2010s. As illustrated by the *Viacom v. YouTube* litigation, as well as other decisions in the influential Second and Ninth Circuits,[59] this body of case law has consistently adopted infringer-friendly interpretations of two key elements of the safe harbor: (1) a high threshold for showing that the defendant failed the no-red-flag knowledge test, largely conflating it with a specific-knowledge requirement; and (2) a high threshold for showing that the defendant failed the no-financial-benefit test, largely exempting business models that indirectly benefit from user infringement. The result is a judge-remade DMCA safe harbor that lies outside any plausible overlap region between the bargaining ranges of Content and Tech at the time of the drafting of the DMCA statute, as reflected by both legislative history and the broader economic context in which the DMCA was negotiated. As shown in Table 5.4, this judicially modified safe harbor effectively provides online intermediaries with a compliance "checklist" that is relatively easy to satisfy and yields a high likelihood that the site will qualify for protection.

The effective reduction of the carefully balanced provisions of the DMCA safe harbors to this easy-to-satisfy checklist leads to outcomes that run counter to the plausible expectations of the drafting parties to the legislative bargain embodied in the DMCA. The resulting state of affairs in which intermediaries can operate with near impunity (or at least can do so for extended periods of time through protracted litigation) is illustrated by the Second Circuit's 2016 decision in *EMI Christian Music Group, Inc. v. MP3*

Table 5.4 DMCA Compliance Checklist

Action Item	Description
1	Maintain a takedown agent who is responsive to takedown notices filed by copyright owners
2	Establish and "reasonably" implement a repeat-infringer termination policy
3	Avoid exercising active control over users' activities (in which case whether the site receives a financial benefit from infringing activity is immaterial)
4	Minimize opportunities to acquire actual knowledge of specific infringing activity on the site

Tunes, LLC.[60] In that case, the defendant provided a service that enabled users to upload to digital "lockers" music that users had located on the internet. The site also provided users with an index of searchable "free" music that could be "sideloaded" into the digital lockers. The site's founder had previously run the music site MP3.com, which had been shut down and ordered to pay $50 million in damages following an infringement lawsuit.[61] He made no secret about the purposes of the new venture, stating: "MP3. com guy back to rejuvenate MP3 business. Largest copyright infringer of all time back at it again."[62] The jury sensibly rejected the defendant's DMCA safe-harbor defense on the ground that it had red-flag knowledge by virtue of willful blindness to users' infringing activity, and awarded the copyright owners $48 million in damages.

Yet the judge overrode the jury's common sense. Relying on statements in the *Viacom v. YouTube* decision holding that intermediaries have no affirmative duty to monitor infringing activity, the judge reversed the jury's finding. While the appellate court ultimately held that the district court had erred in doing so, the case is nonetheless indicative of the almost implausible results some courts have reached in applying the Section 512 safe harbor. In the *MP3 Tunes* litigation, the district court judge's eagerness to grant the Section 512 defense required the copyright owner to undertake a costly and protracted litigation through the appellate level, despite evidence that the site's executives had themselves posted infringing material to the site and had explicitly instructed users that the site's "music is 'legal to download' because '[s]ideload.com [(a searchable index of "free" music)] does not store any music, but rather links to files publicly available [in] other places on the net.'"[63] Anyone casually familiar with the case law on contributory liability—and the founder of MP3 Tunes would appear to meet this standard given his past litigation history—would know that this was statement was false.

5.4.1. A Safe Harbor (Almost) without Bounds

Given the ease with which intermediaries can typically secure the protection of the Section 512 safe harbor, intermediaries have little legal or economic incentive to invest efforts in deterring infringement, which unsurprisingly persists at high levels on those sites. Reported data on takedown notices testify to this fact. As of December 31, 2023, Google reported having received takedown requests from 469,192 copyright owners involving over 5.04 million unique top-level domains, from which over 7.71 billion URLs have been requested to be delisted.[64] As of 2015, the Recording Industry Association of America announced that it had issued takedown notices to Google corresponding to approximately 200 million URLs.[65] While copyright skeptics emphasize the risk that some takedown notices erroneously target non-infringing material (or more precisely, infringing material that *may* qualify as fair use in a fully adjudicated proceeding), those commentators and advocates usually omit to mention that a significant portion of infringing material is likely never detected and hence never triggers a takedown notice at all.

From Content's perspective, the statutory safe harbor in the DMCA, as interpreted by the courts, has effectively reinstated for online intermediaries something akin to the broadly defined judicial safe harbor in the Supreme Court's decision in *Sony Corporation of America v. Universal City Studios, Inc., et al.* in 1984,[66] which had mostly laid dormant since the Court largely rendered it moot in its 2005 decision in *MGM et al. v. Grokster.*[67] As discussed previously, *Sony* had immunized hardware manufacturers or other intermediaries from indirect infringement claims so long as the relevant copying technology was at least capable of a non-infringing use and the defendant did not have specific knowledge of particular infringing activity. While *Grokster* had established a broad definition of contributory liability, encompassing the failure to undertake reasonable measures to impede infringement, it is inoperative if an intermediary meets the qualifying criteria for the DMCA safe harbor. Given the generous judicial redefinition of the DMCA Section 512 safe harbor, it has rendered *Grokster* inoperative almost all of the time.

This state of affairs typically leaves copyright owners without a practically effective remedy against intermediaries that host user-distributed infringing material, even if such material constitutes the overwhelming majority of material on the intermediary's site and the intermediary is well aware of this fact. Given the legislative history and economic circumstances surrounding the negotiation of the DMCA, it cannot reasonably be argued that this outcome was contemplated by Congress when drafting and enacting the DMCA. If that is the case, then the case-law application of the DMCA safe harbor represents a generalized case of judicial misinterpretation for policy purposes.

To be clear, sites that actively solicit and facilitate user infringement, or ignore the notice-and-takedown and repeat-infringer policy requirements, continue to be liable for indirect infringement and a shutdown injunction. This is illustrated by *Columbia Pictures Industries et al. v. Fung*, a 2013 decision in which the Ninth Circuit upheld a shutdown injunction and large damages award against the operator of BitTorrent sites that actively facilitated the unauthorized viewing of motion pictures.[68] Even if copyright owners can ultimately secure a shutdown injunction against an intermediary that does not qualify for the safe harbor, the litigation process required to reach that point can typically involve several years and millions of dollars in legal fees. Moreover, some popular pirate sites located outside the United States, such as the Megaupload and Pirate Bay sites, have attracted tens of millions of users and pose significant difficulties for copyright owners who have sought to shut them down. Megaupload was ultimately shut down,[69] but Pirate Bay has persisted in various iterations, and the founder of Megaupload has successfully resisted extradition to the United States from New Zealand since 2012.[70]

Even if a content owner diligently files, and an intermediary diligently responds to, notice-and-takedown requests, this simply gives rise to a "whack-a-mole" effect in which a content holder files a takedown request, the site operator complies, the infringing material reappears, and the futile cycle repeats. In the first half of 2021, YouTube reported that its automated system had detected 722 million items of infringing content.[71] A filing by the Motion Picture Association of America in 2016 indicated that Disney had sent 34,970 takedown notices for illegal copies of the motion picture *Avengers: Age of Ultron* at a single site during a three-month period, while NBC Universal had sent 58,246 notices for the motion picture *Fast & Furious 7* to a single site during the same time.[72] As these numbers suggest, the notice-and-takedown mechanism has little deterrent effect, while intermediaries have little incentive under prevailing judicial understandings of the DMCA to invest efforts in deterring infringement through more robust means. To the contrary: the intermediary is best off maintaining a technological environment that facilitates (without actively encouraging) file-sharing, which maximizes the user base and, as a result, attracts revenues from advertising and other complementary goods sold through the site.

5.4.2. Evaluating the Remaking of the DMCA Safe Harbor

Through the vehicle of the *Viacom v. YouTube* litigation, I have sought to show that the prevailing judicial interpretation of the DMCA Section 512 safe harbor is implausible as a matter of statutory construction, especially when informed by the legislative history of the statute. That interpretation is also implausible as a matter of political economy given the likely allocation of bargaining power between Content and Tech in the legislative drafting process, which probably favored the interests of Content over Tech or, under conservative assumptions, at least reflected a balance of power between the two constituencies. A Copyright Office report on the Section 512 safe harbor makes a similar observation, noting that "the fact that one of the two principal groups [the content industry] whose interests Congress sought to balance is virtually uniform in its dissatisfaction with the current system suggests that at least some of the [DMCA] statute's objectives are not being met."[73] Consistent with this observation, the one-sided judicial rewrite of the safe harbor has given rise to outcomes that Congress could not plausibly have intended when mediating the legislative bargain between Content and Tech. Moreover, these outcomes come close to rendering copyright protections nothing but a right on paper in digital environments.

Consider the following example. In a 2007 decision, the Ninth Circuit held that, in the case of two entities that provided web-hosting and related services to sites called "illegal.net" and "stolencelebritypics.com" (which contained images reproduced, displayed, and distributed without a license from the copyright owner), there was insufficient evidence to conclude that the intermediary had constructive knowledge of infringing activity for purposes of the red-flag test.[74] This ruling defies both common sense and the legislative history, which shows that the red-flag test was intended to exclude from the safe harbor search engines that refer users to sites that are engaged in infringing activity as indicated by the use of certain "telltale" words. The report of the House Committee on the Judiciary addresses this point specifically: "[P]irate directories refer Internet users to sites that are obviously infringing because they typically use words such as 'pirate,' 'bootleg,' or slang terms in their uniform resource locator (URL) and header information to make their illegal purpose obvious ... safe harbor status for a provider that views such a site and then establishes a link to it would not be appropriate."[75] Ironically, judicial understandings of willful blindness for purposes of applying the red-flag test under the DMCA safe harbor are themselves guilty of willful blindness toward the statute's legislative history.

In the judicially crafted copyright regime put in place by *Viacom v. YouTube* and other similar decisions, copyright owners faced with unauthorized copying on a mass scale now have few practical legal options against entities that would otherwise offer the only litigation target that can result in any meaningful deterrence value. Remarkably, judicial fiat has largely trumped a relatively balanced allocation of enforcement burdens among Content and Tech set forth in the DMCA safe harbor. This is precisely the conclusion reached by the Copyright Office in its Section 512 Report (released in 2020), which observes that "the cumulative effect of courts' interpretations of how an OSP [(online service provider)] qualifies for a particular safe harbor ... has been to increase the burden on rightsholders seeking to enforce their rights online ... ultimately altering the balance of the equities as originally weighted by Congress in 1998."[76] This state of affairs stands in stark contrast to the robust copyright regime that had resulted in Napster's shutdown in 2001, or the broadly defined "inducement by omission" standard of liability that the Supreme Court had set forth in *Grokster* in 2005, which had even imposed an affirmative obligation on intermediaries to undertake reasonable measures to deter infringement. Those decisions are now virtually moot in any practically informed analysis of the liability exposure faced by online platforms for indirect infringement liability.

5.5. Closing Thoughts

Only seven years separated the Supreme Court's 2005 decision in *Grokster*, which established expansive liability under the copyright statute for digital intermediaries that fail to make reasonable efforts to detect and impede user infringement,[77] and the Second Circuit's 2012 decision upholding the district court's expansive reading of the DMCA safe harbor and consequent rejection of the billion-dollar infringement suit brought by major content producers against YouTube.[78] During this same critical time-window, as previously discussed in Chapter 4, lower courts adopted a historically unprecedented understanding of the fair use defense, relying on an expansive interpretation of what is arguably a passing phrase in the Supreme Court's 1994 decision in *Campbell v. Acuff-Rose Inc.*[79] These two acts of judicial fiat are surprising if considered merely as a matter of statutory interpretation, both because they are challenging to reconcile with the legislative intent and history behind these provisions and, in the case of the safe harbor, do not reasonably conform to well-accepted canons of statutory construction. Yet both actions should be unsurprising as a matter of the political economy of copyright law during the transition to a digital content ecosystem. The near-uniform and normatively charged body of commentary from academia, policy advocates, and the press signaled to judges and other policymakers which policy path would converge with the perceived dominant policy preference. The result: a dramatic reduction in the effective scope of copyright protection against unauthorized use and, as a result, a massive transfer of wealth from the producers of content to those who distribute and consume it.

6

The Hesitant Return of Reason

In a trenchant critique in a 2014 case that broke the near-uniformity of judicial enthusiasm for expansive applications of the fair use exemption through the vehicle provided by the transformative use concept, the Court of Appeals for the Seventh Circuit expressed concern that these tendencies were inconsistent with the architecture of the copyright statute. In *Kiennitz v. Sconnie Nation*, the court observed that broad application of the fair use doctrine to shield uses deemed to be transformative would threaten to render moot the statutory adaptation right to which all copyright owners are entitled.[1] Under this right, also known as the derivative right, a copyright extends beyond the original work to encompass specified adaptive uses, such as a translation, dramatization, or motion picture version of the original work, and a catch-all category comprising "any other form in which a work may be recast, transformed, or adapted."[2] While many copyright scholars view the derivative right as an undeserved windfall for content owners, this overlooks the critical role this right plays in supporting the fragile economics of the entertainment and media industry, which relies on the ability to maximize revenues on a franchise that can be developed based on the small minority of releases that are hits. That franchise, which comprises a sequence of related creative properties protected by the umbrella of the derivative right, generates revenues that fund the remainder of releases that fail or barely break even, which in turn provides the monetary support behind a creative ecosystem of writers, actors, directors, and a host of technical personnel. This investment structure—akin to a venture capital fund's portfolio of start-up investments—can be observed in a wide range of content markets, including book publishing, popular music, and motion pictures, all of which tend to exhibit a similarly skewed distribution of commercial outcomes.[3]

As the appellate court observed, an infringing use that is deemed to be transformative and therefore eligible for fair use protection may concurrently and reasonably be deemed transformative for purposes of the catch-all

The Big Steal. Jonathan M. Barnett, Oxford University Press. © Oxford University Press 2024.
DOI: 10.1093/oso/9780197629529.003.0007

category of adaptive uses encompassed by the derivative right, leading to an internal contradiction as a matter of statutory interpretation or, when fair use is upheld on grounds of transformative use, rendering moot the derivative right as specified in the statute.[4] To remedy this unsatisfactory state of affairs, the Seventh Circuit took the view that fair use analysis should dispense with the transformative use concept entirely as an unnecessary and unhelpful supplement to conventional fair use analysis. Arguably, this proposal can be reconciled with the *Campbell* decision since, as I observed previously, that decision did not clearly purport to use the "transformative concept" as anything other than alternative language to refine the existing understanding of criticism and commentary (and in particular, parodic commentary) that can satisfy the first prong of a fair use analysis.

The appellate court's contrarian views represented an "emperor has no clothes" moment by suggesting the self-defeating endpoint to which prevailing trends in copyright jurisprudence would lead if not reversed or significantly qualified. If applied without any reasonable limit, the fair use "exception" would swallow up the copyright "rule" by not only eviscerating the derivative right, as the Seventh Circuit observed, but arguably undermining the ability to bring claims for nonliteral infringement in a wide range of circumstances (or, as the Google Books cases demonstrated, even certain cases of mass literal infringement).

The 2022 edition of the influential Nimmer treatise on copyright specifically endorses the views expressed in the Seventh Circuit's decisions as a necessary intervention to correct certain overreaching applications of the transformative use concept.[5] Reflecting the growing impact of the Seventh Circuit's commentary on the state of fair use jurisprudence, a handful of courts—including, most notably, the Supreme Court in its 2023 decision in *Andy Warhol Foundation for Visual Arts, Inc. v. Goldsmith*—have recently expressed similar concerns in blocking attempts to deploy the fair use doctrine to defend practices that, if upheld, would place in doubt the practical relevance of copyright law in original content markets. Some of these rulings illustrate the extent to which courts' expansive interpretation of the fair use doctrine has enabled business practices that simply appropriate original content for profit and do so in circumstances in which there was no meaningful impediment to a licensing transaction between the copyright owner and infringer. The result is a growing tension in fair use case law between, on the one hand, still-prevailing tendencies to favor a broad understanding of transformative use over competing policy considerations, and, on the other hand, emergent tendencies in some courts to fashion a more nuanced version of fair-use analysis that preserves a meaningful form of property-rights protection for the authors and artists who stand at the historical and conceptual core of U.S. copyright law. As generative AI applications such as OpenAI's ChatGPT and Dall-E services are deployed in textual and visual content environments, it is expected that courts will be forced to continue refining the boundaries of the fair use exemption to preserve meaningful capacities to assert legal exclusivity over creative content.

6.1. *Fox News Network v. TVEyes* (2018): Restoring Balance in Fair Use Analysis

In *Fox News Network, LLC v. TVEyes, Inc.*,[6] decided in 2018, the Second Circuit rejected a fair use defense made by a service that allowed subscribers to use keyword searches to locate content in transcripts of radio and television broadcasts. If a search query found a match, it would provide the user with information on the number of times the keyword appeared in the relevant broadcast and enabled the user to view, download, and email up to 10 minutes of the broadcast. To provide these services, the defendant continuously recorded copyright-protected television programming and compiled that programming in a text-searchable database. Absent a fair use defense, enabling users to view copyright-protected video constituted a clear infringement of the owners' reproduction and distribution rights.

The Second Circuit rejected the fair use defense on the grounds that the transformative use was modest while the market harm was great, given the copyright owner's loss of opportunities to license its content to services such as TVEyes or to offer a similar service independently. To support its decision, the court returned to the seemingly forgotten language of *Harper & Row*, in which the market harm factor had been described as "undoubtedly the single most important element of fair use."[7] However, the court did not bar TVEyes from continuing to maintain and offer its database solely for keyword searches (but excluding the viewing service)—a function akin to the information provided by the HathiTrust service that had been previously upheld by the Second Circuit in one of its two Google Books decisions.[8]

6.2. Locast: The "Non-Profit" Streaming Service (2021)

In a 2021 case, an entity known as the Sports Fan Coalition offered the "Locast" streaming service in 32 regional markets that retransmitted National Football League games and other local broadcast television through the internet without securing consent from, or paying retransmission fees to, the broadcast stations.[9] Locast was owned by a nonprofit entity and characterized users' subscription payments as "donations." In its defense against a copyright infringement lawsuit brought by television broadcasters, Locast argued that its parent entity's nonprofit status qualified for a statutory exemption under the copyright statute, which provides a safe harbor from infringement of the public performance right in the case of transmission by "a nonprofit organization, without any purpose of direct or indirect commercial advantage, and without charge to the recipients of the . . . transmission other than assessments necessary to defray the actual and reasonable costs of maintaining and operating the . . . service."[10] In 2021, a federal court rejected this argument on the grounds that Locast was a commercial operation in practice, as evidenced by the fact that users' so-called recommended donations exceeded costs, and the excess revenues were used to expand operations in new markets.[11] Locast was ordered to cease operations and the television broadcasters were awarded $32 million in statutory damages under the copyright statute.[12]

There is a sequel to the Locast case that illustrates the extent to which the U.S. copyright system has departed from its historical commitment to protect the originators of content assets and, in doing so, has facilitated business practices that favor the private interests of content aggregators over all other constituencies in the creative ecosystem. One of the three directors of Locast was Gigi Sohn, the former president and CEO of Public Knowledge, one of the leading advocacy groups that have sought to weaken copyright protections to promote access to content over all competing policy considerations. The overlapping leadership of Locast and Public Knowledge illustrates the convergence of efforts by advocacy groups and business interests to commoditize content assets in creative markets. Concurrently with the settlement of the Locast litigation in October 2021, Ms. Sohn was nominated to be chair of the Federal Communications Commission (FCC),[13] although she withdrew from consideration in March 2023. The Locast venture may have failed in its gamble that the courts would legalize its profit-generating appropriation of copyright-protected content assets. However, the intersection of commercial and ideological interests in the formation of the Locast venture and the nomination of a former head of a copyright-skeptical advocacy group and director of an infringing streaming service to chair the FCC exemplify the extent to which de-propertization strategies—whether motivated by ideological or profit interests or both—have captured and distorted copyright policy.

6.3. Was Andy Warhol a Serial Infringer? (2023)

In a recently decided case, *Andy Warhol Foundation for the Visual Arts v. Goldsmith*, the Supreme Court addressed the extent to which the fair use doctrine can be used to shield "appropriation art" practices from infringement liability. Specifically, the case involved a series of 16 paintings by Andy Warhol, each of which copied a black-and-white photograph of the musical artist Prince by photographer Lynn Goldsmith. In 1984, *Condé Nast*, a fashion magazine, had licensed from the artist the right to use the image in a single issue and then later retained Warhol to create a color illustration using the image for that issue. Warhol created 15 more color illustrations using the image and, in 2016, *Condé Nast* contracted with the Warhol Foundation to use one of the 15 illustrations on the cover of the magazine in another issue—a use that was not covered by the license with the original artist. Whether this subsequent use infringed upon the artist's right in the original image is a question that stands at the intersection between the fair use exemption and the derivative right.

The case addresses a fact pattern that bears a strong resemblance to the facts addressed by the Second Circuit in its 2013 decision in *Cariou v. Prince*.[14] As discussed previously, the Second Circuit had ruled principally in favor of the appropriation artist (Richard Prince, a celebrity artist) under an application of the fair use doctrine that had adopted an especially broad understanding of transformative use (as part of the first prong of a fair use analysis) and an especially narrow understanding of market harm (the last prong). While the appellate court's ruling was controversial, it is consistent with prevailing tendencies among fair use jurisprudence in federal courts, which have heavily weighted the policy importance of protecting infringing uses deemed to be transformative of original works, while often paying little attention to actual or potential commercial harm to the copyright owner. As illustrated by *Cariou*, the result is a copyright regime in which the fair use doctrine can act as something close to a blank check for infringement of copyright-protected content.

Reflecting the recent judicial pushback against the most expansive understandings of the fair use doctrine, the Second Circuit ruled in the *Warhol* case against the appropriation artist (or more precisely, the Warhol Foundation that manages the Warhol copyright estate). In reaching this outcome, the appellate court rejected the Foundation's transformative use defense and emphasized the fact that Warhol's illustration, which had been widely licensed, had likely displaced portions of the market for the original work (which had been actively licensed by the original artist). Notably, the Second Circuit adopted a more demanding test for finding transformative use, holding that "transformative purpose . . . must, at a bare minimum, comprise something more than the imposition of another's style on the primary work."[15] The contrast with the same court's ruling in favor of the appropriation artist in the *Cariou* case is hard to reconcile on any grounds other than that the court had returned to a more balanced application of the competing first and fourth factors of a statutory fair use analysis. That approach in turn tracks the fundamental balance between access and incentive considerations that has historically driven copyright jurisprudence.

In its decision, the Supreme Court upheld the Second Circuit's ruling and, in doing so, endorsed the trajectory of recent lower court decisions that had placed limits on the scope of the fair use exemption, at least in the case of creative works (as distinguished from the software code at issue in *Oracle v. Google*, in which the Court had arguably endorsed a broad application of the exemption). In particular, the Court upheld the Second Circuit's more demanding threshold for finding transformative use and, echoing the critique expressed by the Seventh Circuit in its 2014 decision in *Kiennitz v. Sconnie Nation*, held that a more demanding threshold was necessary to preserve a meaningful scope of application for the adaptation right accorded to copyright owners by statute.[16] Otherwise, as the Seventh Circuit had observed and as the Supreme Court has now recognized in its own words, "'transformative use' would swallow the copyright owner's exclusive right to prepare derivative works"[17]—an outcome that cannot be justified by any recognized principle of statutory construction.

6.4. The Great American Book Robbery (2023)

The Google Books decisions have been widely lauded in the scholarly community and much of the policymaking community as a creative application of the fair use doctrine to enable access to copyright-protected material without causing undue harm to the profit-based incentives of authors and publishers. Yet the legal precedent set by the Google Books decisions, which immunized the single largest act of mass copyright infringement, has had effects on the copyright system that now place at risk the ability of authors and publishers to deter infringement and extract revenues from literary creations. If fully realized, this threat would unravel meaningful property-rights protections for literary content that stands at the historical core of copyright protection. This threat is illustrated by the actions of an alliance of national library associations and like-minded advocacy groups who have sought to take the rationale behind the Google Books decisions a step further.

To contextualize these developments, recall that the application of fair use in the Google Books litigation relied on the fact that Google only showed "snippets" (one-eighth of a page and a maximum number of total pages) to users, while the HathiTrust project even more conservatively only showed information concerning the number of times, and the pages on which, a particular search term appears in a book. These limitations supported a credible argument that these projects caused no significant economic harm to copyright holders in light of the limited portions of text being displayed to users. As discussed previously, the Google Books project has relied on negotiated licensing agreements to secure consent to display larger portions of original works (and apparently has done so successfully, which casts doubt on widespread arguments that digitized literary databases would be infeasible but for the fair use exemption). However, other entities have sought to "push the envelope" of the fair use exemption by deploying business models that engage in more extensive use of copyright-protected material for commercial purposes—as demonstrated by the infringing uses that gave rise to the *TVEyes* and Locast litigations.

Enter the library associations and associated advocacy groups that have consistently lobbied for weakened copyright protections for authors and publishers. To detour around judicial pushback against further expansion of the fair use doctrine, these entities have lobbied state legislatures to enact laws that impose the equivalent of a compulsory license on book publishers.

A law enacted in Maryland in 2021 provides that any publisher that offers an e-book or recorded version of a book (in the statute's words, "electronic literary products") must offer a license to the e-book or recorded book to public libraries and must do so "on reasonable terms that would enable public libraries to provide library users with access to the electronic literary product."[18] Additionally, the statute specifically precludes any such license from "including a limitation on the number of licenses public libraries may purchase on the same date an electronic literary product license is made available to the public."[19] A similar law was enacted in New York in 2021 but was vetoed by the governor.[20] As of August 2023, similar bills were being or had been deliberated by legislatures in Connecticut, Illinois, Massachusetts, Missouri, Tennessee, and Hawaii.[21]

These state laws are almost certainly invalid under the explicit preemption clause in the federal copyright statute,[22] which is what a federal court ruled in June 2022 in striking down the Maryland law.[23] Nonetheless, these efforts illustrate the extent to which the weakening of copyright protections throughout copyright jurisprudence—and, in particular, through the fair use doctrine—ultimately has placed at risk the ability of individuals and entities to assert legal exclusivity over literary works that stand at the very heart of copyright law. While the Seventh Circuit had raised concerns that the transformative use concept threatened the integrity of the derivative right, as specifically provided by the copyright statute, the compulsory license sought by the library associations threatens the integrity of the reproduction right over literary content.

These consequences are not merely theoretical. During the COVID-19 pandemic, the Internet Archive organization launched a "National Emergency Library" initiative that provided unlimited digital access to more than four million books (including 1.5 million books in copyright) that the Internet Archive had scanned without the consent of the copyright owners.[24] The Internet Archive had already maintained a digital lending library providing online access to these scanned books, but had previously used a wait-list mechanism to "lend" one digital copy for each physical copy that it owned. The Archive had justified its pre-pandemic actions under the fair use exemption on the ground that the unlicensed scanning activities constituted transformative use and its lending policies did not significantly impede sales of the original work due to the one-for-one "lend-to-own" ratio.[25] The argument is legally tenuous since the Internet Archive provides full-view digital access, which is not analogous to the snippet views that had been upheld as fair use in the Google Books litigation. In the case of the Emergency Library, even these contestable defenses were not applicable since the Internet Archive had suspended any wait list and "lent" digital copies without any limitation on the number of copies, which implied significant economic harm and cast doubt on the ability to satisfy the fourth factor of a fair use defense. These legal considerations probably explain why, in response to a suit from major publishers,[26] the Internet Archive elected to discontinue the Emergency Library.

The publishers continued the lawsuit in a challenge to the Internet Archive's "one-for-one" digital lending practices that predated the pandemic. The Archive and its supporters rely on the seemingly attractive claim that digital lending would increase access to literary content and that copyright law should be applied in a manner that permits this practice to continue without liability (and therefore without compensation to authors and publishers of in-copyright titles), especially in light of the Archive's nonprofit status. Two amicus briefs submitted by a total of 48 law professors,[27] and a brief prepared by Harvard Law School's Cyberlaw Clinic,[28] agreed. Even setting aside any imperfections as a matter of law (which are discussed subsequently), this claim suffers from two substantial vulnerabilities as a matter of policy.

First, like all copyright policy positions that focus primarily on reduced access costs, the Archive and its supporters overlook the significant costs incurred to produce and market high-cost content assets and, as a result, overlook the fact that the Archive's practices place at risk the revenue streams that enable publishers to support a wide range of book releases (only a minority of which generate significant profits). Taken to its logical conclusion, a literary market without meaningful copyright protection would force individual authors who are not independently wealthy to exit the market absent support from a philanthropic, governmental, or academic sponsor. As I will discuss subsequently, these adverse effects not only raise economic issues concerning the preservation of market incentives for literary production but, as I discuss in Chapter 15, endanger the institutional preconditions for a liberal democracy characterized by robust discourse on matters of public concern without reliance on potentially conflicted sponsors.

Second, the digital lending model and the associated reductions in copyright protection that would be necessary to enable it as a legal matter favor the giveaway business model used by certain platforms to monetize content assets developed by others. In conjunction with a commercial partner, the Internet Archive follows this same model. While organized as a nonprofit digital library, the Archive has operated a fee-based service for physical libraries that pay the Archive to scan books from the libraries' collections, in exchange for which the Archive provides the libraries with an e-book version (which the Archive also retains for "lending" through its site).[29] During 2011–2020, the Archive reportedly earned approximately $35 million through this service.[30] Additionally, the Archive has maintained a relationship with Better World Books (BWB), a for-profit used bookstore that provides the Archive with books for digitization.[31] BWB was acquired in 2019 by Better World Libraries, an entity reportedly "controlled" by Brewster Kahle, who is the founder and chair of the board of the Archive.[32] The Archive, in conjunction with BWB, apparently uses its digitized content as a revenue source, as suggested by testimony by the Archive's former director of finance that "every single page of the Archive is monetized."[33] In particular, the Archive website features a "Purchase" button that users can click on to purchase from BWB used print copies of certain e-books available through the Archive, which then receives a fee from BWB for each user purchase.[34] While the Archive may be motivated by the objective of expanding access to literary material, it follows some of the same business practices that are used by for-profit content platforms that extract value from third-party content without compensation to the authors and publishers that incurred the costs of producing and marketing that content.

While legal academics in the two previously mentioned amicus briefs supported the position of the Archive, the court disagreed vigorously. In a strongly worded opinion ruling for the publishers on summary judgment, the district court concluded that the Archive's position failed because the conversion of a physical book into an e-book format did not constitute transformative use; rather, it was a "paradigmatic" adaptation captured by the derivative right.[35] Moreover, the court observed that the Archive did not strictly enforce the one-to-one digital lending model since it could not ascertain whether a library removed copies of a physical book from circulation once it had been scanned and made available as an e-book through the Archive.[36] Perhaps most importantly, the court observed that allowing the Archive to freely reproduce in-copyright books without authorization "risks eviscerating the rights of authors and publishers to profit from the creation and dissemination of derivatives of their protected works."[37] This point was especially compelling in this case given the existence of an active licensing market for e-books,[38] which meant that ruling against the Archive could not plausibly reduce access (except to the extent that it enabled copyright owners to charge a positive price for such access—which should be uncontroversial since that is the primary purpose of any copyright system). At least in one court, both common sense and legal precedent have prevailed over the accidental alliance of academic commentators, advocacy groups, and content aggregators in favor of unilateral content appropriation.

6.5. Closing Thoughts

In 2013, then-Register of Copyrights Maria Pallante described how the extreme dilution of copyright protections ultimately betrays any meaningful commitment to the copyright system:

> As the first beneficiaries of the copyright law, authors are not a counterweight to the public interest but are instead at the very center of the equation. . . . Congress has a duty to keep authors in its mind's eye, including songwriters, book authors, filmmakers, photographers, and visual artists. . . . A law that does not provide for authors would be illogical—hardly a copyright law at all.[39]

Pallante's words have proven to be prophetic. The judiciary's largely unbroken enthusiasm for expansive understandings of the fair use doctrine (as well as its broad understanding of the DMCA safe harbor), which in turn tracks largely unbroken enthusiasm among scholarly commentators and advocacy groups for weakening copyright protections, has been motivated by understandable concerns to avoid limiting the use of digital technologies that have dramatically expanded access to content and information. Yet, as a handful of courts have recognized (including most notably the Supreme Court in its 2023 *Warhol* decision), a singular focus on expanding access is not only inconsistent with congressional intent as reflected in the copyright statute, but cannot be reconciled plausibly with the balance between incentive and access concerns reflected in the statute and centuries' worth of copyright case law. Moreover, contrary to widespread characterizations that expanding the scope of the fair use doctrine (and the DMCA safe harbors) necessarily promotes the "public interest," these judicial tendencies have advantaged the private interests of content aggregators while largely ignoring the competing interests of content originators and other individuals and entities that contribute to the often costly and lengthy process of content production and distribution. A one-sided approach to copyright law that always privileges access over incentive concerns places at risk—and facilitates business models that endanger—the ownership protections that are necessary to sustain a robust creative ecosystem.

PART III
UNMAKING PATENT LAW

The unraveling of copyright law relied on the convergence of interests between profit-motivated and ideologically motivated proponents of a weak-copyright regime. In Part III of the book (encompassing Chapters 7–11), I describe the concurrent unraveling of patent law, which was supported by approximately the same coalition of business-motivated and ideologically motivated constituencies that converged upon a common policy objective of weakening IP rights, especially in information technology markets. There is one important difference between the evolution of IP policy in content and technology markets. In contrast to content markets, policymakers did not receive any strong indications of the public's dominant policy preference concerning patent protection since the issue is not especially salient to the average voter (with the important exception of the pharmaceutical markets). Subject to ideological predilections on the part of any individual policymaker, perceived public indifference on most patent-related issues meant that policymakers' preferences were mostly impacted by the preferences expressed by constituencies that exhibited the small-numbers and large-resource characteristics that translate into political impact. In particular, leading firms in information technology industries, together with similarly minded academics and activist organizations, made significant investments in advocacy and lobbying activities to advance a weak-patent trajectory. In Part III's concluding chapter, I show additionally how the erosion of patent protections in the smartphone market by U.S. and European courts and antitrust regulators has been imitated and expanded for mercantilist purposes by courts and regulators in China, resulting in a wealth transfer of significant proportions from innovators to producers and other implementers in the multi-billion-dollar market for wireless communications, computing, and other devices.

7

The Political Economy of Patent Law

During an underdiscussed period of U.S. technology history, the patent system was a legal backwater. From approximately the late 1930s through the 1970s, courts were largely hostile to the enforcement of patents and the antitrust agencies were zealous in enforcing strict limitations on a wide range of patent-licensing practices. As a result, patents were not an attractive mechanism for monetizing the investments in R&D made by the large integrated corporations—such as AT&T, IBM, RCA, and others—that led U.S. technology markets during this period. This state of affairs changed in the early 1980s when a sequence of legislative and judicial changes reinvigorated the U.S. patent system. Unsurprisingly, the market took a renewed interest in using patents as a strategy for extracting returns on knowledge assets, and supporting R&D investment, in technology markets. This strategy was attractive in particular to smaller firms in the biotech market and chip-design segments of the semiconductor market. Within little more than a decade, however, this regime change in the patent system triggered a backlash. Bearing a remarkable resemblance to the political economy of the copyright system, an accidental alliance of thought leaders in the academic and policy advocacy communities, on the one hand, and device producers, certain software developers, financial services firms, and digital intermediaries, on the other hand, converged on an intellectual and legal campaign to undo the shift toward a robustly enforced patent system. The result has largely been the victory of rhetoric and narrative over fact and analysis.

7.1. Regime Shift: The Reinvigoration of the U.S. Patent System

In the late 1970s, the United States found itself in what was widely observed to be an economic malaise characterized by a socially destructive triplet of weak growth, slow productivity, and stalled innovation.[1] The innovation slowdown comprised both a moderate decline in national R&D intensity

The Big Steal. Jonathan M. Barnett, Oxford University Press. © Oxford University Press 2024.
DOI: 10.1093/oso/9780197629529.003.0008

(R&D expenditures as a percentage of gross domestic product) and a significant decline in the number of patents awarded to U.S.-resident inventors on a per capita basis. As of 1979, U.S. R&D intensity was 2.11%, compared to 2.55% as of 1969 and 2.39% as of 1959.[2] As of 1979, 133.7 patents were awarded by the U.S. Patent & Trademark Office (USPTO) per one million U.S. residents, as compared to 248.6 as of 1969 and 247.8 as of 1959.[3] Qualitatively, the 1970s had witnessed the decline of U.S. firms in consumer electronics, such as RCA and Zenith, and the automotive industry, such as Ford and General Motors, that had previously been global innovation leaders.[4] In a report prepared for a congressional committee, two economists observed in 1976 that "[t]here has been a decline in the pace and impact of economic innovation in U.S. industry.... New innovations are not occurring in significant enough numbers, nor are they of transcending import to offset the maturing of older growth industries."[5]

Some commentators attributed the decline in U.S. innovation performance to federal courts that often raised significant obstacles to patent enforcement.[6] During the postwar period, courts were generally unsympathetic toward patentees' infringement claims and antitrust law imposed per se liability rules that targeted (and hence discouraged) a broad range of licensing practices.[7] Others lamented legal obstacles that limited the ability of federal agencies to offer exclusive licenses to, or research institutions to obtain patents on, innovations developed on the basis of federally funded research.[8] Reflecting these various concerns, Congress enacted two major pieces of legislation designed to induce greater confidence in the patent system and, as a result, to bolster incentives to invest in innovation.

In 1980, Congress enacted the Bayh-Dole Act,[9] which lifted previously existing restrictions that had prevented or discouraged recipients from seeking patents arising out of research that had been supported by federal funding. That statute provided the legal basis for the technology transfer industry, which relies on patents to commercialize the research output of universities and other nonprofit research institutions through licensing and other arrangements with commercial entities. In 1982, Congress established the Court of Appeals for the Federal Circuit as the exclusive appellate court for patent litigation,[10] which was designed to provide legal certainty and deter forum-shopping through a uniform body of case law. In the years following its establishment, the Federal Circuit acted decisively to issue decisions (which I discuss subsequently) that strengthened protections for patent owners and, in particular, reaffirmed the injunction as the presumptive remedy following a finding of infringement. Concurrently, the Supreme Court issued in 1980 and 1981 two landmark decisions that clarified the patentability of inventions in the biotechnology and software sectors,[11] respectively.

In short, within only a few years, the patent system was expanded significantly in scope and strength so that it acquired practical relevance as a monetization vehicle in technology markets.

This shift in direction can be illustrated by the Federal Circuit's change in the standard used by courts to determine whether to issue a preliminary injunction to protect a patentee's interests during the pendency of litigation. Prior to the establishment of the Federal Circuit, courts generally only granted preliminary injunctions if the patentee established that its patent was valid "beyond question" and infringed.[12] In a 1987 opinion, the Federal Circuit held that a patentee is entitled to a preliminary injunction if it can establish "a strong likelihood of success in establishing validity and infringement"—a considerably lower threshold than the almost impossible-to-satisfy "beyond question" standard.[13] At the same time, the Federal Circuit reaffirmed in 1988 the long-established principle according to which a patentee that had defended the presumption of validity and demonstrated infringement was entitled in almost all cases to a permanent injunction.[14] In a 1989 decision, the Federal Circuit emphasized this point: "Infringement having been established, it is contrary to the laws of property, of which the patent law partakes, to deny the patentee's right to exclude others from use of his property. . . ."[15] The court added: "[T]he right to exclude recognized in a patent is but the essence of the concept of property."[16] As will be discussed, both the rhetoric and substance of these types of statements would be qualified and then largely rejected by the Supreme Court about two decades later.

The reinvigorated presumption adopted by the Federal Circuit in favor of injunctive relief had concrete real-world effects. In 1986, a federal district court found that Kodak had infringed upon Polaroid's patents relating to the instant camera, which had been pioneered by Polaroid's legendary founder-inventor, Edwin Land. In this David versus Goliath litigation, the court issued an injunction that compelled Kodak to close its instant camera division, resulting in the loss of hundreds of jobs.[17] In 1990, the court awarded Polaroid $909 million (equivalent to $2.14 billion in 2023 dollars) in damages, then the largest ever such award in patent infringement litigation.[18] The lesson was clear: the once nearly dormant body of patent law had been revived and would have to be taken seriously by any potential litigation target, even a company as large as Kodak.

7.2. Effects on R&D, Patenting, and Market Entry

The Federal Circuit's case-law shift, coupled with the "demonstration effect" of the *Polaroid v. Kodak* verdict, increased the expected likelihood that a patent owner could secure a preliminary or permanent injunction against infringing users and, if it prevailed on validity and infringement, could expect to secure a potentially large damages award. These legal developments bolstered a patent owner's bargaining position in licensing or settlement negotiations with third parties that sought to use, or were already using, its technology. Those changed expectations, coupled with the expansion in patent subject-matter eligibility under the Supreme Court's 1980 and 1981 decisions on biotech and software inventions, motivated firms to take a renewed interest in patent-based strategies to extract value from innovation.

That interpretation is consistent with the sharp increase, starting in the mid- to late 1980s, in patent applications and grants at the USPTO, the volume of patent suits filed in federal courts, and, as has not been widely observed, an increase in total and business U.S. R&D intensity. Figures 7.1 and 7.2 show the change during 1970–2005—a period that encompasses enactment of the Bayh-Dole Act in 1980 and establishment of the Federal Circuit in 1982—in the number of patent applications and grants (on a per capita basis) for U.S.-resident inventors and total, federally funded, and business-funded R&D investments as a percentage of total GDP. This period

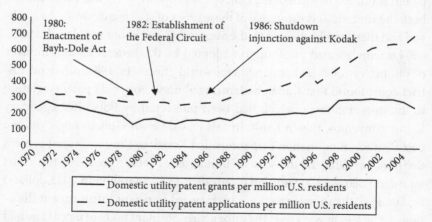

Figure 7.1 U.S. patent intensity (1970–2005).

Source: Author's calculations, based on patent data from USPTO and population data from U.S. Census Bureau.

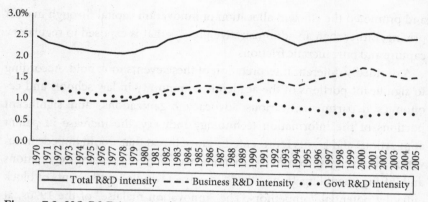

Figure 7.2 U.S. R&D intensity (1970–2005).

Note: R&D intensity measured by R&D expenditures (total, business funded or federally funded) as percentage of U.S. GDP.

Source: National Science Foundation 2021.

is selected to provide a "before and after" picture of the patent and R&D landscape that was available to policymakers and commentators who opined on the effects of the passage of the Bayh-Dole Act in 1980, the Supreme Court's patentability decisions in 1980 and 1981, the establishment of the Federal Circuit in 1982, and the *Polaroid v. Kodak* decision in 1986.

7.3. Origins of the "Patent Failure" Narrative

Given the lackluster innovation performance of the U.S. economy in the 1970s, the increase in patent applications and business R&D intensity might have been viewed as welcome developments as a matter of innovation policy. Commentators might have applauded the significant increase in R&D funding by the private sector (more than offsetting the decline in government R&D funding so that total R&D intensity increased) concurrently with the increase in use of the patent system. Those tendencies are consistent with the view that an increase in the security of property rights for inventors had triggered increased private investment in R&D, resulting in more innovation, just as would be expected following the incentive thesis behind the patent system. Additionally, commentators might have applauded the U.S. innovation system's shift from public to private R&D dollars as the primary source of monetary support, which relieved the economic burden on the public and promoted the efficient allocation of innovation capital through market pricing, rather than an administrative process that is exposed to regulatory capture and bureaucratic frictions.

A decidedly different interpretation of these events took hold. According to significant portions of the academic community in law schools and economics departments, various advocacy organizations, and significant portions of the information technology industry, the increase in patent applications and grants represented a grave threat that would impede innovation by ensnaring technology markets in a "web" of licensing negotiations and infringement litigation initiated to extract windfall settlements or block entry by potential competitors. The "innovation malaise" of the 1970s, at the tail-end of the multi-decade postwar period in which some courts had reduced patents close to a legal nullity, had been quickly forgotten. By the mid-to-late 2000s, economists and legal academics widely asserted that the U.S. economy had been overwhelmed by an unprecedented "explosion" of patent issuance, litigation, and licensing demands that purportedly impeded, rather than promoted, innovation. Books by academics, such as *Innovation and Its Discontents* (published in 2004)[19] and *Patent Failure* (published in 2008),[20] attracted widespread interest in the scholarly community, the press, and, presumably, policymakers. In a widely discussed book, *Against Intellectual Monopoly* (published in 2008),[21] economists Michele Boldrin and David Levine advocated abolishing the patent system entirely, going so far as to analogize supporters of pharmaceutical patents to the "great mass murderers of the 20th Century."[22] As indicated by citations recorded in Google Scholar, each of these books, which were generally written in a style accessible to a reasonably broad audience and published by prestigious publishers, has attracted significant attention. By contrast, two books by prominent academics that tend to favor a robustly enforced patent system, and are also written in a reasonably accessible style and published by comparably prestigious publishers, have attracted far less attention, as indicated by citations (see Table 7.1).

Many scholars and other commentators had a common explanation for this purportedly unfortunate turn of events. It was widely asserted that the Federal Circuit had been captured by some combination of the patent bar and business interests to engineer an excessively strong form of patent protection that would generate monopoly rents for patent owners, raise prices for consumers, and ultimately slow down innovation.[23] In a typical statement, Giovanni Dosi and Joseph Stiglitz asserted that "business firms in

Table 7.1 Citations to Book-Length Assessments of the Post-1982 U.S. Patent System

Book (Authors)	Year of Publication	Publisher	Predominant Policy View on Patent System	Citations (total)	Citations per Year
Innovation and Its Discontents (Jaffe & Lerner)	2004	Princeton	Reform	1659	90.9
Against Intellectual Monopoly (Boldrin & Levine)	2008	Cambridge	Abolition	1969	138.75
Patent Failure (Bessen & Meurer)	2008	Princeton	Reform	1706	119.7
The Patent Crisis and How the Courts Can Solve It (Burk & Lemley)	2009	Chicago	Reform	600	45.28
Justifying Intellectual Property (Merges)	2011	Harvard	Defense	335	29.78
Laws of Creation: Property Rights in the World of Ideas (Cass & Hylton)	2013	Harvard	Defense	32	3.46

Sources: All citations located through Google Scholar as of March 2022 (various dates). For purposes of calculating citations per year, the year of publication is counted in full and the first three months of 2022 are counted. For full citations of books, see References.

general and in particular larger corporations . . . succeeded in inducing the U.S. government to change patent policy in their favor by adopting a stronger patent regime."[24] As I will discuss, this type of claim—which continues to appear widely—is challenged by the fact that most Fortune 500 firms, most large technology firms, and virtually the entire financial services industry have consistently advocated that the Supreme Court or Congress take action to *reverse* the patent-strengthening decisions of the Federal Circuit. Moreover, a patent-skeptical business lobby is nothing new. As I have shown previously, since at least the late 19th century, large U.S. firms (outside the pharmaceutical industry) generally have advocated for changes that would weaken the patent system or halt its extension to new technologies.[25]

It is therefore not surprising to find that the body of purported evidence for widespread assertions among economists, legal scholars, and policy commentators concerning the "failure" of the patent system following the emergence of a strong-patent jurisprudence in the 1980s is weak or, in the best cases, ambiguous. Even at the time these assertions were initially made, a dispassionate assessment of the evidence (which I will subsequently discuss in greater detail) might have recommended skepticism concerning the view that the patent system posed a threat to the innovation economy.

Consider three "macro" trends in the U.S. innovation economy in the years following the shift toward a strong patent regime. First, as shown in Figures 7.1 and 7.2, the increase in patent applications and grants to U.S.-resident inventors starting in the early 1990s (presumably, as the market reacted to the shift in patent case law during the preceding decade) was accompanied by a significant increase in R&D intensity, especially privately funded business R&D intensity. That is consistent with the view that increased patent enforceability had induced not only more patent applications—as emphasized by commentators who expressed concerns over "excessive" use of the patent system—but more R&D investment. Second, contrary to the standard narrative that predicted that expanded use of the patent system would cause U.S. innovation to languish beneath a "thicket" of patent litigation and licensing costs,[26] patent-intensive industries such as biotech and semiconductors have been especially successful in developing transformative innovations and cultivating those innovations through a complex network of innovators, producers, and other implementers. Third, contrary to intuitions that stronger patent protections would raise entry barriers, smaller firms (defined as firms with less than 1,000 employees) have represented increasingly large shares of R&D expenditures as compared to the 1970s, moving from about 5% of all private R&D expenditures as of 1982 (the year in which the Federal Circuit was established) to 21% as of 1992.[27] This dramatic increase in small-firm R&D—something that was never observed during the postwar decades when patent protection was weak and large firms accounted for the overwhelming portion of business R&D expenditures[28]— suggests that the restoration of a robust patent system has both incentivized innovation and enhanced competition, rather than shielding incumbents behind entry barriers, as has been commonly alleged.

Notwithstanding the mismatch between prevailing theory and rhetoric, on the one hand, and the actual performance of real-world markets, on the other hand, an intellectual climate dominated by patent-skeptical commentary by scholars, advocacy organizations, and large platform technology firms has supported a sequence of Supreme Court decisions, starting with the Court's 2006 decision in *eBay Inc. v. MercExchange LLC*[29] and culminating in the Court's 2018 decision in *Oil States Energy Services v. Greene's Energy Group*,[30] that have eroded the secure patent regime put in place by the Federal Circuit. In addition, Congress and antitrust regulators have taken actions under this same intellectual umbrella to "protect" innovation markets from the licensing and litigation strategies of certain purportedly opportunistic categories of patent owners. As I will discuss, it appears in retrospect that it would have been wiser to protect innovation markets against the policymakers that sought to "rescue" them.

7.4. The Political Power of the Stylized Fact

Academic and policy commentators on the patent system have widely attributed a parade of social ills to the restoration of a robust patent regime starting in the 1980s. Each of these assertions constitutes a "stylized fact" that has become an entrenched part of conventional wisdom concerning the U.S. patent system. By "stylized fact," I refer to a factual assertion that is theoretically plausible, supported by a limited number of anecdotal reports, vigorously asserted without qualification (usually accompanied by a salient data point or memorable slogan), widely accepted, and strongly defended when later contested, but rarely subjected by its proponents to close empirical or other objective examination. Additionally, when such stylized facts *are* subjected to examination, these widely assumed facts often turn out to rest on mixed or weak factual grounds. Generally, those critiques are not acknowledged, are dismissed without close examination, or are subjected to exceptionally high standards of proof by "mainstream" commentators.

Scientific progress, including the making of public policy on the basis of factual evidence, is often described as a cumulative process of incremental enlightenment in which carefully formulated hypotheses are tested against data and continuously refined as more evidence is gathered concerning the relevant area of interest. This describes an idealized pursuit of objective knowledge, removed from the distortions that can arise in real-world contexts. As I will show, each of the now-standard set of stylized facts concerning the purportedly harmful effects of a strengthened patent system entered public discourse not through incremental empirical study but rather, consequent to a salient anecdotal event that *might* have indicated a certain defect in the patent system. This was then followed by a mix of academic publications, policy commentary, and industry advocacy that called for urgent action to rectify what was deemed without substantial inquiry to be a significant and confirmed risk. In a closely related scenario, preliminary or limited empirical findings have been used as the basis for sweeping assertions that the patent system "clearly" suffers from a certain flaw or has been captured by a vaguely defined business constituency. In either scenario, a less than fully demonstrated assertion rapidly achieved the status of an established fact because it coincided with the ideological predilections or the economic interests of certain constituencies with congruent policy objectives.

Hence the paradox of the stylized fact: it is both highly contestable as a factual matter but largely shielded by its proponents from the process of continuous testing that is assumed to characterize evidence-based policymaking. This is public policymaking rooted in a combination of ideology and economic interest, rather than dispassionate objective analysis.

This generalized form of confirmation bias (supplemented by robust investment in advocacy and lobbying efforts by ideologically committed and economically interested constituencies) has proven to be a critical tool in translating scholarly critiques of the reinvigorated patent regime into an accessible package of stylized facts on which policymakers have relied in taking actions to weaken patent protections. This symbiosis between the academy, industry, and policymakers has relied upon the fact that these stylized facts not only converge with the policy preferences of ideologically and economically motivated advocates of a weak-IP regime, but are unlikely to conflict with policymakers' interest in accruing reputational capital by tracking what is perceived to be the dominant policy preference. Given that the public does not generally follow patent law closely, policymakers without any prior ideological predisposition are especially likely to be influenced by the advocacy investments of small-number, well-organized, and well-resourced constituencies that have a substantial economic stake in patent policy, especially if those constituencies can make arguments that are reconcilable with a compelling characterization of the public interest. In the pharmaceutical markets, where consumers may have an interest in patent law, the rational preferences of policymakers' constituents for lower prices on existing drugs converge with the policy objective pursued by ideologically motivated proponents of a weak-IP regime. Absent a good-faith willingness to sacrifice political capital for what a policymaker perceives to be the long-term public interest in preserving a robust innovation ecosystem, any policymaker's rational strategy is to support reducing patent protection, which immediately yields reputational goodwill in the political marketplace.

7.5. Concluding Thoughts

As I will show in the following two chapters, stylized facts that lack any compelling real-world analogue have persisted in the discussion and making of patent policy because they conform to the normative preferences pursued by the confluence of ideologically and economically motivated proponents of a weak-patent regime. Those constituencies have generally enjoyed greater advocacy resources than the constituencies that favor a strong-patent regime, as well as complementary thought leadership efforts from the advocacy and scholarly communities. In pharmaceuticals, the sole industry in which supporters of a robust patent regime satisfy the small-numbers and substantial-resource conditions for effective political advocacy, policymakers are likely to observe indications that constituents' dominant policy preferences favor weaker forms of patent protection, complemented by intensive advocacy for weakening (or abolishing) IP protections by ideologically motivated advocacy groups. Across innovation-intensive industries, the thought leadership and advocacy efforts of interested constituencies, mediated through policymakers' pursuit of political goodwill, have resulted in an incremental unraveling of the patent regime that has rolled back much of the shift toward a strong patent regime in the early 1980s. As I will discuss in the following chapters, the result has been a fundamental shift from a patent system that bears a strong resemblance to property-rights systems in which prices are determined by market transactions to a quasi-compulsory licensing system in which prices are largely determined by courts and agencies.

8

The Patent Litigation Explosion and Other Patent Horribles

In this chapter, I identify four categories of stylized facts concerning the purported failure of the patent system since the establishment of the Federal Circuit in 1982. These "patent horribles" have provided the rhetorical, intellectual, and moral basis for taking actions that have significantly limited the force of patent rights. Specifically, these widely adopted assertions in academic and policy discussions appear to have promoted the enactment of the America Invents Act in 2011, the most significant change to the patent statute since 1952. The empirical basis for these widely accepted factual assertions was not thoroughly investigated and, when subjected to more complete investigation after having been widely accepted, each assertion stands in serious doubt or merits considerable qualification. Remarkably, this discrepancy between conventional wisdom and factual evidence has done little to dislodge these entrenched assumptions and, as a result, their influence on patent policy has persisted across all branches of government.

8.1. The Patent Explosion

Starting in the early 2000s, academic and popular discussions of patent policy often referred to the "patent explosion." This phrase has two related meanings. First, the phrase is intended to refer descriptively to the increase in patent applications and grants at the USPTO starting in the early 1990s. Second, the term is intended to convey the normative view that this increase is abnormally large and reflected lax examination standards at the USPTO and an opportunistic use of the patent litigation system by entities that sought windfall jury awards or settlement payments. In a widely referenced book published in 2004, economists Adam Jaffe and Josh Lerner used this phrase in both senses to refer to the "dramatic increase" in the number of patents granted and the normative claim that this "explosion" reflected in

The Big Steal. Jonathan M. Barnett, Oxford University Press. © Oxford University Press 2024.
DOI: 10.1093/oso/9780197629529.003.0009

substantial part the issuance of "patent awards of dubious merit."[1] In short, strengthening the patent system had counterproductively directed the market toward obtaining more patents, rather than investing in more innovation, which in turn generated a transaction-cost burden—attributable to increased litigation and licensing activities—that would ultimately depress innovation. Closer examination shows that both propositions rest on weak or highly contestable factual grounds.

8.1.1. Examining the Evidence

It is important to observe that assertions concerning the purportedly exceptional increase (or "explosion") of patent issuance are almost always based on absolute figures for patent applications and grants drawn from a relatively short period preceding and following establishment of the Federal Circuit. In the same 2004 book publication, Jaffe and Lerner used these absolute figures to support the assertion that, after the establishment of the Federal Circuit in 1982, annual patent applications and grants rose unusually rapidly as compared to any previous historical period dating back to 1840. They rejected the view that the "explosion" in patenting reflected an "explosion in U.S. inventiveness"; rather, they stated that "[i]t is clear that the rapid increase in the rate of patenting has been accompanied by a proliferation of patent awards of dubious merit."[2] A closer examination that takes into account changes in the size of the U.S. population or economy, and the relative participation of foreign as compared to domestic inventors, tells a more complex story.

Figure 8.1 almost replicates the corresponding figure in Jaffe and Lerner's discussion of the patent "explosion," showing total utility patent applications and grants issued by the USPTO from 1860 through 2002. Jaffe and Lerner's data are slightly different because they start in 1840 and include plant and design patents, which represent small to nominal percentages of annual patent applications and grants and can therefore be safely ignored.

For purposes of showing the extent to which the post-Federal Circuit increase in U.S. patenting was exceptional, this presentation of the data is incomplete in two respects. First, it fails to distinguish between patent applications filed by foreign-resident and U.S.-resident inventors at the USPTO. (The USPTO classifies patents based on the stated country of residence of the first-named inventor on a patent application.) Second, even

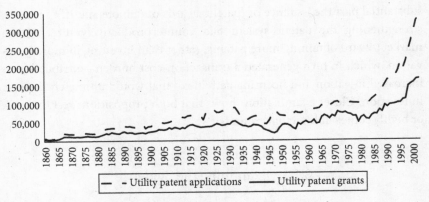

Figure 8.1 Utility patent applications and grants (1860–2002).
Source: Author's calculations based on USPTO data.

excluding foreign-resident patenting activity, the Jaffe-Lerner data do not normalize patent applications and patent grants data based on changes in the size of the U.S. resident population. Both points are important.

Distinguishing between foreign-resident and domestic-resident patenting data is important because an increase in the number of foreign-resident inventors might explain in part the increase in post-Federal Circuit patenting. Figure 8.2 shows why this omission is important. Starting in the mid-1970s, the relative percentage of foreign-resident patent applications increased significantly. By 1986, foreign-resident patent grants had achieved parity with U.S.-resident patent grants and ultimately took a slight lead in 2001 (which has persisted through the present). As of 2002, foreign-resident inventors accounted for almost 51% of total patent grants and almost 45% of total patent applications, reflecting the internationalization of USPTO patenting activity and R&D activity in globalized technology markets. As Figure 8.2 shows, both domestic-resident and foreign-resident patent applications and grants increased steeply starting in the mid-1980s. Hence a substantial reason why the number of patents "exploded" reflects in part the concurrent globalization of R&D activity and the associated increase in foreign patenting at the USPTO. This suggests that the patent surge reflected a welcome development in which technological innovation was growing worldwide, rather than being "burdened" by excessive patenting activity.

To provide the most accurate assessment of the relative increase in patenting activity following establishment of the Federal Circuit, it is necessary to normalize patent applications and grants based on a measure that

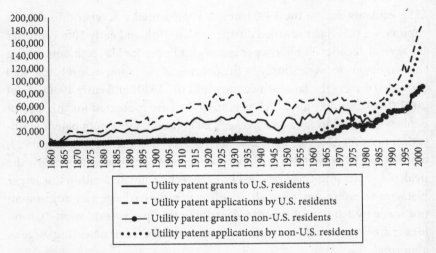

Figure 8.2 Utility patent applications and grants, breakdown by U.S. and non-U.S. residents (1860–2002).

Source: Author's calculations based on USPTO data.

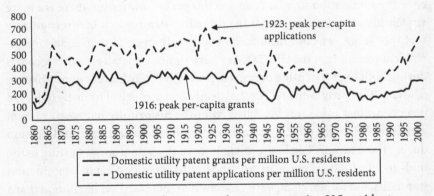

Figure 8.3 Utility patent applications and grants per capita, U.S. residents (1860–2002).

Source: Author's calculations based on USPTO data and U.S. Census data.

accounts for changes in the size of the U.S. population. Figure 8.3 shows annual utility patent applications and grants by U.S.-resident inventors per one million U.S. residents during 1860–2002. A normalized presentation of patenting data for U.S.-resident inventors shows that there was nothing "abnormal" on a per capita basis about the high patenting rates that emerged starting in the early 1990s. Per capita patent application rates for

U.S. residents during the 1990s simply represented a reversion to the per capita rates that had prevailed during the late 19th and early 20th centuries for several decades. Similarly, per capita grant rates for U.S. residents during this same period were simply in the process of reverting to levels that had prevailed during the late 19th century and the 1920s and early 1930s. As of 2002 (the latest date for which patenting data are presented for the "patent explosion" claim in Jaffe and Lerner's 2004 book), per capita patent application rates for U.S. residents had not yet exceeded the record set in 1923, and per capita grant rates for U.S. residents were still materially below the peak per capita grant rate reached in 1916. When situated within this larger historical context but normalized on a per capita basis (an adjustment not made by Jaffe and Lerner in describing the "patent explosion"[3]), it no longer seems reasonable to treat the post–Federal Circuit patenting surge as abnormal.

Jaffe and Lerner also claimed that the increase in patenting during this period reflects a purported decline in USPTO examination standards.[4] As I show subsequently, there is little firm evidence to support the alleged decline in examination standards during this period. Moreover, there is a more straightforward explanation for the surge in patenting volume (recognizing that the "surge" was not historically abnormal), even setting aside foreign-resident patenting at the USPTO. As I have shown in detail elsewhere, courts during both high-patenting periods in post–Civil War U.S. economic history (the late 19th/early 20th and late 20th/early 21st centuries) robustly enforced patents against infringers, as reflected in the historically increased rates at which patents were upheld as valid and found to be infringed in litigation during these times.[5] The best explanation for the patent surge starting in the mid- to late 1980s is not a largely undemonstrated decline in examination standards, but rather, changes in case law that increased the likelihood that a patent would be enforced in litigation (confirmed, as I have shown elsewhere, by data indicating increases in the rate at which patents were upheld as valid when contested in litigation[6]). In both strong-patent periods, the market responded to legal changes that increased the value of a patent by shifting to patents as a strategy for extracting value from R&D investment in certain technology sectors. This explanation is further confirmed by the fact that patenting rates among U.S.-resident inventors declined significantly during the period extending from the late 1930s through the 1970s, when courts were especially unsympathetic to patent owners, antitrust agencies imposed substantial limitations on licensing freedom, and enforcement of patents against infringers was fraught with uncertainty.[7] Rather than representing a largely surmised decline in patent quality, the surge in patenting following establishment of the Federal Circuit most likely represented a rational response to the increase in the likelihood of successfully enforcing a patent (and, if successful, securing injunctive relief) as a result of a change in the governing legal regime.

It can be more reasonably observed that a "patent explosion"—understood as an historically unprecedented increase in the appropriately normalized volume of patent applications and issuance—took place *after* the period during which this assertion was initially made by scholars and other commentators in the early 2000s. Figure 8.4 shows per capita patent grants to U.S. residents and per capita applications by U.S. residents from 1890 through 2019 (the latest year for which the USPTO provides a breakdown of applicants and grants by the inventor's country of residence).

This observation, however, has somewhat greater force concerning patent applications than patent grants (which are ultimately what "counts" as a practical matter). In 2012, utility patent grants to U.S.-resident inventors, on a per capita basis, exceeded the peak previously reached in 1916. However, since 2015, grant volume has largely remained constant, aside from a minor increase in 2019. In 2005, utility patent applications by U.S.-resident inventors, on a per capita basis, exceeded the peak previously reached in 1923, and then increased through 2017, followed by a slight decline through 2019.

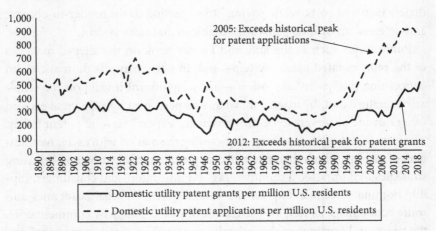

Figure 8.4 Utility patent applications and grants per capita, U.S. residents (1890–2019).

Source: Author's calculations, based on USPTO and U.S. Census data.

Hence, while there appears to have been a significant "explosion" in patent applications by U.S.-resident inventors starting in 2005 and a more limited "explosion" in patent grants to U.S.-resident inventors starting in 2010 (in each case, on a per capita basis), these trends appear to have mostly stalled, although at levels that are still historically high.

8.1.2. Interpreting the Evidence

It is important to keep in mind that the fact that patenting rates have increased (or more precisely, reverted to, and then modestly exceeded, the highest levels that had been previously observed in U.S. patent history) is inherently ambiguous as a matter of social welfare without further analysis. That is, a patent explosion is not inherently a bad thing. Intensive patenting can potentially reflect opportunistic strategies to extract windfall settlements through a combination of litigation threats and licensing demands. But it can also reflect either increased innovative output or the increased use of business models that rely on patents to extract returns from R&D investments, which may facilitate entry by R&D-intensive (and often smaller) firms who would otherwise face high barriers to entry due to large capital requirements. These complications have been largely ignored in prevailing critiques of the post-1982 patent system, which focused on the litigation and licensing costs associated with the strengthened patent system, which are salient and immediately incurred costs, while paying little attention to the harder-to-observe and deferred innovation gains attributable to that same system.

Publications such as the Jaffe and Lerner book on the alleged maladies of the reinvigorated patent system—and, in particular, the dramatic claim concerning the "patent explosion"—had a significant impact on the scholarly literature and, by extension, what was perceived by policymakers and other outside observers to be the consensus "expert" view on patent policy. The view that the patent system was flooding the market with excessive numbers of patents, which then facilitated opportunistic litigation and licensing strategies that imposed a punitive "tax" on innovators and consumers, rapidly dominated scholarship on the patent system by legal academics and some economists, as well as discussions of patent policy by commentators, the press, and portions of the federal judiciary. The "patent explosion" critique soon encompassed related assertions that the patent system was fundamentally "broken" and in urgent need of reform. As I will discuss, each assertion had in common the fact that it achieved widespread adoption among scholars, policymakers, and the press despite having a contestable or largely uninvestigated empirical basis—just like the "patent explosion" thesis that stood at the origin of these views.

If left unchecked initially by the absence of close inquiry, an insufficiently supported assertion in a scholarly discipline can spawn a sequence of overstatements and errors that can be difficult to unravel as an incomplete or even inaccurate proposition acquires the status of received wisdom that is relied upon reflexively by other researchers and rarely is subjected to further examination, whether due to ideological presumptions, cognitive biases, or time limitations on the part of other researchers. Unfortunately, this contingency has been realized in mainstream scholarship by legal academics and economists on the patent system starting in the early 2000s, which adopted without extensive examination the accuracy of the patent explosion thesis. This thesis in turn provided the intellectual foundations for the widespread adoption of three related assertions concerning the post-1982 U.S. patent system: the "patent thicket" thesis, the "junk patents" thesis, and the "patent litigation explosion" thesis. All these assertions have two elements in common: (1) they support the normative position that robust patent protection and intensive patenting impede innovation (and concurrently entrench incumbents); and (2) when examined empirically, these assertions are found to rest on limited or ambiguous evidentiary support. In the aggregate, this implies that much of conventional wisdom on U.S. patent policy has relied on overstated assertions resting on a thin foundation of factual evidence.

8.2. Patent Thickets

Conventional wisdom adopted the proposition that high rates of patent issuance raised the risk of generating a "thicket" of litigation and licensing that would discourage, rather than promote, innovation. This assertion was initially made concerning two legal events that took place in 1980: (1) enactment of the Bayh-Dole Act, which enabled research institutions to seek patents on inventions developed using research funding by the federal government, and (2) the Supreme Court's decision in *Diamond v. Chakrabarty*, which upheld a patent over a genetically engineered bacterium.[8] These two actions removed legal obstacles to using patents as a vehicle for commercializing federally funded biomedical research. To achieve this objective, the Bayh-Dole statute enabled research institutions to use patents to secure profits from the results of federally funded research through licensing and other transactions with business partners. The *Chakrabarty* decision clarified that patent protection extended to biotechnological innovations, which had previously stood in doubt given uncertainty over the scope of the traditional ban on patenting naturally occurring phenomena.

The logic behind the thicket thesis is straightforward. Given that biomedical research had formerly operated in a mostly IP-free environment in which ideas and discoveries could flow freely throughout the scientific community, IP rights would inherently impede that flow and consequently hinder innovation since IP rights holders would have economic incentives to restrict access to scientific discoveries that may have commercial value. While this assertion is plausible, it is no more plausible without factual inquiry than the competing assertion that IP rights would enable researchers to attract capital from outside investors and, as a result, accelerate the conversion of R&D output generated by academic and other research institutions into medical therapies that could improve human well-being. This proposition is especially compelling given historical evidence that legal restrictions on patenting and licensing the results of federally funded research prior to enactment of the Bayh-Dole Act had discouraged interest from industry and commercial partnerships for several decades.[9] The cultivation of economic value and the improvements in human well-being from expanded opportunities and incentives to commercialize federally funded research may exceed, and potentially by a large margin, the increase in transaction costs as a result of the extension of patent rights to biomedical innovations.

8.2.1. Examining the Evidence

The most widely known paper that advanced the patent thicket assertion was a four-page publication in 1998 in the influential journal *Science*, by Michael Heller and Rebecca Eisenberg.[10] This policy brief has become a classic citation for authors who express concern that the proliferation of patents will inhibit innovation (3,817 citations as of January 26, 2024, according to Google Scholar), in some cases referring to this publication as if it were making an authoritative factual statement despite the fact that it comprises theoretical concerns, supplemented by anecdotal examples, that intensive patenting could *potentially* slow down or halt biomedical research projects. This is a possibility theorem that can neither be endorsed nor rejected absent empirical inquiry.

Since publication of the Heller-Eisenberg policy brief, a well-developed body of empirical evidence, and several decades of real-world market experience, now make it possible to evaluate the patent thicket thesis on the basis of factual evidence, rather than merely theory and anecdote. That body of evidence almost uniformly indicates that the thicket thesis has not been realized to any extent sufficient to have a materially adverse impact on biomedical research.[11]

In particular, repeated survey studies of biomedical researchers by Professor John Walsh and colleagues have found little to no evidence that patents, or the necessity to seek a license from, or the prospect of a dispute with, patent owners, have halted or materially delayed research projects.[12] A review of the scholarly literature as of 2006 observed: "The effects predicted by the anti-commons problem are not borne out in the available data" and "[t]he empirical evidence suggests that the fears of widespread anti-commons that block the use of upstream discoveries have largely not materialized."[13] Writing as of 2021, another scholar reviewed the relevant literature and similarly concluded: "[E]mpirical research fails to show that the patenting of research inputs in biotechnology has adversely affected innovation."[14] While researchers have shown that a particular patent-related dispute involving the "Harvard oncomouse" may have slowed research for a certain period of time,[15] one of the authors of that study has concluded in a broader review of the literature that "while it is possible to identify particular cases where patent grants have been associated with what seems to be significant inefficiencies, the more general pattern seems to be that, over time, strong patents operate in parallel (and are complementary to) a large and vigorous domain for open science."[16] Similarly, the authors of the Heller-Eisenberg paper have acknowledged to some extent the gap between anti-commons theory and the real-world conditions in which biomedical researchers typically operate. Eisenberg has recognized that "overall, intellectual property has presented fewer impediments to research than policymakers may have projected on the basis of early salient controversies,"[17] while Heller has stated more guardedly that "the empirical basis for finding that anti-commons effects are stifling innovation remains inconclusive."[18]

What I wrote in a paper published in 2015 remains true today: "At a minimum, there does not currently seem to be compelling support for the anticipated causal sequence extending from increased patenting to increased transaction costs to reduced innovation in biomedical and other scientific research fields."[19] It might have been thought that this discrepancy between theory and evidence would have led the mainstream scholarly and policy discussion to abandon the patent thicket thesis as a once-plausible but now largely rebutted hypothesis. Remarkably, that is not the case in substantial portions of the legal academic literature, policy statements by governmental bodies, and judicial opinions, in which the patent thicket thesis continues to be referenced widely as either an established fact or material risk in any patent-intensive environment.[20] As shown in Figure 8.5, the Heller-Eisenberg policy brief is the most widely cited paper in the patent thicket literature. The next three most highly cited papers are among the few papers that make strong patent thicket assertions or, in the case of a paper by Fiona Murray and Scott Stern,[21] provide empirical evidence of a "modest anti-commons effect" attributed to patenting practices in scientific research. (One of these four highly cited papers, by Carl Shapiro, also observes that

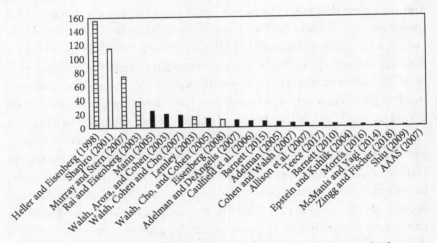

Figure 8.5 Citations per year to representative papers on the patent thicket thesis.

Legend: Solid bars denote papers that find no significant evidence of "patent thicket" effects (or review literature showing no such evidence in the aggregate). Striped bars denote papers that assert or, in the case of Murray and Stern (2007), present evidence of, thicket effects. Bars with a solid border and blank interior denote papers that assert, or find evidence of, thicket effects but identify significant mitigating mechanisms without legal intervention. Extremely short bars are solid.

Notes: All citations located through Google Scholar, as of March 2022 (various dates). For purposes of calculating per-year citations, the year of publication is counted in full and the first three months of 2022 are counted. Citations include self-citations and acknowledgements. "AAAS" refers to American Association for the Advancement of Science.

Sources: See References for full citations to all sources.

private arrangements may mitigate thicket effects.[22]) The remainder of the literature, which generally fails to find evidence of thicket effects, receives far fewer citations.

The conclusion reached by a review of the policy literature in 2006 is apparently and unfortunately still relevant: "[O]ur review of the lively policy debate [concerning "human gene patenting"] and the limited empirical support for the claims that are driving that debate suggest that policymakers may be responding more to a high-profile anecdote or arguments with high face validity than they do to systematic data on the issues."[23]

8.2.2. Interpreting the Evidence

If a hypothesis fails to find support in available evidence, then analytical rigor requires consideration of alternative explanations that exhibit a closer "fit" with that evidence. Given the weak empirical support for the patent thicket thesis, it is appropriate to consider the alternative hypothesis that the extension of patent protection has not only failed to inhibit research and innovation, but has yielded economic and public-health gains by promoting the commercialization of scientific research that might otherwise have been left unexploited. Following the intuitions that drive the thicket thesis, this outcome may seem puzzling: increased patenting would be expected to inhibit subsequent technological development by increasing the transaction costs of accessing knowledge inputs and information exchange within the research community.

The economic realities of innovation markets show that this apparent puzzle is hardly a puzzle at all. There are two reasons.

First, without the prospect of legal exclusivity secured by patents, an outside investor is unlikely to have incentives to place significant funds at stake in commercial development of a technological innovation. This is precisely what occurred during the decades that preceded the Bayh-Dole Act. Federal agencies repeatedly expressed frustration at the inability to attract outside commercial interest in licensing innovations developed at government labs—offered at *zero* royalties—due to legal limitations that barred patent assignments or exclusive licenses.[24]

Second, robust patent protection can *lower* transaction costs by enabling the holders of valuable innovation assets to disclose those assets to potential business partners and, in the course of any ensuing cooperative relationship, to structure each partner's rights concerning the commercial development of those assets. Without patents or some other form of IP protection, the innovator firm (which is typically a smaller start-up in the biomedical context) would be exposed to expropriation by a prospective business partner (which is typically a large integrated company in the biomedical context) that can deploy an existing infrastructure to accelerate product development, testing, production, and distribution. By mitigating expropriation risk, patents and other IP rights facilitate the formation of cooperative business relationships that integrate complementary innovation and commercialization capacities, in the process bringing new products to market at a faster pace and lower cost than would otherwise be the case.

The success of the biotech industry since enactment of the Bayh-Dole Act and the *Chakrabarty* decision in the early 1980s, coupled with the increase in the likelihood of patent enforcement in general under the Federal Circuit, conforms far more closely to this alternative "patent enablement" thesis, as compared to the market failure falsely predicted by the patent thicket thesis. Following the patent enablement thesis, the Bayh-Dole Act, the *Chakrabarty* decision, and Federal Circuit jurisprudence promoted the commercialization of biomedical research by supplying the property-rights foundation that induced private capital to invest the substantial resources required to convert scientific knowledge into approved drugs and therapies.[25] The explosive growth of the biotech industry, which often relies on a network of business relationships among research institutions, scientist-founded start-ups, venture-capital investors, and large pharmaceutical firms, illustrates this proposition. Far from slowing down biomedical innovation and commercialization, the extension of property rights into the "research commons" appears to have incentivized innovation and facilitated commercialization, resulting in favorable impacts in terms of economic welfare and human well-being. Without robust patent protection to preserve reasonable expectations of legal exclusivity in the case of technical and commercial success, prospective investors would almost certainly decline to provide capital to this sector and would move on to other investment opportunities.

Unlike the patent thicket thesis, the patent enablement thesis exhibits a close fit with the actual performance of real-world biotech markets. From 1980 to 2003, over 470 biotech firms went public, and a substantially larger population of firms received tens of billions of dollars in funding from venture capital (VC) firms and other investors.[26] Patents appear to play a key role in eliciting VC investment, as suggested by studies showing that the quantity and quality of a biotech firm's patents increase the likelihood that, and the speed with which, it will receive financing from a VC fund.[27] Evidence collected by David Adelman and Kathy DeAngelis shows that patenting on biotech innovations increased during 1990–2004, but increased especially among universities and was accompanied by robust entry into the biotech industry (usually start-ups founded by academic scientists or through a relationship with a research institution).[28] The shift in innovation toward universities and newer firms contrasts sharply with pharmaceutical development in the postwar decades, when it had mostly taken place in the labs of large integrated incumbents.[29] Consistent with the motivating vision behind the Bayh-Dole Act, these structural changes in the commercialization process strongly favor the thesis that IP rights promoted the monetization of R&D output by rendering investment in biotechnological innovation an economically attractive opportunity, facilitating the infusion of venture capital, entry by biotech start-ups, and, through these vehicles, the conversion of university research into new products for the medical community.

To illustrate concretely the value-enhancing function of patents in the biotech ecosystem, consider the Cohen-Boyer patent, one of the first biotech patents and the first patent to support a commercially available biotech product, synthetic human insulin, which was developed and marketed jointly by Genentech (then a start-up) and Eli Lilly in 1982.[30] This success story is only one of thousands that have emerged from the Cohen-Boyer patent on foundational methods of genetic engineering (specifically, recombinant DNA techniques), which Stanford University licensed widely and at rates that were perceived to be "below market" given the foundational technology covered by the patent. Contrary to the thicket thesis, the issuance of a patent for this building-block technology did not impede the development of medical innovations that have in turn relied on that technology. Just the opposite occurred. Through negotiated licensing relationships, the Cohen-Boyer patent provided the legal tool for disseminating the underlying technology to hundreds of firms and other entities, which in turn relied on this property-rights framework to secure funding from VC investors and to negotiate production and distribution relationships with large pharmaceutical firms that could supply the capital and expertise necessary to convert a medical innovation into a clinically and commercially viable product. Far from impeding the flow of information, the Cohen-Boyer patent facilitated and structured the flow of information from the university to start-ups to VC investors and business partners, providing the basis for a robust ecosystem comprising investors, innovators, and other parties required to commercialize a biopharmaceutical innovation. With various iterations, this model has been replicated many times over in the subsequent evolution of the biotech industry, resulting in a continuous flow of new drugs and other medical therapies.

8.3. Junk Patents

The patent explosion and patent thicket assertions reflected concerns that the "excessive" quantity of patents being issued by the USPTO, exacerbated by the dispersed ownership of those patents, would slow down innovation under the burden of increased licensing and litigation costs. In a related assertion, scholars and commentators widely claimed that the increase in patent issuance reflected in part a reduction in the standards being applied by USPTO examiners to screen out low-value patents that did not meet the patentability threshold as defined by statutory and case law.[31] Put more simply, it was (and is) asserted that the USPTO had adopted a "rubber stamp" approach that dramatically lowered the bar for patent applications. Following this line of argument, the market observed that the USPTO had relaxed examination standards, concurrently with a reduction in patentability standards at the Federal Circuit,[32] and then responded by investing more resources in patent applications, drawing in lower-quality applicants that might otherwise have been screened out.

Various agencies and think tanks adopted the junk patents thesis. In 2003, the Federal Trade Commission (FTC), in a widely referenced report, expressed concern that low-quality patents "contribute to the patent thicket" and can "deter follow-on innovation and unjustifiably raise costs to businesses and, ultimately, to consumers."[33] A report issued in 2004 by the National Research Council stated, with some qualification: "There are several reasons to suspect that more issued patents are deviating from previous or at least desirable standards of utility, novelty, and especially non-obviousness."[34] These initially qualified views converted rapidly into an intellectual consensus that the USPTO was "flooding" the market with low-value patents. A 2009 report released by the Brookings Institution suggested little doubt that this problem was widespread and severe: "Critics across the political spectrum complain of a crisis in quality in the patent system . . . officials all but rubber-stamp the applications that come across their desks."[35]

.These assertions yielded practical effects that have substantially altered the playing field in patent infringement litigation. Conventional wisdom that the PTO was acting as a rubber stamp was one of the principal rationales behind enactment in 2011 of the America Invents Act (AIA), the first major U.S. patent legislation in approximately 60 years. The statute provided for the establishment of the Patent Trial & Appeals Board (PTAB), which significantly expanded opportunities to challenge the validity of an issued patent. The result is that any patent owner seeking to enforce a patent must now expect to face significantly increased litigation costs in a "two-front" litigation landscape involving both an infringement claim in federal district court and a challenge to the patent's validity filed by the alleged infringer in the PTAB.

8.3.1. Examining the Evidence

Remarkably, the empirical literature had not provided compelling evidence to support the junk patents thesis at the time of the enactment of the AIA in 2011, and still failed to do so as the PTAB commenced operations in 2013. Writing in 2015, Michael Frakes and Melissa Wasserman observed: "Despite the fact that major changes in the patent system are driven by concerns that the Agency [(the USPTO)] allows too many invalid patents to issue, there exists little to no compelling empirical evidence that any particular feature of the system drives the PTO to overgrant."[36] The authors do present in the same paper empirical evidence showing an examiner bias toward patent over-issuance due to budgetary pressures to reduce repeat filings;[37] however, this finding does not appear to rely on any elements of the patent examination process that are specific to the period following the strengthening of patent rights and purported reduction in examination standards in the early 1980s.

The contested state of the empirical literature concerning patent quality appears to have been largely overlooked by an academic and policy consensus that advocated vigorously for reforms to address a "junk patents" problem but generally did not inquire rigorously whether the assumed problem existed at any reasonable level of confidence. Concerns over "junk patents" were often illustrated by anecdotal examples in which the USPTO had issued patents for inventions that seemed to lack much if any inventive contribution. The list of "silly patents" is entertaining: a patent for swinging on a swing,[38] a patent for a method of playing with a cat with a laser,[39] and a patent for a crustless sandwich.[40] However, the critical question was whether the USPTO was *systematically* issuing low-quality patents. This question cannot be addressed merely by focusing on a few salient errors that would inherently arise in any patent examination system that operates under limited resources. Relatedly, a rigorous empirical examination would have necessitated showing that examination standards at the USPTO had fallen relative to previous years, since it was argued that a decline in examination rigor had contributed to the purportedly exceptional increase in patent issuance starting in the 1980s.

Like the patent explosion thesis, widespread adoption of the junk patents thesis can be traced back to imperfections in an academic publication. In 2001, Cecil Quillen and Ogden Webster published an empirical study that claimed that the USPTO had issued patents for as many as 97% of applications filed during 1993–1998.[41] This implausibly high percentage was later revised by the authors (and an additional coauthor) in a 2002 publication, with a newly estimated grant rate of approximately 85% of applications filed.[42] Both the original and revised estimates in the Quillen and Webster studies (and especially, the original estimate) have been widely referenced to support the assertion that the USPTO grants the vast majority of the applications that are brought before it. Both studies were referenced in the previously mentioned 2003 FTC report[43] and 2004 National Academy of Sciences report,[44] which expressed concerns over the claimed issuance of low-quality patents by the USPTO. In 2008, a law review publication observed that "[a] growing chorus of voices is sounding a common refrain: the patent office is issuing far too many bad patents."[45]

Yet factual accuracy cannot be a function of the number or intensity of voices making a particular assertion. Even the reports by the FTC and the National Academy of Sciences, which otherwise emphasized the risk posed by low-value patents, indicated appropriately that firm evidence for this purported risk was not yet clear. Specifically, both reports referenced a subsequent publication that had contested the methodology used in the Quillen and Webster studies and reached a lower estimated grant rate of 75% for the period 1994–1998.[46] Differences in estimated grant rates reflect different approaches to address the complicating fact that U.S. patent law allows applicants to file "continuation," "continuation-in-part," and "divisional" applications that result in multiple "child" applications flowing from a single "parent" application that establishes priority. Using a more nuanced approach that reflects these continuation applications, Ron Katznelson found that the estimated annual grant rate during 1981–1998 (the period during which patent strength increased under the Federal Circuit) increased from 60% to 76%, which is significant but substantially below the 85% and 97% figures that had been reached in the Quillen and Webster studies.[47] A subsequent empirical study found that, for patent applications filed during 1996–2005, the average grant rate had *declined* to 71%.[48] Putting these studies together suggests that, even if examiners may have applied a looser patentability standard in the 1980s through the mid-1990s, the USPTO had likely returned to a stricter standard by the time the AIA was enacted in 2011 and the PTAB opened for business in 2013.

8.3.2. Interpreting the Evidence

Even if it is accepted that the grant rate under the Federal Circuit increased by a certain significant amount (at least through the mid-1990s), it is still not clear that this increase necessarily reflects a decline in patent quality.

Two studies that find evidence of an over-granting bias attribute the bias to factors that would have been present both before and after the purported reduction in examination standards starting in the early 1980s (specifically, agency pressures to reduce repeat filings[49] and examiner age[50]). Studies published in 2004 and 2006 claimed to find evidence of a lack of examination rigor at the USPTO as reflected by lower grant rates at the European Patent Office (EPO) for patent applications that had been granted at the USTPO.[51] However, these studies also showed that this difference was largely caused by higher percentages of applications being withdrawn by EPO applicants, rather than being denied by EPO examiners.[52] In particular, the difference in USPTO and EPO average grant rates may simply reflect the fact that USPTO applicants have no incentive to withdraw an application because of an idiosyncratic feature of the U.S. patent system that does not allow USPTO examiners to definitively reject an application. Hence, withdrawal of a patent application would irrationally forfeit the option of refiling an amended application at a later time based on the earlier priority date.[53] A study published in 2008 ultimately concludes that procedural and substantive differences in the examination process across major patent offices pose an intractable "apple/oranges" problem that precludes attributing with any reasonable confidence comparative differences in grant rates to differences in examination rigor.[54]

In short, the state of empirical knowledge concerning patent quality at the time of the enactment of the AIA and the inauguration of the PTAB remained unsettled. There was no firm evidence specifically showing (1) a significant and persistent decline in examination quality following the increase in patent applications and issuance starting in the early 1980s, which (2) was reasonably attributable to a decline in examination standards at the USPTO (as distinguished from other preexisting elements of the patent examination process). To be clear, it may nonetheless be the case that the U.S. patent examination system exhibited features that resulted (or continue to result) in significant underscreening of lower-quality patent applications,[55] although it is important to specify (as is not always the case) some reasonably objective measure of patent quality. It may also be the case that mechanisms can be designed to improve patent quality without undermining the efficacy of patents as an incentive and monetization mechanism. Subject to those caveats, it remains the case that, at the time of the enactment of the AIA and the creation of the PTAB, policymakers relied on a factual assumption—namely, the junk patents thesis—that lacked a compelling factual foundation.

8.4. The Patent Litigation Explosion

The purported explosion in patent issuance was widely held to be accompanied by not only a flood of low-value patents, but also an explosion of patent litigation. Both claims were logically derived from the underlying claim that the Federal Circuit had lowered the standards that patent owners must meet when defending the validity of an issued patent in litigation and, by implication, the standards that patent examiners apply when reviewing a patent application. Together these two effects were presumed to have imposed economic harms by incentivizing opportunistic entities to acquire patents for purposes of securing exorbitant damages awards or settlement payouts on the basis of patents that should never have been issued in the first place. The alleged result was a surge of nuisance litigation that burdened and discouraged innovation, precisely contrary to the intent of the patent system.

Like the patent thicket and junk patents claims, the patent litigation explosion was a plausible claim based on a quick read of available evidence. During the 1990s, the number of patent infringement suits filed annually doubled, and continued to increase during the following decade, rising from about 2,500 suits filed in 2000 to over 3,500 suits in 2011.[56] (Since 2017, the number of patent infringement suits has fluctuated within a range of 3,600 to 4,000 each year.[57]) These trends were noted with concern by academics and policy commentators, including in the previously mentioned book-length publications by Jaffe and Lerner (published in 2004)[58] and Bessen and Meurer (published in 2009).[59] Scholarly and policy commentary widely agreed that the expansion of patentable subject matter by the Supreme Court, the increased enforceability of patents since the establishment of the Federal Circuit, and the lure of patent damages had led to an exceptional and burdensome increase in the volume of patent litigation.

In 2013, the White House issued a report stating that "[t]he increased prevalence of . . . patent suits . . . in recent years stands in contrast to the 20th century, when suits for patent infringement were relatively rare."[60] The statement is substantially accurate, aside from the use of the word, "rare," which is somewhat of an overstatement. However, the key question is whether the increase in patent litigation activity since the 1990s had been historically exceptional once any such increase is appropriately normalized to allow for comparisons across time periods. Specifically, it is necessary to assess the number of patent infringement suits as a percentage of either the number of patents issued or the number of patents in force during any particular period. (The latter measure is more accurate since it takes into account the fact that a large portion of patents lapse prior to the end of the statutory term due to failure to pay maintenance fees.) Using these relative measures casts doubt on the "litigation explosion" thesis. As noted by Congresswoman Marcy Kaptur during legislative deliberations on a patent reform statute in 2007, the number of patent infringement suits filed as a percentage of patents issued was 1.45% in 1993 and remained virtually unchanged at 1.47% in 2006, with no rate higher than 1.71% in the intervening years.[61] That does not seem like much of an explosion.

Subsequent empirical research has confirmed Kaptur's skepticism (and rebutted still-prevailing conventional wisdom among scholarly and policy commentators), showing that the absolute rise in the number of patent infringement suits starting in the 1990s through the present was historically unexceptional when assessed in relative terms, given the approximately concurrent rise in the number of issued patents. As shown by Ron Katznelson in exhaustive (and almost entirely overlooked) historical research that covers a full century spanning 1923–2013, "patent litigation intensity," whether measured by the number of patent infringement suits filed relative to the number of issued patents or the number of patents in force, was not materially higher during the period following establishment of the Federal Circuit as compared to previous periods in U.S. history since 1923.[62] The only exception to this finding is 2011–2013, when patent suits surged; however, as Katznelson and other scholars have observed, this was due to a technical change in federal civil procedure that limited the ability to consolidate multiple defendants into a single infringement litigation.[63] In historical research that extended into the 19th century, Christopher Beauchamp discovered that the rate of patent infringement litigation per patents issued had been highest during a surge in patent litigation in the mid- to late 19th century,[64] again suggesting that the surge in patent litigation following establishment of the Federal Circuit was hardly the exceptional event widely described as such in academic and policy commentary.

These findings do not purport to contest claims that patent litigation increased in absolute terms following establishment of the Federal Circuit. However, they do show that this increase was historically unexceptional—in fact, it should have been expected—given the concurrent increase in the number of patents that were issued and in force (which, as shown previously, was itself not particularly exceptional on a normalized basis until the early 2010s). Hence, the widely expressed view that an unprecedented "patent litigation explosion" had occurred, which therefore demanded urgent policy action, was largely unfounded.

8.5. Policy Payoff: The America Invents Act

A stylized fact will persist and enjoy increasing adoption if it is a *useful* fact in supporting arguments for a particular policy objective that is both (1) supported by a strong and stable coalition of interested constituencies, and (2) not resisted by a comparably strong and stable coalition of interested constituencies. As a general rule, it is probably the case that the more useful the stylized fact for the policy objectives pursued by interested constituencies, and the weaker the resistance mounted by opposing constituencies, the less scrutiny will be allocated to verifying the accuracy of that stylized fact.

The "patent thicket," "junk patents," and "litigation explosion" assertions, which are all extensions of the underlying "patent explosion" thesis, provided useful stylized facts for the grand alliance of ideologically and profit-motivated constituencies that advocated for policy actions to shrink the volume of issued patents and to discourage patent litigation by increasing the obstacles faced by patent applicants and litigants in the examination and litigation processes, respectively. The constituencies that supported these policy actions exerted significant influence over policymaking entities (and were consistent with normative views that predominated in the scholarly community), while constituencies that resisted those actions exerted considerably weaker influence. As a result, there was little interest in examining closely the reliability of the factual claims made by commentators and advocates who asserted that the reinvigorated patent system posed a grave threat to the U.S. innovation economy.

The patent-skeptical constituencies that were strong adherents of the patent explosion thesis, and the related claims that fall under its intellectual umbrella, achieved a landmark policy outcome in the legislative arena with the enactment of the AIA on September 6, 2011,[65] the most significant amendment to the patent statute since passage of the Patent Act of 1952.

The AIA represented the culmination of legislative deliberations starting in 2005,[66] which had been preceded by congressional hearings on patent reform dating from 2001.[67] In 2007, a U.S. Congressman introduced a patent reform bill, which later matured into the AIA, and referred to concerns over patent quality and litigation abuses, specifically citing the book by Jaffe and Lerner.[68] To address patent quality concerns and deter opportunistic litigation to enforce low-quality patents, the AIA established the PTAB, an administrative tribunal within the USPTO that provides several mechanisms through which the validity of an issued patent may be challenged.

8.5.1. The PTAB in Action

Among the mechanisms provided by the PTAB to challenge an issued patent, the most commonly used is the *inter partes* review (IPR) mechanism, which enables any party to challenge the validity of an issued patent on grounds of lack of novelty or non-obviousness (in both cases, due to a previously issued patent or other "printed publication" that had not been considered by the examiner),[69] even if that party would not otherwise have standing to do so under the "case or controversy" requirement in federal court. The IPR mechanism not only removes the customary standing requirement to challenge the validity of an issued patent, but also allows such challenges to take place at any time during the life of the patent, starting nine months after issuance.[70] The absence of any time limit on filing an IPR challenges differs from

EU post-grant opposition proceedings (which the PTAB's advocates had lauded), which require that an opposition must be filed *within* nine months after issuance of a patent.[71] Moreover, in the IPR process, a challenged patent does not enjoy the statutory presumption of validity, as in patent infringement litigation. Together these changes have created a cloud of insecurity throughout the life of a patent issued by the USPTO—again, to an extent that goes beyond any such uncertainty arising from opposition proceedings in other major jurisdictions.

Since implementation by the USPTO starting in 2013, the PTAB mechanism has proven to be a potent tool in the hands of firms that are, or expect to be, targets of a patent infringement suit. When a patent owner files an infringement suit in federal district court, a defendant can respond by opening a "second front" at the PTAB, which raises the patentee's costs of pursuing its suit and, by anticipation, may deter the suit in the first place. This strategy is commonplace. In 2022, the USPTO reported that more than 80% of IPR petitions were filed in conjunction with a pending district court litigation (typically initiated by the patent owner).[72] Based on data reported as of 2019, a firm that seeks to defend a patent through the litigation process must now expect to incur the costs associated both with a federal district court litigation, which can range from $700,000 to $4,000,000 depending on the amount at risk, and a PTAB proceeding, which can total an estimated $400,000 to $650,000.[73] When the defendant is a large technology firm that has abundant litigation resources and the patentee is a start-up that faces significant budgetary constraints, the economic realities of sustaining a multi-venue litigation process may induce settlement on terms favorable to the infringer, or may deter the patentee from bringing an infringement suit at all. (This imbalance can be mitigated in certain cases by the availability of third-party litigation funding entities.)

Data on PTAB outcomes suggest that it is often prudent for a patentee to settle rather than proceed to a fully adjudicated PTAB proceeding, especially if the challenger prevails at the "institution" stage (equivalent to a plaintiff surviving a defendant's motion to dismiss on summary judgment in civil litigation). During 2015 through 2019, slightly more than 60% of all petitions were instituted,[74] with a modest decline to 56% and 59% in 2020 and 2021, respectively, followed by a sharp increase to 67% in 2022.[75] For some technology classes, institution rates (as of 2022) for petitions were higher, rising to 77% in biopharmaceuticals as compared to 68% in the electrical/computer category.[76] During the life of the PTAB through 2022, 8,578 patents were challenged, of which 33% (2,749 in total) were partially invalidated and 10% (890 in total) were fully invalidated.[77] Put differently, among all patents targeted by petitioners since the PTAB opened for business through 2022, 57% survived with all claims intact.

8.5.2. Evaluating the PTAB's Performance

The normative implications of the PTAB's performance to date are ambiguous. Without further inquiry, the success rate of PTAB petitioners that challenge issued patents might be interpreted to mean that the PTAB is working as intended by identifying a significant number of low-value patents with claims that do not meet the patentability threshold. Alternatively, these findings might be interpreted to mean that the PTAB is sometimes being used offensively as a tool by incumbents to impede entry by innovators or, given the costs involved in a PTAB challenge, to compel small-firm innovators to enter into favorable settlements with large-firm infringers.

Without settling this question, it is nonetheless possible to gain some insight into these issues by considering the composition of the pool of entities that regularly file challenges at the PTAB. As shown in Figure 8.6, the firms that filed the most petitions during 2013–2021 included some of the largest firms in the world, specifically Samsung, Apple, Google, Intel, and

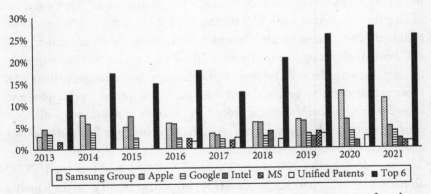

Figure 8.6 PTAB petitions filed by top six petitioners, as percentage of total petitions (2013–2021).

Notes: Filings for each petitioner include filings by subsidiaries.

Source: Unified Patents 2013-21, in each case based on data "aggregated" from the USTPO website and "enriched" by Unified Patents.

Microsoft, in addition to Unified Patents, an intermediary that files PTAB petitions on behalf of its clients (which, based on the organization's website, consist of a mix of larger and smaller technology companies[78]). The concentration of PTAB petitions among these six entities has intensified over time. In 2013, the first full year in which the PTAB was in operation, these entities constituted 12.5% of all petitions filed at the PTAB; in 2021, that percentage had climbed to almost 26%. These percentages decline by only a modest amount if Unified Patents' petitions are excluded.

It is notable that the lead PTAB petitioners were generally among the leading advocates, or were members of trade organizations that advocated, for the AIA statute that established the PTAB. To be clear, most of these firms are among the most commonly named defendants in patent infringement litigations filed in federal court[79] and hence would naturally be expected to be among the most frequent users of the PTAB mechanism. Some PTAB petitions, or the threat of a PTAB petition, may constructively play a defensive function by deterring nuisance infringement suits, consistent with the rationale behind the PTAB. Nonetheless, the predominance of these large technology firms among the petitioner population raises concerns that those firms may sometimes be using the PTAB mechanism to deter legitimate infringement suits brought by small-firm and individual innovators with limited litigation resources. It is worth noting that, during 2014–2022, slightly more than half of PTAB petitions filed each year challenged patents held by operational entities, as distinguished from the non-practicing entities (NPEs) most commonly associated with nuisance patent litigation.[80] Moreover, out of all petitions filed at the PTAB during 2014–2022, almost 16% have been filed in the life sciences sector,[81] in which NPEs are generally not active.

Concerns about opportunistic use of the PTAB are further supported by the fact that some large technology firms have opposed changes to the PTAB process that seem to be consistent with basic due-process principles and were designed to correct certain procedural features that favored challengers over petitioners. The response of several large technology firms in response to one of these reforms is telling.

In two decisions in 2018 and 2020, the PTAB had held that the USTPO director may decline to institute an IPR petition, in part based on whether there was a pending district court proceeding concerning the same patents being challenged in the petition.[82] Subsequently, USPTO director Andrei Iancu exercised his statutory authority to designate those PTAB decisions as "precedential," which means they became binding on the PTAB going forward. In response, Apple, Cisco, Google, and Intel sued the director for allegedly exceeding his statutory authority,[83] accompanied by an open letter from information technology trade associations and advocacy organizations urging Congress to investigate the USPTO's actions.[84] While the suit was dismissed in November 2021,[85] large technology companies did not concede this point and instead sought to reverse these procedural changes made under USPTO director Iancu through legislative action, lobbying for the "PTAB Reform Act," a Senate bill that was introduced in June 2022 and would have precluded the USPTO director from declining to institute an IPR petition based on a pending district court litigation.[86] Although this legislation did not move forward, USPTO director Katherine Vidal adopted in 2022 the policy that institution should not be denied because there is a concurrent district court proceeding, so long as the IPR petition "presents compelling evidence of unpatentability" or the petitioner is pursuing different grounds for unpatentability in the district court proceeding.[87] Based on data reported by the USPTO, these policy shifts have had little practical effect: in 2019, 2020, 2021, and the first quarter of 2022, only 1%, 4%, 11%, and 2%, respectively, of all institution determinations at the PTAB resulted in a denial due to concurrent district court proceedings.[88]

Based on existing evidence, it is difficult to ascertain the mix of PTAB petitions that are being used legitimately to block and deter nuisance infringement litigation, on the one hand, and PTAB petitions that are being used illegitimately to suppress and deter meritorious infringement litigation, on the other hand. Yet it is important to observe that a substantial percentage of PTAB petitions do not target the NPEs that were widely viewed as being the primary source of opportunistic patent licensing and litigation strategies. Given these empirical uncertainties concerning the operation of the PTAB, coupled with underlying uncertainties concerning whether there was ever a significant "junk patents" problem in the first place, the intensive use of the PTAB mechanism by large technology incumbents, and the unusual lack of any time limit on filing a PTAB petition, there are reasonable grounds for concern whether the PTAB in its current form represents an improvement in the U.S. patent system.

8.6. Closing Thoughts

The prevailing narrative of the U.S. patent system for the past several decades is a story of decline in which the patent system was captured by entities that use patents for opportunistic purposes and, as a result, place an inefficient burden on the innovation economy. The narrative comprises a series of dramatically characterized policy failures, including the patent explosion, patent thickets, junk patents, and the patent litigation explosion assertions. Remarkably, the empirical evidence for these widely asserted claims is weak: the increase in patent applications and grants starting in the late 1980s was not historically unprecedented (at least through the mid-2000s), market participants typically seem to anticipate and resolve patent thickets through contractual devices, the evidence that examination quality declined at the USPTO is ambiguous, and the increase in patent litigation is the naturally expected result of the increase in patent issuance. Available evidence does not appear to support the widely held view that the reinvigoration of the patent system starting in the early 1980s was a policy mistake that harmed the U.S. innovation economy. As will be discussed subsequently, there are strong reasons to believe that just the opposite was the case.

9

Patent Trolls and the Demise
of the Injunction

In early 2006, corporate America was worried. Strangely enough, the source
of concern was a patent infringement litigation brought by an obscure entity,
NTP, against a corporate giant, RIM, the manufacturer of the then-ubiquitous
Blackberry mobile communications device. The litigation was of interest because the parties had not settled and NTP had a reasonably strong chance
of being able to secure an injunction against Blackberry given that NTP
had already prevailed on validity and infringement. The result might have
been a shutdown of the Blackberry service, on which businesses, government agencies, and millions of individuals then relied. At the eleventh hour,
the parties settled for an amount ($612.5 million) that was widely criticized
as being disproportionately large relative to the perceived value of NTP's
patent, which covered an essential component of the Blackberry device for
which RIM did not then have a non-infringing substitute component.[1]

Whether or not this amount was in fact excessive, the Blackberry litigation and settlement were widely viewed as evidence for a perceived pattern of opportunistic patent litigation undertaken by certain types of patent
owners. These entities, known variously as patent-holding companies,
patent-assertion entities, or non-practicing entities (all of which I refer to as
NPEs), acquire and hold patents for licensing purposes and turn to litigation
when necessary. In the favorable version of this strategy, the NPE engages in
licensing to monetize the R&D investment underlying its patent portfolio
(and, in the most favorable version, the NPE is an entity formed directly by an
inventor for licensing purposes). In the unfavorable version of this strategy,
the NPE acquires a patent portfolio solely for the purpose of bringing a nuisance infringement suit against cash-rich targets in the hopes of securing a
windfall settlement. This strategy is more likely to succeed if a patent owner
can credibly threaten a "shutdown" injunction against a licensing or litigation target, which may induce the target to settle for an inflated amount to
avoid disruption to its business. Reflecting the disrepute associated with this

The Big Steal. Jonathan M. Barnett, Oxford University Press. © Oxford University Press 2024.
DOI: 10.1093/oso/9780197629529.003.0010

business practice, these types of "license-or-litigate" patent owners are commonly known as "patent trolls" in much of the tech industry and IP policy community.

If these opportunistic types of practices characterize a substantial portion of the total universe of patent litigation, then this would constitute a matter of urgent policy concern. That would mean that the patent system no longer functions principally as a mechanism to compensate innovators for the costs and risks borne in the R&D process, but rather, as a rent-seeking mechanism that rewards entities that are most skillful in navigating the litigation and settlement process. While that conclusion has been widely adopted in a significant portion of popular, policy, and scholarly commentary, it is important to assess the strength of that view by examining carefully the evidence that is most commonly referenced to support it.

Just as in any field of civil litigation, the patent system is inherently liable to abuse, so long as judges and juries can make errors and litigation is costly. There is no doubt that a material amount of litigation has been brought by firms that are principally in the business of licensing patents and, if necessary, are willing to litigate them against allegedly infringing parties. There is also no doubt that a certain portion of those licensing entities are engaging in those strategies for opportunistic purposes. However, it is also the case that a certain portion of infringement suits brought by NPEs promote the constructive purpose of defending the IP rights that support a licensing-based business model for monetizing R&D investments, which both disseminates technology to intermediate users and delivers returns to inventors who lack the capacities to commercialize the innovation independently. Ironically, the plaintiff in the Blackberry suit illustrates this "good NPE" scenario, since NTP (the plaintiff) was an entity co-founded by an engineer who had been awarded about 50 patents for mobile email and related inventions, which NTP then sought to license to device makers and telecom carriers.[2]

The characteristics of the NTP entity in the Blackberry litigation stand in tension with conventional wisdom concerning NPE litigation, which assumes that virtually all such litigations constitute an opportunistic business tactic undertaken by enterprising non-inventors, who impose a socially unproductive tax borne by "legitimate" businesses and ultimately consumers. These types of views appear throughout academic and policy commentary. In 2003, an FTC report on the patent system observed that NPEs "can successfully employ a hold-up strategy without fear of retaliation."[3] In 2006, four Supreme Court Justices joined a concurring opinion in *eBay Inc. v. MercExchange LLC* that observed, citing the same FTC report, that firms that acquire patents only for licensing purposes can use injunctions "as a bargaining tool to charge exorbitant fees to companies that seek to buy licenses to practice the patent."[4] In 2013, a report issued by the White House concluded that NPE litigation accounts for 60% of all patent infringement lawsuits, "significantly retard[s] innovation in the United States and result[s] in economic 'dead weight loss' in the form of reduced innovation, income, and jobs for the American economy."[5] In that same year, President Obama issued an executive order instructing regulators to take action against "patent trolls."[6] In 2015, a Supreme Court majority expressed adverse views of NPEs, stating that "[s]ome companies may use patents as a sword to go after defendants for money, even when their claims are frivolous."[7] In 2016, the FTC issued a study on patent assertion entities, reaching a more nuanced conclusion that "[n]uisance infringement litigation . . . can tax judicial resources and divert attention away from productive business behavior," while recognizing that "infringement litigation plays an important role in protecting patent rights."[8] Clearly there was a policy consensus concerning NPEs across multiple branches of government.

NPE litigation is one of the most extensively studied and analyzed areas of patent infringement litigation. Surprisingly, a closer look at that rich body of evidence shows significant ground for uncertainty concerning the factual basis for the monolithically adverse characterization of entities that are commonly placed within the NPE category. This is not to deny that *some* NPEs engage in bad-faith litigation and licensing practices that are socially unproductive. However, the evidence does suggest that the NPE patent litigation landscape encompasses a range of entities and practices, many of which do not fall into that category and therefore do not merit the same legal treatment.

Refining our empirical understanding on these points is important since the blanket assumption that NPEs are a significant if not predominant source of abusive patent litigation has provided some of the most potent intellectual support for substantial across-the-board changes in patent protection that apply to all patent owners. Notably, these changes include the elimination of the long-standing presumption that patent owners are entitled to injunctive relief against adjudicated infringers. If NPEs do not consistently or predominately engage in opportunistic litigation (while still recognizing that some NPEs do engage in such practices), then constraining the availability of injunctive relief to deter this practice—and, as will be discussed, even extending a de facto bar on injunctive relief to certain entities that fall outside the NPE category—would constitute a case of judicial overreach, especially if there is reasonable confidence that courts can deploy existing tools of civil litigation to deter misuse of patent infringement litigation.

9.1. Does NPE Infringement Litigation Really Destroy $83 Billion a Year?

Much of academic and policy discussion concerning various elements of IP policy have been driven by a memorable slogan or data point. This pattern is exemplified in public discourse concerning the "patent troll problem," which, at least in its early stages, relied to a substantial extent on the assertion that patent litigation brought by NPEs imposes tens of billions of dollars in social costs annually.

These discussions often relied on the work of James Bessen and Michael Meurer, who used an event-study methodology to estimate the losses incurred by public firms that are the targets of infringement litigation. The results were initially presented in a book published in 2008.[9] An event study examines the "abnormal returns" of the stock of a publicly traded corporation during a certain period before and after a particular unforeseen event, based on the assumption that stock price movements are a reasonably accurate proxy for changes in firm value attributable to that event. Using this methodology, the 2008 book concluded that shareholders in large public firms outside the pharmaceutical and chemical industries are generally made worse off by the patent system, although Bessen and Meurer noted that this may not be the case for individual inventors and the owners of smaller firms that are not publicly traded (which were not covered by the study).[10]

In a widely referenced finding, a subsequent paper published by the authors (with Jennifer Ford) in 2011 stated that public firms targeted by infringement suits brought by NPE plaintiffs incurred in the aggregate $83 billion annually (during 2007–2010) in direct and indirect costs as a result of these suits, as measured by changes in market capitalization during a five-day window around the time of the filing of an infringement suit against these firms.[11] Those costs were equivalent to approximately one-quarter of annual U.S. industrial R&D spending. The authors estimated that in the aggregate "lost wealth" attributable to NPE suits against publicly traded firms amounted to approximately $500 billion during 1990–2010.[12] Those dramatic results supported the conclusion that NPE patent litigation represents a "very large disincentive to innovation."[13] In another widely referenced finding, Bessen and Meurer published a paper in 2014[14] asserting that defendants faced with infringement litigation brought by an NPE collectively incurred as a result $29 billion in the narrower category of direct costs (defined to include litigation costs and settlement amounts or monetary judgments) in a single year. This result was based on a database of selected NPE lawsuits and confidential surveys of defendants in patent infringement litigation, in both cases provided by RPX, a "defensive patent aggregator" that sells a form of insurance against patent infringement lawsuits brought by NPEs and other entities.

As shown in Figure 9.1, all three publications attributing high economic costs to NPE litigation have been widely cited for the view that NPEs impose substantial economic costs. Outside academia, both the $29 billion and $83 billion estimates have been widely referenced in the business and technology press[15] and appeared in an influential 2016 report by the FTC on patent assertion entities.[16] However, the reliability of these estimates has been questioned by several scholars. In a critique of the 2008 book, Rosemarie

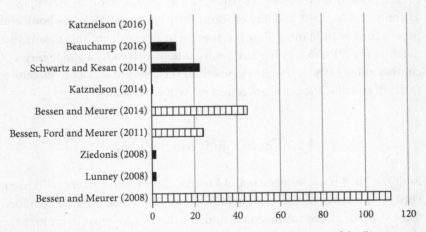

Figure 9.1 Citations per year to papers on the economic costs of the "patent explosion."

Legend: Solid bars denote papers that find no significant evidence that the increase in patent litigation since the early 1980s imposes high economic costs likely in excess of benefits. Striped bars denote papers that present evidence for this thesis. Extremely short bars are solid.

Notes: All citations located through Google Scholar, as of March 2022 (various dates). For purposes of calculating per-year citations, the year of publication is counted in full and the first three months of 2022 are counted. Citations include self-citations and acknowledgements.

Sources: For full citations to all sources, see References.

Ziedonis cautioned that Bessen and Meurer's results only measure costs borne by firms that are defendants in NPE suits and must be offset against potentially greater benefits attributable to the patent system in the form of increased innovation and commercialization.[17] Jay Kesan and David Schwartz have questioned the $29 billion estimate of direct costs in the 2014 paper on various methodological grounds, including the presumptive treatment of settlement or damage amounts as "costs" when some of those amounts may represent payment for infringing use of a validly issued patent, in which case the damages amount efficiently remunerates the innovator, as the patent system contemplated.[18] As I will discuss shortly, Glynn Lunney[19] and Ron Katznelson[20] undertook extensive analysis that identified significant drawbacks to the event study methodology on which the 2008 book and 2011 paper relied.

Yet this subsequent body of critical scholarship, much of it involving painstaking empirical research, has elicited little attention in the academic literature. Aside from the Kesan and Schwartz paper, these critiques of Bessen and Meurer's widely cited claims have been discussed infrequently: as of March 2022, Google Scholar reports three citations for Katznelson's two papers, 22 citations for Ziedonis's paper, and 28 citations for Lunney's paper, as compared to 1,593 and 639 citations for Bessen and Meurer's book and papers (one with Jennifer Ford), respectively. Remarkably, this means that much of the NPE debate has been substantially driven by a single series of contributions early in the development of the relevant scholarly literature, with little qualification made to reflect subsequent research.

9.1.1. Event Study Methodology

Both the 2008 book by Bessen and Meurer and the 2011 paper by Bessen, Ford, and Meurer measure changes in the market value of publicly traded firms sued for patent infringement and, for this purpose, use as a proxy the abnormal returns observed during a five-day period around the announcement of the filing of the lawsuit. This is an unreliable proxy. A short-term stock-market reaction to the announcement of a patent infringement lawsuit may not provide an accurate measure of the actual loss in the litigation target's value over a more economically relevant time horizon. Various developments may emerge in the litigation after the five-day reaction window: the suit could be dismissed, resolved by settlement, or adjudicated in favor of the alleged infringer. Moreover, as Lunney pointed out,[21] research by financial economists shows that markets tend to overreact to "bad news" in the short term, which means that relying on short-term market responses is prone to yield exaggerated estimates of the losses attributable to a particular infringement lawsuit.

The 2011 study by Bessen, Ford, and Meurer attempts to address this issue by also measuring changes in stock market value during a longer 25-day window. However, this is not an especially satisfactory solution since virtually no litigation resolves within such a short period. Any arbitrageurs who bought the stock "on the dip," anticipating investors' overreaction to the suit announcement, would not be able to impact the firm's stock price within this period. Moreover, suppose that a defendant is sued, suffers a large decline in the value of its stock, but then prevails later in the suit, after which, everything else being equal, the stock returns to its pre-suit value. As that hypothetical illustrates, changes in a defendant's stock price after announcement of the suit but prior to its final disposition are unlikely to provide a reliable proxy for the lasting effects on economic value attributable to a particular NPE litigation.

This deficiency can only be addressed by examining stock price movements over the course of an entire litigation lifecycle. In surprisingly overlooked research, Ron Katznelson did so. He replicated the 2011 study's methodology and applied it to the stock price movements of a limited number of the same firms as used in the study, but over a full litigation timeline through case disposition (including settlement). Remarkably, the result runs *contrary* to the results in the 2011 study: the target firms' market value not only fully recovered but achieved positive net performance during this period. While Katznelson's study involves a selected number of firms, it nonetheless casts doubt on the reliability of the event-study methodology used in the 2008 book and 2011 paper as a proxy for the net long-term effects on firm value reasonably attributable to NPE lawsuits involving publicly traded firms.

9.1.2. Private v. Social Losses

Even hypothetically assuming the $83 billion amount is an accurate measure of the economic loss suffered by a publicly traded target of a patent infringement suit, it is often overlooked that this amount does not reflect the *net* economic impact on the economy attributable to any such suit. As suggested by

Rosemarie Ziedonis in a review of Bessen and Meurer's 2008 book,[22] there is no reason to believe that a decline in a specific defendant-firm's value consequent to the announcement of a patent infringement lawsuit reliably reflects a decline in total economic value. If a manufacturing company must pay damages to consumers it injured as a result of negligent business practices, the resulting decline in the company's value would not qualify as a social loss; rather, this simply represents an efficient internalization of the social costs that the firm imposed on others. Similarly, so long as the infringed patent incentivized innovation and commercialization activities that otherwise would not have been undertaken (or would have been undertaken less efficiently), then the litigation target's loss in economic value does not constitute a social loss. It may even represent a social *gain* to the extent the lawsuit enables the innovator (whether directly or through the NPE) to capture a return on its R&D investment and bolsters confidence by other innovators (and investors who fund innovators) that the patent system provides a robust mechanism for capturing returns on R&D efforts. The bottom line: even assuming for the sake of argument the accuracy of the $83 billion amount as a measure of the event-specific change in value in a defendant firm attributable to a particular NPE infringement suit, this amount by itself says little about the net impact of NPE litigation on the economy as a whole.

9.2. Are NPEs Responsible for Most Patent Litigation?

A critical claim that has driven policy actions to address the "NPE problem" is the assertion that "patent trolls" (meaning, the subset of NPEs that deploy opportunistic litigation tactics) represent a majority of patent infringement litigation. This assertion appeared in a widely publicized report released by the White House in 2013, which, citing a seven-page working paper (that has apparently never been subsequently published in an academic journal), stated that NPEs had accounted for 60% of all patent infringement lawsuits in 2012.[23] A 2015 report by the Electronic Frontier Foundation similarly stated that "[p]atent trolls now make up a majority of patent litigation."[24] A 2023 report by Unified Patents, a provider of patent litigation insurance, reports that NPEs represent 58% of all patent infringement litigation filed in federal district courts.[25] Such a high incidence of NPE litigation activity would appear to support the thesis that the U.S. patent system is "broken" and has been converted from a socially constructive vehicle to incentivize inventors to a socially unconstructive vehicle to enrich strategic litigants. It is therefore critical to look closely at empirical evidence relating to this point.

The relevant body of evidence—especially formal evidence published by peer-reviewed journals and independent governmental entities—paints a substantially different picture as compared to the influential White House report and accompanying working paper that appeared in 2013. To be clear, some of this evidence (which will be discussed subsequently) derives from more recent studies that were unavailable to earlier commentators and policymakers. However, an under-publicized report issued concurrently in 2013 by the Government Accountability Office (GAO) had already reached substantially smaller estimates of total NPE litigation activity, finding that NPEs had initiated 24% of all patent infringement suits filed as of 2011.[26] The GAO's estimate was consistent with the findings reached by a peer-reviewed study published in 2013 (and which had been similarly overlooked in the widely publicized White House report), which had found that NPE litigation constituted between 12% and 28% annually of patent infringement litigation during 1995–2011.[27] Those estimates must cast some doubt on the reliability of the 60% figure relied upon by the White House and then widely publicized by the press and advocacy organizations.

Critically, the GAO report also found that the largest portion of the increase in patent infringement litigation was not due to increased litigation by NPEs, but rather increased litigation by operational companies.[28] This has two important implications. First, it suggests that much of the increase in patent infringement litigation, at least through the early 2010s, cannot be reflexively attributed to entities principally engaged in patent acquisition for licensing and litigation purposes. Second, it suggests that much of that increase in patent litigation reflected in part the fact that, as patent enforceability had increased due to changes in federal case law, some operational firms had shifted toward monetization strategies that relied on licensing and enforcing patents. This account is consistent with evidence that, as noted in Chapter 8, much of the perceived "explosion" in patent litigation reflected a concurrent increase in patent issuance, which in turn reflected both an increase in patent enforceability due to Federal Circuit decisions and an increase in use of the patent system by foreign-resident inventors. As shown by Christopher Beauchamp (as discussed previously),[29] a historical perspective shows that absolute increases in total patent litigation in the wake of the establishment of the Federal Circuit are not historically exceptional when normalized for the increase in the total number of patents in force.

The White House report and the GAO report provide the upper and lower bound, respectively, for the fairly wide range of estimates of the portion of patent litigation attributed to NPEs by an extensive scholarly, policy, and trade literature. Notwithstanding these varying estimates, empirical research (encompassing the period from the mid-1990s through the mid-2010s) has established two points: (1) NPEs are a material portion (but, based on most studies, less than a majority) of the patent litigation landscape as measured by suits filed annually; and (2) NPE litigation has represented an increasing portion of all patent infringement litigation since approximately the mid-2000s through at least the mid-2010s. Table 9.1 lists various estimates of the

Table 9.1 Selected Empirical Studies on NPE Litigation as a Percentage of Total Patent Infringement Litigation (2000–2018)

Source	Period of Litigation Sample	NPE Suits as Share of Litigation Sample	Are NPEs a Majority of the Sample in at Least One Year?
Chien (2009)	2000–2001, 2006–Mar. 2008	10%, 20%	No
Allison et al. (2009)	2008–2009	28%	No
Chien (2013)	2010–2012	29%, 45%, 62%	Yes
Govt. Accountability Office (2013)	2007, 2011	17%, 24%	No
Jeruss et al. (2012)	2007, 2011	22%, 40%	No
Cotropia et al. (2014)	2010, 2012	18%, 44%	No
Feldman et al. (2013)	2012	59%	Yes
Mazzeo et al. (2013)	1995–2011	Ranges 12%–28% annually	No
Miller et al. (2018)	2000–2017	Early 2000–2009: approx. 15% (annually); 2010–2017: approx. 45% (annually).	No

Notes: For studies that cover multiple years, the NPE market share is listed in respective order corresponding to each year (or group of years) in the second column. Studies may use different definitions of NPEs. All studies relied on the Lex Machina patent litigation database (formerly the Stanford Intellectual Property Litigation Center database), except Mazzeo et al. (2013), which relied on a patent litigation database maintained by PwC, a major accounting firm, and Chien (2013), which relied on data provided by RPX, a patent litigation insurance provider. Some studies examined all patent infringement suits filed in federal district court during the years indicated; others examined a randomly compiled sample of such suits. Most studies excluded lawsuits that did not involve a utility patent or did not assert at least one infringement claim.

Source: For full citations, see References.

shares of all patent infringement suits initiated by NPEs. Some disparities (even in a single year) are so substantial that it suggests significant differences in these studies' methodology, NPE definition, and datasets.

The existing body of empirical research reflects the fact that our most informed understanding of the volume and objectives of NPE litigation is substantially less precise, and the underlying reality is substantially more complex, than has often been assumed by legal and economics scholars, policymakers, and the trade press. In particular, it appears that conventional wisdom on NPEs has made two key overstatements. First, as indicated initially by the GAO report and then confirmed by other research, conventional wisdom may have substantially overestimated the volume of litigation that can be reasonably attributed to NPEs, or at least NPEs that are engaged in opportunistic strategies. Second, conventional wisdom may have assumed unjustifiably that NPEs are presumptively engaged in an opportunistic strategy to extract settlement windfalls at the expense of operational companies, as distinguished from the intermediation functions that constructively match the holders of innovation assets with entities that can most efficiently convert those assets into viable products. That is, even if a material portion of current infringement litigation is attributable to NPEs, this does not necessarily raise policy concerns unless it can also be confirmed that NPEs typically or often litigate for opportunistic purposes.

A key difficulty in achieving consensus concerning the extent to which NPEs in general, and opportunistic NPEs in particular, are a source of patent infringement litigation is the complexity of defining NPEs in a manner that is neither over- nor under-inclusive. In an important study, Christopher Cotropia, Jay Kesan, and David Schwartz studied over 7,500 patent lawsuits in 2010 and 2012 and then placed patentee-plaintiffs in various entity categories.[30] Using this methodology, the authors found significant heterogeneity among entities that are typically placed under the "NPE" label, encompassing patent acquisition and licensing firms, licensing divisions of operating companies, entities that engage in R&D and license out inventions, patent aggregators, academic technology transfer entities, failed start-ups, and individual inventors.[31]

This meticulous research delivered a complex picture that departs from the one-size-fits-all categorization of NPEs as "patent trolls" engaged in serial nuisance litigation against operational companies. Specifically, the authors found that NPEs that primarily or only acquire patents for licensing and litigation purposes constitute a lower percentage of all infringement suits when compared to previous estimates that had used broader NPE definitions that captured individual inventors and, in some cases, certain entities with significant R&D activities.[32] As this study illustrates, painting all NPEs with the broad sweep of the "patent troll" brush is likely not only to overstate the percentage of infringement litigations brought by NPEs engaged in socially unconstructive strategies, but also to overlook the socially constructive functions played by other NPEs.

To be clear, NPEs constitute a significant portion of total patent litigation activity, and a nontrivial portion of NPE litigation is likely driven by opportunistic objectives. This is unsurprising. As in any area of civil litigation, it is inevitable that some entities—including both operational and licensing entities—would sometimes abuse the litigation process. But the key point is that both the total quantity of NPE litigation and the extent to which such litigation is being undertaken for socially unconstructive purposes remain unclear. Exemplifying this ambiguous state of affairs, a 2019 study released by the National Bureau of Economic Research found that acquisitions of patents by NPEs had positive effects on upstream innovation while exerting adverse effects on downstream follow-on innovation.[33] Hence it is challenging to make any general statement about whether NPE activity is a "net plus" or "net negative" for the innovation ecosystem. These complexities are overlooked in policy discussions that take at face value widely repeated assertions that NPEs are the single most important driver of patent infringement litigation and engage almost entirely in opportunistic litigation strategies. The nuanced landscape of real-world patent litigation and licensing practices stands in contrast to the simplistic narrative that has supported sweeping policy changes impacting a broad range of patent owners, whether NPEs or not.

9.3. The Legal Payoff: *eBay v. MercExchange*

Dramatic episodes such as the NTP/RIM litigation appeared to support the view that the patent system had been captured by an army of plaintiffs' lawyers with nothing more than a laptop, a patent, and a post office box. Shortly after the NTP/RIM settlement, the Supreme Court decided *eBay v. MercExchange LLC*,[34] which addressed the standard that courts should apply in determining whether to issue an injunction against an infringing party. Prior to *eBay*, it had been settled law that a permanent injunction would issue in all cases in which a patent had been found valid and infringed, other than exceptional cases in which an injunction would threaten the public interest. In a 1908 precedent, *Continental Paper Bag Co. v. Eastern Paper Bag Co.*, the Supreme Court had also held that a patentee that did not "practice" its patent was still entitled to "insist upon all the advantages and benefits which [patent law] promises," including eligibility for injunctive relief upon a successful defense of validity and showing of infringement.[35] In a concurring opinion in the *eBay* case, Chief Justice Roberts and Justice Ginsburg recognized the long-standing practice of near-automatic injunctive relief: "From at least the early 19th century, courts have granted injunctive relief upon a finding of infringement in the vast majority of cases."[36] The presumption favoring permanent injunctions against adjudicated infringers was so well-rooted in U.S. case law that it persisted during the multi-decade postwar period in which courts had been especially hostile to patent infringement claims.[37] At the time of the *eBay* decision, the presumption was alive and well: in the year prior to the decision, courts had granted an injunction in all of the cases in which patentees had sought a permanent injunction against an adjudicated infringer.[38]

In *eBay*, the Court lifted that well-settled presumption and required that courts use a four-factor test to determine whether an injunction should issue even after a patent owner had defended validity and demonstrated infringement. At the time of the decision, the extent to which the Court's ruling would have a significant effect on patent infringement litigation was not clear. The reason for doubt lay in a divergence of opinion within the Court, as reflected in two concurrences that provided, respectively, narrow and broad understandings of the practical implications of a unanimous decision authored by Justice Thomas.

The concurring opinion by Chief Justice Roberts and Justice Ginsburg counseled lower courts that "a major departure from the long tradition of equity practice [of granting permanent injunctions upon a finding of validity and infringement] should not be lightly implied."[39] Another concurring opinion, authored by Justice Kennedy and joined by three other Justices, observed by contrast that an "industry" had emerged in which patents were being abused for purposes of opportunistic litigation by entities that were not engaged in any business other than licensing and litigating patents. In light of those developments, the Kennedy concurrence suggested that courts, when applying the multi-factor *eBay* test, should consider whether monetary damages would be sufficient compensation since those entities were solely pursuing licensing fees, rather than market share as would be the case if the patentee were an operational company. Additionally, the concurrence suggested that courts, in exercising the discretion granted by *eBay*, should be wary of granting injunctive relief in cases in which a patent relates to a small component of a larger systems product.[40] These suggestions seemed to stand in tension with the Court's unanimous opinion in the case, which had rejected any categorical rule concerning the availability of injunctions, specifically admonishing the lower court for having "appeared to adopt certain expansive principles suggesting that injunctive relief should not issue in a broad swath of cases."[41]

The *eBay* decision elicited substantial press coverage, which focused on the opportunistic strategies of so-called patent trolls.[42] The dominant tenor of public discourse concerning "patent trolls" may have had an effect on the lower courts' interpretation of *eBay*. Christopher Seaman exhaustively examined infringement cases during the seven-and-a-half-year period following *eBay* (2006–2013) and found a consistent pattern that reflects the predominant influence of the Kennedy concurrence and, in particular, its entity-specific approach to awarding injunctive relief. At the district-court level, NPEs secured injunctive relief 16% of the time, while all other patentees secured injunctive relief 80% of the time.[43] Additionally, Seaman found that practicing patentees that did not secure injunctive relief tended to be firms that were not in direct competition with the infringer,[44] suggesting that the lower courts had in practice adopted a collateral rule barring injunctive relief for practicing patentees when the infringer was not diverting revenues from the patent owner's core business. Clearly the "patent troll" concept had captured a key element of patent law jurisprudence.

More recently, some courts have extended the rationale behind *eBay* to litigations involving operational companies that are in direct competition with each other. In the headline patent infringement dispute between Apple and Samsung during the mid-2010s, in which Apple alleged that Samsung had infringed upon certain patented elements of the iPhone, Apple prevailed on validity and infringement, but the federal district court declined to issue a permanent injunction. Given that the infringed patents related to a component of a complex multi-component product, the court held that, for purposes of showing irreparable harm (one of the factors under *eBay*'s four-factor test for injunctive relief), Apple was required to show that the infringing features "drive consumer demand for Samsung's infringing products"[45] (known as the "causal nexus" requirement). While the Federal Circuit subsequently rejected the lower court's application of the causal nexus requirement,[46] Apple's inability to secure an injunction immediately against an infringing firm and direct competitor is indicative of a legal environment in which the property-like features of a patent have been substantially eroded. The shutdown injunction against Kodak's entire instant-camera division in 1986, after it was found to have infringed patents held by Polaroid, is by now a faint memory and an improbable outcome today in federal patent infringement litigation.

The lower courts' application of *eBay* has implemented a fundamental change in patent law without legislative action. Effectively, the post-*eBay* patent system operates as a two-tier system in which certain patent owners— practicing patentees in direct competition with the infringer—are entitled to injunctive relief with a substantial likelihood, while all other patent owners (with the possible exception of nonprofit research institutions) have little prospect of securing injunctive relief in federal district court. In the case of multi-component products (which encompasses the bulk of the computing and communications industry), at least some courts would apparently deny an injunction to all patent owners. This differential treatment based on patentee type and invention type is in contravention of the plain language of the Court's unanimous opinion in *eBay*, which had specifically counseled lower courts *not* to adopt categorical rules denying injunctive relief to certain entities.

9.4. Closing Thoughts

The impact of the *eBay* decision, which in turn reflects an existing body of scholarly writing and policy advocacy that has sought to limit the availability of injunctive relief, has been remarkable. Based on a widespread but overstated view that "patent troll" litigation is pervasive and licensing-based business models almost never have constructive social value, some members of the Supreme Court joined a concurring opinion that has had ramifications that may be significantly broader than even they could have expected. Post-*eBay* case law has instituted a weakened property-rights regime that advantages producers, distributors, and platforms that operate under integrated structures in which competitive advantage often derives principally from economies of scale and scope. At the same time, this "IP-lite" regime disadvantages vertically disintegrated entities that focus on R&D and require patents to earn returns on innovations that drive forward the broader tech ecosystem. These counterproductive distributional effects—shifting wealth from innovators to implementers, and often, from entrants to incumbents—raises significant doubts whether the retraction of injunctive relief from patent infringement litigation in broad segments of the patent landscape has advanced the public's interest in a robust innovation economy. In seeking to deter purportedly opportunistic patentees by adopting a rule that limits the availability of injunctions across the patent system generally, the Court may have inadvertently protected the Goliaths against the Davids of technology markets.

10

The Patent Holdup Conjecture

The accidental alliance between the forces of ideology and interest in IP policy is vividly illustrated by the confluence of antitrust and patent law involving "standard-essential patents," commonly known as "SEPs." These patents cover foundational technologies in wireless communications standards, which are developed through standard-setting organizations by major chip suppliers, handset producers, telecom carriers, and other stakeholders in the digital ecosystem. These standards are the basis for the device interoperability that is a ubiquitous feature of consumer electronics markets. Without industry-wide convergence and adoption of common standards, an HP printer might be unable to communicate with a Lenovo laptop, and the user of a Samsung Galaxy phone might be unable to communicate with the user of an Apple iPhone.

As a condition for inclusion of a particular technology in a standard, the standard-setting organization typically requires that the contributor commit to license its patents that protect the technology on a "fair, reasonable and non-discriminatory" basis (commonly known as the "FRAND" commitment) to all interested parties. The FRAND commitment governs licensing transactions between firms that hold SEP portfolios relating to wireless communications devices (and are typically the source of the key technological innovations behind those devices), on the one hand, and producers and telecom carriers that use SEP-protected technology in handset devices and other equipment, on the other hand. Since that time, the industry has developed, through the standard-setting process, the 2G, 3G, 4G/LTE, and now the 5G wireless communications standards. Each new wireless technology generation has provided users with increasing capacities to deliver audio, video, textual, and other content at high speed and quality.

Since approximately the mid-2000s, competition regulators in commercially significant jurisdictions, and in particular the United States and the European Union (and, as will be discussed in Chapter 11, the People's

The Big Steal. Jonathan M. Barnett, Oxford University Press. © Oxford University Press 2024.
DOI: 10.1093/oso/9780197629529.003.0011

Republic of China), have sought to re-engineer the global marketplace for SEPs in wireless communications technologies. In particular, regulators have claimed that SEP owners are inherently in a position to "hold up" device producers and demand "exorbitant" royalty rates and other terms. Based on this assertion, regulators and courts have taken actions to limit SEP owners' ability to secure injunctions against infringers and have cast doubt over the enforceability of widely used SEP licensing contracts and related business arrangements. These policy initiatives inherently depress the value of SEPs and therefore operate to the advantage of SEP licensees, which encompass device manufacturers that are among the world's largest companies. Remarkably, there is little evidence that patent holdup occurs systematically and abundant evidence that SEPs have been licensed at consistently modest rates that promote the dissemination of wireless technologies. As a result, there is substantial concern that policy interventions by competition regulators to correct what appears to be a conjectural form of market failure have skewed the commercial playing field in a manner that favors device producers over the firms that have driven innovation in the wireless tech ecosystem. This is a form of privately interested wealth redistribution in the guise of publicly interested competition policy.

10.1. The Structure of the Smartphone Market

To appreciate antitrust and patent policy debates concerning SEPs, it is necessary to appreciate the division of labor in the wireless communications market between firms that specialize in research and development, which are principally chip suppliers, and firms that specialize in integrating technology inputs into handsets and other physical devices distributed and sold to consumers. This can be most clearly illustrated by comparing the "R&D intensity" of firms that predominate in each of these sectors. "R&D intensity" measures the percentage constituted by a firm's R&D expenditures out of the firm's total sales revenues. As shown in Table 10.1, firms that lead in R&D intensity also tend to lead in the number of SEPs that these firms have declared as being essential to the 3G and 4G/LTE wireless technology standards. Handset sales are shown for both 2019 and 2022 to show Huawei's market position before exiting much of the global handset market in 2020 as a result of the imposition of U.S. sanctions.

Table 10.1 Division of Labor in the Wireless Communications Industry

Firm	R&D Intensity (2021)	Primary Activity in Wireless Market	Percentage of Declared 4G/5G SEP Families (2021)	Percentage of Declared 4G SEP Families above "Value Threshold" (2021)	Global Market Share, Handset Units (Q4 2019)	Global Market Share, Handset Units (Q4 2022)
Qualcomm	19.8%	CD	16.4%	63%	n/a	n/a
Ericsson	17.4%	CD	4.3%	46%	n/a	n/a
Nokia	18.3%	CD	7%	41%	n/a	n/a
Huawei	22.4%	CD, DP	12.8%	39%	15.2%	n/a
LG	1.5%	CD, DP*	8.5%	35%	n/a	n/a
Samsung	7.7%	CD, DP	10.1%	38%	18.8%	19.4%
Apple	7.1%	CD*, DP	2.3%	28%	20%	24.1%
ZTE	3.1%	DP	8.7%	25%	n/a	n/a
Xiaomi	5.7%	DP	1.9%	n/a	8.9%	11%
Vivo	n/a	DP	3.1%	n/a	n/a	7.6%
Oppo	n/a	DP	3.1%	24%	8.3%	8.4%
Honor	n/a	DP	n/a	n/a	n/a	n/a

CD = chip design; DP = device production.

Notes: In the second column, the asterisk next to "DP" in the case of LG reflects the fact that it exited the handset business in 2021; and the asterisk next to "CD" in the case of Apple reflects the fact that it only recently invested substantially in developing in-house chip-design capacities for the iPhone. In the fifth column, "value threshold" reflects the extent of patent coverage in the highest-value global jurisdictions (for further explanation, see Tech+IP Advisory 2022, 25–26) and hence applies a "value adjustment" to assessments of technological leadership based solely on patent counts.

Sources: For R&D intensity, author's calculations based on 2021 annual reports or other investors' materials made available by each company. For percentage of declared SEPs, Tech+IP Advisory 2022. For global market share, IDC Worldwide Quarterly Mobile Phone Tracker 2022.

10.2. The FRAND Commitment

The FRAND commitment to which SEP owners are subject can be understood as a loosely defined principle that mediates licensing relationships between the key stakeholders that stand on each side of the industry's division of labor. These stakeholders include, on the one hand, leading SEP owners and wireless innovators such as Qualcomm, Nokia, and Ericsson, and on the other hand, leading SEP licensees and hardware manufacturers such as

Huawei, Xiaomi, Apple, and Samsung. While there has never been a firmly settled definition of the FRAND principle, it has historically operated akin to a good-faith principle that has supported the development of market norms concerning the range of royalty rates and other licensing terms that conform to the FRAND principle.

The origins of the FRAND principle can shed some light on its substantive content.[1] In the late 1980s, the European Union promoted the launch of a cross-border wireless communications network, which challenged the national monopolies previously enjoyed by national telecom carriers and equipment suppliers. The European Telecommunications Standards Institute (commonly known as ETSI), the entity formed to develop standards for this network, initially sought to impose a "licensing by default" standard that would have barred patent owners from seeking injunctive relief against infringers. Patent owners (most notably, Motorola, a lead innovator in cellular telephony) successfully resisted both the proposed ban on injunctions and an effort by national telecom carriers to require royalty-free licensing. The FRAND principle, together with a commitment to disclose all essential patents to ETSI, represented a compromise between the interests of net IP users, which contended that SEP owners would have market power and therefore advocated for constraining the range of royalty rates open to negotiation by SEP licensors and licensees, and net IP producers, which asserted that SEP owners would operate in a competitive market and therefore any such constraints would be unnecessary (subject to a commitment by the SEP owner to license all device producers at the negotiated royalty rate). The precise meaning of the FRAND principle was left to be determined through individualized negotiations between licensors and licensees as the underlying technology would be deployed across computing and communications markets.

10.3. The Patent Holdup Conjecture

Starting approximately the mid-2000s, competition regulators took actions to intervene in SEP licensing in wireless technology markets based on some device producers' allegations that SEP owners—which encompass firms that have led technological innovation in the wireless ecosystem—were purportedly engaging in an opportunistic strategy known as "patent holdup."

Following the patent holdup thesis, a SEP owner could exploit the fact that device producers had made costly investments in an established standard to demand exorbitant licensing terms for continued access to SEP-protected technologies. Having no feasible alternative to the standard, the device producer would be forced to capitulate to the terms dictated by the SEP owner. If left unchecked, patent holdup would inflate royalty rates, which would then inflate device prices and in turn constrain the growth of markets for wireless communications devices.

Regulators largely accepted at face value these concerns about the imminent or realized risk of patent holdup, often making reference to a small number of publications that had appeared in economics journals and law reviews. Those publications presented theoretical models in which patent holdup could arise, but offered no systematic evidence of this practice in real-world markets. Additionally, commentators theorized that each SEP owner would exert pricing power when setting licensing rates for its patented component technology, which in the aggregate would result in a "royalty stack" of double-digit licensing rates and exorbitant device prices for consumers.[2] Assertions of holdup and stacking effects subsequently appeared in influential reports and other statements by antitrust agencies, such as a 2007 policy statement by the FTC and the Department of Justice (DOJ) Antitrust Division,[3] a 2011 report issued by the FTC,[4] a 2012 speech by a DOJ antitrust regulator,[5] and a 2013 joint policy statement by the FTC, DOJ Antitrust, and the National Institute for Standards and Technology (NIST).[6]

Illustrating this rapid convergence toward a policy consensus, regulators at DOJ Antitrust, the FTC, and the European Commission jointly authored an article in 2013 expressing concerns over the threat posed by patent holdup practices.[7] A 2014 working paper authored by lawyers at WilmerHale (outside counsel to Apple and Intel, as disclosed) and a vice president at Intel purported to find evidence of double-digit royalty rates—specifically, "patent royalties in excess of $120 on a hypothetical $400 smartphone"[8]—based on a summation of major SEP owners' announced rates (but specifically excluding consideration of cross-licensing and rate negotiations that can significantly reduce announced rates).[9] In a 2016 speech by Margrethe Vestager, the EU commissioner for competition, the same claim reappeared, specifically referring to the same working paper: "Patents and standards are very important in the world of mobile devices. One recent study shows that

120 dollars of the cost of each smartphone comes from paying royalties for the patents it contains."[10]

As the patent holdup and royalty stacking assertions were increasingly adopted in the academic and policymaking communities, this stylized fact acquired persuasive force. Remarkably, regulators and courts that relied upon these mostly theoretical assertions paid little attention to whether these academic conjectures had any rigorous basis in empirical fact. In hindsight, this turned out to be a critical oversight.

10.4. The Regulatory Campaign against SEP Injunctions

Relying on the patent holdup and royalty stacking theories, antitrust regulators invested extensive efforts to preclude SEP owners from seeking injunctive relief against infringing parties, which are typically the device producers located at midstream and downstream points on the technology supply chain. The logic was straightforward: if a SEP owner could never legally preclude a device producer from using its technology, then the holdup problem would be resolved and, in the case of infringement, the SEP owner could be made whole through monetary damages. For ease of reference, Table 10.2 lists the principal regulatory actions and judicial determinations through which this outcome has largely been achieved.

Table 10.2 Selected Regulatory Statements and Judicial Rulings in the European Union, United Kingdom, and United States Concerning Injunctive Relief and Other Issues Relating to Standard-Essential Patents (2007–2023)

Year	Jurisdiction	Agency or Court	Action
2007	USA	FTC, DOJ	Expresses patent holdup concerns and opines that SEP owners are not entitled to injunctions under the FRAND commitment
2011	USA	FTC	Same
2013	USA	FTC	Files complaint against Google/Motorola Mobility for pursuing injunctive relief to enforce SEPs in violation of FRAND commitment
2013	USA	DOJ, USPTO	Expresses patent holdup concerns and opines that SEP owners are not entitled to injunctions under the FRAND commitment

Table 10.2 Continued

Year	Jurisdiction	Agency or Court	Action
2014	USA	Fed. Cir.	States that injunctions for SEP owners are limited to "unwilling licensees"
2015	USA	DOJ	Grants "business review letter" to standard-setting organization that would mostly bar SEP owners from seeking injunctions
2015	EU	CJEU	Recognizes availability of injunctions in event of "unwilling licensee"
2017	UK	UK High Court	Same
2019	USA	DOJ, USPTO, NIST	"Clarifies" 2013 statement by FTC/USPTO; rejects patent holdup concerns and no-injunction rule
2020	USA	DOJ	"Updates" 2015 business review letter to reflect low risk of patent holdup and importance of preserving injunctive relief
2020	UK	UK Supreme Court	Affirms 2017 High Court decision (see above)
2021	USA	DOJ, USPTO, NIST	Releases but later withdraws draft revised policy statement that emphasizes patent holdup concerns and largely bars injunctions for SEP, with a limited exception for "unwilling licensees"
2021	USA	FTC, ITC	FTC Chair and Commissioner intervene in ITC proceeding to argue against issuing exclusion order against devices that infringe SEPs.
2023	EU	DG Comp	Releases proposal that conditions right to enforce SEPs on having registered the SEPs with a government-run registry and agreed to a government-run FRAND determination (using an aggregate royalty cap)

CJEU = Court of Justice of the European Union; DG Comp = Directorate-General for Competition; DOJ = Department of Justice; FTC = Federal Trade Commission; ITC = International Trade Commission; NIST = National Institute for Standards & Technology; USPTO = U.S. Patent & Trademark Office.

Sources: European Commission 2023; Federal Trade Commission and U.S. Department of Justice 2007; Federal Trade Commission 2011; U.S. Department of Justice and U.S. Patent & Trademark Office 2013; Letter from Makan Delrahim 2020; Letter from Renata B. Hesse 2015; U.S. Department of Justice 2019, 2021; *In the Matter of Motorola Mobility and Google Inc.*, Docket No. C-4410, July 23, 2013; *Apple, Inc. v. Motorola, Inc.*, 757 F.3d 1286 (Fed. Cir. 2014); Case C-170/13, *Huawei Techs. Co. v. ZTE Deutschland GmbH* 2014 E.C.R. 477 ¶¶ 61-67; *Unwired Planet International Ltd. et al. v. Huawei Technologies (UK) Co. Ltd. et al.*, [2017] EWHC 2988 (Pat); *Unwired Planet International Ltd. et al. v. Huawei Technologies (UK) Co. Ltd. et al.*, [2020] UKSC 37.

Courts in major jurisdictions have issued rulings on injunctive relief for SEP owners that have largely conformed to regulators' policy objectives. In 2012, a widely discussed decision by the influential Judge Richard Posner suggested that SEP owners cannot seek injunctive relief outside exceptional circumstances.[11] In 2014, the European Commission identified circumstances in which the holder of a standard-essential patent could be subject to liability for abuse of dominance under competition law for seeking injunctive relief against an alleged infringer.[12] These legal positions were refined and attenuated by the Court of Appeals for the Federal Circuit in 2014[13] and, in a more explicit manner, by the European Court of Justice in 2015[14] and the UK Supreme Court in 2020.[15] Those courts all recognized that a SEP owner is entitled to seek injunctive relief when a prospective licensee refuses to negotiate in good faith (which can be demonstrated by showing that a licensee had rejected a "FRAND-compliant" royalty rate). Since 2018, British, Dutch, and, most often, German courts have granted injunctions to SEP owners following this "unwilling licensee" exception.[16] However, no U.S. court has so far granted an injunction to a SEP owner (reflecting the influence of the *eBay* decision), which means that the owners of SEP portfolios covering foundational technologies in wireless communications cannot expect to stop infringing use in the U.S. market and are restricted to seeking monetary damages through the costly and lengthy litigation process.

The erosion of the property-rights backstop and the institution of a quasi-compulsory licensing regime for the enforcement of SEPs distorts the market pricing of SEP-protected technologies by shifting bargaining leverage in licensing negotiations from licensors to licensees. The reason is straightforward: licensees face no material prospect of being denied access to the SEP owner's technology and, assuming sufficient litigation resources, may rationally elect to infringe and then invite litigation from the patent owner rather than negotiate a license. While an "almost-no-injunction" patent regime eliminates the risk of patent holdup by licensors, it facilitates "patent hold*out*" by licensees, which in turn distorts the prices of SEP-protected intellectual assets and does so in a manner that systematically favors implementers over innovators. The result is a wealth transfer from R&D-intensive firms that drive technological innovation in wireless communications to device manufacturers that are often far larger and have abundant cash reserves and competitive advantages in production, marketing, and distribution.

This makes little sense as a matter of innovation or competition policy. Even if consumers may enjoy short-term cost-savings from these regulatory

interventions (assuming competitive conditions compel a device manufacturer to pass on to consumers some of the savings in royalty rates), it is unlikely such short-term gains would outweigh the long-term losses that arise
from unraveling the property-rights infrastructure behind the licensing
relationships that have sustained R&D investment by wireless innovators
and have facilitated the dissemination of wireless technology among device
makers around the world.

10.5. FTC-plus-Apple v. Qualcomm

On January 17, 2017, the international regulatory campaign to preempt the
risk of patent holdup in SEP-intensive markets culminated in the landmark
lawsuit brought by the FTC against Qualcomm. The FTC's suit proceeded
concurrently with litigations initiated three days later by Apple against
Qualcomm, including an antitrust and patent infringement lawsuit filed by
Apple in federal district court and a lawsuit filed eight days later by Apple
in China for alleged abuse by Qualcomm of its "dominant market position"
under Chinese competition law.[17] Supported by amicus briefs filed by advocacy groups and academics in law and economics, the coalition of the FTC
and one of the world's largest companies illustrated vividly the convergence
among academia, industry, and policymakers in the effort to implement a
weak-IP legal regime for global wireless technology markets. It is hard to find
a clearer rebuttal of the common assumption that stronger patents are always
a means to block entry and secure monopoly rents for incumbents. This case
seemed to illustrate precisely the opposite dynamic.

Throughout these litigations, Apple and the FTC inherently had the upper
hand since, given the unavailability of injunctive relief, Apple could (and
did) withhold payment of billions in dollars in licensing fees even as it continued to make use of Qualcomm's patent-protected technology in Apple
iPhones and other devices sold in the retail market. This behavior is perfectly
rational under a regime of weak IP rights. Absent any reasonable prospect
that a court would issue an injunction remedy, a well-resourced and technically sophisticated user's best strategy is to delay licensing negotiations, withhold payment, and compel the SEP owner to enter into a protracted litigation
that may result in a favorable settlement (with an opportunity to contest the
validity of the SEP owner's patent portfolio, in federal court or through the
PTAB). So long as the likelihood of a court awarding enhanced damages for

willful infringement is sufficiently low (which is generally the case[18]), the alleged infringer has little to lose by declining to enter into a license with the SEP owner. Even if the infringer ultimately loses in the infringement litigation, it can expect to pay approximately the same amount in damages (which are calculated based on a "reasonable royalty" standard) that it would have paid if it had agreed to a license up front, less legal fees (which may be viewed as the price paid for the opportunity to invalidate the patent or to reach a below-market settlement). Given this asymmetrical playing field, the SEP owner may elect to save on litigation costs and settle for a rate that does not reflect the patented technology's market value, especially if it lacks sufficient resources or alternative revenue streams to sustain a protracted litigation process.

Apple's stalling tactics in its litigation with Qualcomm replicated its strategies in two major litigations in which it previously had been sued for patent infringement by innovators of wireless communications technologies. In 2012, in a patent infringement suit brought by Motorola against Apple, the district court found that Apple had used the litigation process as a delaying tactic to distort the licensing rate that could be reached by the parties in negotiations. Specifically, the court found that Apple's intentions "became clear only when Apple informed the court . . . that it did not intend to be bound by any rate that the court determined" and concluded that Apple was attempting to use the litigation to set "a ceiling on the potential license rate that it [(Apple)] could use for negotiating purposes."[19] In a litigation brought in 2013 by Samsung against Apple for patent infringement, the International Trade Commission (ITC) determined that "Apple has failed to negotiate in good faith by engaging in 'reverse patent hold-up'"[20] (a tactic that is now usually called "patent holdout"). Yet Samsung's victory on the merits in the proceeding—the ITC upheld Samsung's patents and found that Apple had infringed the patents—was for naught. Just as the FTC would effectively defend Apple's business interests in its licensing dispute against Qualcomm in 2017, the U.S. Trade Representative (USTR) did the same in the 2013 dispute with Samsung by taking the rare step of blocking the ITC's issuance of an exclusion order against the infringing Apple devices.[21]

It is important to appreciate the extent of harm that could have been caused to the wireless technology ecosystem (and the broader ecosystem that relies on wireless communications technologies) if the FTC had succeeded in its litigation against Qualcomm. While Apple settled its suit with Qualcomm (after Apple failed in an attempt to secure technically equivalent chipsets from Intel), the FTC prevailed at trial against Qualcomm and secured a district court order that would have required Qualcomm to renegotiate hundreds of existing licenses with device producers and to offer new licenses to direct competitors in the chip market.[22] This far-reaching order would have endangered the economic viability of Qualcomm's licensing-based business model, degraded the value of its crown-jewel IP assets, and most likely would have compelled a sale of Qualcomm to an integrated technology company that could monetize Qualcomm's technological assets by embedding those assets within a hard-to-replicate product ecosystem. (Broadcom, an integrated chip maker, made a bid for Qualcomm during the Apple and FTC litigations that might have succeeded but for intervention by the U.S. government on national-security grounds.)

The court's ruling tracked the preference for theory over fact that has predominated in much of scholarly and policy commentary concerning patent holdup risk in wireless markets. Specifically, the court relied heavily on a mostly theoretical model of market harm presented by the FTC's lead witness (a coauthor of the 2007 paper that is most often cited by patent holdup theorists[23]), largely dismissed empirical evidence submitted by Qualcomm's lead expert witness (who had testified that the DOJ's theory of competitive harm failed to describe negotiating outcomes in real-world wireless SEP markets, which exhibit consistently modest royalty rates for SEP licensors[24]), and placed considerable weight on inherently conflicted testimony submitted by Qualcomm's licensees concerning purportedly "exorbitant" royalty rates.[25] In 2020, the Ninth Circuit rejected the district court's finding of antitrust liability in all respects and found in particular that certain portions of the opinion were irreconcilable with governing Supreme Court precedent.[26]

10.6. Facts v. Dogma in SEP Policy

Regulatory and judicial interventions in SEP licensing markets rely on widely accepted theories that SEP-intensive markets suffer from an inherent risk of patent holdup and royalty stacking. Yet there is one inconvenient fact: the real-world wireless communications market has yet to conform to these theories during the several decades that it has been in operation. Far from being a case of market failure, the SEP-intensive wireless device market offers a case of exceptional market success, exhibiting not only increased output and declining prices (adjusted for quality),[27] but an impressive record of continuous innovation and widespread adoption that is obvious from everyday experience.[28] This success suggests that the royalty rates paid by device makers to SEP owners are not especially burdensome, resulting in retail prices that make smartphones accessible across a broad range of income segments.

Multiple empirical studies confirm this intuition. Using various methodologies and data sources, these painstaking studies have estimated that aggregate royalty rates paid to patent licensors by the producers of smartphones and other SEP-dependent devices fall within a range of 3%–5% of the average retail device price.[29] Moreover, empirical studies have found that the aggregate royalty rate paid to SEP owners has remained approximately constant throughout the period from 2007 through 2016.[30] That result runs contrary to the patent holdup thesis, which anticipates that SEP owners would *increase* rates as manufacturers become more deeply locked into the technology standard.

These findings cast doubt on the factual reliability of the patent holdup and royalty stacking theories, which in turn casts doubt on the policy actions that were taken on the basis of these theories. The disconnect between the regulatory consensus and market performance tracks the disconnect between the academic consensus and empirical evidence. As Figure 10.1 shows, empirical studies (denoted by an "E") that cast doubt on the patent holdup and royalty stacking theories have not been widely referenced in the academic literature (with the limited exception of a 2015 paper by Alexander Galetovic and coauthors) when compared to the number of references to the four most highly cited papers that provide a mix of theoretical and anecdotal arguments in support of the patent holdup and royalty stacking assertions.

If empirics fail to support a prevailing theory, then the scientific method demands revisiting the theory to identify why it generated false expectations. In the case of patent holdup theory, the likely defect is easily identified. The theory relies on a simple model in which the patent owner seeks to maximize its payoffs in a single-round licensing game and licensees have no alternative to the patent owner's technology. It is then virtually tautological to anticipate that the IP owner will set the royalty rate so that it captures virtually all the economic surplus, leaving no more than "crumbs on the table" to keep device producers in business. In real-world markets, however, this prediction is falsified. It is customer-facing device producers, rather than R&D-intensive chip suppliers, that capture the largest portion

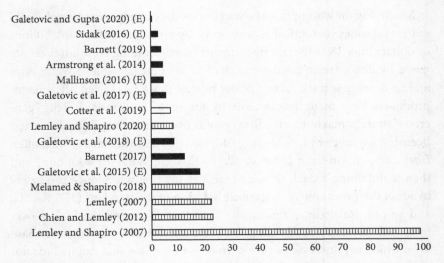

Figure 10.1 Citations per year to selected published scholarly articles on patent holdup and royalty stacking.

Legend: Solid bars denote papers that find no significant evidence for the "patent holdup" or "royalty stacking" thesis or contest it on theoretical grounds; striped bars denote papers that assert, or present anecdotal evidence for, this thesis; solid white bars with a black border assert, or present anecdotal evidence for, this thesis but acknowledge significant limitations. Extremely short bars are solid. Sources followed by "E" present formal empirical evidence; all other sources present a combination of theoretical or anecdotal arguments, sometimes supplemented by reviews of empirical evidence.

Notes: All citations located through Google Scholar, as of March 2022 (various dates), on a per-year basis since the year of publication. For this purpose, the year of publication is counted in full and the first three months of 2022 are counted. Citations include self-citations and acknowledgements. Note that Armstrong et al. (2014) is not a published paper; however, it is included because it has been discussed regularly by scholars and policymakers.

Sources: For full citations to all sources, see References.

of the revenues in wireless device markets. As of 2005, Apple captured approximately 53% of the "measured value" (defined as gross profit, equal to the difference between net sales and cost of goods sold) from U.S. sales of the Apple Video iPod 30G.[31] As of 2010, Apple captured approximately 58.5% of the value from sales of the Apple iPhone 4 and 30% of the measured value from sales of the Apple iPad.[32] As of 2016, Apple captured approximately 42% of the measured value from sales of the iPhone 6 and 7 devices, as compared to 34% for Samsung on the Galaxy 6 and S7 devices and 42% for Huawei on the Huawei P8 and P9 devices.[33] All other firms in these supply chains captured single-digit percentages of the measured value from sales of these devices.

Modifying the assumptions behind the model can explain why real-world markets disobey theoretical expectations. Upstream firms that sink billions of dollars into R&D (before investments or any binding commitments are made by downstream producers) elect to offer "reasonable" royalty rates and to develop a track record of *not* raising those rates even after device producers have made investments in adopting the standard. This "generous" strategy maximizes the firm's profits over the course of a *multi*-period licensing sequence by first seeding adoption of a new standard (which often faces competition from other standards that are vying for adoption) and then maintaining a track record of fair dealing that will induce producers to adopt their technology in the next iteration of the standard (3G, 4G, 5G, and so on). Relatedly, a repeat-play firm that offers "reasonable" royalty rates will maximize device adoption over time, which grows the user base from which royalty revenues are sourced—a user base that can include not only individual users but also, in the 5G environment, an expanding range of businesses that deploy wireless-enabled technology for a variety of commercial applications. Moreover, maintaining a stable stream of licensing revenues enables the licensor to continuously fund R&D investments that are made several years prior to the launch of the subsequent iteration of the standard. In this repeated sequence of interactions between licensors and licensees, demanding "exorbitant" royalty rates would likely be self-defeating for anyone other than a single-play licensor. This richer theoretical model of a multi-period game and reputational feedback effects accounts for both the relatively modest and constant SEP royalty rates observed in real-world wireless device markets.

10.7. Patent Holdup Theory Persists

Notwithstanding strong evidence to the contrary, the stylized facts of patent holdup and royalty stacking still play a prominent role in regulators' statements and actions concerning SEP licensing, as well as some academic commentary. Regulators and academic commentators often continue to analyze the competitive effects of SEP licensing at a mostly theoretical level and pay limited attention to empirical evidence or the actual characteristics of real-world smartphone markets. Puzzlingly, academic theorists often still make assertions that holdup and stacking are imminent risks while incompletely describing the contrary body of empirical evidence or dismissing such evidence through cursory analysis of a single study or a limited number of studies.[34]

Even the well-respected National Bureau of Economic Research (NBER) has published at least two papers that reiterate the patent holdup and royalty stacking theories without acknowledging empirical evidence that challenges these theories. In a 2016 NBER paper, two economists asserted, without bringing specific evidence, that "the 'Internet of Things' is a new and growing area where royalty stacking and patent holdup appear to be very real dangers."[35] In a 2020 NBER paper, an EU competition regulator and the same two economists stated that the FTC had presented evidence in its suit against Qualcomm showing that Qualcomm had obtained "unreasonably high royalties for its standard-essential patents,"[36] again without acknowledging empirical studies showing that SEP owners earn modest royalties in the aggregate, leaving the bulk of the value generated by smartphone technology to customer-facing device producers.

The glaring divergence between antitrust theories, on the one hand, and real-world evidence and business realities, on the other hand, did finally achieve some recognition among the regulatory community. A turning point took place in November 2017, when Assistant Attorney General Makan Delrahim, then the head of the DOJ's Antitrust Division, announced a change in the Division's policy concerning SEPs in light of (among other factors) the meager evidence supporting patent holdup concerns.[37] In 2019, the DOJ, together with the USPTO and the NIST, "clarified" (and effectively retracted) a 2013 policy statement issued by the FTC and the USPTO that had emphasized patent holdup concerns and suggested that SEP owners generally should not be entitled to injunctive relief against infringers.[38] In the 2017 and 2019 statements, other statements by Assistant Attorney General Delrahim,[39] and interventions by the DOJ in several antitrust cases (including most notably, the FTC's suit against Qualcomm[40]), the Division expressed the unconventional view that patent holdup did not constitute a material risk calling for antitrust action. Rather, the Division took the position that a greater risk was posed by "patent hold-*out*" by large device producers, who, given the absence of any realistic prospect of an injunction, have incentives to use patented technology and then contest the patent or effectively renegotiate licensing rates through judicial and regulatory processes.[41]

Ultimately, the DOJ's policy shift in the late 2010s appears to have had limited long-standing effect. An executive order issued by President Biden in July 2021 stated that the DOJ and the USPTO "are encouraged to consider whether to revise their position on the intersection of the intellectual property and antitrust laws," including specifically by revising the 2019 joint statement.[42] In December 2021, the DOJ Antitrust Division (together with the USPTO and the NIST) issued a revised draft policy statement that, if adopted, would have largely retracted the 2019 policy statement on SEPs and reverted to the approach expressed in the 2013 policy statement, which had emphasized patent holdup risks and had advocated a near-complete ban on injunctive relief for SEP owners.[43] The DOJ proposal elicited formal letters expressing opposition from a former U.S. International Trade Commissioner, two former Chief Judges of the Federal Circuit, all three prior commissioners of the USPTO, two former heads of DOJ Antitrust, and three former heads of the NIST.[44] Ultimately, the agencies announced that both the draft 2021 policy statement and the 2019 policy statement had been withdrawn,[45] leaving a vacuum in which current policy at the U.S. antitrust agencies on wireless SEP licensing remains unclear.

That vacuum has now been filled by EU competition regulators, who have reverted to a renewed focus on the purported risk of patent holdup and royalty stacking as wireless technologies are deployed in the "Internet of Things," including but extending beyond smartphones and other communications devices to encompass automotive and other wireless-enabled market segments. Reflecting long-standing concerns over holdup and stacking risks, the Commission issued in 2023 a proposal that would effectively institute a quasi-mandatory and government-run "conciliation" process to determine FRAND royalty rates and provide a mechanism to agree upon an aggregate royalty cap for all SEPs encompassed by a particular standard.[46] The proposal (which, as of July 2024, had not yet been definitively enacted) is quasi-mandatory since participation in this FRAND determination process would be a prerequisite for bringing any legal action to enforce a SEP against an infringing party, although the rate determination would not be binding. Running counter to the strong presumption in competition law favoring the use of market mechanisms to set asset prices, as well as the long history of privately formed and administered patent pools and standard-setting organizations in information technology markets, this proposed regime would compel the market to operate in the shadow of rates determined through a costly administrative process inherently prone to calculation error, delay, and industry capture.

10.8. The Enabling Role of Patents in Wireless Markets

The treatment of SEP licensing markets by antitrust regulators in the United States and other jurisdictions has principally relied on stylized theoretical models that have yet to find compelling factual support. Any meaningful commitment to evidence-based application of the antitrust laws would have concluded that SEP licensing is not a market that merits a high degree of regulatory scrutiny. This misapplication of the antitrust laws in the face of factual evidence to the contrary is not simply a wasteful misallocation of agency resources, but can have significant adverse consequences for the wireless-enabled ecosystem by placing at risk the patent-dependent transactional mechanisms that have enabled innovation, disseminated wireless technology broadly, and enhanced competitive conditions in the global wireless communications market.

The symbiotic effects of property rights and contract in sustaining both innovation and competition in the smartphone ecosystem can be illustrated by the history of Qualcomm, which is still generally recognized as the leading innovator of chip designs for the smartphone market. Founded in 1985 by Irwin Jacobs and a group of six other engineers and scientists, Qualcomm pioneered the use of CDMA (code-division multiple-access) technology.[47] This breakthrough enabled the leap from mostly voice and text transmission using the 2G/GSM standard (which had been selected and mandated in the late 1980s by the European Commission[48]) to the reliable transmission of video, audio, and other data in the 3G and 4G/LTE (and now 5G) wireless standards. At the outset, Qualcomm was a small company that sought to persuade U.S. telecommunications firms to abandon the existing TDMA (time-division multiple-access) standard. To do so, it entered into an alliance with PacTel Cellular, a telecom carrier, to build a prototype system, including handset devices that demonstrated that the CDMA technology outperformed dramatically the existing TDMA standard. Following the prototype's success and demonstrated superiority to the TDMA standard, Qualcomm was able to persuade major U.S. telecom carriers to adopt its technology.

Patents played a critical role in this success. There are two reasons. First, without patents, it is unlikely that Qualcomm could have disclosed its technology as freely to potential customers and business partners, many of which were sophisticated firms that posed a substantial expropriation risk

224 UNMAKING PATENT LAW

since they typically had deep technical expertise, combined with substantially greater financial resources and an existing production and distribution infrastructure. Second, patents supported Qualcomm's use of a licensing-based strategy to monetize its R&D assets. Patents supported this strategy by protecting Qualcomm against uncompensated usage of its technology. The same is true of other chip-design innovators that rely substantially on licensing structures to monetize R&D, including Arm, Ericsson, Nokia, and others. The broad dissemination of wireless technology through a licensing apparatus not only yields returns to innovators in the wireless communications industry, but enhances competitive conditions in the device-production market, which in turn promotes favorable pricing for consumers. In lieu of undertaking R&D independently to replicate the functionalities required to offer a competitive device, any prospective manufacturer can license much of the required technology from a handful of licensors, with the assurance that any such technology complies with the governing standard and will therefore deliver the interoperability expected by users.

It is certainly the case that patents impose costs in the form of licensing and litigation-related expenses that would not otherwise be incurred by device makers. To assess the policy implications of this observation, however, it is necessary to consider how firms would respond, and how the market structure would adjust, in a counterfactual scenario where patent protection is withdrawn or substantially curtailed. This analytical step is rarely undertaken by commentators and policymakers who advocate weakening SEP enforcement. Absent reliable patent protection, innovators would be unable to monetize R&D through licensing structures and would be compelled to adopt vertically or systems-integrated structures in which returns on R&D can be captured through economies of scale or scope. In turn, this would lead to a market environment in which innovation and commercialization processes take place principally within stand-alone "lab-to-market" pipelines that can only be maintained by the largest firms. That outcome would tend to promote industry concentration and limit technology dissemination, which may in turn inhibit interoperability. While weakening SEP enforcement may reduce input costs in the short term for device manufacturers, which may result in some reduction in device prices for consumers (depending on competitive conditions), it runs the risk of inducing a market structure that comprises a handful of "walled gardens," rather than the current structure in which lead innovators broadly distribute technology among device producers. Licensing and litigation-related expenses may be a small price to pay for a market that exhibits a virtuous combination of high levels of innovation performance and competitive intensity.

10.9. Closing Thoughts

Licensing transactions in standard-essential patents constitute the unseen "plumbing" behind wireless-enabled devices in the computing, communications, automotive, and other industries. From the inception of mobile communications in the 1990s through the current emergence of the Internet of Things, the development and deployment of wireless technologies have relied on a patent-intensive business model that disseminates technology from firms that specialize in developing innovations to firms that integrate innovations into devices for end-users. Based on mostly theoretical assertions of market failure in the form of patent holdup and royalty stacking, regulators and courts in the United States, the European Union, and (as will be discussed) China have taken action to intervene in transactions between licensors and licensees. Without a sound basis in empirical fact, these interventions have placed at risk an efficient infrastructure for sustaining innovation incentives and disseminating innovations broadly among producers and consumers.

11

China and the Accidental Alliance

In the previous chapter, I showed how large device manufacturers and other net IP users in technology markets have successfully undertaken lobbying and advocacy activities to secure legal changes that have weakened the ability to enforce and license patents in wireless markets. This strategy has an obvious business rationale: weakening patents decreases the bargaining leverage that can be exerted by innovators when negotiating with implementers and other users over the terms of access to technology inputs. In this chapter,[1] I show that this same rationale can account for policy actions taken by the People's Republic of China (and, to some extent, other East Asian jurisdictions) concerning patent licensing and enforcement in wireless communications markets. These policy actions appear to be part of a broader objective to eliminate local device producers' reliance on technology inputs supplied by foreign firms or, when that is not technologically feasible, to minimize those firms' royalty obligations to foreign technology suppliers.

The importance that China places on the legal treatment of IP rights, and the closely related objective to achieve technological independence and leadership in geopolitically strategic industries, reaches the highest levels of government. In 2016, the Chinese State Council announced formation of a cross-agency effort dedicated to "formulating guidelines for the cross-border licensing and transfer of intellectual property rights."[2] In January 2021, President Xi Jinping stated that China should "rigorously protect IP [to] safeguard indigenous Chinese R&D on core technologies in key fields."[3] In December 2021, the Chinese government released the 14th Five-Year Plan for National Information, which specifically identifies the goal of creating "a closed-loop innovation mechanism with 'technology research and development—standard research and formulation—industrial application."[4]

In pursuit of these objectives in the wireless communications industry, Chinese regulators and courts have often deployed the substance and rhetoric of the patent holdup and royalty stacking theories that were developed by U.S.-based academics and adopted and promoted by regulators at U.S. and European antitrust agencies. These conjectural models of market

The Big Steal. Jonathan M. Barnett, Oxford University Press. © Oxford University Press 2024.
DOI: 10.1093/oso/9780197629529.003.0012

failure have provided the basis for Chinese courts and regulators to adopt IP and IP-related antitrust policies that impose an across-the-board discount on the price of critical technology inputs in wireless markets or, in certain cases, determine the price of those inputs directly. The result is a global convergence of interests and views concerning patent and competition policy in wireless communications markets among much of the scholarly and advocacy communities, competition regulators in the most commercially significant jurisdictions, and some of the world's largest technology firms. There is one constituency, however, that stands outside this accidental alliance: the firms that are most responsible for the technological innovations that underlie wireless communications markets.

11.1. Competition Law and the IP Balance of Trade

China, South Korea, and Taiwan each runs a negative "IP payments" deficit of various proportions: meaning, they pay more in IP royalties and other related payments for IP assets (excluding revenue from patent sales) than they receive. By contrast, the United States enjoys a large IP payments surplus. In 2020, China, South Korea and Taiwan each exhibited a negative IP balance of trade (−$29.29 billion for China, −$2.9 billion for South Korea, and −$2.44 billion for Taiwan), while the United States enjoyed a significantly positive IP balance of trade at $70.9 billion.[5] Japan enjoyed a more modest surplus of $14.8 billion, while the EU exhibited a significant negative IP trade imbalance (−$67.9 billion), although certain EU member countries (most notably, Germany) individually enjoyed a positive IP trade imbalance ($20.2 billion). As shown in Figure 11.1, these tendencies in the IP balance of trade have largely been consistent during the two-decade period starting in 2020, although the gap between the United States and China has expanded since the mid-2000s. Note that these data have limitations insofar as they do not capture IP transfers that are not formalized or are bundled within a larger transaction, but may encompass copyright license fees for creative assets that fall outside technology markets.

IP payment deficits provide a powerful motivation for governmental entities in the relevant jurisdiction to use the instruments of patent and antitrust law as a tool to limit the enforcement and licensing capacities of foreign IP owners. This is especially true in jurisdictions that do not operate under rule-of-law constraints. Policy actions that limit the enforcement and

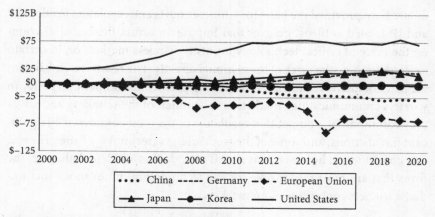

Figure 11.1 IP balance of trade (2000–2020).

Note: IP balance of trade refers to payments received for use of IP assets, less payments made for use of IP assets.

Source: Values calculated based on World Bank data for payments and receipts for use of intellectual property, available at https://data.worldbank.org/indicator/BM.GSR.ROYL.CD (payments) and https://data.worldbank.org/indicator/BX.GSR.ROYL.CD (receipts).

licensing capacities of foreign IP suppliers are likely to reduce the royalties and other payments made to those suppliers by domestic producers and other firms, mitigating the jurisdiction's negative IP payments balance and earning political goodwill for courts and regulators. Put differently, the tools of patent and competition law can be used for mercantilist purposes to renegotiate the terms of trade in IP assets for the benefit of local net IP users and to the detriment of foreign net IP suppliers.

To illustrate how regulatory policymaking in a particular jurisdiction can improve the IP balance of payments, Table 11.1 shows actions by competition regulators in China, Korea, and Taiwan against Qualcomm for purported violations in connection with its patent licensing practices and the remedies that were granted, either initially or following appeal. In the smartphone market, these jurisdictions are principally populated by device producers that are located at intermediate points on the supply chain and that rely on foreign suppliers such as Ericsson, Nokia, and Qualcomm for the chipsets, chip designs, and other technology required to assemble 3G, 4G, and now 5G-enabled devices. For the remainder of this chapter, I will focus on the actions taken by Chinese regulators and courts, which reflect an effort to limit SEP enforcement and influence SEP licensing terms to the advantage of licensees. These legal actions effectively transfer wealth from foreign firms

Table 11.1 Selected Enforcement Actions by Competition Regulators in East Asian Jurisdictions Concerning Qualcomm's Patent Licensing Practices (2009–2017)

Year	Regulator	Fine/Remedy	Local Device Mfrs/Licensees	Country's IP Balance of Trade
2009	KFTC (Korea)	$243M (reduced to $200M on appeal)	Samsung, LG	−$4.1B
2009	JFTC (Japan)	Behavioral	Sharp, Sony	+$4.68B
2015	NDRC (China)	$975M; reduced royalty rates	Huawei, ZTE	−$20.9B
2016	KFTC (Korea)	$868M (under appeal)	Samsung, LG	−$2.12B
2017	TFTC (Taiwan)	$778M (reduced to $93M)	HTC	−$4.13B

JFTC = Japan Fair Trade Commission; KFTC = Korea Fair Trade Commission; NDRC = National Development and Reform Commission; FTC = Federal Trade Commission; TFTC = Taiwan Fair Trade Commission.

Notes: "Year" denotes the year in which the remedy was initially issued. Information on balance of trade and local device manufacturers is as of the same year. Dollar amounts are nominal values (unadjusted for inflation).

Sources: Balance of trade data (except for Taiwan) sourced from World Bank, https://data.worldb ank.org/indicator/BM.GSR.ROYL.CD (payments) and https://data.worldbank.org/indicator/ BX.GSR.ROYL.CD (receipts). For Taiwan, data sourced from OECD, Balanced International Trade in Services (2005–2021) (charges for the use of intellectual property n.i.e.), https://stats.oecd. org/Index.aspx?DataSetCode=BATIS_EBOPS2010. Other information as follows: for China, see Randewich and Miller 2015; for Japan, see Tibken 2019b; for Korea, see Yang 2019; for Taiwan, see Lee and Nellis 2018.

that are the principal source of technology inputs in the smartphone market to domestic producers, assemblers, and other firms that make use of those inputs in the downstream segments of the market. These actions also benefit foreign device makers that outsource production in the relevant jurisdiction and therefore similarly favor legal changes that depress the royalty rates paid to IP suppliers.

11.2. Competition Law as a Geopolitical Instrument

It is widely observed that the Chinese government has sought to secure technological independence, parity, and leadership relative to the U.S. and other Western economies.[6] As part of this broader project, the Chinese government has sought to promote the adoption of indigenous technology standards for critical computing and communications markets, including standards in wireless communications, DVD players, audio/video "codec" standards, local area networking, optical media storage, and cloud computing.[7] Most recently, it has sought to do so in the case of automotive chip standards.[8] These efforts have mostly been unsuccessful. In the wireless communications market, China initially sought to replace the globally dominant W-CDMA standard with an indigenous TD-CDMA standard, and to replace the globally dominant WiFi standard with an indigenous WAPI standard. Both initiatives failed, in part due to resistance by local device makers or telecom carriers because the indigenous standard could not replicate the technical features and performance capacities of the globally dominant standard.[9] As a result, Chinese producers of wireless-enabled computing and communications devices have generally continued to rely to a significant extent on foreign-sourced technology, for which a license fee is owing to patent owners. In light of this technological constraint and resulting cost burden, Chinese courts and regulators have taken actions through patent and competition law to lower (directly or indirectly) the royalty rates that local device manufacturers must pay to the foreign holders of patent-protected technology inputs that are necessary to produce standard-compliant computing or communications devices.

11.2.1. Regulatory Actions

Until recently, there were three competition regulators in China: the Ministry of Commerce, National Development and Reform Commission, and State Administration for Industry and Commerce. In 2018, competition enforcement was consolidated in a single agency, known as the State Administration of Market Regulation (SAMR). Several elements of Chinese competition law have enabled regulators to take actions to impact the royalty rates for patent-protected technologies in wireless markets.

First, Chinese competition law (unlike U.S. antitrust law) provides regulators with authority to take legal action against a firm for "excessive" prices.[10] In 2012 and 2017, draft guidelines issued by the Anti-Monopoly Commission of the State Council specifically affirmed that IP rights are subject to the anti-monopoly law's prohibition of "unfairly high" pricing by firms deemed to hold a dominant market position.[11] This principle has been adopted by SAMR concerning IP licensing specifically in guidelines issued in 2020 and IP "abuse rules" issued in 2022.[12]

Second, draft guidelines concerning IP rights issued in 2012 by a Chinese competition regulator broadly define the circumstances under which an IP owner that has a "dominant market position" can be obligated to offer a license to third parties on reasonable terms.[13] The same principle appeared in draft IP "abuse rules" issued by SAMR in 2015, which provide that a SEP holder's refusal to license "on reasonable terms within the process of standardization" constitutes an abuse of dominant position absent "due justifications."[14] A similar principle appears in IP guidelines issued by SAMR in 2020 and intellectual property "abuse rules" issued by SAMR in 2020 and 2022, which impose a duty to deal on IP holders that are deemed to hold a dominant market position, absent limited exceptions.[15] This goes well beyond U.S. antitrust law, which only imposes a duty to deal in limited circumstances involving both an existing and profitable business relationship and a refusal to deal lacking any legitimate business justification.[16]

Third, and most specifically, draft IP abuse rules issued by SAMR in 2020 and 2022 provide that the owner of a SEP that has a "dominant market position" must conform to the FRAND principle and identify practices such as refusal to license, tying, and price discrimination as violations of the FRAND principle, subject to certain exceptions.[17] So long as a SEP owner is deemed to hold a "dominant market position," these rules appear to effectively impose something close to per se liability concerning SEP licensing practices that would be subject to the far more demanding rule-of-reason treatment under U.S. antitrust law. Moreover, decisions by Chinese courts and regulators suggest that SEP owners are generally treated as holding a dominant market position,[18] which would then trigger these limitations on the permitted range of licensing activities.

Chinese regulators have made use of these tools to intervene in licensing agreements between technology suppliers (usually foreign firms) and device producers (usually domestic firms). Most notably, in 2015, regulators brought an abuse of dominance action against Qualcomm on the ground that Qualcomm charged "excessive" royalty fees and engaged in anticompetitive tying practices. Qualcomm resolved this enforcement action by agreeing to pay a fine of approximately $975 million. It was also required to lower substantially the royalties paid by China-based 3G and 4G handset device makers for licensing Qualcomm's patent portfolio (specifically, by assessing a royalty on only 65% of the device sale price).[19]

This strategic use of competition law as a device for collectively negotiating IP royalty rates advances China's interest in lowering the input costs incurred by its local device producers that rely on technology inputs sourced from foreign owners. Given the size of the Chinese market for mobile communications devices, the ramifications of the Qualcomm settlement—or any other effort to use competition law to reset royalty rates for IP inputs in the Chinese market—inherently has global ramifications. The rates secured by Chinese regulators on behalf of local device producers could be treated as the "market rate" in future licensing negotiations, judicial determinations of "reasonable royalty" damages in future patent infringement actions, and the settlement of antitrust enforcement actions in other jurisdictions. Consistent with this possibility, the headline-grabbing fine assessed against Qualcomm by Chinese competition authorities in 2015 was followed by large fines being assessed against Qualcomm in 2016 and 2017 by competition authorities in Korea and Taiwan, respectively. The strategic deployment of competition law on behalf of net-IP users in a major jurisdiction may have impacted royalty rates in other jurisdictions, resulting in implicit wealth transfers from IP licensors and innovators to IP licensees and device producers. While these policies may advance the particular interest of a jurisdiction that is a net-IP user in the technology supply chain (as well as foreign firms that contract with producers in that jurisdiction), it does not advance the global interest in preserving the property-rights infrastructure that supports the incentive and funding mechanisms behind a robust innovation economy over the long term.

11.2.2. Judicial Actions

With some exceptions, Chinese courts in cases involving SEPs have largely followed the weak-patent policy trajectory established by Chinese competition regulators (who in turn track and accelerate the policy trajectory followed by regulators in the United States and the European Union).

The earliest FRAND rate determination decision by a Chinese court, *Huawei v. InterDigital*, involved InterDigital Communications (IDC), a U.S.-based patent licensing entity that brought a patent infringement suit against Huawei, China's flagship wireless device and equipment producer. In this case, IDC had filed a patent infringement suit against Huawei in U.S. district court and sought an exclusion order against Huawei at the International

Trade Commission (ITC), a U.S. administrative agency. Huawei responded by filing lawsuits in Chinese courts alleging violations of Chinese competition law and seeking a FRAND rate determination.[20] IDC lost the Chinese litigation, both in the lower court and on appeal, and as a result, was forced to pay approximately $3 million in damages to the alleged infringer in connection with the cause of action under competition law.[21]

Taking into account the SEP owner's FRAND commitment, the court found that IDC had violated competition law through excessive pricing, illegal tying of SEPs and non-SEPs, and seeking an injunction for patent infringement in U.S. federal district court and an exclusion order in the ITC.[22] In its order, the appellate court imposed a fine against IDC and determined the FRAND royalty rate for IDC's 2G, 3G, and 4G patents as 0.019% of the device sale price,[23] which contrasts sharply with both announced royalty rates for SEPs held by other companies on the same wireless standard (ranging from 0.8% to 3.25%) and reported royalty rates of 1.5% and 1% offered by Huawei and ZTE (two China-based companies), respectively, for licensing wireless SEPs.[24] In short: IDC's effort to enforce its SEP rights in China resulted not just in a legal loss, resulting in judicially ordered reduction in the royalty rate paid by its licensees, but in being compelled to pay a fine simply for attempting enforcement.

11.2.2.1. Injunctive Relief

Various statements by Chinese courts provide further indication of the uniformity with which Chinese governmental entities have pursued a weak-patent policy concerning SEPs and, like U.S. antitrust regulators, have sought to impose a de facto prohibition on injunctive relief for SEP owners.

In 2015, draft guidelines released by Chinese competition regulators provided that a SEP holder that requests injunctive relief against an alleged infringer may be deemed to violate the competition laws if the request is deemed to have been made for the purpose of compelling a licensee to accept "unfairly high" royalties or other "unreasonable" terms.[25] In 2016, the Supreme People's Court attenuated this position by providing that a SEP owner is not entitled to an injunction if it violates its FRAND commitment by offering a non-FRAND-compliant rate during the course of negotiations with an alleged infringer.[26] Given that a SEP owner would generally lack assurance concerning what a hypothetical court would likely deem to be a FRAND-compliant royalty rate, this standard probably discouraged SEP owners from seeking injunctions against infringers.

In 2017 and 2018, the Beijing and Guangdong High Courts, and in 2020, the Chinese competition regulator issued more balanced guidelines that establish a presumption against injunctive relief but allow for rebuttal of the presumption if an alleged infringer is unwilling to pay a "reasonable" royalty or does not negotiate in "good faith."[27] This approach resembles approximately contemporaneous court decisions in the European Union, the United Kingdom, and, to a lesser extent, the United States, which conditioned the no-injunction presumption on good-faith negotiation by the prospective licensee (the "willing licensee" standard).[28] However, the EU and UK decisions established a reasonably well-defined sequence of steps that a SEP owner can follow to identify with reasonable confidence whether a potential licensee is acting in bad faith, in which case the SEP owner can seek an injunction without risk of liability under competition law. By contrast, Chinese courts' reliance on a vaguely defined standard of "reasonable" royalty or "good faith" negotiation makes it difficult to predict judicial outcomes, and therefore SEP owners are most likely reluctant to seek injunctive relief. In a departure from these infringer-friendly tendencies, Chinese courts in 2017 and 2018 granted injunctive relief against Sony and Samsung, respectively.[29] Notwithstanding these two decisions (which unusually involved China-based firms as the SEP owner-plaintiff), there is a low likelihood that SEP owners can secure an injunction from a Chinese court in patent-infringement litigation, and even attempting to do so risks triggering a counterclaim under competition law that can result in the *patent owner* being held liable (as IDC discovered in its infringement litigation against Huawei).

11.2.2.2. Reasonable Royalty Determinations

The use of competition and patent law by Chinese courts and regulators for mercantilist purposes is most clearly illustrated by statements and actions that directly set royalty rates between SEP owners and local device manufacturers.

In 2008, the Supreme People's Court issued an advisory opinion that any patent included in a national standard requires its owner to offer licenses to all implementers and, in the case of infringement, entitles the owner to a royalty rate that is "significantly lower than the normal amount."[30] While the first element of that statement is consistent with prevailing understandings of the FRAND obligation that governs SEP licensing, the second element is not. Similarly, draft guidelines released by a Chinese competition regulator in 2009 held that a patent owner whose patents are included in a standard must either offer its patents at a zero royalty or a royalty "significantly lower than a normal rate."[31] The subsequent version of those guidelines, as issued in draft form in 2012[32] and then finalized in 2014, dropped the zero-royalty option and the "significantly lower than" language and instead provided that a SEP patent should be licensed at a FRAND rate.[33] In 2018, however, the High People's Court of Guangdong issued guidelines that provided that reasonable royalty determinations in SEP infringement litigation should set a rate that reflects the "ex ante" value of the patent prior to its inclusion in the standard.[34] This approach (which replicates proposals made by certain U.S.-based scholars[35]) would arguably deprive the patent owner of any of the value generated by the standardization process, which, by implication, would then flow exclusively to producers and other intermediate users that adopt the standard but contribute little to its development.

Chinese courts' implicit devaluation of SEPs and other patents included in technology standards through damages methodologies in infringement litigation appears to have achieved its objective. As observed by one researcher, the application of the reasonableness standard by Chinese courts in determining monetary damages for SEP owners translates into judicially determined "royalty rates [that are] lower than other countries, especially the United States and Europe."[36] This effectively reduces the value of SEPs or other patents included in a standard, both for purposes of determining damages in infringement litigation and in the broader context of licensing negotiations that take place "in the shadow" of potential litigation. This approach secures short-term cost-savings for users of existing technologies—in this case, local device producers (and potentially end-users, depending on competitive conditions)—at the price of reduced incentives to invest in the development of future technologies. So long as China remains a net-IP-user in the wireless communications device market, this is a rational application of competition law that reduces input costs for local manufacturers and replicates, using a political system unconstrained by rule-of-law and separation-of-powers principles, the same wealth-shifting strategy that has been employed by device producers in lobbying, advocacy, and litigation activities in U.S. and European jurisdictions.

11.2.2.3. Extra-Territorial Jurisdiction

In a more recent development in SEP infringement litigation, Chinese courts have sought to act as the exclusive global jurisdiction to adjudicate disputes between SEP owners and implementers. Chinese courts have pursued this objective through three tools: (1) anti-suit injunctions (ASIs) that prevent parties from seeking recourse in foreign courts; (2) reasonable royalty orders that purport to apply globally; and (3) choice of law rulings that subject FRAND disputes to Chinese law. Given the enormous size of the Chinese market as a portion of the global wireless device market, this multi-pronged strategy potentially places Chinese courts in a position to exert significant influence over the worldwide price of technology inputs for the benefit of manufacturers and other intermediate users.

In 2014, as described previously, a Chinese court held that IDC, a patent licensing entity, had violated competition law by pursuing an exclusion order in the ITC, a U.S. administrative entity, and filing an infringement suit against Huawei in U.S. federal district court (when IDC was allegedly still engaged in negotiations with Huawei concerning a license to IDC's Chinese SEPs).[37] In connection with this ruling, the court also held that IDC's FRAND commitment to the standard-setting organization would be interpreted under Chinese law,[38] an approach that stands in contrast to courts in other jurisdictions, which have typically interpreted a FRAND commitment under the law selected by the standard-setting organization. This effectively converted the parties' litigation into a dispute to be resolved exclusively in Chinese courts and subject to Chinese law.

The Chinese court's decision in the Huawei/IDC litigation constituted an implicit ASI insofar as it signaled that parties may be subject to competition law liability by initiating a concurrent infringement action against Chinese patent owners outside China. Following the court's decision, it published an article that candidly advocates a mercantilist approach to the application of competition and patent law. Referring to Huawei's strategy of seeking an ASI in Chinese courts in response to the lawsuits and administrative actions undertaken by IDC against Huawei in U.S. federal court, an article published by the Guangdong court reportedly stated that Qui Yongqing, the Chief Judge of the Guangdong Higher People's Court, "believes that Huawei's strategy of using anti-monopoly laws as a countermeasure is worth learning by other Chinese enterprises. Qui suggests that Chinese should bravely employ anti-monopoly lawsuits to break down technology fortresses and win space for development."[39]

Expressing similar sentiments, President Xi Jinping reportedly stated in a 2020 speech: "Intellectual property is a core factor for competitiveness on the international stage, as well as a focal point of international dispute.

Table 11.2 Reported Anti-Suit Injunctions Sought in SEP Litigations in Chinese Courts (2020–2021)

Month/Year	SEP Owner	Alleged Infringer (HQ Location)	Granted?	Location of Foreign Litigations
Aug. 2020	Conversant (USA)	Huawei (China)	Yes	Germany
Sept. 2020	InterDigital (USA)	Xiaomi (China)	Yes	Germany, India
Sept. 2020	Conversant (USA)	ZTE (China)	Yes	Germany
Oct. 2020	Sharp (Japan)	Oppo (China)	Yes	Germany, India, Japan
Dec. 2020	Ericsson (Sweden)	Samsung (Korea)	Yes	Belgium, Germany, Netherlands, USA
Jan. 2021	Nokia (Finland)	Lenovo (China)	No	Germany

Sources: Cohen 2023; Colangelo and Torti 2023; European Union 2022; Nikolic 2022; Yu, Contreras, and Yang 2022, 1588. This table also appears in Barnett 2023, 302.

We need to have the courage and the capacity to stand up for ourselves."[40] Consistent with these policy signals from Chinese government leaders, Chinese courts in 2020 and 2021 issued several ASIs that barred SEP owners from seeking relief in courts outside China. Table 11.2 describes all ASIs that were reportedly sought in Chinese SEP litigation. In the following discussion, I describe in more detail two selected litigations that resulted in ASIs against the SEP owner.

11.2.2.4. Conversant/Huawei Litigation
In the Conversant/Huawei litigation, Huawei sought an ASI in the Chinese court on the same day that Conversant, a U.S.-based SEP owner, had been granted an injunction in its patent infringement litigation against Huawei in a German court. Since the German court had determined a FRAND licensing rate that was 18.3 times the rate by the Chinese court,[41] the Chinese court's intervention had the effect of reducing substantially the royalty obligation borne by a local device manufacturer. In the IDC/Xiaomi litigation, Xiaomi sought an injunction barring IDC from enforcing an injunction in connection with an infringement suit that IDC had filed against Xiaomi in

India (which in turn had been initiated in response to a legal action initiated by Xiaomi in a Chinese court to determine the FRAND royalty). In response, the Chinese court issued an order barring IDC from seeking injunctive relief or a FRAND rate determination from any other court while the Chinese proceeding was ongoing. A statement from the court described explicitly the mercantilist objectives behind this decision, explaining that the decision to issue an ASI against IDC "effectively safeguarded my country's high-tech enterprises' participation in intellectual property rights in transnational competition."[42] This is another case in which the judicial system has been deployed explicitly for purposes of international trade strategy.

11.2.2.5. Sharp/Oppo Litigation

The Sharp/Oppo litigation was initiated by Oppo, a China-based device producer, in response to a patent infringement suit filed in Germany by Sharp, a Japan-based SE owner, and involved a petition by Oppo asking the Chinese court to determine a global FRAND royalty rate.[43] The Chinese court issued an ASI barring Sharp from continuing to pursue the German litigation. While the German court issued an injunction against Oppo with respect to the Chinese litigation, Sharp agreed to abide by the Chinese court's ruling.[44] In 2021, the Supreme People's Court affirmed the right of Chinese courts in SEP licensing disputes to set global FRAND royalty rates on a global basis.[45] In 2022, the Supreme People's Court recognized the decisions in *Huawei v. Conversant* and *Oppo v. Sharp*, which resulted in the issuance of ASIs, as two of the 10 "big, typical IP cases" of the year, an action that signals to other courts that these cases should be viewed as a form of guidance or quasi-precedent.[46] As described by Mark Cohen, the language used by the Supreme People's Court in endorsing these cases conveys an intent to make active use of the judicial apparatus as a mechanism for engineering royalty rates in the global market for SEP royalty rates. Cohen writes:

> The SPC [(Supreme People's Court)] . . . describes this case [*Oppo v. Sharp*] as "providing strong judicial guarantees for enterprises to fairly participate in international market competition" and considers these cases [(*Oppo v. Sharp* and *Huawei v. Conversant*)] to be indications of the transformation of the court from a "follower of property rights rules" into a "guide of international intellectual property rules" and that it is of "great significance."[47]

To be sure, courts in the United States have also issued ASIs in connection with determinations of a global FRAND royalty rate.[48] These decisions were based on legal principles that instruct courts to make a trade-off between comity principles, designed to reduce frictions with litigation in other domestic or foreign courts involving the same or similar issues, and litigation efficiency, which may recommend consolidating determination of a legal issue in a single venue. Following these principles of deference, the Court of Appeals for the Second Circuit rejected an antitrust claim against a group of Chinese vitamin C producers on the ground that the producers were purportedly compelled under Chinese law to collude for export purposes.[49] By contrast, Chinese Civil Procedure Law does not require deference to a foreign court's determination in a parallel proceeding and does not require consideration of international comity principles in determining whether to issue an ASI.[50] Moreover, Chinese courts have only issued ASIs concerning foreign judicial proceedings, unlike common-law jurisdictions that issue ASIs against both domestic and foreign proceedings.[51] Given these differences, Mark Cohen has argued that Chinese ASIs should be distinguished from ASIs issued by courts in the United States and other common-law jurisdictions since Chinese courts use them as a "tool by a non-independent . . . judiciary at the urging of China's political leadership."[52]

More recently, there are indications that Chinese policymakers have effectively shifted the use of ASIs or equivalents from the judiciary, operating largely under patent law principles, to regulators, operating through competition law. In January 2021, a Chinese court unusually declined to grant an ASI sought by Lenovo, a Chinese OEM that had been sued for SEP infringement by Nokia.[53] Subsequently, however, Chinese competition regulators issued draft IP abuse rules that specifically prohibit a firm with a dominant market position from violating the FRAND commitment in connection with licensing SEPs. Following these rules, such behavior could include "unfairly request[ing] the court or relevant department to make or issue a judgment, ruling, or decision, prohibiting the use of relevant intellectual property rights, forcing the licensee to accept unfairly high prices or other unreasonable restrictions."[54] Additionally, the rules contemplate that the regulator may seek the equivalent of an ASI through administrative action,[55] a step consistent generally with Chinese competition law, which empowers regulators to take actions against business practices that occur outside China but have anticompetitive effects on the domestic Chinese market.[56]

11.3. Antitrust Mercantilism

In the aggregate, the actions taken by Chinese courts (and potential actions that may be undertaken by Chinese competition regulators) have created a hospitable environment in which local device producers can make use of legal proceedings—and in particular, competition law and the FRAND rate determination process—as a mechanism for reducing the royalty rate owed to foreign IP owners, deterring SEP owners from bringing enforcement actions against infringers in China, and even deterring SEP owners from initiating infringement litigation against China-based firms in adjudicative venues located outside China.

Specifically, the Chinese legal environment is attractive to producers in two important respects. First, as discussed previously, Chinese competition law provides for a cause of action on grounds of "excessive" pricing, which in the SEP context is modified to encompass claims that the pricing or other terms of a SEP license are not compliant with FRAND licensing principles. A cause of action for "excessive pricing" under antitrust law is not available in U.S. law and is rarely recognized by European courts. Second, Chinese courts have shown a willingness to set royalty rates that apply on a global basis, so long as there is a sufficient connection to China, which has sometimes been derived based merely on the fact that negotiations between the licensor and licensee took place in China.[57] Third, when Chinese courts have set SEP royalty rates under the FRAND standard, those rates have tended to be lower than SEP royalties set by courts outside China,[58] which explains why China-based firms that are defendants in SEP infringement litigations initiated in foreign courts take action to shift FRAND rate determination to Chinese courts. For example, in *Huawei v. IDC*, as noted previously, the Chinese court set SEP royalty rates of 0.019% for Huawei's 2G, 3G, and 2G/3G/4G devices;[59] by contrast, in *TCL v. Ericsson*, the Central District of California stipulated royalty rates of 0.090%, 0.224%, and 0.314% for everywhere in the world except the United States and even higher rates in the United States.[60]

Second, Chinese courts' approach to FRAND determination, coupled with a willingness to treat "excessive" pricing as a competition law violation and to issue ASIs to frustrate recourse by SEP owners to foreign courts, provides a potent set of tools to reduce the royalty rates owing by downstream producers to the upstream innovators that hold the required technology inputs for wireless communications devices. Courts' implementer-friendly methodologies for determining a FRAND royalty and willingness to assert extraterritorial jurisdiction effectively operate as a mercantilist mechanism that transfers economic value from foreign IP and technology holders to domestic producers through the judicial process. These concerns led to the filing in February 2022 of a complaint by the European Union against China at the World Trade Organization (WTO), in which the European Union asserted that China had violated its commitments under WTO rules by issuing ASIs (enforced in at least one case by punitive fines of approximately $150,000 per day) against EU-based SEP owners who had brought patent infringement suits against Chinese device producers and by refusing to publish decisions in which Chinese courts had issued those injunctions.[61]

This use of competition law for mercantilist purposes is illustrated perhaps most clearly by a 2021 decision by a Chinese court in a litigation involving Hitachi, a Japanese firm that owns over 600 patents relating to the production of Neodynmium-iron-boron (NdFeB) magnets (widely used in consumer electronics devices, electric vehicles, and wind-power generation), and an alliance formed by several China-based firms to negotiate licensing terms with Hitachi.[62] Prior to these negotiations, Hitachi had already licensed its patent portfolio to more than 10 companies worldwide, including eight Chinese companies. After negotiations with Hitachi broke down, one member of the alliance filed suit against Hitachi under competition law for alleged "abuse of dominance" by virtue of its refusal to license its patents.

While Hitachi's patents were not SEPs, the court found that the patents covered inputs that were essential to the relevant market and therefore Hitachi could be deemed to occupy a dominant market position. Based on these determinations, the court concluded that the patent owner's refusal to license constituted an abuse of its dominant position that restricted competition in the relevant market. This conclusion seems contestable since the patent portfolio had already been licensed to eight China-based firms so the competitive harm attributable to its refusal to license additional firms seems unclear. In any event, the court's expansive application of the essential facility doctrine to a patent portfolio in the Hitachi litigation is consistent with Chinese courts' readiness to use competition law as a vehicle to re-engineer the split of economic value among innovators (usually foreign firms) to implementers (usually domestic firms), usually to the advantage of the latter.

11.4. Apple, Inc., and China, Inc.

Actions by Chinese competition regulators and courts have put in place a legal understanding of the FRAND commitment—specifically, as reflected in the judicially suggested range of "reasonable" royalty rates—that operates to the advantage of local companies that specialize in the production segments in the smartphone supply chain. By logical extension, this regulatory and judicial approach toward FRAND operates to the competitive advantage of any firm that operates in the China market and similarly occupies the midstream and downstream segments of the supply chain. For these foreign firms, China's policy of devaluing SEP royalty rates is a welcome development.

Among these firms, Apple is the clearest beneficiary. There are two reasons. First, Apple is a net-IP user in the smartphone market, focusing on the production, distribution, and branding functions that are closest to the retail point of sale. Hence, in general, it would be expected to favor weaker forms of patent protection in any jurisdiction, which is consistent with its advocacy and lobbying behavior. Second, Apple derives a significant portion of its sales in the China market (generally ranging from 15% to 20% of its quarterly revenues during 2012–2023[63]) and produces more than 90% of its devices through contractors located in China.[64] As a result, Apple would be expected to have a preference for weaker patent protections in China, just as it has expressed a preference for weaker patent protections in the United States. Both expectations are confirmed. Apple has taken actions, both directly and indirectly, to harness the apparatus of Chinese competition law in an effort to reduce its royalty rate obligations to its largest chip supplier.

This is most clearly illustrated by a sequence of events that occurred in January 2017 (parts of which were described previously in Chapter 10). In that month, a multi-front international litigation strategy was launched against Qualcomm, consisting of antitrust claims filed by Apple and allied competition regulators in China and the United States in connection with Qualcomm's SEP licenses with device manufacturers. On January 17, 2017, the FTC filed an antitrust suit against Qualcomm in the Northern District of California;[65] on January 20, 2017, Apple filed an antitrust suit against Qualcomm in the Southern District of California;[66] and, on January 27, 2017, Apple's Chinese subsidiary filed two lawsuits against Qualcomm in China, alleging that Qualcomm's licensing practices violated Chinese competition law.[67] In the space of a single month, Apple's principal chip supplier (and the lead innovator in the global wireless industry) faced antitrust lawsuits from government regulators and one of the world's largest companies in the two geographic markets that accounted for the bulk of its royalty revenues.

Apple's strategy was ambitious in its scope, clear in its intent, and potentially devastating in its impact if successful. The evidence of intent is well-documented. Internal Apple documents presented in April 2019 by Qualcomm in its opening statement at trial in Apple's lawsuit against Qualcomm (and publicly available through the Scribd database[68]) illustrate a strategy to harness the litigation process to devalue Qualcomm's IP assets and push down the royalty rate.[69] Those documents suggest that Apple sought to use litigation as a tool to "Reduce Apple's Net Royalty to Qualcomm," as reflected by language stating that Apple "[c]onsider nonpayment of royalties [to Qualcomm] by CMs [(contract manufacturers)]" and that it would be "[b]eneficial to wait to provoke a patent fight" until after Apple's existing licenses with Qualcomm would expire.[70] Relatedly, these documents suggest that Apple sought to enter into "favorable, arm's-length 'comp' licenses"[71] with other firms, presumably to create a record of comparable licenses that could be used to argue in any future litigation that Qualcomm's royalty rate offers did not conform to the FRAND standard. At the same time, these documents suggest that Apple recognized the superior quality of Qualcomm's patent portfolio compared to other SEP licensors, specifically stating that "Qualcomm patents (SEPs and non-SEPs) on average score higher compared to the other, largely non-U.S.-based licensors."[72] This evidence suggests a combined licensing and litigation strategy designed for purposes of, in the words of one such internal Apple document presented at trial, "[r]eshaping FRAND" to "[d]evalue SEPs"[73]—that is, presumably to impose a legal ceiling on the royalty rate it would owe to SEP licensors in the smartphone market.

Through U.S. and Chinese competition law, it appears that Apple sought to secure legal outcomes such that Qualcomm would be compelled to license direct competitors in the chip supply market (the remedy that was issued by the U.S. district court in the FTC litigation, although stayed and then overturned on appeal[74]) or, as a second-best outcome, operate subject to an interpretation of the FRAND commitment that would significantly truncate the range of "reasonable" royalty rates. Relying on patent holdup and royalty stacking theories, Apple argued that its legal arguments were consistent with the public interest in preserving competitive markets. In fact, the opposite is likely the case. If Apple and its regulatory allies had been successful in these litigations, the chip segment in the smartphone supply chain would likely have been commoditized and then virtually all economic surplus would have flowed to device makers that hold brand goodwill and difficult-to-match complementary assets in the form of global production and distribution infrastructure. This wealth transfer from innovators to implementers would have appropriated profits from the chip-design specialists that deliver the innovations on which the smartphone supply chain relies. While this outcome would have reduced Apple's input costs and increased its profits, compelling innovators to operate at "break-even" levels cannot plausibly support a robust innovation ecosystem over the medium to long term.

For a net-IP user such as Apple, the skeptical approach taken by Chinese competition regulators and courts toward patent enforcement and licensing in wireless device markets has provided a useful mechanism to reduce technology input costs that it bears either directly or, more commonly, indirectly through its China-based contract producers. This same rationale would apply to any multinational technology firm that specializes in the production and distribution segments of the consumer electronics supply chain and, like Apple, has significant production and sales activities in China. Since this is true of virtually all major branded device manufacturers in the computing and communications device markets, there is a strong commonality of interests between major technology producers in general and Chinese regulators who rationally pursue the objective of minimizing the fees that must be paid by domestic device producers to the foreign sources of critical technology inputs. The convergence of economic interests among midstream and downstream firms in the wireless device supply chain (which include some of the world's largest companies) and the Chinese government's geopolitical interest in reducing technology input costs for local device producers has provided a stable political coalition to support the use of judicial and regulatory tools to raise the costs of enforcing and licensing IP rights.

11.5. Closing Thoughts

Enforcement actions by competition regulators in China (and, to some extent, other East Asian jurisdictions) indicate that, at least with respect to SEPs in wireless communications markets, the existing accidental alliance of ideologically motivated proponents of weak IP rights and profit-motivated device producers has expanded to form a triangular relationship that encompasses regulators in jurisdictions that principally execute the production and distribution functions in the global technology supply chain. Just as large technology firms raise concerns about patent holdup and royalty stacking, so too do competition regulators in jurisdictions that are net users of IP assets in the wireless communications ecosystem. In both cases, any evaluation of assertions concerning allegedly "unreasonable" rates or other terms being "imposed" by IP owners must take into account the fact that these assertions strategically advance the economic interests of entities and jurisdictions that run a negative IP trade balance in the wireless technology ecosystem. These entities' and jurisdictions' narrow interest in minimizing input costs runs counter to the broader interest in preserving the incentive and funding structures that sustain a continuous flow of innovations in the global technology ecosystem.

PART IV

THE HIDDEN COSTS
OF FREE STUFF

Digital platforms and technologies have laudably conferred benefits on consumers in the form of dramatic reductions in the costs of accessing immense inventories of creative content and powerful computing and communications technologies. These reductions in access costs reflect in part consistent reductions in the strength of IP protections over approximately the past two decades. Yet a short-term focus on access costs overlooks the innovation, investment, and transactional mechanisms that sustain innovation in the long term. In this part, I identify the social costs—which can vary by industry and entity type—that arise in a weakened property rights environment that prioritizes access to the existing stock of innovations over sustaining the future flow of innovations. This policy approach discourages innovation and investment in the biopharmaceutical sector and, in other technology and content markets, favors vertically and systems-integrated entities over smaller and less integrated entities that specialize in innovation and rely on stand-alone monetization strategies. The commoditization of content under a weak-IP regime endangers the economic viability of an independent press that is a critical component of robust liberal democracies.

12

How Free Stuff Distorts Innovation and Competition

In the earlier years of the internet, many users took the view, whether explicitly or implicitly, that a regime of lax to nonexistent copyright enforcement was necessarily consistent with the public interest, as evidenced by the mass support for platforms and other websites that advocated vigorously against the SOPA and PIPA legislation to bolster copyright enforcement in 2012. As illustrated by the expansive application of the fair use exemption and DMCA safe harbor, much of the federal judiciary has adopted the same view toward widespread usage of file-sharing sites, apparently reflecting the assumption that a profitable business model that expands access to informational goods is inherently aligned with the public interest. In the patent context, there are relatively few policymakers who are willing to vigorously defend the public interest in robust patent protections for pharmaceuticals or medical devices or recognize the public interest in preserving robust patent protections in the computing and communications industries. To the contrary: since approximately the mid-2000s virtually every branch of the federal government—encompassing the Supreme Court, Congress, and the antitrust agencies—has consistently taken actions that raise obstacles to the enforcement and licensing of patents. Throughout this period, thought leaders in academia, think tanks, and advocacy groups have promoted and applauded this across-the-board relaxation in IP protections.

In this chapter, I argue that this intellectual climate, often characterized by a narrow range of reflexively IP-skeptical and IP-hostile views, overlooks a fundamental divergence between the private interests of technology implementers and content aggregators, who rationally seek to reduce the costs of accessing the existing *stock* of technology and content assets, respectively, and the public interest in sustaining the continuous *flow* of new (and especially disruptive) technology and content assets that characterizes a robust innovation ecosystem.

The Big Steal. Jonathan M. Barnett, Oxford University Press. © Oxford University Press 2024.
DOI: 10.1093/oso/9780197629529.003.0013

The weak-IP trajectory that policymakers have pursued (and many scholars and other commentators have widely advocated) in patent and copyright law, and IP-related areas of antitrust law, over approximately the past two decades places at risk the incentive, funding, and other transactional structures that induce markets to make efficient choices in allocating resources to a diversity of business models for supporting and monetizing creative and technological innovation. In particular, the erosion of the property-rights infrastructure behind innovation markets—a term I will use to encompass both content and technology markets—has advantaged intermediaries, implementers, and other entities that primarily occupy the midstream and downstream segments of the content and technology supply chain. At the same time, this policy shift has disadvantaged innovation specialists—including research institutions, start-ups, and large firms that rely on licensing-based revenue models—that primarily occupy the upstream segments of the supply chain and monetize knowledge assets through discrete "stand-alone" transactions. The implicit limitations on the feasible range of strategies for extracting value from knowledge assets in a zero or weak-IP environment harm innovation and competition by limiting the range of firms and individuals that can feasibly participate in the content or technology ecosystem. Over any policy horizon other than the short term, a "free stuff" approach to IP rights ultimately is not free at all.

This is not a straightforward argument to present since it relies on a nuanced interaction between IP rights, organizational form, and market structure over an extended time period.[1] The benefits of weakened IP protections are immediate and tangible—"free stuff"—while the benefits of robust IP protections are deferred and less salient—"more, different, and better stuff." It would be far simpler to argue that substantially reducing the strength of IP protections in content and technology markets has not had an adverse effect on creative output or technological innovation since neither appears to have declined materially during this period (although there may be difficult-to-assess adverse effects on the "quality" of that output in creative markets and, as I will discuss, more observable adverse effects on the types of entities and innovation projects that can attract risk capital in technology markets). There is no shortage of musical and video output on YouTube, Instagram, and TikTok, pharmaceutical innovation has not come to a halt, and there are probably too many apps for smartphone devices. More objectively, the percentage of U.S. GDP constituted by R&D expenditures (known as national R&D intensity) has not declined since the erosion of patent protections starting in about 2006 through 2020, moving from 2.54% as of 2006 to 3.4% as of 2021.[2] Hence, it might seem to be the case that digital platforms, hardware manufacturers, and other large integrated firms that vigorously sought to limit copyright and patent protections have done the public a service by showing that substantial innovation can persist and grow without the transaction and other costs inherent to a formal property-rights system.

If that conclusion were true, the conventional incentive justification for robust IP rights would be nothing but intellectual cover for a self-interested effort by originators and owners of content and technology assets to secure monopoly rents at the expense of consumers and business users. Substantial portions of the academy have adopted some version of this interpretation, which has tracked or influenced court decisions and policy actions to a significant extent, forming a tight confluence of overlapping views across predominant portions of industry (with a qualified exception for biopharmaceuticals), academia, and government concerning the appropriate direction of IP policy.

This consensus is mistaken.

Since approximately the late 1990s in the case of copyright and the mid-2000s in the case of patent law, firms in content and technology markets have been compelled to adapt to a reduction in the force of IP protections. While some firms and other entities have been able to do so with success, others have not. Firms that embed an innovation within a larger suite of products and services that is difficult to replicate—for example, a search engine, a content aggregation site, or a device manufacturer—can often capture returns on the innovation indirectly even if it is not securely protected from imitation as a legal matter. However, firms and individuals that deliver a technological or creative innovation as a stand-alone asset may struggle to capture value from that asset in a weak or zero-IP environment, especially if the development and commercialization costs are especially large and the imitation costs are especially small. These include firms and other entities that stand at the heart of many innovation markets, such as chip developers, biotech start-ups, research universities, and content production entities. In each of these cases, the conventional incentive thesis applies: the innovator is exposed to expropriation by any firm that can replicate the exposed asset and then distribute it at a reduced price or give it away as part of a larger product-and-services bundle. While Microsoft could extract value from an internet browser that it developed at great cost and then integrated into the Windows OS at no additional charge to users, Netscape, which pioneered the technology and sold it as a stand-alone product, could not. Hence Netscape lost market leadership once Microsoft's imitate-and-giveaway strategy reduced Netscape's crown-jewel asset to a commodity. The absence of IP protections over the browser technology favored the larger second-mover that maintained an integrated suite of products and services, which outperformed the smaller first-mover that had pioneered the innovation but relied on an IP-dependent strategy in which the innovation was monetized as a stand-alone product.

Microsoft's strategy in response to the threat posed by Netscape is hardly exceptional. As I described in a previous book, technology history shows that large incumbents have often used "fast second" strategies to imitate innovations developed by individual inventors or small firms.[3] The innovator often has little chance of survival when faced with the incumbent's potent commercialization capacities and infrastructure, which in turn translate into economies of scale and scope that are difficult to match. Counterintuitively, it is sometimes the absence of robust IP rights that can act as an entry barrier that protects incumbents against more innovative but smaller and less integrated entrants. Weak-IP environments tend to be in-hospitable for firms and other entities that seek to monetize technological or creative innovations through direct-to-user delivery or through contrac-tual relationships with other firms that specialize in certain elements of the commercialization process. In both cases, the innovator must reveal a por-tion of its technology and, absent technical barriers to reverse engineering, is exposed to imitation by actual or potential competitors. To avoid this fate, the innovator is compelled to integrate vertically by moving into production and distribution, horizontally by constructing a bundled product-and-services system, or by acquisition with a firm that is already integrated on one or both of those dimensions. The result is a transactionally impoverished ecosystem dominated by large integrated entities that can execute the innovation and commercialization process internally and are protected from the competi-tive threat posed by smaller and less integrated entrants that cannot feasibly do so. This outcome represents a step backward as a matter of innovation and competition policy.

12.1. Diverse Strategies for Monetizing Innovation

To understand how weak-IP protections can endanger the transactional diversity and innovative vigor of content and technology markets, it is

Table 12.1 Principal Strategies for Monetizing Innovation Assets

Strategy	Description	Requires Robust IP Rights?	Requires Complementary Non-IP Assets?	Examples
Direct monetization	Stand-alone delivery of the content or technology asset	Yes	No	Disney, MS Windows, ARM (chip design)
Indirect monetization	Embedded delivery of the content or technology asset	No	Yes	Internet Explorer, Apple iPhone's Siri function
Giveaway monetization	Giveaway delivery of the content or technology asset, which promotes sales of a complementary good or service	No	Yes	Bluetooth, YouTube, Google Search, Waze

necessary to consider the full range of monetization strategies that firms can construct to extract returns from innovation, assuming robust enforcement of IP protections. Once this theoretical baseline is in place, it is possible to appreciate how constraining IP protections truncates the feasible range of monetization strategies and in turn can give rise to adverse effects on innovation and competition. Broadly speaking, there are three types of mechanisms through which individuals or firms can earn positive returns from informational assets, whether in content or technology environments. Table 12.1 sets forth these mechanisms and key comparative parameters.

12.1.1. Direct Monetization

A firm directly extracts revenues by selling the right to use the asset, whether by outright sale or a license. This model is illustrated in the content markets by a firm such as Disney, which directly sells access to its content to retail users through the sale of a ticket at a movie theater, the sale of a physical storage medium (for example, a DVD) or a digital download, or access to a streaming or similar service (for example, the Disney+ streaming platform). In wireless technology markets, this model is approximated by a firm such as ARM, which sells access to its chip architecture through licenses to firms that design semiconductors for the mobile communications device market.

A more familiar example is Microsoft Windows, which is delivered on a stand-alone basis to home and business users, in exchange for a subscription fee, subject to the terms of the end-user license. This monetization strategy is common to the software industry and, in content environments, subscription streaming services such as Netflix in video content or Spotify in musical content.

12.1.2. Indirect Monetization

A firm indirectly extracts revenues by embedding the technology in an asset that is otherwise difficult to reverse-engineer. This embedded-IP strategy is illustrated by automotive manufacturers, which incorporate technological innovations into a complex multi-component product system that is not amenable to rapid and low-cost imitation and can only be produced and distributed on a mass scale by entities with ample funding and deep technical expertise. These considerations probably explain why the automotive industry generally has not relied significantly on patents and, at least in the U.S. market, historically engaged in cross-licensing arrangements among the small handful of large competitors that once dominated the industry.[4] A more current example would be the various functions embedded in a mobile operating system, which constitutes a systems-integrated product and services ecosystem that is not readily amenable to replication by anyone but the most technically sophisticated and well-financed competitors. Hence, Apple can extract revenues on its voice-activated assistant, Siri, by embedding it within the Apple iPhone, rather than assessing a separate fee for users to access it. The same can be said of the Google Maps and Waze traffic applications within the Android ecosystem—applications that Google developed or acquired at significant cost but for which it assesses no fee from end-users.

12.1.3. Giveaway Monetization

A firm indirectly extracts revenues through a giveaway strategy in which the technology is distributed at a zero or below-market price to promote the sale of complementary goods and services that are sold at a positive price and are at least partially shielded from imitation. The two-sided giveaway model comprising a "free" IP asset and a complementary "pay" asset can be illustrated by the monetization strategy behind the Bluetooth wireless communications technology. The principal owners of patents relating to the Bluetooth technology formed a consortium, the Bluetooth Special Interest Group, to distribute their pooled technology on a royalty-free basis with the intent of seeding adoption and then earning returns through the sale of Bluetooth-enabled proprietary devices.[5] An example in the content industry is academic research, which is given away when posted on non-commercial sites such as the Social Science Research Network or published in academic journals that pay no fee to authors or the authors' employers. These giveaway practices are only feasible for the content producers—in this case, academics and universities—because higher education generally relies on a bundling strategy in which research is published and distributed without generating revenue for its authors, while a complementary good, teaching services, are sold at a positive price to students, who in part select institutions based on their scholarly reputation.

Firms can engineer a potentially infinite variety of business models using these building-block strategies of direct, indirect, and giveaway monetization strategies. Absent collusion or some other entry barrier, it would be expected that competitive markets would converge upon the maximally efficient mix of monetization strategies and then continuously adjust that mix as economic and technological conditions change. Just as firms can compete on price and quality, so too firms can compete by crafting different business models for extracting returns from content or technology assets and learning through trial-and-error which models are most efficient.

The diversity of organizational forms that markets can develop for delivering and monetizing knowledge assets can be illustrated by the radio market. Some firms operate on a traditional ad-based terrestrial model; other firms operate on a satellite-based subscription model; and other firms offer streaming and other internet radio services, which in turn comprise ad-supported and subscription-based models. As shown in Table 12.2, each market segment has selected a different business model that reflects different distribution strategies and revenue sources, which is determined in part by the availability of technological capacities to regulate and therefore price usage. For example, all business models other than ad-supported terrestrial radio were not feasible prior to the technological innovations that enabled satellite radio, and subsequently, internet-based streaming services.

Table 12.2 Business Models in Radio/Music Streaming Markets

Music Distribution Service	Direct Monetization	Giveaway Monetization	Primary Revenue Source	Examples
Terrestrial radio	No	Yes	Ads	FM, AM stations
Satellite radio	Yes	No	Subscription	SiriusXM
Non-interactive streaming	No	Yes	Ads	Pandora, YouTube
Interactive streaming	Yes	No	Subscription	Spotify, Apple Music, Amazon Music

Notes: Presentation of information is simplified and does not reflect that Pandora and YouTube also offer subscription services and Spotify also offers an ad-free service. "Interactive" streaming refers to music streaming services in which the user does not individually select musical titles (although the user may select a musical genre), akin to a non-digital radio service; "non-interactive" streaming refers to music streaming services that enable users to select particular musical titles.

12.2. The Adverse Effects of Weak IP Rights

Policy changes that weaken IP protections interfere in the market-driven selection and development of business models for monetizing innovation by discouraging innovators from adopting direct monetization strategies that rely on the secure enforcement and licensing of IP rights, which is necessary to support business models that involve the stand-alone delivery of creative or technology assets to end-users. This has two adverse consequences as a matter of both innovation and competition policy.[6]

First, the weakening of IP rights compels firms to adopt giveaway or indirect monetization strategies that do not rely on IP rights, even when direct monetization may be a more efficient or, for certain types of firms or technologies, the only feasible option. In certain technology environments, weakening IP rights tends to disadvantage smaller or less integrated R&D–focused entities that excel in innovation but lack (or elect not to acquire) the complementary assets required to support indirect or giveaway monetization strategies. Second, weakening IP rights tends to favor entities that specialize in the aggregation and distribution of content and technology assets over entities that specialize in the origination of those assets. This impoverishes the innovation ecosystem over time by shifting value toward firms that excel in integrating knowledge assets into commercially viable products and services, while shifting value away from firms that excel in generating those knowledge assets in the first place.

This is not merely a distributional effect about allocating the "economic pie"—that is, the value generated by creative and technological innovation— among producers and users of innovation. Rather, over any period other than the immediate short term, the distortion in the feasible range of monetization strategies can shrink the economic pie through two effects. First, a weak-IP regime may undermine the incentives of innovation specialists to enter the market (or compromise those firms' ability to secure the risk capital that is necessary to enter), which may "dry up" the innovation pipeline on which implementers and other intermediate users rely. Second, a weak-IP regime may have adverse competitive consequences by preventing the use of licensing-based business models in which IP-protected knowledge assets are distributed broadly among a large population of intermediate users, which in turn can lower barriers to entry by producers and other firms into the relevant goods or services market.

To illustrate the consequences that can result from reducing the strength of IP protections, consider the previously discussed decision, *Viacom International, Inc. v. YouTube, Inc.*[7] That decision adopted a generous definition of the DMCA safe harbor, which resulted in digital platforms bearing a nominal portion of the enforcement burden and leaving copyright owners with almost no practically meaningful mechanism to deter the mass circulation of infringing content through file-sharing services. This interpretation of the statute effectively compels content owners to abandon direct monetization for a giveaway monetization strategy. This is illustrated by the fact that large content owners now typically elect to receive a share of the revenues generated by user uploads of infringing material on YouTube (through a program known as "Content ID," which I discuss subsequently), rather than engaging in a futile notice-and-takedown cycle that cannot deter user infringement. Given the intermediary's low liability exposure under courts' expansive reading of the DMCA safe harbor, the content owner cannot credibly threaten to seek injunctive or even monetary relief against the platform and hence stands in a weak negotiating position with an entity that hosts infringing content but has ample litigation resources. Remarkably, this enables the *infringer* to dictate the split of ad revenue generated by use of the copyright owner's content assets. This wealth transfer from content originators to aggregators reflects the fact that originators cannot easily adapt to a weak-IP environment, while aggregators thrive in it.

The critical question is whether this implicit intervention in the mix of feasible monetization strategies—in particular, the effective limitation on the use of direct monetization strategies to capture returns on content production—advances not only the private interests of content aggregators and individual users in lower input costs, but also the public interest in a robust innovation ecosystem that induces continuing investments of capital, time, and other required resources by originators (and, indirectly, entities that fund originators) in the production and distribution of new content. The same question arises in technology environments. Technological innovations constitute inputs that are required by intermediate users, such as manufacturers, distributors, and other implementers, which embed those inputs in products purchased by end-users (whether businesses or individuals). Intermediate and end-user constituencies have an interest in lowering the costs of acquiring technology inputs by limiting the force of patents and other relevant IP protections, which limits innovators' ability to make any credible threat to deny access to infringing users and facilitates entry by imitative competitors. The dominant policy consensus that generally favors weaker IP protections implicitly assumes that the private interests of producers, distributors, and individual users in reducing access costs through weaker IP protections necessarily coincide with the public interest in a robust technology ecosystem that preserves incentives for entrepreneurs and investors to continue deploying capital to innovation-intensive projects.

It now remains to consider whether this prevailing policy preference for weaker IP rights, which necessarily reduces access costs but truncates the range of viable monetization strategies (and, in turn, the range of viable organizational forms) in innovation markets, rests on persuasive grounds over a medium- to long-term policy horizon. I will address this question by assessing both "simple" and "complex" cases that can arise in content and technology markets.

12.2.1. The Simple Case

The "simple case" against substantially weakening IP rights arises whenever direct monetization is the only viable strategy for capturing returns on innovation and, as a result, limiting IP protection prevents innovators from attracting investment capital to fund the innovation and commercialization process. This follows the classic incentive case for IP rights, which anticipates a significant decline or even halt in innovation investment if IP rights are substantially weakened or withdrawn. This standard argument for IP rights is overstated in light of the fact that a substantial number of technology and content environments can sustain innovation through certain types of business models that do not rely, or do not rely substantially, on IP rights. Yet this classic argument does apply persuasively in other technology and content environments where, absent a complete (and often economically implausible) reliance on public or philanthropic funding, innovators would have difficulty securing the funding necessary to execute the full sequence of innovation and commercialization actions that are necessary to develop an innovation and embed it in a technically and commercially viable product.

In the biopharmaceutical industry, compelled use of a giveaway monetization strategy in response to a withdrawal of patent protection would generally be economically infeasible since firms would struggle to capture returns on new products that are exceptionally costly to develop, test, and produce (compounded by the high risk of failure) and far cheaper to imitate. While government funding plays an important role in basic biomedical research, there is generally no feasible business model to support the complete process of research, development, testing, production, and distribution without robust IP protections (or other forms of legal exclusivity[8]) against imitators. It is estimated that a pharmaceutical innovator faces total capitalized costs through market release of $1.46 billion on average and a low success rate (only about 11.8% of all drug projects survive clinical trials).[9] By contrast, a generic entrant faces an almost 100% success rate (since the drug's safety and efficacy have already been demonstrated), incurs low R&D costs, and is relieved from most testing costs under the Hatch-Waxman Act (which provides that the generic firm can rely on testing data developed by the originator and must only show bioequivalence with the brand-name drug to receive regulatory approval for entry after the end of the patent term).

In content markets, the same incentive logic would apply to big-budget motion pictures. If a studio were compelled to give away, or could not preclude unauthorized distribution of, its newest animated movie (which now typically has a budget exceeding $100 million dollars), there would be few if any feasible avenues for the studio to recover returns on its investment and, as a result, few if any incentives to invest in projects of that magnitude. The costs of copying and distributing a digital copy of any motion picture are nominal and, again, commercial success has already been demonstrated. This does not necessarily mean that the total volume of content production in general would cease or even fall dramatically in the absence of robust IP protection, although, if measured as a function of production costs, "quality" would almost certainly decline. This reflects the fact that a weak-IP environment would truncate the feasible range of content investments by deterring or precluding investment in the highest production-cost projects, resulting in efficiency losses relative to a secure property-rights environment in which investment choices are made free of the distortions that arise from expropriation risk. In short, YouTube would still be full of thousands of entertaining home videos, but major motion pictures would rarely be undertaken.

These two paradigm examples from technology and content markets—biopharmaceutical innovation and high-cost content production—support a more general proposition. *Weak-IP environments are unlikely to be economically viable whenever the costs of development and commercialization are relatively high, replication costs are relatively low, and firms cannot feasibly shift to non-IP-dependent monetization strategies.* This is a fatal combination that drives away investment capital in the absence of a secure property-rights infrastructure. Conversely, this also implies that, so long as economic conditions are favorable, investment capital will flow back to these fields whenever a secure property-rights infrastructure is restored.

That is precisely what occurred in the U.S. biotech industry after three key policy actions in 1980: (1) the Supreme Court's decision in *Diamond v. Chakrabarty*, which upheld the patentability of genetically engineered biological forms;[10] (2) the issuance by the USPTO of a patent on a foundational gene-splicing method (the "Cohen-Boyer" patent);[11] and (3) enactment of the Bayh-Dole Act, which removed legal constraints that had impeded patenting and commercial exploitation of research funded by the federal government. Concurrent advancements in genetic engineering starting in the mid-1970s (including Cohen and Boyer's breakthrough innovation) undoubtedly were a necessary precondition to the technological viability of the industry. However, this was not a *sufficient* condition for the emergence of a market in funding and commercializing biotech innovations, which required a secure institutional mechanism to ensure exclusivity over any new product and, as a result, to elicit investment by VC funds and large pharmaceutical firms to support the costly and lengthy development and testing process. That additional condition was fulfilled by the *Chakrabarty* decision, the USPTO's issuance of patents for biotechnological inventions (at the time, a pioneering step among national patent offices), and the removal of patenting and licensing restrictions through the Bayh-Dole Act. The market responded to this policy shift by directing investment toward the then-nascent bio-tech market, resulting in the release in 1983 of synthetic human insulin, the first genetically engineered medical product.[12] That development would be followed by the blossoming of the U.S. biotech industry and the release over the next decades of hundreds of new biotechnological products, resulting in not only economic returns for innovators and investors, but also public-health returns for society in general.

12.2.2. The Complex Case

In markets outside the life sciences, the economic case against substantially weakening IP rights is often more complex, and the standard incentive thesis encounters exceptions that apparently cast doubt on the necessity of IP protections in these innovation environments. That is because many firms in these markets can extract returns through indirect or giveaway monetization strategies that offer viable business models for capturing returns on innovation without substantial reliance on IP rights. Google has earned healthy returns on its continuous and significant investments in its search-engine technology through both giveaway and indirect mon-etization strategies. In a giveaway monetization strategy, Google cross-subsidizes the free provision of search services by attracting user traffic to offer targeted ad services to paying businesses. In an indirect moneti-zation strategy, Google embeds its search-engine technology within a complex product ecosystem that is challenging to replicate. Contrary to the standard incentive thesis, substantially reducing IP protections in this market may not result in appreciable reductions in aggregate investment in innovation since some firms already rely on (or could shift toward) non-IP-dependent indirect or giveaway monetization strategies. Firms that are unable to adapt will be compelled to exit the market, and innovation capital will flow toward firms that are able to sustain giveaway or indirect monetization strategies that are well-suited to a weak-IP environment. Based on these types of observations, it is often asserted that IP protections, or at least robust forms of IP protection, are unnecessary in information and communications technology industries.

This assertion, however, rests on the assumption that non-IP-dependent monetization strategies are always more or equally efficient than direct mon-etization strategies that are not viable under a weak-IP regime. There are no theoretical or empirical grounds to support such an across-the-board assumption. Precluding firms from adopting direct monetization strategies can distort competitive conditions by favoring larger and more integrated firms that have complementary assets that can be used to support indirect and giveaway monetization strategies to extract returns from innovation without secure IP protections. Since those complementary assets often comprise capital-intensive production and distribution facilities, a weak-IP environment may raise an implicit entry barrier to smaller and less integrated entities that specialize in innovation and cannot feasibly build or acquire production and distribution facilities. The result may be a market structure that compares unfavorably with the competitive conditions under a legal regime with more robust enforcement of IP rights.

These relationships between IP protection, monetization strategies, and market structure can be illustrated by comparing the structure of the U.S. software industry prior to, and after, the extension of IP protection to software.[13] During the early decades of the computing industry following World War II, software was not protected by IP rights. Starting in the early 1960s, the Copyright Office began accepting registrations of software programs,[14] although there remained significant doubt concerning the enforceability of software copyrights until a 1980 amendment to the copyright statute,[15] which was followed by the extension of patent protection in a 1981 Supreme Court decision.[16] When software lacked secure IP protection, commercial investments in software development were typically monetized by being bundled with a larger complex hardware system. As a result, software development was mostly conducted in-house by large hardware manufacturers or undertaken on a customer-specific basis and a small scale by software development specialists. Once copyright protection was extended to software, entry barriers fell: independent software developers emerged that operated on a large scale by supplying software programs on a stand-alone basis through sales of physical media or internet downloads to hundreds of millions of businesses and home users.

Contrary to the skeptical views often expressed toward IP rights in software, secure IP rights (together with concurrent technological changes) enabled the de-bundling of the packaged hardware and software model that had prevailed in the industry, which in turn had favorable consequences as a matter of both innovation and competition policy. This is even true to a certain extent of open-source software, which relies on a copyright license to enforce the terms of the license whenever the code is distributed and

modified by subsequent licensees. Counterintuitively, the extension of secure IP rights to software expanded the market by providing a tool through
which developers could block imitation and, as a result, secure a return on
their R&D investment by entering into relationships directly with businesses
and home users, rather than being compelled to monetize R&D investment
indirectly through hardware-plus-software product bundles or directly
through client-specific software development projects. In turn, the emergence of a property-rights structure that enabled industry-wide licensing of
software had favorable competitive effects on the hardware market, where
producers could now feasibly enter without having to incur the costs of independently replicating incumbents' existing hardware-plus-software
bundles. Moreover, given software developers' interest in maximizing sales
by offering hardware-agnostic products, business and home users enjoyed
increased product choice by acquiring the ability to create various hardware-
software combinations for different purposes.

This example of the manner in which strengthening IP rights not only
facilitates innovation but lowers entry barriers and enhances competitive
conditions illustrates a broader point. *A weak-IP environment truncates the
feasible range of business models and, in particular, compels innovators to shift
from direct to indirect and giveaway monetization strategies that may limit
access to technology inputs; a strong-IP environment enables innovators and
investors to freely select the most efficient mix of monetization strategies for
any particular innovation asset.*

Surprisingly, weaker IP regimes may therefore yield a more concentrated
market, dominated by a handful of integrated firms that can fund and execute the innovation and commercialization process internally. As a matter
of competition policy, this "walled gardens" business model compares unfavorably with the licensing-based business models observed in some patent-
intensive segments of the ICT sector. As described in Chapter 10, a handful
of lead innovators in the wireless communications market specialize in semiconductor chip design and extract returns on those efforts through licensing
relationships with all device producers that are willing to pay the royalty fee,
including entrants that may lack significant R&D capacities. Without secure
IP rights, those licensing arrangements would not be viable due to expropriation risk from actual or potential competitors, and the market would likely
be dominated by a smaller group of firms that maintain an integrated suite of
R&D, production, and other commercialization capacities to support indirect or giveaway monetization strategies.

This line of argument implies that any significant reduction in IP protections can, in certain circumstances, have adverse effects on both innovation and competition by distorting the business models that firms must construct to extract returns from knowledge assets in a weak-IP environment. These effects can be illustrated by two attempted acquisitions in the semiconductor industry that took place against the backdrop of antitrust litigation and other policy actions that had cast a legal cloud over the enforcement and licensing of patents in this industry.

12.2.2.1. Broadcom/Qualcomm (2017–2018)

Qualcomm, the widely recognized pioneer in the wireless communications technologies that underlie the 3G, 4G, and 5G wireless communications standards, is an innovation specialist that focuses on the design and production of chipsets for wireless communications devices. To monetize this investment, Qualcomm relies on a patent-dependent licensing business model that has been the target of antitrust regulators around the world. As discussed previously, this campaign culminated in suits brought against the company in January 2017 by the FTC, which targeted key elements of Qualcomm's licensing-based business model on antitrust grounds. If successful, the FTC's suit would have endangered the economic viability of this business model—in particular, the FTC's position that Qualcomm had a "duty" under antitrust law to license its patent portfolio to direct competitors in the chip supply market. As Qualcomm's antitrust litigation did not appear to be headed toward a rapid resolution, Broadcom, an integrated chip manufacturer that maintains a diverse suite of hardware and software products, made an offer in November 2017 to acquire Qualcomm for $103 billion.[17] Qualcomm's exposure to a potential loss in the antitrust litigation may have prompted Broadcom's bid to acquire it, and most likely at a price discounted to reflect the legal attack on the company (exacerbated by the refusal of Apple, its single largest customer, to pay billions of dollars in royalties during the litigation). Ultimately, the Broadcom acquisition was blocked by the U.S. government on national security grounds.

The Broadcom offer to purchase Qualcomm may be interpreted as a preemptive market response to the risk of a legal decision that would have limited the ability to enforce and license standard-essential patents in wireless communications markets. Consistent with this view, some equity analysts argued that Broadcom intended, if it closed the acquisition, to migrate away from Qualcomm's licensing model and extract more revenue from physical chipset sales.[18] Indeed, Broadcom had criticized what it described as Qualcomm's "broken" licensing-based business model.[19] If the acquisition had been consummated and the analysts' prediction had been realized, the result may have been a market structure in which some of Qualcomm's technology would have been deployed internally within its new owner's corporate structure, rather than being distributed among all producers as in a licensing-based model. As a result, access to the technology inputs required to enter device production would have been limited, resulting in less competitive market conditions as compared to the conditions under a reasonably secure legal infrastructure for enforcing and licensing patents.

12.2.2.2. Nvidia/Qualcomm (2020)

In 2020, Nvidia, an integrated chip manufacturer, sought to acquire Arm, which, as described previously, is a UK-based company that develops and licenses the chip architecture that is used by virtually all chip designers and producers in the wireless communications market.[20] Like the attempted Broadcom/Qualcomm acquisition, this transaction may have been motivated by the vulnerability of the target's licensing-based model in a legal environment in which regulators and actual or prospective licensees regularly challenge the enforceability of IP licenses on antitrust and other legal grounds. Regulators' concerns over the transaction derived from the possibility that Arm, as a subsidiary of an integrated chip manufacturer, may have had incentives to abandon the licensing-based business model that involves distributing technology to producers that could be competitors of Nvidia. In the face of resistance from EU and U.S. competition authorities, the transaction was withdrawn in 2022.

In the case of both the Broadcom/Qualcomm and Nvidia/ARM transactions, it does not appear that a weak-IP regime that substantially limits patent enforcement and licensing capacities would necessarily promote a more innovative and competitive technology ecosystem. Rather, any such limitations may have the opposite effect by leading firms to consider shifting away from disaggregated business structures that monetize innovation through licensing relationships and toward integrated business structures in which innovation is principally monetized internally within end-to-end commercialization pipelines. The logic is straightforward in the case of both transactions. Once innovators such as Qualcomm and Arm can no longer rely on a reliable IP infrastructure to capture returns on their knowledge assets through direct monetization strategies in the form of licensing, concerns over expropriation risk compel innovators to shift toward business models in which innovation is monetized internally through indirect monetization models (as in the case of Broadcom and Nvidia), even if this is not always the most efficient strategy for doing so. Collectively, these responses to a weak-IP environment can result in a market structure that exhibits reduced innovative and competitive intensity as compared to the likely structure of markets that operate under more secure property-rights protections.

12.3. The Case for Business-Model Agnosticism

In general, whether firms choose to adopt any particular monetization strategy (or a hybrid form that combines elements of multiple strategies), including business models that rely substantially on IP rights and models that do not rely on such rights at all, should be a matter of indifference from the perspective of innovation and competition policy. So long as market conditions are not distorted by collusion or other anticompetitive tactics, markets will reward firms that adopt the most efficient mix of monetization strategies, while punishing all others. To appreciate this point, it is helpful to compare the diversity of strategies used to monetize investment in the development of operating systems in three information technology markets: personal computers (PCs), mobile communications devices, and servers. Those strategies are presented in Table 12.3 for ease of reference and then are discussed separately below.

12.3.1. PC Operating System Market

Consider the competition between Microsoft and Apple in the operating systems (OS) segment of the home computing market in the 1980s. Microsoft's Windows OS was licensed to all interested computer producers willing to pay the licensing fee, while Apple's Mac OS was never licensed since Apple produced its own hardware. Apple elected an indirect monetization strategy in which the OS was embedded in Apple hardware, while Microsoft adopted a partial giveaway strategy in which the application programming interfaces (APIs) to the Windows OS were licensed at a zero royalty to developers, while the Windows OS was licensed at a positive royalty to OEMs. Microsoft's more open strategy prevailed as Windows became the industry standard in the PC

Table 12.3 Selected IP Monetization Strategies in Operating System Markets

Market	Firm/Strategy	Firm/Strategy	Firm/Strategy
Personal computers	*Microsoft*: partial giveaway (APIs licensed to developers at zero royalty; closed-source license for OS to OEMs)	*Linux*: giveaway (open-source license for OS)	*Apple*: indirect (OS embedded in hardware)
Mobile communications devices	*Microsoft*: direct (closed-source license for OS to OEMs)	*Google/Android*: partial giveaway (open-source license to Android OS, subject to contractual conditions)	*Blackberry, Apple*: indirect (OS embedded in hardware)
Servers	*Microsoft*: direct (closed-source license for OS to OEMs)	*Linux*: giveaway (open-source license for OS, IBM sponsorship)	*IBM*: indirect (Linux OS embedded in server hardware)

Notes: API = application programming interface; OEM = original equipment manufacturer; OS = operating system.

market, while Apple suffered for having adopted what appears to have been an excessively closed monetization strategy.

12.3.2. Mobile Operating System Market

A similar dynamic occurred in the OS segment of the mobile computing market in the late 2000s. Promptly after launch in 2008, Google's open-source Android OS—released to handset makers and telecom carriers at no charge under an open-source license, subject to certain contractual conditions (as discussed previously in Chapter 4)—swiftly displaced the closed-source OSs used by then-leading device makers such as Nokia and Blackberry, which had adopted an indirect monetization strategy in which the OS was embedded within the producer's hardware. However, this should not be interpreted to mean that only giveaway monetization strategies are viable in the mobile OS market. Apple's indirect monetization strategy (in which it embedded the iOS in Apple hardware and did not license it to other producers) was successful in securing significant market share in the smartphone market, making Apple the only current alternative to Android-based handset providers. In this case, both partial giveaway (Google) and indirect monetization (Apple) strategies prevailed and now support competing business models within the mobile OS market.

12.3.3. Server Operating System Market

In other circumstances, markets have rewarded entities that have modified what the market judged to be an excessively generous giveaway strategy. Like most other open-source projects,[21] the Linux OS struggled initially to achieve adoption. However, it was able to achieve substantial adoption in the server computing market—dominated by Microsoft's Windows OS, distributed under a closed-source license to hardware manufacturers—once for-profit entities made substantial investments of funding and personnel in the Linux ecosystem. Starting in the mid-1990s, Red Hat distributed "free" copies of Linux together with user manuals and technical support for a fee,[22] and in 2000, IBM committed to contribute over $1 billion in funding to the Linux Foundation and concurrently dedicated extensive personnel to internal Linux development initiatives.[23] Effectively, IBM and Red Hat adopted Linux as part of a hybrid monetization strategy in which the development and maintenance of the free IP asset (the Linux OS) was cross-subsidized by proprietary hardware sales in the case of IBM and support services in the case of Red Hat (among other corporate contributors to the Linux ecosystem). Specifically, IBM subsidized the development of the Linux OS and then embedded it within its hardware, constituting an indirect monetization strategy, while Red Hat subsidized the development of the Linux OS, which promoted adoption and supported the sale of Red Hat's complementary services, constituting a giveaway strategy. At the same time, Microsoft Windows remains the most widely used OS in the server market,[24] resulting in a state of affairs in which giveaway, indirect, and direct monetization strategies (implemented through open-source and closed-source licenses, respectively) coexist by offering consumers differentiated bundles of complementary software, hardware, and support services.

The fluid transactional solutions observed across various technology environments, or among different firms in the same technology environment, illustrate how competitive forces continuously refine different business models in a manner akin to the familiar process through which markets refine different pricing strategies. This analogy yields an important policy implication. Just as the state in market-driven economies generally does not take steps to intervene in the trial-and-error process through which buyers and sellers make pricing choices, so too the state in market-driven economies should not take steps that impede or distort the trial-and-error process through which innovators (and investors in innovators) craft monetization strategies. The reason is one and the same: there is no one-size-fits-all approach to monetize innovation efficiently, and the best approach can only be discovered through the bottom-up process of market discovery. That process demands a business-model-agnostic approach to IP law and policy (including IP-related antitrust law) that preserves the ability of market participants to choose from the full range of feasible monetization strategies in any particular innovation environment.

A legal regime that does not provide secure IP protections violates this principle. In tangible goods markets, pricing decisions take place based on the institutional foundations of a legal regime that provides secure enforcement of property rights and contractual agreements. So too in intangible goods markets. Weak-IP regimes that limit the enforcement of IP rights, IP licenses, and other IP-dependent arrangements distort markets' organizational choices by effectively discouraging firms from selecting direct monetization strategies in which IP assets are distributed as discrete assets—for example, medicines sold in a pharmacy or movies distributed through a streaming service—to intermediate or end-users. Truncating the set of viable distribution strategies cannot in general yield a preferred policy outcome since there is no reason to believe that giveaway and indirect monetization strategies consistently outperform direct monetization strategies as a matter of innovation and competition policy. Adopting weak-IP policies that effectively force firms to monetize knowledge assets by embedding them within a broader product and services bundle, or giving them away as part of a cross-subsidization strategy, raises entry costs and, as such, may advantage producers and other entities that are in the best position to adopt and implement those strategies, while disadvantaging all other firms and, in particular, the innovation specialists that are best positioned to generate those knowledge assets in the first place.

Intermediaries in content and technology environments tend to be advantaged in two respects by legal changes or business strategies that devalue—or, in business terminology, commoditize—IP assets. First, commoditization of IP assets reduces the intermediary's input costs (in some cases, pushing down those costs to zero). Second, commoditization can shift the point in the business ecosystem from which value is extracted toward non-IP-dependent segments in which the intermediary has a competitive advantage. For example, YouTube thrives under a weak-copyright regime since this both eliminates its input costs by commoditizing content and drives the locus of competition to the online advertising market in which it excels. In the smartphone market, Apple thrives under a weak-patent regime since this reduces its royalty payments to upstream chip suppliers and drives the point at which economic value is extracted to the distribution and marketing segments in which Apple excels. The losers in both cases are the innovators that stand at the apex of the supply chain and deliver the content or technology inputs on which aggregators and implementers rely to deliver commercially viable products and services to the target business and home-user markets. Precluding innovators from earning market-determined returns on their investments in a reasonable secure property-rights environment, and shifting a substantial portion of the economic surplus within the content or technology ecosystem to firms that do not invest significantly in innovation, would not seem to be a sustainable policy for a knowledge-driven economy.

12.4. How Weak IP Distorts Innovation Markets

Conventional policy wisdom has generally assumed that weaker IP rights favor the public interest by expanding access and reducing the monopoly rents that would otherwise by enjoyed by "Big Pharma" or "Big Media." This is a short-sighted policy that is unlikely to result in a net public gain in a significant range of technology and creative environments. The private interests of aggregators and implementers in minimizing input costs, reducing litigation costs, and raising entry barriers through weaker IP rights are unlikely to be aligned with the public's interest in a sustainable knowledge ecosystem that supports a continuous flow of new technology and content assets over the longer term, rather than only maximizing access to the stock of existing technology and content assets.

In the life sciences industries and certain high production-cost content markets, the anticipated result is straightforward. Absent IP rights, firms would have limited expectations that the costs of innovation could be recovered in the face of anticipated imitation and would therefore struggle to raise funds for developing new products and services. In many information technology segments, the result is more complex. While some firms can monetize innovation through non-IP-dependent business models, a weak-IP regime still distorts the innovation landscape by diverting capital away from entities that excel in innovation but lack the complementary assets required to support giveaway or indirect monetization strategies. This distortionary effect is likely especially to impact start-ups, research institutions, and other R&D–focused entities that rely on IP rights to monetize knowledge assets through relationships with producers, distributors, and other entities situated at midstream and downstream points on the commercialization pathway. Under a weak-IP regime, innovation may persist in certain industries at "reasonable" levels, but it is likely to concentrate among larger and more integrated entities that can sustain non-IP-dependent business models that extract returns through giveaway or indirect monetization strategies. As I discuss in the following sections, the result is likely to be a skewed knowledge ecosystem that favors larger integrated firms that tend to focus on incremental improvements to existing technologies, rather than smaller and R&D–specialist entities that tend to focus on disruptive innovations that challenge existing technologies. As a matter of both innovation and competition policy, this is a suboptimal outcome.

12.4.1. Evidence: Distortions Based on Entity Type

As I have discussed extensively in previous work, these proposed relationships between IP strength, organizational form, and market structure are consistent with evidence from six decades of U.S. technology history.[25] To illustrate this point, Figure 12.1 shows the distribution of R&D expenditures by U.S. firms during 1957–2021, organized by firm size (large v. small). For this purpose, large firms are firms with more than 1000 employees.

Broadly speaking, there have been three patent regimes during the period shown in Figure 12.1: (1) from the 1950s through the 1970s, courts generally did not enforce patents consistently and there were significant antitrust constraints on patent licensing; (2) during the early 1980s through the mid-2000s, courts enforced patents with significantly greater consistency (principally due to the influence of the Federal Circuit) and antitrust constraints on patent licensing were substantially relaxed; and (3) during the mid-2000s through the present, courts have re-imposed obstacles to patent enforcement (principally due to the influence of the Supreme Court) and antitrust

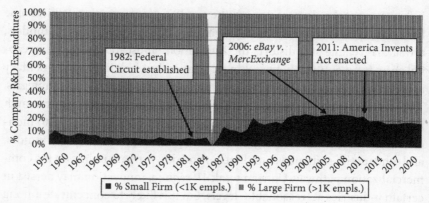

Figure 12.1 R&D expenditures by entity type (1957–2021).

Notes: R&D expenditures reflect expenditures on R&D performed by companies in the U.S. and funded by any source except the federal government. Starting in 2008, R&D expenditures only reflect expenditures funded by companies. Data is missing for 1985.

Sources: National Science Foundation, Company and other (except Federal) funds for R&D, by industry and size of company, 1957-98; National Science Foundation, National Center for Science and Engineering Statistics, Research and Development in Industry (annual reports, 1999-2007); National Science Foundation, National Center for Science and Engineering Statistics, Business R&D and Innovation (annual reports, 2008-2021).

regulators have constrained licensing in certain industries, especially wireless communications markets.

As Figure 12.1 shows, R&D expenditures in the private sector have always been skewed toward large firms. However, there have been significant variations in the degree of concentration of R&D expenditures across large and small firms. During the decades following World War II through the 1970s, when courts were reluctant to enforce patents, small firms represented only 5%–7% of private R&D expenditures. By contrast, during the strong-patent period that followed enactment of the Bayh-Dole Act in 1980 and establishment of the Federal Circuit in 1982, there was a surge in small-firm R&D expenditures. As of 2011, small firms represented approximately one-quarter of private R&D expenditures, as compared to about 5% as of 1980. Notably, the small-firm percentage started to decline in the early 2010s and, since 2012, has stood at 18%–19%. While this percentage is still substantially above the levels that prevailed during the 1950s through the 1970s, it represents a material decline relative to the levels that had been reached during the late 1990s and the following decade.

Throughout this period, fluctuations in the portion of R&D expenditures by small firms appear to follow changes in the force of patent protection. With a limited time-lag, the falloff in small-firm R&D expenditures follows judicial decisions—most notably, the Court's 2006 decision in *eBay v. MercExchange*, which largely denied injunctive relief to non-practicing and certain other entities[26]—and enactment of the America Invents Act in 2011 that materially weakened patent protections. This is consistent with a recent empirical study finding that the reduction in the availability of injunctions following the *eBay* decision reduced U.S. firms' likelihood of engaging in technology licensing to monetize returns on innovation, which in turn adversely impacted in particular smaller firms in "discrete" technology segments.[27]

While other contributory factors certainly play a role in these developments (and therefore these observations are merely suggestive of any potential causal relationship), changes in the composition of R&D expenditures among differently sized firms in response to changes in the strength of patent protection are consistent with theoretical expectations. As patent protection weakens, smaller firms, which tend to rely more substantially on patents in certain industries (and are especially reliant when using a licensing-based business model), reduce R&D expenditures, apparently in response to lower expected returns on innovative activity, whereas the same is not true for large firms, which can often rely on non-IP strategies for capturing returns on innovation outside the life sciences. While the evidence is not definitive, it is consistent with the view that the market responds to reductions in the strength of IP protection by shifting capital from smaller to larger firms, which, in certain technology markets outside the life sciences, can secure returns on innovation even without a secure IP infrastructure. When patent protection is restored to stronger levels (as in the period from the 1980s through the mid-2000s), the market can freely allocate innovation capital without the transactional distortions induced by a weak-IP regime. The result is as expected: an increased diversity of transactional forms—in particular, increased participation by smaller firms in the R&D market—emerges during this period. Contrary to standard expectations, these trends suggest that strengthening patent protection lowered entry barriers and reduced market concentration.

12.4.2. Evidence: Distortions Based on Innovation Types

Whenever patent protections are weakened, the allocation of innovation capital—that is, the available pool of capital that is or could be allocated to innovation activities—would be expected to flow toward larger and more integrated firms, which have greater capacities to capture returns on innovation through non-patent-dependent strategies. The same effect should be expected concerning the allocation of innovation capital across different types of innovation projects. As patent protections are weakened, innovation capital should flow toward entities that undertake innovation projects that are more amenable to non-patent-dependent monetization strategies and away from projects that are less amenable to those strategies.

While still preliminary, there is evidence that the market is responding in this manner to the increasing inability to reliably enforce and license patents. This distortion in the allocation of innovation capital raises significant policy concerns since it appears to divert capital away from patent-dependent fields that can deliver especially high social returns. Specifically, there is suggestive evidence that the weakening in patent protections since approximately the mid-2000s has led to a distortion in the allocation of venture capital across innovation sectors, favoring non-patent-dependent over patent-dependent sectors. In an important study of the distribution of VC investments in U.S. firms during 2004 to 2017, Mark Schultz found that VC investors had shifted away from patent-dependent markets, such as biopharmaceuticals, medical devices, and IT hardware, and toward non-patent-dependent markets, such as social media, consumer finance, and food and leisure.[28] To be clear, these investment trends reflect in part the influence of contemporaneous economic and technological changes; however, it is worthy of note that these trends conform to the expected effect of reductions in the strength of patent protection on VC funds' investment decisions.

The Schultz study finds that the share of VC funding being invested in the most patent-intensive sectors fell dramatically from 50.5% in 2004 to about 25.1% in 2015. That significant shift in investment priorities coincides with the legal shift toward a weaker patent system starting with the *eBay* decision in 2006 and culminating in the enactment of the America Invents Act in 2011 and the launch of the Patent Trial & Appeals Board in 2013. It is especially concerning that the biopharmaceutical and medical-device industries lost a substantial share of total VC investment during this period (shifting, respectively, from 19% and 10% of VC funding as of 2004 to 15% and 6% of VC funding as of 2017), raising concerns over not only economic costs in the form of inefficiently allocated resources, but also non-economic costs attributable to reduced investment in pharmaceutical and medical technologies. Similarly, VC investment in semiconductors (a market in which some leading innovators

Table 12.4 Changes in Venture Capital Investment in U.S. Industry
(2004–2017)

Industry	Share of VC investment (2004–2008)	Share of VC investment (2013–2017)	Percent change
Non-patent-intensive sectors			
Financial services	1.6%	4.1%	147.1%
Food and beverage	.4%	1.5%	248.5%
Healthcare information technology	1.2%	2.6%	112.6%
Restaurants, hotel, and leisure	.4%	1.4%	266.5%
Software	25%	40%	57.6%
Total	28.6%	49.6%	
Patent-intensive sectors			
Computer hardware	3.4%	1.2%	−63%
Healthcare devices and supplies	10.7%	6.2%	−42.6%
Biopharmaceuticals	15.6%	12.4%	−20.1%
Semiconductors	3.4%	.6%	−82.7%
Total	33.1%	20.4%	

Notes: All values are rounded. The study relies on the USPTO's definition of "patent-intensive" industries, which encompasses (among others) computer and peripheral equipment, communications equipment; other computer and electronics products; navigational, measuring, electromedical, and control instruments; semiconductors and other electronic components; basic chemicals; electrical equipment, appliances, and components; medical equipment and supplies; pharmaceutical and medicines; other chemical product and preparation; and machinery (U.S. Patent & Trademark Office 2016, 23–25 Table 3).

Source: Schultz 2020, 32 Table C.

use patent-dependent, licensing-based business models) fell precipitously during this same period, which raises both economic concerns and, given the strategic importance of this sector, national-security concerns (see Table 12.4).

12.4.3. Implications: Why Distorting Innovation Markets Matters

It may be objected that, even if weak-patent protection drives innovation away from firms and industries that rely on patent-dependent business models, the resulting funding and innovation gap can be filled either by large firms that often do not rely on patents or, in the case of patent-dependent sectors such as the life sciences, publicly funded research entities. This objection may seem reasonable in light of the considerable R&D expenditures of the largest technology firms (both in absolute terms and as a percentage of revenues) and the billions of dollars distributed annually by the federal government for research purposes. Yet an innovation ecosystem that consisted solely of large firms and publicly funded research entities would likely underperform substantially compared to innovation ecosystems that make available robust IP protections and can therefore support a broader range of entities to execute the innovation and commercialization process.

The reason is twofold. First, an innovation regime that relied principally on public funding would likely excel in generating basic research but would struggle in converting that research into technically and commercially viable products that can deliver value to consumers. Without legal exclusivity (and in the absence of technological equivalents to secure functional exclusivity), no investor would be willing to risk the billions of dollars required to convert basic research into a new pharmaceutical product that can survive clinical testing and reach market release. Historical experience testifies to the social costs of overlooking this basic point. During the decades following World War II, the federal government lavishly funded R&D, but industry generally showed little interest in commercializing federally funded research and, in some cases, adopted policies designed to avoid any possible involvement with federally funded researchers or research entities. The culprit: federal funding policies that largely barred agencies or recipients of federal research funding from seeking patents, or exclusively licensing patents, on federally funded research.[29]

To be clear, this period produced groundbreaking technological advances in defense-related aerospace, computing, and communications fields, However, as I have shown in previous research, once federal R&D funding was cut back (starting in the late 1960s) from the unsustainable levels that had prevailed during the Space Race, key measures of R&D performance declined significantly, including R&D intensity (the percentage of GDP reflected by total R&D expenditures), business R&D intensity (the percentage of GDP reflected by firms' R&D expenditures), and R&D employment intensity (the percentage of firms' total personnel reflected by firms' R&D personnel). These measures then shifted back upward following reinvigoration of the patent system in the 1980s, which apparently induced firms and investors to place capital at stake in technological innovation.[30] As suggested by this "rise and fall" pattern of the U.S. innovation economy during the period from World War II through the 1970s, an innovation economy that relies principally or substantially on public funding is likely to excel in basic research, underperform in commercializing innovations, and impose a tax and debt burden that is unsustainable over any significant period of time. That is not a long-term recipe for innovation success.

Second, while it is true that large firms in the life sciences and information technology industries typically spend abundant sums on research and development, the business management literature shows that large firms often struggle to execute the most disruptive forms of innovation. As observed by Kenneth Arrow,[31] large-firm managers tend to be averse to supporting projects that will render obsolete existing products, especially if those products are generating stable cash flows. By contrast, a start-up has incentives to challenge an incumbent by developing an innovation that displaces the incumbent's technology, rather than developing a mere improvement, which would likely be replicated by the incumbent.

This asymmetry in incentive structures may explain why small-firm innovators have been a disproportionate source of breakthrough innovations in U.S. technology history, encompassing inventions such as the telephone, the airplane, FM radio, air conditioning, xerography, synthetic human insulin, CDMA wireless communications, and many other examples.[32] In light of this history, William Baumol observed that "it is plausible that perhaps *most* of the revolutionary new ideas of the past two centuries have been, and are likely to continue to be, provided more often by those independent innovators who essentially operate small-business enterprises."[33] As I and others have shown, the exemplary innovation performance of smaller firms explains why large technological firms often implicitly outsource certain types of R&D through repeated acquisitions of start-ups.[34] Given the fact that small-firm innovators in certain industries often rely on patent protection to overcome incumbents' advantages in production, distribution, and most other competitive parameters[35] (or to negotiate the terms of partnerships and acquisitions with incumbents on a level playing field), a legal regime that weakens patent protections may sustain innovation but is likely to suffer from a lack of disruptive innovation that delivers the most significant steps forward in technological advancement.

12.5. Closing Thoughts

In this chapter, I have argued that the weakening of IP protections distorts innovation markets by precluding firms from freely engineering business models for extracting value from investments in creative and technological innovation. Those models differ across markets and are continuously being adapted in response to changes in economic and technological conditions. Hence any limitation on IP protections, which constrains the freedom to choose from the full set of transactional structures, endangers markets' ability to select the most efficient mechanisms for monetizing innovation assets. In turn, these distortions in markets' transactional choices may have adverse effects by endangering the viability of certain types of firms (especially smaller or less integrated firms) or certain types of innovation projects that rely on IP rights to achieve commercialization. Secure IP rights avoid these potential distortions by enabling markets to freely craft organizational structures for funding and supporting the innovation and commercialization process. Just as firms in a particular industry converge on, and then continuously adjust, efficient prices through the trial-and-error process of market competition, so too firms select and continuously adjust efficient transactional structures in the same manner. Policy actions that truncate IP protections skew these choices by constraining the menu of feasible monetization strategies and, in particular, by foreclosing the monetization strategies that are often used by innovation specialists that stand at the heart of knowledge ecosystems.

13

How Weak IP Rights Shield Incumbents and Impede Entry

In the previous chapter, I argued that substantially weakening IP rights distorts innovation markets by favoring firms that adopt integrated structures for monetizing R&D investments and disfavoring firms that specialize in R&D but rely on relationships with third parties to execute the commercialization process. This gives rise to the counterintuitive implication that weak IP rights (or the absence of IP rights) can operate as an entry barrier that shields incumbents against potential threats posed by smaller and less integrated innovators, while strengthening IP rights can lower entry barriers and enhance competition. In this chapter, I explore these surprisingly complementary relationships between IP rights, innovation, and competition through four paradigm "Illustrations" drawn from technology markets.

In *Illustrations 1* and *2*, I describe circumstances in which a weak-IP regime bolsters entry barriers and shields incumbents against competitive threats posed by smaller but more innovative entrants. This is a "lose-lose" policy outcome: weakening IP rights reduces innovation incentives (at least among smaller and less integrated firms) but protects incumbents by shielding them against more innovative rivals. In *Illustrations 3* and *4*, I describe circumstances in which strengthening IP rights promotes innovation (especially among smaller and less integrated firms) but lowers entry barriers by facilitating technology dissemination through licensing arrangements between innovators and intermediate users, which in turn promotes entry in the downstream production market. This is a "win-win" policy outcome: strengthening IP rights bolsters innovation, but also promotes competition by lowering the technical and capital requirements to achieve entry in the production market. Contrary to standard assumptions, weak IP rights can sometimes lower both innovative and competitive intensity, while strong IP rights can have the opposite effect.

The Big Steal. Jonathan M. Barnett, Oxford University Press. © Oxford University Press 2024.
DOI: 10.1093/oso/9780197629529.003.0014

13.1. Illustration 1: Sonos v. Google

It has long been argued that patent protection and other forms of IP rights can be used by dominant firms to block entry and suppress competition. While this is a plausible contingency under certain circumstances, patent protection can have the opposite effect by facilitating entry by smaller firms that have strong innovation capacities but limited capital or expertise to execute the commercialization process independently (or at least, as efficiently as larger firms with established production and distribution capacities). When this is the case, a patent can enable the innovative entrant to challenge incumbents, who can outperform the entrant in every non-innovation segment of the supply chain and, as a result, may have the ability not only to imitate the entrant's technology, but to produce and distribute that technology on a mass scale at a substantially lower cost. This theoretical intuition is consistent with multiple survey studies, which find that larger firms (outside the pharmaceutical and chemical industries) tend to place a relatively low value on patents as a device for appropriating value from R&D investments,[1] and that smaller firms tend to place a high value on patents, especially in industries such as IT hardware, medical devices, and biopharmaceuticals.[2]

These divergent valuations likely arise in part from disparities in large firms' and small firms' access to the complementary non-IP assets that are typically required to convert innovations into commercially viable products or services. A large integrated firm has in place a well-developed financing, production, and distribution infrastructure that is costly to replicate. As a result, the integrated firm can capture returns on R&D investment even if the innovation is not legally protected, so long as most potential imitators are unable to replicate the firm's full package of related products and services at a comparable cost. Alternatively, a large firm may have a protected complementary asset that generates revenues that can support a giveaway distribution strategy to fund development, production, and distribution of the unprotected innovation asset. Neither strategy can be executed by a smaller firm that has robust R&D capacities but has not developed substantial commercialization capacities or lacks an excludable complementary asset that can support a giveaway distribution strategy for its IP asset.

A patent can play a critical function in leveling this uneven playing field between incumbents and entrants in technology markets. This contingency is vividly illustrated by a sequence of infringement litigations involving Google and Sonos.

In 2020, Sonos, a pioneer in the home audio systems market, brought suit at the U.S. International Trade Commission (ITC) against Alphabet (Google's parent) for allegedly imitating Sonos's technology and incorporating it into various Google devices, including in particular Google's home speaker product.[3] Sonos is a public company with over 1,800 employees and a market capitalization of $2.15 billion as of December 2023; Alphabet is a public company with over 150,000 employees and a market capitalization of $1.75 trillion as of December 2023. According to Sonos, Google was able to imitate Sonos's technology by securing information in the course of negotiating a potential licensing deal with Sonos in connection with Google's home music service. The ITC determined that certain of Google's products, including its "smart speakers," replicated certain patented features of Sonos's technology, although newer redesigns of those products did not. These findings, and the limited exclusion order, were upheld in 2024 by the Court of Appeals for the Federal Circuit.[4]

The interaction between Sonos and Google is precisely the type of information exchange that exposes an innovator to expropriation by a counterparty with significant resources and technical sophistication. Firms that specialize in innovation often seek to cultivate the value of their technology through external relationships with holders of complementary assets (rather than having to replicate each of those complementary assets independently, a challenging undertaking). Sonos adopts a hybrid commercialization strategy insofar as it both produces audio system hardware and, as occurred in its interactions with Google, enters into partnerships and other relationships with firms that hold complementary assets. However, as the Sonos/Google litigation demonstrates, entering into negotiations for this purpose is a perilous exercise, especially if the counterparty has sufficient resources and expertise to imitate the innovator's technology once it has been disclosed in the course of negotiations. The innovator can attempt to protect against a counterparty's anticipated opportunism by limiting disclosure (which may impede valuation of the innovator's technology), relying on reputation effects that may discipline a counterparty if it engages regularly in interactions with other innovators, or maintaining a portfolio of patents and other IP rights to deter unauthorized usage.

Without a robust patent portfolio (and in the absence of sufficiently powerful reputation effects), Sonos faced a classic free-rider scenario in which the value of an innovation is mostly captured by intermediate users rather than the originator. Assuming that Google replicated important functionalities of Sonos's home speaker products, Sonos could not remain competitive on price, because Google had presumably not incurred comparable R&D costs and, most critically, could cross-subsidize the prices of its "smart speakers" with the cash flow generated by its core search business. By contrast, Sonos had incurred significant R&D costs to develop those functionalities and, unlike Google, did not have a sufficient cash flow stream from other products to support a cross-subsidization strategy. As a result, Sonos's only remaining recourse was the patent system. Sonos's general counsel described the simple rationale behind its case against Google: "This is just trying to level the playing field with the big actors and not let them abuse the competitive situation by just taking what we invented for free, because it wasn't free for us to invent it."[5]

After significant litigation costs and two years of delay, Sonos secured a decision in its favor. In January 2022, the ITC issued an exclusion order against Google, finding, as noted previously, that Sonos's five litigated patents (covering certain features of its home speaker products) were valid and had been infringed by certain Google devices.[6] In June 2022, the U.S. Customs Service determined that Google had violated the order by importing products that infringed at least two Sonos patents,[7] and, in September 2023, the ITC rejected an infringement claim that had been filed in response by Google.[8] (As noted, the Federal Circuit upheld in 2024 the limited exclusion order issued by the ITC against Google.[9]) In a concurrent infringement litigation, a federal district court ruled in October 2023 that certain of Sonos's asserted patents were invalid and rejected a previous jury award of $32.5 million in damages.[10] As of this writing, Sonos has appealed the court's ruling.

Sonos's infringement claims (and lengthy efforts to enforce those claims) are far from an outlier. Other smaller technology companies have alleged that large technology companies have copied their innovations, either after the disclosure of information in a business pitch or in the context of a supply relationship or other business partnership. At least three infringement and trade-secret claims have recently been brought against Apple concerning alleged copying of medical monitoring innovations that can be used in conjunction with Apple mobile devices, including suits brought by Masimo (which invented and patented a pulse oximeter for use with Apple mobile devices), AliveCor (which invented and patented an electrocardiogram device for use with the Apple Watch), and Valencell (which developed a heart-rate monitor for use with wearable devices).[11] In December 2023, Masimo secured an exclusion order in the ITC against Apple smart watches, based on the ITC's finding that a feature in Apple's smart watch infringed upon Massimo's patent-protected technology. Apple subsequently redesigned the watches to remove the infringing feature and has appealed the exclusion order.[12] At the time of this writing, Apple has also filed patent-infringement claims and sought an order to block Masimo's release of its "Freedom" smart watch that includes Masimo's patented blood-oxygen measurement technology.[13]

If Masimo ultimately prevails in its patent-infringement litigation against Apple, it will be an exception to the predicament faced by small-firm innovation specialists that bring infringement suits against an allegedly infringing large integrated firm. Even when an innovator brings an infringement claim under patent or trade secret law, it is difficult to prevail since the infringer may claim that it had already developed the innovation (which rebuts a trade secret claim), may bring a patent infringement counterclaim, or may argue that its alleged copy constitutes an improvement that falls outside the scope of the patent. Moreover, given the modest prospect of securing a permanent injunction in cases involving multi-component technologies, a large infringer that has the resources to sustain a protracted litigation can exert bargaining leverage in settlement negotiations with the patent owner. This infringer-friendly state of affairs is compounded by the fact that the alleged infringer can file, or threaten to file, a petition in the PTAB to challenge the validity of the inventor's patents. In this scenario, the absence of secure patent protection acts as an implicit mechanism for enabling an integrated incumbent to appropriate value from a specialized innovator's R&D investments, especially when the innovator lacks the expertise, capital, or infrastructure that would be necessary to monetize its R&D investment independently.

13.2. Illustration 2: Netflix v. YouTube

Weak-IP regimes can distort innovation markets by implicitly favoring firms that have complementary non-IP assets that can be used to capture returns on innovation in the absence of legal exclusivity, while raising entry barriers to firms that specialize in innovation and lack the complementary assets required to convert an innovation into a commercially viable product or service. This distortion in the mix of viable organizational types may result in a market structure that is less competitive as compared to the market structure that would likely arise under a stronger IP regime in which entry could be achieved by relying primarily on an IP-protected portfolio of knowledge assets, coupled with an associated licensing infrastructure. In turn, this distortion in the range of feasible monetization strategies may distort the range of feasible innovation projects by favoring projects from which value can be extracted in a zero or weak-IP environment.

The distortionary effects of reduced IP protections on innovation choices and competitive conditions can be illustrated by comparing two real-world markets for video content: in one of these markets, copyright owners can largely deter unauthorized usage; in the other, they cannot. For purposes of this exercise, I will compare (1) "free" video-sharing services, which operate in an environment in which copyright is insecure due to the absence of meaningful legal or technological obstacles to user infringement; and (2) paid video streaming services, which operate in an environment in which copyright is secure due to technological controls that impede unauthorized usage and contractual agreements that support royalty payments to copyright owners.

In the video-sharing market, YouTube users (excluding subscribers to YouTube's licensed video-streaming service) can access abundant content of variable quality in exchange for a zero fee and modest search costs. By contrast, users of a paid streaming service such as Netflix can access substantial content of more consistent quality in exchange for a subscription fee and lower search costs. While the YouTube service relieves the user from any out-of-pocket expenditure, the quality of the content (at least as measured objectively by the size of production budgets) fluctuates considerably, ranging from amateur videos to high-budget motion pictures, and content is delivered with ads (absent payment of a fee to block ads) and is displayed at variable levels of quality and convenience (for example, a single movie may be delivered in multiple segments). Netflix must incur significant costs to license content or produce original content (it spent an estimated $17 billion on content production in 2021[14]), which it then delivers to paying subscribers in a curated ad-free environment. The same is true for streaming services such as Amazon Video, which spent an estimated $10.7 billion in 2021 on content production and acquisition.[15] (As discussed subsequently in Chapter 16, YouTube now spends significant amounts paying individual content creators by sharing a portion of the advertising revenue associated with creators' videos.)

It is sometimes argued that the abundance of content on free online sites such as YouTube demonstrates that copyright protection is not necessary to support creative production and, specifically, that an ad-based giveaway model can feasibly support content production even if users do not pay to consume it. This line of argument suffers from two difficulties.

First, this argument relies on a "manna from heaven" assumption. That is, it ignores the fact that the highest production-cost content being viewed on unlicensed services such as YouTube would not have been produced but for the ability of content production companies to earn a return on their investment through licensed streaming services such as Netflix and Amazon (as well as theatrical exhibition and other paid distribution channels), which in turn relies on maintaining exclusivity through technological or contractual means. As of year-end 2022, the estimated number of worldwide users on the YouTube platform exceeded 2.5 billion,[16] which far outpaced the estimated number of worldwide users on any other paid streaming service (approximately 247 million for Netflix, 200 million for Amazon Prime Video, 150 million for Disney+, 95 million for HBO Max, 63 million for Paramount+, and 48 million for Hulu[17]), suggesting that the industry as a whole relies on a minority of paid subscribers to cross-subsidize a majority of non-paying users on unlicensed services. Hence there remains a concern that the supply of *new* high-production-value content would decline if prevailing levels of legal or technological exclusivity were ineffective in enabling streaming services to sustain subscriptions from a sufficient population of paying viewers.

Second, content markets that rely on ad-based business models that give away content produced by others may be prone to higher concentration relative to markets that support subscription-based business models in which direct payments from users fund original content production, whether directly or indirectly through royalty payments to copyright owners. Until the recent rise of TikTok, YouTube had few competitors among general-purpose online sites that display user-uploaded content, whereas Netflix must compete with Amazon, Hulu, and, more recently, Apple TV, Disney+, Peacock, and other paid streaming channels. Figure 13.1 illustrates visually this difference in market structure and concentration between licensed and unlicensed markets for online content.

Apparent differences in market concentration can be derived from differences in the level of exclusivity over content assets in the ad-supported video-sharing market and the subscription-based video streaming market. In an environment in which content is available to all due to the absence of effective IP protections or any technological substitute to regulate unauthorized replication and distribution, no video service can compete on the basis

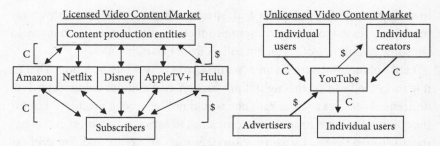

Figure 13.1 Structural differences in licensed and unlicensed markets for video content (simplified).

Legend: "$" denotes monetary payments; "C" denotes transmission of content.

Notes: Under "Licensed Video Content Market," the image is intended to reflect that (1) content flows from streaming services to subscribers and payments flow from subscribers to streaming services; and (2) content flows from production entities to streaming services and payments flow from streaming services to production entities. Under "Unlicensed Video Content Market," "individual users" appear twice to reflect the fact that some users both upload content to, and view content on, the platform.

of its content inventory, which would simply match the content that could be found on any other site. As a result, *competition shifts from the market for content production and acquisition to the market for content aggregation and curation.* However, the aggregation and curation services market is prone to converge on winner-take-most outcomes since users minimize search costs by using a single platform that contains the largest volume of content, adjusted for variety, quality, and ease of service. Advertisers will then tend to converge on the site that attracts the greatest number of users (adjusted in some cases for the type of users preferred by certain advertisers), resulting in a winner-take-most outcome for some period of time.

This exercise in the relationship between IP rights and market structure supports a broader point. The apparent "success" of certain markets in supporting continuing innovation—whether in a content or technology market—absent robust IP protection may hide the efficiency losses attributable to the non-IP-dependent strategies that firms are compelled to adopt in this environment. Put differently, even if certain firms can construct workable and even lucrative business models under a weak-IP environment, this does not demonstrate that the relevant market is operating under a maximally efficient property-rights regime. Under a weak-IP regime, firms must adopt non-IP-dependent monetization strategies that can feasibly extract returns from innovation assets in the absence of legal exclusivity. However, these adaptations (and the implicit inability to select freely across the full range of monetization models) may impose efficiency losses that would not arise under a more secure IP regime. Since video content that is uploaded by users to online platforms has limited protection against unauthorized replication and distribution, both as a legal and technological matter, video-sharing sites generally cannot compete on the basis of unique content inventory. As a result, competition shifts from the market for video production and acquisition to the market for video aggregation and curation services, which tends to converge for some period of time on a dominant supplier that maximizes users' inventory choice and minimizes users' search costs. Any savings in litigation, access, and other transaction costs attributable to the withdrawal of copyright protection must therefore be weighed against *other* social costs attributable to the non-IP-dependent business model that prevails in the absence of copyright. The result may be a market that exhibits higher concentration levels, and potentially weaker competitive conditions, as compared to the content distribution market that would prevail under a more secure IP regime.

To be clear, the prevailing distribution platform in an unprotected content market may remain exposed to competition from smaller services, differentiated services that target particular market niches, or potential competition from new services and therefore should not be presumed to exercise market power without further inquiry. Reflecting this contingency, YouTube now faces competition in the video-sharing market from TikTok and Instagram. Yet even this change in competitive conditions in the online video-sharing market reflects in part the fact that IP-free innovation environments are often compelled to adopt some form of practical exclusivity, whether implemented through legal or technological means or a combination of both mechanisms. As will be addressed in greater detail in Chapter 16, each of these three leading video-sharing sites now voluntarily recognizes implicit IP rights by offering payments to leading video creators to appear exclusively on its platform, which in turn means that these sites are competing in part on the basis of partially differentiated content inventories. Moreover, YouTube has invested in acquiring licensed content and producing original content. The enhanced competitive intensity, increased product differentiation, and renewed production of original content observed in the current video-sharing market has arisen in connection with the re-emergence of synthetic IP rights in lieu of formal IP rights that remain largely ineffective as a practical matter, an outcome that is consistent with theoretical expectations concerning the complementary relationships between property rights, innovation, and competition.

13.3. Illustration 3: Microsoft v. Apple

Conventional wisdom holds that weakening IP protections necessarily expands access, lowers entry barriers, and, as a result, enhances competitive conditions. Yet it is possible to identify real-world circumstances in which this proposition is falsified, resulting in a "lose-lose" policy outcome in which weakening IP rights both disincentivizes certain types of innovation and detracts from competitive conditions by raising entry barriers to certain types of firms. The early years of the home computing industry illustrate how strengthening IP rights can lower entry barriers, increase user access, and improve product choice by enabling innovators to adopt licensing strategies that distribute innovation assets broadly, rather than embedding them within a "walled garden" product ecosystem.[18]

Table 13.1 presents the different monetization strategies pursued by Apple and Microsoft at the onset of the personal computing industry in the 1980s and early 1990s. Apple pursued a mostly closed monetization strategy: it integrated its proprietary OS into Apple hardware and developed peripheral hardware devices and software applications internally, offering users a highly integrated hardware-software bundle.[19] In contrast, Microsoft adopted a

Table 13.1 Principal Monetization Strategies in Personal Computing Markets (approx. 1981–1994)

Firm; OS	Operating System	Investment in Promoting External Development of Hardware and Software Applications	Extent of Dependence on Secure IP Rights to Appropriate Value	Market Share of PC Suppliers (1981, 1994)
Microsoft (MS-DOS; then Windows)	Direct monetization (OS licensed to OEMs)	High	High	Almost 20%; approx. 80%.
Apple (Mac)	Indirect monetization (OS integrated into Mac hardware)	Hardware: low Software: moderate	Low	Approx. 10%; approx. 15%.

OEM = original equipment manufacturer; OS = operating system.
Source: For the last column on the right, see Baldwin 2021, 21.

substantially open monetization strategy in which it licensed its crown jewel asset, the MS-DOS (and later Windows) OS, to any original equipment manufacturer (OEM), facilitated third-party development of peripheral devices, and provided software developers with access to its OS APIs on a royalty-free basis (together with technical support), which reduced the costs of developing applications for the Microsoft OS.[20]

As shown in Table 13.1 (far right-hand column), Microsoft's more "generous" monetization strategy prevailed. Licensing the Windows OS to OEMs on a non-exclusive basis enabled Microsoft by the early 1990s to secure its position as the leading OS provider in the PC market. In addition, Microsoft actively promoted the development of peripheral devices by other firms and released the Windows APIs to software developers on a no-fee basis, which cultivated a large inventory of Windows-dedicated programs and peripherals that in turn promoted user adoption of Windows-compatible PCs over Apple's Mac device.

The comparison of Apple's and Microsoft's monetization strategies rebuts any necessary relationship between "more IP" and "less access." Microsoft's monetization strategy relied on IP rights to support its OEM licenses but was more open than Apple's strategy in two respects: (1) it licensed out the Windows OS to all OEMs willing to pay the licensing fee, and (2) it made more extensive efforts to facilitate third-party development of complementary hardware devices and software applications. By contrast, Apple generally adopted a more "closed" strategy that bundled the OS into its proprietary hardware, internally developed certain peripheral hardware devices, and made less extensive efforts in facilitating external development of software applications. Critically, Microsoft's greater reliance on a more open monetization strategy relied on IP rights to "expose" its IP assets to third parties who would then have incentives to develop complementary applications that increased the value of the Windows OS and enabled Microsoft to secure a dominant position in the personal computing OS market.

This strategy benefited not only Microsoft in the OS market but also hardware producers and end-users in the PC market. By making the Windows OS available to all interested licensees, Microsoft's licensing-based business model lowered entry costs for "clone" OEMs, which drove down retail prices and diverted market share away from higher-priced machines offered by the PC pioneer, IBM.[21] Tellingly, IBM had once resisted extending IP rights to software because it anticipated that doing so would enable formation of a stand-alone market in software that would threaten the hardware/software bundling strategy that IBM had deployed during the decades in which it had led the global mainframe and computing industry.[22] IBM's expectations were correct. The incremental extension of copyright to software programs in the 1970s, through actions of the Copyright Office culminating in an amendment to the copyright statute in 1980, enabled the distribution of software as a stand-alone product and the subsequent proliferation of hardware/software combinations that increased product variety and lowered aggregate costs for end-users.

This is an especially clear illustration of the manner in which strengthening IP rights not only induces increased innovation, as would be expected, but also has favorable effects on entry costs (in this case, in the PC hardware and software markets) and, as a result, on retail prices paid by end-users. This result runs counter to the standard intuition that reducing IP protections always advances the public interest by maximizing access to existing knowledge assets. Far from restricting access, inflating prices, or entrenching incumbents, the use of IP protection to protect software enabled the disaggregation of the computing market into complementary hardware and software segments and lowered entry costs in both markets. As IBM had correctly anticipated, IP rights were a critical element behind these developments that ultimately led to its withdrawal from the PC market that it had pioneered. Secure copyright protection for software applications made it feasible for developers—most notably, Microsoft—to operate outside an integrated supply chain, which ultimately benefited billions of consumers and businesses worldwide who enjoyed increased supply, increased variety, and lower prices in the personal computing market.

13.4. Illustration 4: The Dolby Sound Story

Scholarly and academic discussions often characterize IP licensing as a "tax" that limits access to creative and technological assets and generates rents for IP owners, ultimately at end-users' expense. This view myopically focuses on the royalty payments paid to licensors without identifying and evaluating feasible non-IP-dependent structures for generating the funds required to sustain the same or greater level of innovation and commercialization activities that are supported by the purportedly "burdensome" IP licensing model. This oversight is critical because the alternative feasible structure is often a vertically integrated product and services ecosystem that can only be established and maintained by a handful of companies, resulting in higher entry barriers and a more concentrated market structure. IP-dependent licensing structures not only generate the funds that support the entities that originate innovations, but also enable those entities to engage with a variety of partners that specialize in the production, distribution, and other activities that are required to convert an innovation into a technically and commercially viable product. Without a secure IP system for safeguarding intellectual assets, those interactions are likely to raise expropriation risks that lead firms to monetize innovation assets through integrated structures that minimize knowledge leakage during the commercialization process. Far from burdening the innovation ecosystem, patent-mediated transactions can counterintuitively lower the costs of information exchange and, in doing so, enable an efficient division of labor across the supply chain and disseminate creative and technology assets broadly among producers and distributors.

The counterintuitive effects of IP rights on competitive conditions can be illustrated by the monetization strategy adopted by Dolby, the originator of the most widely used audio sound systems for purposes of cinematic theatrical exhibition and a variety of consumer electronic devices. In the mid-1960s, Ray Dolby invented a music recording and transmission system that included a pioneering noise-reduction system, marketed as the "Dolby NR" system and designed for use in sound-recording equipment and cassette tape players. The Dolby corporate group has principally monetized its inventions through a licensing-based business model, as a result of which its technology has been adopted by manufacturers of devices for recording and playing music.[23] In connection with the transition away from analog sound systems, Dolby developed digital audio technologies that became the industry standard in DVD systems, movie theaters, home theaters, PCs, and digital television sets.[24] Disseminating its technology through licensing relationships with hardware manufacturers enabled Dolby to secure a position as the industry-standard audio system in each of these market segments while generating licensing royalties that it used to fund innovation across technology generations.[25]

Contrary to the common caricature of the licensor as a monopolist that sets exorbitant fees at will, which then translates into high prices for consumers, Dolby reportedly elected to "cut royalties to the bone" and charge all licensees the same rate.[26] Another source observes that Dolby adopted the policy of charging the "same very low royalty rate" to all licensees in order to cultivate "a very large royalty base."[27] This policy might seem irrationally altruistic given the fact that there are few alternatives to Dolby's audio technology that are both technically comparable and have a recognized consumer brand. Yet this "generous" licensing approach rests on a sound business rationale. The originator of a new technology that lacks independent production and distribution capacities may expect to maximize revenues by adopting a low royalty rate that maximizes the speed and extent of adoption by producers and consumers, which in turn maximizes the device sales from which the licensor can extract a royalty to fund R&D. According to a historical account of the Dolby corporate group, licensing "allowed the company to focus on its core competency in technology development, while leaving the high-volume manufacturing, distribution and marketing to the experts."[28] Even after the originator's technology has achieved widespread adoption, it must continuously invest in developing improvements to maintain a continuing revenue stream and to deter potential competitors that can introduce competing and potentially superior technologies. So long as the originator is a repeat-play firm, it has a rational interest in developing a record of consistently "reasonable" licensing terms, which enhances the likelihood that it will be able to successfully license enhancements to its existing technologies.

Throughout U.S. patent and antitrust history, courts and regulators have often sought to intervene in licensing transactions to "protect" consumers from the purportedly high licensing fees extracted by "monopolist" licensors.[29] Yet there is remarkably little factual basis for this widespread assumption, which typically reflects an idealized licensing model in which an IP monopolist faces no competitive threats and seeks to maximize revenues during a single technology generation. Yet real-world licensing markets are typically populated by firms that either face competition in markets that have not yet settled on a single dominant technology, or operate in a repeat-play environment in which even current market leaders seek to maximize revenues over multiple technology generations. Within this context, licensors—even licensors such as Dolby that enjoy strong market positions— have incentives to accrue reputational goodwill by offering "reasonable" and stable royalty rates. That stock of goodwill can be used to promote adoption of the licensor's current technology and, in the future, adoption of extensions of its current technology (without which the underlying R&D investment cannot be monetized).[30] This long-term licensing strategy relies on a legal infrastructure that supplies a reliable mechanism for enforcing and licensing IP-protected assets, which generates revenue streams that fund innovation and supports a transactional infrastructure that facilitates dissemination of the technologies generated by those investments. Broad-based access to technology inputs through licensing transactions can have favorable competitive effects by lowering technical entry barriers into the relevant product or services market, which in turn may enhance competitive conditions in the retail market for end-users. In these circumstances, policy interventions that weaken the ability to enforce and license patents and other relevant IP rights reverse these effects.

13.5. Closing Thoughts

It is common to assume that there exists an inherent tension between innovation policy, which relies on legal or technological exclusivity to generate the anticipated profits required to incentivize innovation in the face of potential imitators, and competition policy, which generally seeks to maximize access by entrants and end-users to existing technology and creative assets. A transactional approach to IP rights—that is, an approach that recognizes the enabling function of IP rights in overcoming transaction-cost obstacles to information exchanges among innovators, investors, and other business parties—shows that robust enforcement of IP rights and IP-dependent contractual arrangements can promote both innovation and competition in a wide variety of real-world circumstances. By implication, policy changes that impede the enforcement and licensing of IP rights can reverse these effects by impeding firms' ability to monetize innovation assets through licenses and other contractual relationships, which may induce firms to monetize innovation through self-contained business models that limit the circulation of knowledge assets, raise entry barriers, and protect incumbents.

14
Free Stuff Gets Dangerous

The IP skepticism that has dominated scholarly and policy commentary concerning IP policy (including IP-related antitrust policy), and which has supported the across-the-board weakening of patent and copyright protections, has sometimes made an exception for IP rights (in particular, patents) concerning the pharmaceutical and biotech industry. This "pharma qualification" may reflect the fact that the empirical case for patents in the pharmaceutical industry is especially compelling, reflecting the exceptionally large costs involved in developing, testing, and mass-producing a new pharmaceutical product, the high risk of project failure, and the long period from conception through market release. It has been estimated that the total average costs of a new biopharmaceutical product, incorporating the costs of failed projects, exceeds $2.8 billion,[1] while the time to develop a product through market launch typically exceeds a decade.[2] Those costs are exacerbated by the low rate of project success: as of 2011, average success rates for pharmaceutical drug projects ranged, depending on the therapeutic category, from 2.38% to 29.77%.[3] By comparison, the costs of replicating a new successful product are substantially lower and, by definition, include none of the costs and risks of failed projects. Moreover, the costs of imitation are subsidized by the Hatch-Waxman Act,[4] which enables generic entrants to secure regulatory approval after having demonstrated bioequivalence with the brand-name drug (rather than having to replicate the costly testing process completed by the producer of the brand-name drug). In short, biopharmaceutical innovation is an exceptionally high-cost, high-risk endeavor that is unlikely to persist absent secure legal protection against unauthorized imitation.

The reliance of biopharmaceutical development on patent protection is supported by several bodies of empirical evidence. First, several landmark survey studies—conducted at roughly 10-year intervals since the late 1980s through the late 2000s—find that biopharmaceutical firms view patent protection as a "but for" condition for making R&D investments and do so more consistently than virtually any other industry.[5] Unlike certain segments of

The Big Steal. Jonathan M. Barnett, Oxford University Press. © Oxford University Press 2024.
DOI: 10.1093/oso/9780197629529.003.0015

the information technology industries, the strong preference for patent protection persists among large integrated firms. Second, evidence on the advocacy activities of firms in different industries on patent-related litigation before the U.S. Supreme Court shows that the biopharmaceutical industry, unlike the information technology industry, consistently and uniformly takes positions that support strong patent protection.[6] Third, several empirical studies involving large samples of different countries find that increases in the strength of a country's patent protection stimulate local investment in pharmaceutical R&D, so long as a country has reached a sufficiently high level of economic development and educational attainment.[7]

The empirical literature aligns with an almost universal business consensus that a sufficient portfolio of pending and issued patents is typically necessary to induce VC investors to fund the costly tasks required to bring a new biopharmaceutical product to market, encompassing innovation, testing, production, and distribution. Unlike much of the information technology industry, there are few business models in biopharmaceutical markets that do not rely on patent protection, and hence, even large integrated firms generally cannot substitute toward non-patent-dependent business models in response to significant reductions in IP coverage or other forms of legal exclusivity. This simple fact casts great doubt on the arguments made by some commentators and policymakers who express skepticism concerning the necessity for patent protection to sustain biopharmaceutical innovation, often dismissing it as an unjustified windfall for private industry.[8]

Notwithstanding the strong theoretical, empirical, and business case for patents in the biopharmaceutical industry, policymakers are continuously under pressure to reduce the strength of patent protection in this sector given the strong policy preference among consumers, insurers, and other constituencies for lower drug prices. Pressures to implement weaker forms of patent protection are especially strong in countries that have a well-developed generic pharmaceutical industry and therefore have a clear economic interest (at least in the short term) in reducing or eliminating IP rights that may constrain the industry's growth. If policymakers blindly followed these widely shared preferences for weaker patent protection for pharmaceuticals, the business case for investment in this sector would stand in great doubt and the global public-health ecosystem would almost certainly suffer from a meager flow of new drugs and therapeutics. To preserve incentives to invest in the biopharmaceutical sector and maintain a robust biomedical innovation ecosystem, the United States and other countries have sought over approximately three decades to establish a global baseline of minimum patent protections in pharmaceutical markets through the vehicle of the "TRIPS" agreement (which came into effect in 1995),[9] to which all members of the World Trade Organization (WTO) must commit.

In an unprecedented shift, the U.S. government has recently pursued, or advocated for, two key policy actions that would considerably weaken patent protections for certain pharmaceutical innovations: (1) a "waiver" of IP rights concerning vaccines and treatments for COVID-19; and (2) an expansion of "march-in" rights under the Bayh-Dole Act (which enables the government to compulsorily license a patented product covered by the statute). Given the strong empirical case for patent protection in the pharmaceutical sector, this sharp policy turnaround appears to reflect an extension of the ideologically driven and factually indifferent IP-skeptical approach that has driven the dilution of IP protections in content and technology markets over approximately the past two decades.

14.1. The COVID-19 IP Waiver

In October 2020, the governments of India and South Africa made a submission to the WTO seeking a waiver of certain provisions of the TRIPS agreement concerning medical products and technologies to prevent and treat the COVID-19 disease,[10] the source of the pandemic that spread across the world from late 2019 through mid-2022. The concept of the COVID IP waiver was the culmination of several years of lobbying by certain developing countries for international organizations to weaken patent protections in the medical field (including, for example, a report released in 2016 by the UN High-Level Panel on Access to Medicines, which stated that IP rights are incompatible with human rights[11]). The United States and other countries that are the principal source of pharmaceutical innovations (as well as the World Intellectual Property Organization) had consistently resisted this position on the grounds that it would undermine incentives to continue investing in future pharmaceutical innovation (while access concerns could be addressed separately through differential pricing, subsidies, and other mechanisms).

In May 2021, the Office of the U.S. Trade Representative (USTR) announced its support for the waiver[12]—effectively, a governmental revocation of IP rights covering vaccines that reflected billions of dollars of private investment of risk capital, principally by companies based in the United States and Europe (and, in some cases, partially funded with government support). The USTR not only endorsed the waiver proposal but was arguably at the forefront of an effort to secure international support for it. In this endeavor, the USTR enjoyed strong backing from developing countries (in particular, Brazil, India, and South Africa, which have significant generic drug industries) but faced resistance from certain European countries, such as the United Kingdom and Switzerland that (like the U.S.) are innovation leaders in the pharmaceutical industry. In June 2022, the WTO announced that the IP waiver had been adopted concerning "patented inventions necessary for COVID-19 vaccine production and supply," subject to certain limitations.[13] In February 2023, the USTR requested that the U.S. International Trade Commission (ITC) undertake a study on the COVID-19 "diagnostics and therapeutics market" and related issues, including "how existing TRIPS rules and flexibilities can be deployed to improve access to medicines."[14] The study was requested in connection with a potential extension by the WTO of the COVID-19 IP waiver and expansion of the waiver to cover not only vaccines but COVID-19 diagnostics and therapeutics. In October 2023, the ITC released its report, which failed to find definitive evidence that IP rights posed a significant impediment to access to COVID-19 diagnostics and therapeutics.[15]

In light of the qualifications to the waiver as adopted by the WTO, some commentators and advocacy groups have expressed doubt whether the waiver substantially enhances the ability to make use of IP-protected technologies related to the COVID-19 vaccine. Nonetheless, the USTR's decision to depart from the TRIPS baseline of global patent protection in the life sciences—a policy position it has continued to endorse by contemplating an extension and expansion of the waiver—represents an unprecedented departure from several decades of agency policy. Given the substantial extent to which pharmaceutical innovation relies on the property-rights infrastructure provided by the patent system, the IP waiver and the signal it sends concerning the security of patent rights in the global marketplace are likely to have three adverse impacts on the development and commercialization of new vaccines and do not necessarily accelerate access to existing COVID-19 vaccines.

First, the IP waiver is likely to discourage investment in the development of new or improved vaccines, a high-cost, high-risk undertaking that cannot elicit funding without a secure expectation of market exclusivity in the unlikely event of success. As is true of biopharmaceutical development in general, the development and commercialization of a new vaccine is a capital-intensive and labor-intensive process that requires specialized facilities, personnel, and expertise.[16] In particular, the development and production of the COVID-19 vaccines necessitated billions of dollars of capital investment, in addition to personnel and physical plant on the part of biopharmaceutical companies, supplemented by government funding in the case of some companies.[17] Without secure IP protection and the expected returns that can be secured as a result of the exclusivity arising from such protection, there is significant doubt that these companies could have justified to shareholders making these exceptionally large investments. An IP waiver would counterproductively encourage pharmaceutical firms to shift resources *away* from vaccine development and toward other therapeutic categories that do not operate under similar legal encumbrances.

Second, the IP waiver is likely to impede the ability of smaller firms to attract capital for the development of vaccines that, like other biopharmaceutical products, typically necessitate partnerships with larger firms to execute the capital-intensive testing, production, and distribution process that leads to market release. These partnerships supported the development and launch of three of the most widely distributed COVID-19 vaccines, including the BioNTech/Pfizer, Moderna, and Astra-Zeneca vaccines. In the case of BioNTech and Moderna, the smaller firm developed the vaccine and then, in each case, partnered with larger firms (as in the BioNTech/Pfizer partnership) or contract manufacturers or distributors (as was the case for Moderna) for purposes of testing, production, and distribution. In the case of the Astra-Zeneca vaccine, the vaccine was developed by researchers at Oxford University's Jenner Institute, which partnered with Astra-Zeneca to execute the commercialization process. Patents typically play a critical role in supporting relationships in the biotech industry between small firms and large firms, or between research institutions and commercial firms, by protecting each partner against expropriation of its knowledge assets and, in the process, enabling relationships that efficiently combine complementary IP and non-IP assets to develop, test, produce, and deliver a safe, effective, and commercially viable product.

Third, as observed in the ITC's 2023 report concerning a potential extension of the COVID-19 IP waiver, it is not clear that a waiver facilitates production and delivery of the vaccine by third parties.[18] The reason is that a patent owner subject to a compulsory license is unlikely to be especially eager to cooperate in the sharing of technical know-how and related expertise that are necessary to produce and deliver a vaccine in a safe and effective manner. By contrast, keeping the patent regime in place preserves the property-rights infrastructure that enables parties to structure, through the combination of contractual agreements and IP rights, mutually beneficial relationships that safeguard the patent owner's intellectual assets while disseminating those assets to production and distribution partners.

Given these adverse impacts on the investments and partnerships required to support vaccine development and commercialization, there must be significant concern that the USTR's support for the COVID-19 IP waiver is likely to discourage the biopharmaceutical industry from allocating capital to this segment of the life-sciences industry and, in particular, is likely to discourage investment in start-ups that often play a critical role in the innovation stages of the drug development process. Even if it were believed that governmental and philanthropic funding would be sufficient to support the innovation stages of the drug development process, this does not address the necessity to secure funding and operational expertise to execute the capital-intensive and labor-intensive testing, production, and distribution stages of that process. There is little reason to believe that publicly funded entities could replicate the capital-market discipline and other incentive structures that drive profit-seeking firms to execute those tasks as efficiently as possible. Contrary to the intentions of policymakers, the COVID-19 IP waiver is likely to discourage and impede investment by the private sector in this segment of the biomedical innovation ecosystem.

14.2. How Patents Helped End the COVID-19 Pandemic

During the COVID-19 pandemic, advocates for the IP waiver argued that patents were obstructing the development, production, and distribution of vaccines that could save human life. Closer scrutiny of the mechanisms through which vaccines were developed for COVID-19 supports precisely the opposite conclusion. The patent system, in conjunction with public funding both before and during the pandemic, facilitated and promoted the innovation, production, and distribution of vaccines that accelerated the end of the pandemic and saved the lives of millions of people.

The scientific origins of the BioNTech/Pfizer vaccine lie in decades of academic and commercial research into the use of mRNA-based methods to develop and produce vaccines,[19] as distinguished from conventional methods that rely on producing inactive or weakened versions of the relevant virus (typically grown in chicken eggs or mammalian cells). However, the more immediate origins of the BioNTech/Pfizer vaccine derive from the formation in 2008 of a biotech startup, BioNTech, by two German scientists who secured VC funding to support the development of mRNA-based vaccines.[20] As part of these efforts, BioNTech had partnered with Pfizer on the development of an mRNA-based vaccine against influenza. This relationship enabled BioNTech, a small R&D–focused firm, to access the powerful commercialization capacities of its large-firm partner in order to execute the necessary testing, production, and other tasks involved in making and distributing a drug on a mass scale. Following the onset of the coronavirus pandemic in early 2020, the two companies decided to apply their existing know-how to develop a vaccine against COVID-19. In a period of less than 12 months, the two companies reportedly incurred over $1 billion in development and testing costs.[21] The vaccine was first approved on an emergency basis by UK regulators in December 2020, which was followed by approvals in many other countries.[22]

BioNTech holds a patent portfolio comprising over 200 patent "families" that it exclusively or jointly owns or licenses from other entities.[23] As stated in BioNTech's 2021 annual report, the company's portfolio includes patents that are specifically directed at "various features of mRNA structure" and "various formulations for mRNA delivery," pending patent applications directed at specific features of the company's COVID-19 vaccine, and licenses for technologies "relating to certain lipids and/or lipid nanoparticles and formulations used in" the vaccine.[24] As in other small firm/large firm partnerships that are common in the biotech industry, patents and pending patent applications played a critical function at two juncture points in the relationship between BioNTech and Pfizer, which in turn enabled each firm to contribute its specialized capacities toward accelerated development of a COVID-19 vaccine.

First, a patent portfolio provided a mechanism to secure legal exclusivity against potential imitators in the event the development project was successful and the product was released into the market. Without that assurance, neither BioNTech nor Pfizer would have had rational business justifications to invest in this costly undertaking since success would simply have invited the entry of imitators who had not borne any part of the R&D costs. Second, patents (or, more generally, the availability of patent coverage) supported the ability of BioNTech to secure VC funding for its early development efforts and subsequently to enter into a partnership with Pfizer. In the BioNTech/Pfizer relationship, BioNTech's patent portfolio functioned as a device for enabling a mutually beneficial partnership between a firm that specialized in innovation and a firm that specialized in the complementary non-innovation capacities required to convert an innovation into a technically and commercially viable product. The synergy between these two firms' specialized innovation and commercialization capacities ultimately benefited the public, which received an effective vaccine at a faster pace than would otherwise have been possible, representing an immense social gain as a matter of both innovation and public health policy.

Even recognizing that patent rights play a critical role in supporting investment incentives in the biopharmaceutical industry, it might nonetheless be argued that it is worthwhile in certain cases to incur the costs of reduced innovation in the future in exchange for increased access to existing drugs in the present. Yet it is not clear that there is always a strict dichotomy between facilitating access and supporting R&D and commercialization incentives. Perhaps ironically, the COVID-19 pandemic—precisely the type of exceptional case in which it might seem to be appropriate to prioritize short-term access over longer-term incentive concerns—illustrates the manner in which access can be improved while preserving the legal security of patent rights.

While commentary has often focused on the formal adoption of the IP waiver, it is sometimes overlooked that the waiver was only adopted as the pandemic was subsiding (in mid-2022), and hence the existing patent system was left in place during most of the period in which COVID-19 vaccines were developed, produced, and distributed. The coronavirus pandemic therefore provides an opportunity to assess whether patent protections impeded access as proponents of the IP-waiver have suggested.

The answer is clearly not. There are several reasons.

First, large developed countries donated hundreds of millions of doses of the COVID-19 vaccine to the COVAX program administered by the United Nations, which had distributed in total 1.43 billion doses to developing countries as of April 2022.[25] Second, three leading vaccine producers (Pfizer, Moderna, and Johnson & Johnson) pledged to provide approximately 3.5 billion doses at cost or a discount to middle- and lower-income countries.[26] As of April 2022, it was reported that there was a glut of COVID-19 vaccines and, in light of this fact, the world's (and India's) largest vaccine producer had elected to stop production,[27] strongly suggesting that concerns over limited access to the vaccine were unfounded. Third, some vaccine producers entered into licenses with producers in developing countries. For example, Astra-Zeneca and Johnson & Johnson licensed their technology to producers in India, South Africa, and South Korea.[28] Pfizer granted 35 manufacturers the right to produce generic versions of Pfizer's COVID-19 antiviral pill (which relieves symptoms in patients who contract the virus) for the purpose of expanding access to the treatment in lower- and middle-income countries.[29]

It is important to observe that patents facilitated these transactions and therefore expanded access since, without legal exclusivity, the original producers would likely have been unwilling to disclose their technology to other firms given the inability to regulate and price usage of their technology. Moreover, the ability to enter into structured licensing and other business relationships enabled innovators and manufacturers to negotiate contractual terms governing the provision of know-how without which a licensee may be unable to exploit the technology being licensed. Contrary to advocates' claims that patents limited dissemination of vaccine technology and impeded access among users, it appears that patents may have had precisely the opposite effect, in addition to supporting the incentives to make the R&D investments without which the vaccine would never have been developed at all.

14.3. Proposed Expansion of "March-In Rights"

The Bayh-Dole Act enables recipients of federal research funding—principally, academic research institutions—to seek patents on innovations developed using that funding. This reflects the underlying rationale behind the statute, which seeks to harness the private market's profit-seeking incentives to accelerate the conversion of federally funded research into commercially viable products. The statute constitutes a key part of the institutional infrastructure behind a biotech ecosystem that relies on a mix of public funding, VC risk capital, and contractual relationships among scientist-founded start-ups and large pharmaceutical firms. The statute's removal of restrictions on patenting the fruits of federally funded research is qualified by a march-in rights provision, which enables the government in certain circumstances to compel the owner of a patent on technology that derives from federally funded research to grant a "nonexclusive, partially exclusive, or exclusive license" to a "responsible applicant or applicants."[30] The march-in rights provision applies only in specified circumstances, which principally arise in cases where the patent owner or licensee has not taken sufficient steps "to achieve practical application of the subject invention" or there are "health and safety needs which are not reasonably satisfied."[31]

Since enactment of the Bayh-Dole Act in 1980, the federal government has never exercised its rights under the march-in rights provision, and it has commonly been understood that it would do so in only the most exceptional circumstances. Eight petitions have been filed with the National Institutes of Health to exercise the march-in rights provisions, and those petitions have been rejected in every case after a finding that the relevant product market did not suffer from any supply constraints.[32] Recently the understanding that the march-in rights provision can only be exercised in the most exceptional circumstances has been unsettled by a policy shift toward using this provision as a tool for regulating drug prices. In September 2021, a report issued by the Department of Health and Human Services (HHS) indicated that HHS was considering petitions to make broader use of the federal government's march-in rights provisions under the Bayh-Dole Act.[33] In March 2023, HHS and the Department of Commerce took a step further and announced that an "Interagency Working Group for Bayh-Dole" would "develop a framework for implementation of the march-in provision," including articulating criteria and processes for exercising march-in rights under certain circumstances.[34] In December 2023, the National Institute of Standards and Technology released for public comment draft guidelines that set forth the factors that an agency may consider when determining whether to exercise march-in rights under the Bayh-Dole Act, including "the reasonableness of the price and other terms at which the product is made available to end-users."[35]

Advocates for using the march-in right provision more expansively have taken the view that these rights may be exercised if the government determines that a patent owner or a licensee is demanding "unreasonably" high prices for patented drugs and other products that derive from federally funded research. This position purports to rely on the statute's definition of "practical application," which includes language that the patented invention is being made "available to the public on reasonable terms."[36] This interpretation of the statute would effectively convert the march-in rights provision into a form of price regulation, an objective that is hard to reconcile with the fact that the Bayh-Dole was enacted to *remove* governmentally imposed limitations that had historically discouraged private industry from investing in developing and commercializing innovations derived from government-funded research. The authors of the statute, former Senators Robert Dole and Evan Bayh, had specifically contested this expansive interpretation of the statute,[37] which virtually rebuts any credible argument that this interpretation reflects legislative intent at the time of the statute's enactment.

This novel understanding of the march-in rights provision would cast a cloud of legal insecurity over any drug developed using innovations derived from federally funded research, since there is no settled methodology for determining objectively whether any particular price is "reasonable" and hence no ability to predict whether the government would exercise its march-in rights and, if it did so, whether any such action would be likely to withstand scrutiny in court. The prospect that the government might exercise its march-in rights in anything other than the most exceptional circumstances would likely discourage pharmaceutical companies from partnering with academic research institutions (which are almost universally funded in part through federal research grants), effectively undermining much of the intended purpose of the Bayh-Dole Act to facilitate the conversion of academic research into technically and commercially viable products by harnessing the profit motivations of private investors. In 1997, the National Institutes of Health (NIH) had identified this risk when declining to grant a march-in petition, stating: "In exercising its authorities under the Bayh-Dole Act, the NIH is mindful of the broader public health implications of a march-in proceeding, including the potential loss of new health care products yet to be developed from federally funded research."[38]

Historical experience supports concerns that expanded use of the march-in right would have unfavorable effects on private investment in the biopharmaceutical industry. During a period extending from the 1950s until passage of the Bayh-Dole Act in 1980, research funded by federal agencies generally could not be used to support patent applications by, or even exclusive licensing to, private entities, or could only do so under cumbersome restrictions (which differed across agencies).[39] These policies rested on the expectation that making federally funded research available to any interested party on a non-exclusive basis would lower entry barriers and therefore promote both competition and innovation in technology markets. The market behaved otherwise. As observed by federal agencies and congressional committees, private industry generally exhibited little interest in developing commercial applications of federally funded research under these limitations that effectively barred exclusivity over any successful end-product. The reason is straightforward. Without exclusivity, the prospect of securing a profit from investing capital and personnel in commercialization was doubtful given third parties' ability to imitate any successful product developed, even partially, from federally funded research. As of 1980, it was estimated that only about 5% of federally owned patents were being exploited.[40] In short, the government's open-access policies had resulted in a zero-development outcome.

There is no reason to believe that firms in today's market would react differently if regulators were to adopt the proposed broad understanding of march-in rights, which would effectively constrain a patent owner's exclusivity over the use of any drug or other therapeutic developed from research funded by the federal government. Any such firm would be exposed to the risk that a regulator could determine, and private parties could allege, that the drug was being distributed at "unreasonable" prices or other terms that prevent "practical application," which would therefore trigger the march-in right. In anticipation of this contingency, many firms would likely choose to avoid or limit relationships with academic research institutions, unless the institution were willing to covenant that the research it sought to commercialize had not been supported by federal funding. Given the ubiquitous role played by federal funding in academic biomedical research, it is doubtful any research institution would be able to provide such assurances to a commercial partner. The result would be an effective rollback of the Bayh-Dole Act in a broad range of circumstances and, as a result, a substantial impediment to relationships involving the conversion of academic research into commercially viable products in the biomedical sector. The loser would be the public-health system and the hundreds of millions of patients that it serves (not to mention the billions of patients around the world that indirectly benefit from pharmaceutical innovations developed by the U.S. biomedical industry).

14.4. Cautionary Lessons from Japan

It may be reasonably objected that we cannot exclude a plausible counterfactual world in which patent protections are substantially weakened, either directly or indirectly (through limitations on patent owners' pricing and licensing freedom), but yet pharmaceutical innovation proceeds at robust levels. (We also cannot exclude the counterfactual world in which patent

protections are substantially increased and pharmaceutical innovation proceeds even more robustly.) While this objection—as would be the case for
any counterfactual proposition in the social sciences—cannot be definitively
rebutted, the weight of the evidence concerning the role of patent protection
in supporting biopharmaceutical innovation casts doubt on its plausibility.
In particular, an imperfect natural policy experiment in Japan provides
strong reasons for caution in making policy changes that would significantly
cut back on the patent rights and other forms of legal exclusivity that currently protect pharmaceutical innovations against unauthorized imitation.

During the 1970s and 1980s, the Japanese pharmaceutical industry was
a world leader in drug innovation.[41] Using "new chemical entities" (NCEs)
as a measure of new drugs, Japan-headquartered companies accounted for
15% of all NCEs released internationally during 1971–1980 and 29% during
1981–1990. Thereafter, Japan's pharmaceutical industry went into decline, as
evidenced by its declining share of NCEs: 9% during 1991–2000, 9% during
2001–2010, and 7% during 2011–2020. By contrast, during this same period,
the U.S. share of NCEs increased from 31% during 1971–1980 to 64% during
2011–2020. During approximately the same period, Japan's pharmaceutical
industry exhibited a decline in both innovation inputs, as evidenced by a
decline in pharmaceutical R&D investment (whether measured as a share
of GDP or as a share of global pharmaceutical R&D expenditures), and
outputs, as evidenced by a decline in NCEs and "triadic" biopharmaceutical patents (patents filed in the EU, Japan, and U.S. patent offices). During
1987–2018, Japan's share of global pharmaceutical R&D expenditures fell by
one-half (from 14.1% to 7.3%), while the United States increased its share by
one-quarter (from 30% to 40%).

While several non-IP-related factors contributed to the decline of the
Japanese pharmaceutical industry, it happens to coincide with an effective
devaluation of pharmaceutical patents during the same period. Starting in
1982, Japan introduced strict price controls for pharmaceuticals.[42] While this
type of policy—which indirectly reduces the value of patent protection by
substituting a government-imposed price for a market-determined price—
enabled policymakers to accrue reputational goodwill by satisfying their
constituencies' preferences for lower drug prices, it may have contributed
to the sharp decline in investment in the Japanese pharmaceutical industry
and the resulting decline in drug development. The logic is straightforward.
As price controls reduced expected returns on drug development, capital
shifted toward other industries (or pharmaceutical firms focused resources

on existing drugs), which ultimately injured Japan's biomedical innovation ecosystem by "drying up" the pipeline of new drugs. Over the longer term, this may have resulted in a significant net aggregate welfare loss for Japanese consumers, with adverse effects on public health. It should therefore be a matter of some concern that the U.S. Congress, in the Inflation Reduction Act of 2022, imposed the equivalent of price controls on drug prices by setting "maximum fair prices," or requiring rebates on the prices, for certain branded drugs purchased by the federal government for the Medicare system.[43] The price controls can be applied starting seven to ten years after a new drug has been on the market.[44] While this policy intervention delivered political goodwill in the short term for policymakers, this de facto truncation of patent protections on certain drugs may adversely impact the long-term innovation performance of the U.S. life sciences market.

14.5. Closing Thoughts

Theory, evidence, and history support the view that a rigid IP-skeptical approach in biopharmaceutical policy risks giving rise to significant adverse impacts on innovation, competitive conditions, and public health. Unlike many information technology markets, the biopharmaceutical industry has few if any viable business models that do not rely on a secure portfolio of IP rights (comprised principally by patents and trade secrets) to deter imitators that have not borne the unusually high costs and risks inherent to innovation and commercialization in this field. In particular, patents are especially critical for start-ups that have played an important function in converting scientific research into new drugs and other therapeutics since the extension of patent protection to biotechnological innovations by the Supreme Court in 1980 and the enactment of the Bayh-Dole Act by Congress in that same year. Recent policy proposals, including in particular the COVID-19 IP waiver and the expanded understanding of march-in rights under the Bayh-Dole Act, threaten to unravel the intricate network of transactional arrangements that harness the specialized innovation and commercialization capacities of smaller and larger firms in the biopharmaceutical ecosystem. Policy actions that would reduce significantly, or even eliminate, patent protections are hard to reconcile with an approach that relies on evidence, rather than ideology, to guide innovation policy.

15

Free Stuff and the Decline
of the Free Press

Political theorists in the classical liberal tradition have long expressed the
view that property rights are a foundational right because they safeguard
all others in a liberal democracy. This view of property rights is commonly
traced back to John Locke, who argued that civil society derives from
individuals' interest in securing their property from expropriation. Writing
in 1689, Locke stated: "The reason, why men enter into society, is the preservation of their property; and the end, why they chuse and authorize a legislative, is that there may be laws made, and rules set, as guards and fences
to the properties of all the members of the society, to limit the power, and
moderate the dominion, of every part and member of the society."[1] While
Locke's conception of property rights focused on individuals' cultivation of land and other physical assets (what Locke called "[t]he Labour of
[a Man's] Body, and the Work of his Hands"[2]), James Madison extended this
idea to intangible assets. Writing in one of the Federalist Papers in 1788,
he stated: "[T]he faculties of men, from which the rights of property originate . . . is [sic] the first object of government."[3] In another Federalist Paper,
Madison had applied this concept specifically to IP rights, stating: "The
copyright of authors has been solemnly adjudged, in Great Britain, to be
a right of common law. The right to useful inventions seems with equal
reason to belong to the inventors. The public good fully coincides in both
cases with the claims of individuals."[4] This view was ultimately reflected
in language proposed by Madison and accepted for inclusion in the U.S.
Constitution, which authorizes Congress "[t]o promote the Progress of
Science and useful Arts, by securing for Limited Times to Authors and
Inventors the exclusive Right to their respective Writings and Discoveries."[5]
Exercising this authority, Congress promptly enacted a copyright statute
in 1790.

The foundational view of property rights within a liberal democracy
reflects the proposition that a society in which property rights are not

The Big Steal. Jonathan M. Barnett, Oxford University Press. © Oxford University Press 2024.
DOI: 10.1093/oso/9780197629529.003.0016

respected is a society in which "might makes right": that is, the most powerful, whether private or governmental entities, can use force to seize assets belonging to others with impunity. In the IP context, the case for property rights is especially pressing since, absent reverse-engineering barriers due to secrecy or technical difficulties, intellectual assets are inherently exposed to imitation and usage without consent. As this book has argued (in particular, in Chapters 4 and 5), the federal judiciary (and by inaction, the U.S. Congress) has acted contrary to these elementary principles in applying the copyright statute to digital content markets. Rather than taking steps to protect the fruits of authors' and other artists' "faculties," the courts have engaged in intellectual acrobatics to apply the copyright statute in a manner that undermines any reasonably effective legal recourse for the holders of content assets against digital intermediaries that facilitate, and profit from, infringement by millions of individual users. The result has been a substantial erosion of property rights in digital content markets and a transfer of wealth from individuals and entities that originate content to intermediaries and individuals that distribute and consume it.

In this chapter, I examine how weakened copyright protections for print and online news publications lead to outcomes that raise concerns relating to the incentive mechanisms that support certain forms of content production, which in turn place at risk the critical function played by an independent press in a robust liberal democracy. In particular, I discuss how a weak-copyright environment commoditizes news content, which compels market actors to shift the main point of revenue extraction from the delivery of news content sold directly to users to the aggregation of such content for purposes of gathering user data for sale to advertisers. In the news context, "aggregation" can encompass a range of reproduction and distribution activities, including the reproduction and dissemination of headlines and excerpts (with or without explicit attribution but typically including a link to the original source), sometimes combined with a paraphrase of language from the original source. While platforms and users may benefit in the short term from zero-cost access to news content, the ecosystem in general is likely to be harmed over any longer period if entities engaged in the gathering, analysis, and distribution of news content can no longer secure adequate remuneration to support those costly activities. The result may be an environment in which the quantity of news is abundant but the average "quality" of news (as measured by accuracy, breadth of analysis, or other parameters) has deteriorated.

15.1. The "News Wants to Be Free" Fallacy

Content environments that operate under weakly enforced copyright regimes face a fundamental difficulty. If the absence of secure property rights and the proliferation of unauthorized copying sufficiently reduces the returns to content originators, then content aggregators are prone to run out of original content or, more specifically, original "high-value" or "professional" content that is costly to produce.

At the start of the commercialization of the internet, this was *not* the prevailing prediction. It was widely asserted that markets would adopt open-access business models and support content production through advertising. Some academics even argued that artists would be content to live on digital tips through "voluntary payment models"[6] or, as suggested by Arianna Huffington (the founder of the *Huffington Post*, a leading online news aggregator), communities of "citizen journalists" would sustain the flow of news by using the distribution platform provided by digital intermediaries.[7] The view that it was no longer necessary to maintain exclusivity over content was adopted not only by IP-skeptical academics and advocates, but also by a large number of news sites, which mostly did not use subscription-based models, instead adopting no-fee, open-access models to attract a large base of readers from which it was expected that significant ad revenue could be generated.[8] Conventional wisdom held that the "democratization" of information access could be reconciled with not only viable but profitable business models.

It is now clear that the ad-based news model has failed in most cases. As of 2014, more than 70% of all daily newspaper sites in the United States had adopted some form of a paywall to implement a digital subscription strategy, as compared to almost none in 2010.[9] In 2017, 69% of a sample of 200 newspapers in the United States and six European countries used some type of a paywall.[10] Even a prominent newspaper such as the *New York Times* struggled to turn a profit using a purely ad-based model and in 2011 adopted a "soft" paywall (that is, a paywall that allows a limited number of "free" articles before requiring a paid subscription).[11] Flagship newspapers in major cities have sometimes only survived financially as a result of "trophy" investments by extremely wealthy individuals, while other digital news publications regularly appeal to readers for philanthropic "micro" contributions. Even once-successful "digitally native" online news publications are now facing significant distress, as illustrated by *Buzzfeed News*, a prominent online news site that shut down in April 2023.[12] Ironically, the money-losing sites include

HuffPost,[13] the popular online news site founded by the same Arianna Huffington who had espoused the view that journalism would thrive by relying on content delivered by amateur "citizen" journalists.

In retrospect, the failure of the ad-only model is not surprising since the newspaper industry had mostly relied for decades on a mix of subscription, single-payment, and ad-derived revenues,[14] suggesting that a purely ad-based model is not economically efficient and, at least in a digital environment, perhaps not even viable. The failure of the ad-based digital news model has led online news publishers to adopt various subscription-based strategies in which some, most, or all content is only available to paying users,[15] effectively reverting to the mixed subscription/ad-based model that had generally prevailed in the industry. However, with the exception of certain specialized business news publishers that appeal to higher-income readerships, such as the *Wall Street Journal* and the *Financial Times*, this shift in strategy has generally not yielded sufficient revenues, apparently reflecting the unwillingness of many consumers to pay for access when news can be obtained at no cost through other sites. Only a minority of actual and potential readers report being willing to purchase a subscription to a news website,[16] while news publishers report difficulty in retaining existing subscribers, resulting in high "churn rates."[17]

Figure 15.1 presents data compiled by the Reuters Institute for the Study of Journalism, which shows that only a small percentage of users in most selected countries reported having purchased a subscription for online news

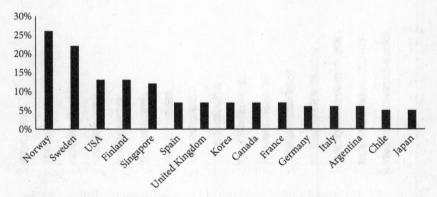

Figure 15.1 Percentage of surveyed users who purchased online news subscriptions (2018, selected countries).
Notes: Total survey sample in each market = 2000.
Source: Newman et al. 2019, 33.

in 2018. Among nine developed economies (including the United States) for which data had been collected since 2013, the average percentage of users paying for online news in each country had remained stable each year at approximately 11%.[18]

Figure 15.2 shows the decline in the economic fortunes of the U.S. news industry in a weak-copyright, mostly-free news environment during 2005–2020. Since 2005, total industry revenues (including subscription and advertising) have fallen by more than half, although the decline has moderated since the early 2010s. While the newspaper industry has earned increasing revenues from digital advertising, this is not sufficient to offset the decline in revenues from subscriptions and print advertising (including classified ads). According to data compiled by PwC on the global newspaper industry during 2011–2022, total circulation revenue held constant at approximately $60 billion, while advertising revenues declined from almost $80 billion to $70 billion.[19] In the U.S. newspaper market, the Pew Research Center found that total circulation revenue through 2020 has similarly held constant at approximately $10 billion, but total advertising revenues have fallen far more steeply, declining from almost $49 billion as of 2000 to below $10 billion through 2020 (based on estimated data since 2013).[20]

The result of this decline in total revenues in the news industry has been the closure of hundreds of newspapers and, among surviving newspapers, a reduction in the number of journalists and the frequency of publication.[21] During 2004–2018, approximately 1,800 local newspapers in the United

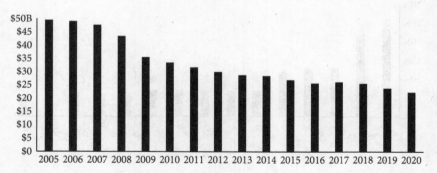

Figure 15.2 Estimated annual revenues of U.S. newspaper publishers (2005–2020, $B).

Note: Figures are not adjusted for inflation.

Source: Statista, Estimated aggregate revenue of U.S. newspaper publishers from 2005 to 2020 (based on data from U.S. Census).

States closed.[22] During 2008–2019, the number of personnel employed in the U.S. newspaper industry fell by almost 50% (from 71,000 to 35,000), while the number of personnel employed in a broader category of news-producing industries fell by almost 25% (from 114,000 to 88,000).[23] These adverse effects are offset to a limited extent by the emergence of digital "native" news sites, which have taken advantage of the reduced entry costs in a digital environment where it is no longer necessary to establish an infrastructure for the printing and distribution of physical copies. However, this model too has struggled to achieve economic viability. Leading digital native media firms, such as BuzzFeed and Vice Media, announced substantial layoffs in 2019 through 2022, and, as noted previously, BuzzFeed announced that it was shutting down its news division in April 2023.[24]

The financial struggles of digital native news sites suggest that the industry still struggles to identify a viable business model even when a publication is not burdened by an existing print-based legacy infrastructure. There can be little doubt that the news industry as a whole is economically worse off—that is, the industry's total revenues from subscription, advertising, and other sources have declined—than had been the case prior to the advent of a digital content environment.

This funding shortfall underlies some observers' and (as suggested by survey evidence) consumers' concerns that the quality—as measured imperfectly by accuracy, depth of analysis, and breadth of coverage—of news content has fallen, even if total quantity has increased due to lower entry costs, resulting in an infusion of amateur or quasi-amateur news content in the form of blogs and other online formats.[25] Even acknowledging the high quality of some blogs and other digital formats, a downward shift in the average quality of news content should be expected as entry costs fall. Absent a substitute for the funding mechanisms that previously sustained investments in news content production, news publications must shift to lower-cost forms of content production or "curate" news produced by others to regularly deliver new content. This is the type of strategy that has been adopted by some digital native sites and automated news feeds that make significant use of headlines and "ledes" (the opening sentence of a news story) that link to content on other sites. Some evidence (including a 2010 study by Pew Research and a 2011 report by the Federal Communications Commission[26]) indicates that news sites have increasingly relied on official press releases by governments or corporations, rather than independent reporting, due to a lack of funding, resulting in reduced numbers of reporting personnel.

Commentators have also expressed concern over funding pressures that have led news publications to reduce investments in investigative journalism,[27] which involves factually detailed reporting that may not appeal to a broad audience but addresses the public interest in a robust independent press that closely scrutinizes public-sector and private-sector activities. The reduction in the quality of news content can have important non-economic effects given the critical role that a vigorous press can play in promoting an informed citizenry and robust self-government in democratic societies.

There are two constituencies in the digital content economy that *have* profited from the free, ad-based model advocated by IP-skeptical policy advocates, endorsed by some scholars, and initially adopted by much of the news industry. These are individual users (at least as measured by the volume, rather than quality-adjusted volume, of accessible information) and digital intermediaries such as search engines, content aggregators, and social networking sites, which appropriate headlines, ledes, and excerpts of various lengths from original-source news sites.[28] A report issued by the European Commission in 2012 observed that the most successful entities in the digital news ecosystem were "aggregation services like Google News, or services which manage large amounts of readers with low-cost user-generated news ... [or] provide links to news headlines from other sources."[29]

Consistent with this view, the economic fortunes of content producers and content aggregators have moved in opposite directions during the news industry's transition to a digital environment. While newspaper publishers' revenues have been plunging, online ad industry revenues have grown vigorously. Online ad revenues have largely flowed to leading platforms, while the news industry has suffered dramatic declines in revenues from print ads (in particular, classified ads) and has been unable to make up the shortfall through online ad revenue.[30] This trend is illustrated by the declining percentage that the newspaper industry's advertising revenues represent out of total advertising revenues. As of 1997, the newspaper industry's advertising revenues represented 34.6% of global advertising revenues; as of 2012, its share had fallen to 19.8%.[31] By 2020, digital and print newspapers represented only 5.7% of global advertising expenditures, while mobile and desktop internet advertising represented over 52%.[32] As these trends suggest, the transition from a print to a digital environment and the associated erosion of copyright protections have adversely impacted news publishers, who are often unable to capture sufficient returns on their investments in producing content, while benefiting entities and individuals who consume and, in the case of online platforms, typically distribute that same content at no cost.

15.2. Fair Use and the Decline of the News Industry

The "free lunch" business model—use content produced by others without payment while retaining all the economic benefits—deployed by leading digital platforms has been promoted by judicial expansion of the fair use doctrine, which substantially reduces any legal risk associated with purportedly "transformative" uses of copyright-protected content by content aggregators. Generous application of the fair use doctrine reduces the input costs borne by news aggregator sites, which would otherwise be compelled to enter into licensing transactions with original-source news sites or to incur the costs of operating an original-source news site. At the same time, an expansive fair use doctrine threatens the ability of content suppliers—in this case, news organizations—to capture sufficient remuneration to cover the costs of gathering information and delivering content to target audiences. In response, it is often argued that publishers benefit indirectly from aggregation platforms because platform users may "click through" to the original-source news site, which then earns revenue based on the agreed-upon split with the platform. If this were true, then it might be plausible to argue that aggregators' practices do not cause material economic harm "on net" to news publishers and therefore might qualify for the fair use exemption, even if the "market harm" prong of a fair use analysis were rigorously applied (which is often not the case in copyright infringement litigation).

These conjectures, however, do not describe the actual economics of digital news markets. A 2020 study of the digital news ecosystem concluded that "[t]he prospect of sharing in Google and Facebook's advertising revenues to finance journalism has 'disappeared.'"[33] While news sites may sometimes benefit from click-throughs that originate on a platform, this does not appear to be the typical case (and even when some click-through revenue flows to the platform, the split with the content aggregator typically favors the latter[34]). For many readers, the headlines and short excerpts that appear in a news feed (in both cases, content originated by third-party news publishers) provide sufficient information so that the reader does not click through to the underlying news website.[35] A 2014 Pew Research study finds that "few Facebook visitors . . . end up also coming to a [news] site directly"[36] and a 2020 Pew Research study found that 50% of respondents, and a majority of respondents aged 18–29, reported that social media sites or search engines were their principal source of news.[37] A 2019 report by the Reuters Institute for the Study of Journalism concluded that Facebook "remains by far the most important social network for news,"[38] a statement that is consistent with the fact that, across 12 major geographic markets, Facebook was the social media platform most commonly used for news in every year from 2014 through 2022.[39]

The harsh realities of the digital news landscape raise an important legal implication. If aggregators are mostly substituting for news organizations, rather than principally being a gateway that delivers traffic to news organizations' websites, then there is no credible doctrinal argument that the fair use doctrine covers aggregators' use of snippets and other excerpts from publishers' news sites. It may be objected that the use of headlines and brief excerpts qualifies as "de minimis" usage; however, the legal viability of de minimis defenses to copyright infringement[40] is unclear and, in any event, some aggregators' replications of news content go beyond a brief headline or short phrase that could plausibly quality for de minimis treatment. Moreover, some federal courts have specifically rejected fair use defenses in the case of seemingly nominal uses of copyright-protected content when the infringing use was deemed to have caused commercial harm to the copyright owner.[41] As a policy matter, aggregators would object that, absent the fair use exemption from infringement liability, they would face infeasible logistical burdens in licensing content from so many news sources and, as a result, end-users would have access to far more limited content. Given platforms' technological capacities, this is not a credible position. If a search engine can auction ad space on millions of sites in nanoseconds and simultaneously deliver location-specific ads to hundreds of millions of individual smartphones, laptops, and other devices, it would seem that aggregators can support a licensing system in which news sources would be compensated in micro-payments for the use of headlines and excerpts.

15.3. Licensing Alternatives to the Fair Use Exemption

The argument that a broad fair use exemption is necessary to support the dissemination of news content in digital markets is difficult to reconcile with the existence of successful mechanisms for micro-licensing transactions involving the use of digital images. Image licensing services such as Getty Images, Shutterstock, and iStock license millions of images to online users worldwide, with a range of pricing options based on the image and type of usage (including zero-royalty options for certain images). A sequence of natural legal experiments provides reason to believe that these types of licensing arrangements would have emerged across the digital content landscape if courts had applied copyright protections more vigorously. Specifically, legislation that limits intermediaries' ability to make use of news content without payment, or legal actions that increase intermediaries' legal exposure for such actions, have sometimes induced intermediaries to enter into licensing agreements under terms negotiated with the entities that fund the production of that content. For example:

- In 2019, the European Union amended its copyright law (the Copyright Directive[42]) to bar aggregators from using news content (except for "individual words or very short extracts," which may include certain types of "snippets"[43]) without seeking the consent of the copyright owner. Subsequently, Google entered into licensing agreements with over 300 European news publishers.[44]
- In 2010, Australia enacted a law requiring that designated digital platforms pay news publishers for "core news content" (subject to mandatory arbitration if the platform and publisher cannot agree on licensing terms).[45] Subsequently, Facebook and Google negotiated licensing deals with multiple Australian news providers.[46]
- Threatened with copyright lawsuits in 2023 over the use of news and other copyright-protected content in the ChatGPT service, Open AI entered into licensing agreements with the Associated Press and other major news organizations.[47] At approximately the same time, Apple was reportedly discussing licensing arrangements with major news publishers for purposes of its generative AI service.[48]

These transactions rebut the common view that broad application of the fair use doctrine is a precondition for news aggregation services and the social media industry more generally. The prevailing expansive judicial interpretation of fair use simply eliminates an input cost and logistical burden that content aggregators and consumers would prefer not to bear. Even in the context of licensing transactions between aggregators and publishers for longer-form uses of the licensed content, the availability of the fair use exemption distorts the terms of those transactions to the licensee's advantage since aggregators retain the outside option of not entering into a licensing transaction and still being able to earn advertising revenues through short-form uses of publishers' content that can credibly be deemed fair use (and would therefore require the rights holder to undertake a costly and lengthy litigation process to rebut that defense).

It might nonetheless be argued that this effective subsidy to aggregation services promotes the public's interest insofar as it improves access to news and therefore, on these non-economic grounds, it is worthwhile to limit the revenues of news organizations to subsidize access by users. This argument is unpersuasive. If news organizations are not reaping the economic value generated by investments in fact-gathering, writing, and editorial activities, then, everything else being equal, those efforts must decline, resulting in a fall in the quantity or quality of news coverage. While it is difficult to measure quality objectively, the public appears to believe that the trustworthiness of news content has declined. Polls find that the average level of trust in the news in various countries has fallen and is especially low in the case of news that is accessed through search engines or social media sites.[49] Far from benefiting the public—as commentators who prioritize access over incentives would argue—the erosion of copyright protections has potentially harmed the public by inducing news coverage that may be of lower quantity and quality (whether measured imperfectly by accuracy, depth, and breadth of coverage) as compared to institutional environments characterized by more robust levels of legal and technological exclusivity. This outcome raises significant policy concerns not only as a matter of economic efficiency, but also as a matter of preserving an informed citizenry that is essential to a well-functioning liberal democracy.

15.4. Reality Bites: Utopian Alternatives to Copyright

Copyright skeptics would insist that there exist alternative mechanisms to support news organizations' production incentives even under a weak-IP regime in which content cannot be securely safeguarded. Two main arguments were initially proposed by IP-skeptical academics, policy advocates, and the tech industry, which insisted that copyright (or at least, robust copyright) was not necessary to support content production incentives in a digital environment. First, it was argued that content production and distribution costs were dramatically lower in a digital environment, in which case the necessary returns required to induce investment were reduced. Second, it was argued that the revenue streams that were still necessary to support content production could be secured through mechanisms other than IP rights (principally, through ad-based revenue models).

Neither argument is persuasive upon closer examination.

Let's start with the first argument. The costs of a news organization can be allocated among content production (news gathering, verification, and editorial) and distribution activities. While it is true that reproduction and distribution costs are dramatically reduced relative to a physical marketplace, the cost-savings relative to a print publication can be overstated. There are three reasons. First, legacy newspapers usually continue to maintain print operations.[50] (This consideration is not relevant in the case of digital native news sites.) Second, the costs of generating content are largely unchanged by the transition to a digital environment, which does not appreciably lower the costs required to employ skilled personnel for the purposes of gathering information and writing and editing a news article. This is especially true of investigative and other long-form reporting, which has unusually high costs and extended timelines compared to shorter-form reporting. Third, news organizations in a digital environment must make substantial investments in acquiring and maintaining the necessary technological infrastructure and associated personnel to operate effectively in a digital environment. These costs increase if a news organization wishes to sell ads directly, rather than relying on an intermediary, which enables the news site to retain a substantially greater portion of ad revenues.[51] This is partly why local newspapers, which typically cannot bear the costs of assembling the infrastructure required to sell directly to advertisers, have fared especially poorly in the transition to a digital environment.[52]

The second argument fails as well. At the onset of the internet, it was widely argued that content producers could generate revenue streams even in a weak-IP environment by giving away content to generate a user base that could then be used to elicit revenue from advertisers. This argument might appear to be supported by the ad-based business models that have been widely and successfully deployed in broadcast television and radio predating by decades the advent of digital communications. But these are false precedents. These ad-based content markets differ from the ad-based models used by content aggregators since broadcast TV and radio operators enter into licenses with content owners, whereas online news aggregators rely on the fair use exemption to claim that a license is unnecessary (or simply ignore copyright considerations altogether). As a result, these historical ad-based models provided a revenue stream to support continued content production.

That revenue stream is exactly the element that is missing in the digital ecosystem, which therefore lacks a sound economic foundation for a creative ecosystem that maintains a constant stream of original high-cost, high-value content. The market has already proved this point, as demonstrated by the fact that the most successful original-source news websites have adopted complete or partial paywalls, abandoning original efforts to construct a viable content business model that only sourced payments from advertisers, while in some cases making additional recourse to philanthropic support from foundations or extremely wealthy individuals. It is hard to find a more compelling rebuttal of the widely held view in academic and policy circles that exclusivity (or at least, a robust form of exclusivity) is unnecessary to support the production of creative output in digital environments.

15.5. The New Patronage Model

In the absence of a robust property-rights foundation to secure revenues from the sale of news content, the digital news market has been compelled to adopt two strategies to preserve economic viability.

First, as discussed previously, some news websites have shifted from mostly ad-based giveaway models to mostly or entirely subscription-based delivery models. This model appears to work effectively for a small number of specialized business news publications that appeal to higher-income readerships. However, as noted previously, available evidence indicates that most readers (and especially younger readers) are unwilling to purchase a subscription for news. This is consistent with widely reported findings that news feeds on open-access social media platforms such as Facebook, Instagram, X (formerly Twitter), and Google are among the most common sources of news. Surveys by the Reuters Institute for the Study of Journalism found that, in 2013, 69% of U.S. respondents reported using online media as a news source each week, as compared to 47% for print; in 2022, those values had changed to 67% and 15%, respectively.[53] Additionally, in the 2022 survey, respondents aged 18–24 expressed a preference for accessing news through social media and search sites, rather than news-specific websites or apps.[54] More recently, subscription models have emerged to support sites managed by individual journalists or commentators who use platforms such as Substack, or digital native sites that focus on highly specialized areas of interest to certain audiences. Notwithstanding these limited pockets of success, it remains the case that subscription-based business models appear unable to support general news sites that seek to attract a broad user base.

Second, news publications have sought various forms of sponsorship from philanthropic or corporate interests to cover at least a portion of the missing revenue stream lost to widespread unauthorized usage. More specifically, the news industry now sometimes makes recourse to patronage-type arrangements to generate the revenue streams required to support the costs involved in the production and distribution of high-quality news content in a digital environment. These arrangements encompass acquisitions of news organizations by extremely wealthy individuals (such as the acquisition in 2013 of the *Washington Post* by Jeff Bezos, the founder of Amazon), financial grants from philanthropic foundations,[55] or nonprofit consortia that support investigative journalism projects,[56] and financial support from leading search engines and online content aggregators.

Having successfully pursued a legal strategy to impede the robust enforcement of copyright, which undermines the direct monetization models on which the news industry had relied, digital aggregators have been compelled to fund and support alternative financing, production, and distribution models to sustain a robust flow of news content. It appears that Facebook (Meta Platforms) and Google (Alphabet) are now among the largest sources of philanthropic funding for the journalism industry. As of late 2020, the Tow Center for Digital Journalism reported that Facebook and Google had collectively committed $816 million in total to support digital journalism.[57] Table 15.1 provides a list of Google's and Facebook's known monetary grants or commitments to the media and journalism industry since 2011. The list does not purport to be comprehensive. Unless otherwise indicated, all dollar amounts reflect commitments; information concerning amounts actually granted is incomplete.[58]

Google's initial news-funding initiative targeted European media or media-related organizations through the Digital News Initiative (DNI), with a focus on projects to develop data-analysis methods, automated content production, and related technologies for improving content production and monetization in a digital environment.[59] In 2018, Google announced a $300 million commitment to the Google News Initiative, a worldwide

Table 15.1 Philanthropic Commitments by Google and Facebook to Digital Journalism (Selected, 2013–Present)

Years	Funder	Program	Geographic Coverage	Commitment
2013–2015	Google/Alphabet	Digital Publishing Innovation Fund	France	€60 million (granted)
2015–2019	Google/Alphabet	Digital News Initiative	Europe	€150 million (granted)
2018–present	Google/Alphabet	Google News Initiative	Worldwide	$300 million
2019–present	Facebook/Meta Platforms	Meta Journalism Project	Worldwide	$300 million; additional $100 million committed in 2020

Notes: Unless otherwise indicated, the table does not reflect the extent to which committed amounts in the bottom two rows have been granted and disbursed.

Sources: Associated Press 2013; Brown 2019, 2020; Google News Initiative 2020, 2021.

extension of the DNI, with a similar focus on promoting technical and business-model innovation in news gathering, analysis, and distribution.[60] By contrast, Facebook has focused its grants on supporting local journalism, which has been impacted most adversely by the digital transition. In 2020, Facebook announced $100 million in grants to local news organizations as part of the Facebook (now known as the Meta) Journalism Project, in addition to an existing $300 million commitment.[61]

Patronage and sponsorship mechanisms for supporting digital news production constitute second-best adaptations to an environment in which property-rights arrangements are insecure and news organizations are unable to capture the value generated by investment in news production and distribution. These mechanisms necessarily rely on the profit-motivated interests or ideological predilections of large corporations, well-endowed foundations, governments, or wealthy individuals, which may imperil the editorial autonomy of media organizations. The end result is ironic. The same firms that have led advocacy efforts to weaken copyright protections in digital markets are now among the largest patrons of digital journalism. News producers are now reliant to some extent on the aggregators that have promoted the weak-IP regime that (among other factors) renders those producers unable to generate the revenues necessary to cover the costs required to produce high-quality news coverage.

15.6. Closing Thoughts

At the onset of the internet, an IP-skeptical consensus envisioned a digital forum of vigorous news reporting that would virtually eliminate access costs without any diminution in the quantity and quality of news output. Real-world markets have declined to conform to these utopian speculations. The absence of an effective legal mechanism to regulate access to news content has undermined the ability of many news producers to capture sufficient returns to meet the test of economic viability. This development is not only an economic loss but a social loss with significant implications given the important role played by an independent press in a liberal democracy. While patronage mechanisms can mitigate the adverse effects in output that can arise in a weak-IP environment for news production, they are no more than a second-best mechanism that cannot rival the economic and therefore editorial independence the press can enjoy in a stronger-IP environment. While subscription models may offer a viable solution for specialized news segments, they raise access concerns and do not appear to function effectively in general news segments. Barbara Ringer, a Register of Copyright, communicated eloquently the extent to which a robust free press relies on robust copyright protections: "Freedom of speech and freedom of the press are meaningless unless authors are able to create independently from control by anyone, and to find a way to put their works before the public."[62] In what may ultimately be its greatest failing, the popular rush to dismantle copyright among much of the academy, judiciary, and the broader public has overlooked this critical relationship between property rights and intellectual and political freedom.

PART V
REMAKING IP RIGHTS

This book has provided a political-economic account for the across-the-board reduction in the strength of IP protections in content and technology markets over approximately the past quarter-century. This interest-group analysis suggests that the widely applauded shift toward weak IP protections has disserved the public interest by undermining the ability to form markets in content and technology assets, which in turn adversely impacts individuals and entities that monetize innovation through stand-alone transactional mechanisms. This final part looks forward and considers efforts and proposals to rectify the persistent "IP deficit" in creative and technology environments. Specifically, I discuss how content markets have developed technological and contractual substitutes to promote the formation of markets in digital content assets, even in the continuing absence of secure formal IP protections. I also set forth a simple set of proposals to restore the robust property-rights baseline that is necessary to sustain a robust flow of creative and technological innovation in the digital ecosystem.

16

The Inevitability of Property Rights

Since the advent of digital technologies for replicating and distributing content, it has been widely argued that IP rights, or at least robust IP rights, are no longer necessary to support creative output. The purported irrelevance (or limited relevance) of property rights has been advanced by scholarly commentators, policy advocates, and much of the tech business community, as the intellectual basis for disfavoring robust enforcement of copyright against digital intermediaries that facilitate mass infringement. In this chapter, I show that this proposition is challenged by the evolution of business models used in digital content markets. Specifically, I show that in markets for musical content and short-form video content, leading intermediaries have been compelled to adopt some form of property rights—understood broadly to encompass technological and contractual mechanisms to establish exclusivity over intangible assets—to provide remuneration to content producers and sustain a robust flow of high-value creative output. Far from being irrelevant, as asserted by academic commentators and thought leaders, property rights (whether implemented formally or informally) have proven to be essential in maintaining the robust flow of content that drives a well-functioning creative economy.

16.1. The Persistent IP Deficit

Property rights are typically associated with formal legal entitlements, such as property deeds and titles, issued by governmental authorities. However, as institutional economists have long understood, property rights can be understood functionally as any mechanism through which individuals or entities can restrain unauthorized usage by third parties of a particular asset.[1] Hence, even in a jurisdiction that lacks a formal property registry (or has a registry but legal enforcement is not feasible), the occupant of a piece of land can assert a de facto property right that enables it to regulate usage by third parties, so long as it can achieve this objective through the use of other

The Big Steal. Jonathan M. Barnett, Oxford University Press. © Oxford University Press 2024.
DOI: 10.1093/oso/9780197629529.003.0017

legal rights, security measures, or business relationships. As is also the case with a formal property right, the strength of a holder's functional property right will depend on the tools it has available to block or otherwise regulate unconsented usage and the investments made by the holder in acquiring and implementing those tools. In the aggregate, the effective level of property rights protection in any particular market will be a function of both formal property rights issued by the state and informal property-like mechanisms developed by the market, in each case depending on holders' capacities to enforce those "rights" against third-party users.

This point is important in assessing the "IP deficit"—that is, the difference between the practically available level of IP coverage and the socially efficient level of IP coverage—under which innovators operate in any particular content or technology market. Suppose it is determined that the existing level of formal copyright protection (or more precisely, the practically enforceable level of copyright protection) in the software market is insufficient to deter high piracy rates and to support incentives to invest in software development. Based solely on this observation, it would not be persuasive to conclude that it is necessary to strengthen formal copyright protection to cure the incentive shortfall and mitigate underinvestment in software development. That is because the software industry has developed an extralegal strategy that partially corrects for limitations on the use of copyright to deter piracy. Specifically, developers have largely migrated away from distributing software through physical media or digital files, which are easily copied, and instead principally distribute software through the "software as a service" (SaaS) model. The SaaS model (which encompasses apps in a smartphone or other computing devices) frustrates piracy because the provider can deny access at any time and will do so as soon as a contractually required payment is not made. While this mode of distribution has important business and technological advantages (specifically, it enables the provider to frequently update its service, customize service and pricing for different users, and technologically enforce the terms of the governing license), it also offsets the practical challenges to enforcing formal property rights over software in the face of mass infringement.

It is important to note, however, that the SaaS model only *partially* mimics copyright protection in a hypothetical world of perfect enforcement. This is because the SaaS model cannot mimic the "trade-ability" of a formal property right. This characteristic is critical because it enables holders *to divorce control over an intangible asset from use of the asset*, which in turn enables an abundance of financing, licensing, assignment, and other value-creating transactions that would otherwise be infeasible. Without this characteristic, particular content or technology markets might still deliver substantial returns to individuals and firms engaged in innovation activities, so long as innovators have the technical means to deny access to non-paying users. However, the potential size of the market would be substantially limited— and therefore the funds available to support innovation would be substantially limited—since innovators could not enter into business-to-business relationships or partnerships with investors, lenders, or other firms for which denial of access is generally an inadequate mechanism for assuring exclusivity over the innovation asset.

In short, *it is the market-determined combination of formal IP rights, technological tools, and contractual instruments that unlocks the maximal value embedded in an innovation asset.* This point can be illustrated by the remarkable turnaround of the Marvel franchise.[2] In 1996, Marvel had entered corporate reorganization in the wake of the decline of its then-principal market, print comic books. As part of its restructuring, Marvel decided to shift strategy and attempt to cultivate the commercial value of its comic book characters by entering the motion picture market. To do so, it entered into a series of transactions that relied on Marvel's copyright interests in its portfolio of characters. Initially, Marvel entered into licensing agreements with major production studios, which produced successful motion pictures featuring Marvel characters in the early 2000s. Marvel then decided to set up its own studio so it could capture the maximal value from deploying its characters in the motion picture medium. Since this undertaking required significant capital, it entered into a $525 million loan transaction with Merrill Lynch, for which Marvel posted its copyright portfolio as collateral in the event it defaulted on payment. With these funds, Marvel produced several more blockbuster hits and was ultimately acquired by Disney in 2009 for approximately $4 billion.

Marvel's remarkable turnaround in less than 15 years illustrates the critical function played by IP rights, in conjunction with contractual agreements and technological protections, in enabling the holder of an intangible asset to cultivate its commercial value even in cases where exclusivity can be maintained technologically at the final point of consumption. To regulate users' access to a physical movie theater or a streaming service, the holder of a creative property such as a Marvel motion picture relies on technological controls: physical security barriers in the case of a movie theatre and digital security barriers in the case of a streaming service. At the point of sale, these technological (and associated contractual) controls act as the functional equivalent of a property right, which enables the formation of a market that can reflect the value of creative goods through the pricing mechanism. The continued flow of high-value, high-cost content into that market in turn relies on a secure copyright apparatus to block unauthorized copying and distribution. The sequence of production, marketing, and distribution activities that led up to the Marvel theatrical releases—an undertaking that necessitated hundreds of millions of dollars in investment capital—relied on secure expectations by investors, lenders, and other market participants that Marvel would be able to enforce its legal rights to deter unauthorized copying or distribution. Without a robust IP infrastructure, a company like Marvel would have little capacity to raise capital to support the investments necessary to cultivate the value of its intangible assets, which would remain dormant, leaving not only content holders but also consumers worse off as a result.

16.2. The Inevitability of Property Rights

Unlike land or other tangible goods markets, the argument for property rights in intangible goods markets is often not straightforward since individuals and firms may have, or could potentially develop, other mechanisms that can be used to regulate access and capture returns on innovation. Yet there remains a robust case for formal IP rights even in markets in which firms have access to extralegal mechanisms for regulating access by third parties. The reason lies in the fact that any policymaker or outside observer is unable to identify the most efficient combination of property rights, contract, technology, and other mechanisms that individuals and firms can use to extract value most efficiently from intangible assets. A "baseline" of robust formal IP protections—which any owner may choose to waive partially or fully—allows the market to determine the maximally efficient combination of formal and informal property rights for any particular innovation and to continuously adjust that combination in response to changing economic and technological factors. Hence, limitations on IP rights inherently give rise to the risk that an innovator, or the holder of an innovation asset, may be compelled to adopt a second-best business model that does not fully extract the value embedded in an innovation. When IP protections are restored, markets are free to put together any combination of IP rights, contract, and technology to capture returns on innovation, and will through trial-and-error discover the combination that most efficiently extracts value from the underlying asset. This proposition can be illustrated by the evolution of the digital music and short-form video markets.

16.2.1. Digital Music Market

Following the launch of the Napster platform in 1998, copyright protections declined drastically in strength given the inability to enforce copyright against individual users and, even after Napster was shut down by judicial order, to deter the entry of new file-sharing platforms. Unsurprisingly, revenues from sound recordings plummeted in the face of competition from a zero-price alternative. It has been widely observed that some artists operating under this weak-copyright regime could still earn revenues through live performance, which in turn is often used as the basis for the policy conclusion that copyright is unnecessary to incentivize musical production, which can be supported by ticket sales.[3]

That conclusion is premature. This apparently successful adaptation to a weak-copyright environment masks two potentially significant deficiencies.

First, a performance-dependent business model leaves untapped significant additional value that could be extracted through IP-protected sound recordings that are distributed through radio or streaming services or licensed for other uses. A performance-dependent business model precludes the formation of a complete market in the underlying creative asset, which in turn frustrates the formation of financing, distribution, marketing, and other transactions that are predicated on an underlying property right.

Second, the inherently limited number of live-performance venues (in contrast to the theoretically unlimited number of recorded-music titles that can be offered by an online vendor) means that a performance-dependent business model will provide meaningful remuneration to a substantially smaller number of artists, as compared to an environment in which copyright protection over recorded music remains robust. Consistent with this expectation, I have found in previous research that the distribution of live-performance revenues in the U.S. concert market in the post-Napster years tended to skew heavily toward older artists who had already established a "brand" in the pre-digital market under secure copyright protections, which had generated sufficient sound-recording revenues to support substantial marketing expenditures.[4] Other empirical research has similarly found that live-performance revenues for popular music tend to be concentrated among a small handful of superstar artists.[5]

The evolution of the music industry from the "Napster shock" through the present shows that the industry did not recover due only to live-performance revenues, which have always been available as a source of income for performing artists, but rather through the combination of live performance and *licensed* streaming services that deliver remuneration to copyright owners for music played on those services. This is a licensed transaction anchored in the digital performance right provided by the copyright statute. Pioneered by Apple starting with the launch of the iTunes service in 2003, a streaming service relies on a combination of technology, contract, and copyright to protect the exclusivity of its licensed musical assets and to generate revenue from users, which is then split with the record label and the artist. This distribution vehicle, used by leading platforms such as Spotify, Amazon Music, and Apple Music (the successor to iTunes), has delivered significant revenue streams to copyright owners and, through licensing transactions grounded in reasonably secure copyright portfolios, restored the mix of funding from sound recordings and live performance that support production, marketing, and other activities in musical content markets. As shown in Figure 16.1, annual sound recording revenues (which include streaming subscriptions, digital downloads, and physical media) in the U.S. market have substantially recovered from a low of $6.7 billion in 2014 to $14.9 billion in 2021, as

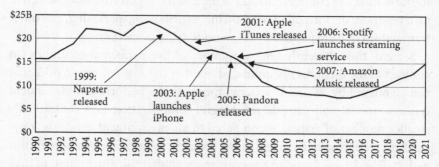

Figure 16.1 Fall and comeback of the recorded music market (1995–2021, U.S. sound recording revenues, $B).

Note: Revenues shown exclude revenues from terrestrial and satellite radio.

Source: Recording Industry Association of America.

compared to the previous inflation-adjusted high of $23.72 billion in 1999, the year in which Napster was launched.[6]

The funding sources that have supported the formation and maintenance of music-distribution platforms have delivered gains to users in the form of improved convenience and improved reliability (and, compared to a physical media environment, confers gains on users by de-bundling the record album and enabling a wider variety of delivery formats and pricing levels). To be clear, industry data show that piracy persists to a significant extent in online music markets, principally through unlicensed ad-supported streaming services and "stream-ripping" services that enable users to extract a permanent copy of digital music from a streaming service.[7] Nonetheless, as compared to the years following the launch of Napster, piracy has been reduced through licensed streaming services that operate within the legal framework of property rights and contract, supplemented by technological safeguards. In a world in which all music would be freely available, the market for online music consumption would most likely have continued to be dominated by ad-based platforms that offer a user experience that is generally characterized by lower convenience, reduced reliability, and, aside from the handful of stars that earn substantial live-performance revenues, limited remuneration for the artists and record labels who supply content to the music ecosystem.

16.2.2. Short-Form Digital Video Market

The evolution of digital markets for short-form video content distributed on platforms such as YouTube, Instagram, and TikTok illustrates that, even in the case of leading digital intermediaries that successfully operate under ad-supported giveaway models, a property-free environment fails to sustain a robust flow of original high-value content to attract the user base that elicits interest from paying advertisers. Somewhat ironically, YouTube, the defendant in the *Viacom v. YouTube* litigation that expanded the contours of the DMCA safe harbor, best demonstrates this proposition since it has launched several initiatives through which payment is made to the owners of existing content or the originators of new content that is displayed on YouTube's site. These payment mechanisms mitigate the distortions arising from the absence of robust IP rights, but nonetheless do not replicate an institutional environment in which copyright protections are securely enforced and asset values are determined through market transactions undistorted by expropriation risk.

16.2.3. Content ID

In 2007, YouTube started developing the Content ID program, approximately one year after it had been acquired by Google. Content ID is an automated detection service that identifies infringing material owned by entities that are eligible to enroll in the service (which include large content owners or individual artists represented by music licensing entities). Content ID provides copyright owners the option to request that YouTube take down detected infringing content, or to leave it on the site but share with the copyright owner a percentage of the advertising revenue attributable to the infringing content.[8] According to YouTube, content owners enrolled in Content ID typically choose the second option.[9] This is consistent with the fact that major record labels and motion picture studios—the large entities that are eligible for the Content ID program—appear to have ceased filing significant numbers of takedown notices with Google (YouTube's parent) as of 2014 (according to data made available by Google),[10] the year in which Viacom and other content owners settled their litigation with YouTube. Effectively, it appears that, for larger content owners, YouTube has agreed to bear part of the burden of detecting infringement through the Content ID program, with the qualification that content owners may elect not to send a takedown notice in exchange for a share of the advertising revenue generated by infringing content.

According to YouTube, it has paid $9 billion to rights holders through the Content ID program since its inception through 2022.[11] Nonetheless, it would be erroneous to conclude that Content ID has restored the economic equivalent of robust property-rights protections for content owners on YouTube. As observed by the U.S. Copyright Office, the effective rates paid by YouTube to content owners (that choose not to take down the infringing content through the Content ID program) are reportedly "far below market rates on competing [streaming] services."[12] As of May 2024, one industry source reported that an artist receives on average $0.00087 per view through YouTube's Content ID, which compares unfavorably with average rates per stream on licensed streaming platforms: $0.01 on Apple

Music, $0.003–$.005 on Spotify, and $0.004 on Amazon Music.[13] As of 2023, another industry source reported the following values: $.0006 per view on YouTube, as compared to $.0043 per stream on Spotify and $.004 on Amazon Music.[14] Based on those 2023 rates, an artist would have to secure the following number of views or streams to earn one dollar: 1,456 views on YouTube, 229 streams on Spotify, and 249 streams on Amazon.[15] Given these compensation levels, it is unsurprising to learn that the total income earned by the overwhelming majority of creators on YouTube is reportedly insignificant.[16]

The apparently low rates paid through Content ID reflect in part the bargaining leverage enjoyed by YouTube (and other unlicensed music sites) in light of the expansive DMCA safe harbor crafted by the courts, which shields YouTube from any material risk of either a shutdown injunction or monetary damages even if it regularly hosts infringing material. In the absence of any such threat, YouTube only has to offer a small to nominal sum to make the content owner better off relative to continuing to incur the costs of making takedown requests that have nominal deterrent value. Hence, even when the copyright owner receives some compensation for the unauthorized use of its content, the price does not reflect market value since the owner has no practical ability to deny access to its content or, so long as the intermediary would likely qualify for the DMCA safe harbor, to secure damages. This also distorts the royalties paid to artists by content distribution sites, such as Spotify, Apple Music, and Amazon Music, which must adjust user fees in light of the availability of zero-price unlicensed streaming services, which in turn depresses the amount paid to artists and other content owners.

To be clear, Content ID represents a meaningful attempt by one of the market's largest digital content intermediaries (and probably the largest single repository of infringing content) to provide an avenue for certain content owners to earn some return on their investments in content production and promotion. Yet, without a credible threat by copyright owners to deny access or secure damages, the royalty rates and other terms agreed upon between content suppliers and digital intermediaries are inherently distorted downward by the availability of free content on unlicensed sites against which the content owner has little legal recourse. Put differently, while Content ID mitigates the absence of robust property rights in digital content markets, it is an imperfect substitute that does not correct the distortion in asset values in a constrained property-rights environment in which content holders have limited capacities to impede unauthorized usage. In short, the IP deficit persists.

16.2.4. Original Content Initiatives

The business history of YouTube validates concerns that ad-based giveaway models, even when supplemented by some payments to content owners through mechanisms such as Content ID, will struggle to support a sustainable flow of high-value content production. YouTube has undertaken several initiatives to support and promote original content production through direct payment to short-form content producers and, concurrently, has launched subscription-based streaming services with originally produced long-form content.

YouTube Originals, which operated during 2016–2022, funded original content production in an unsuccessful effort to build a subscription-based streaming service. YouTube Creators provides individual creators with the ability to create personalized channels through which the creator receives a percentage of the advertising revenues collected by YouTube on the creator's channel. Other short-form video platforms, including Instagram, TikTok, and Spotify, operate similar initiatives in which individual creators are paid for distributing original content through the platform.[17] YouTube Music is a subscription music-streaming service that competes with platforms like Spotify and is fully licensed by content owners. Unlike the free YouTube music service, it offers users features such as ad-free viewing, the ability to build playlists, and a curated user experience—that is, YouTube subscribers pay a fee for convenience features that are not available on YouTube's free, ad-supported, and unlicensed service.

These initiatives, all of which involve payments to content owners and creators, constitute an implicit recognition by one of the largest digital intermediaries that individuals and entities that supply the distribution pipeline with original content must receive meaningful remuneration to maintain incentives to engage in what is often a costly and lengthy process of creative production. While YouTube management has recognized this market reality, it remains overlooked or dismissed by much of the academic and policymaking community, which continues to express skepticism concerning the necessity for copyright or other meaningful property rights in digital content markets.

16.3. Concluding Thoughts

The partial reversion of the music and short-term video content markets to traditional models for funding content illustrates the inherent limitations of the ad-based giveaway model. Unsurprisingly, digital intermediaries have discovered that the content pipeline will "run dry"—or more precisely, will be populated mostly by low-value or already existing content—absent sufficient financial incentives to induce the production of new high-value content. Virtually all content markets that have recovered to some meaningful extent from the "shock" of the digital revolution have done so through a mix of informal and formal property rights that enable the formation of markets in content assets, which in turn generate revenue streams to support content production. As illustrated by the rise of licensed music and video streaming services, the performance of real-world digital content environments shows that well-functioning markets that support a robust flow of content production are generally compelled to assemble a property-rights infrastructure—understood broadly to encompass legal, technological, and contractual devices that enable content owners to regulate and price access to some significant extent. The same argument can be made for licensed platforms in electronic books, digital images, and other creative media. Contrary to the widespread characterization of copyright as an unnecessary "tax" that impedes access for users and delivers windfalls to the content industry, it supplies the property-rights foundation that is the precondition for incentivizing markets to devote capital to the production and distribution of original content, which in turn delivers compensation to the artists that ultimately drive any successful creative ecosystem.

17

Reinvigorating IP Rights and
the Innovation Ecosystem

It is beyond the scope or intention of this book to set forth a comprehensive set of proposals to reinvigorate IP protections in content and technology markets. However, to provide some insight into how IP protections can be bolstered in a constructive manner that promotes the public interest in a sustainably robust innovation ecosystem, I propose in this discussion discrete changes to copyright and patent law that would substantially restore the market's confidence in the security of IP rights in content and technology markets. Enhancing the legal security of IP rights would expand the freedom of action enjoyed by market stakeholders—encompassing innovators, creators, investors, and other entities that support the commercialization process—to devise the most efficient transactional structures for implementing the innovation and commercialization process. These proposed changes share in common the fact that they are administratively straightforward to implement (assuming the emergence of a political coalition to put them into practice) and focus on restoring the most foundational elements of a meaningful property-rights system for a knowledge-based economy.

17.1. Copyright: Enabling Markets in Digital Content

At the onset of the digital economy, it was widely asserted that robust enforcement of copyright would impede the development of the internet by burdening intermediaries and other distribution platforms with the costs and risks associated with the licensing and litigation activities inherent to any formal property-rights system. This view has been reflected in copyright jurisprudence since that time, in particular as illustrated by courts' expansive understanding of the fair use exemption from direct infringement liability and the DMCA safe harbor from indirect infringement liability. Each

The Big Steal. Jonathan M. Barnett, Oxford University Press. © Oxford University Press 2024.
DOI: 10.1093/oso/9780197629529.003.0018

of these safe harbors has been interpreted so broadly that the practical significance of copyright stands in serious risk, especially in light of technological developments that have continuously reduced the costs of quality-equivalent copying and transmission of creative content. As discussed previously in Chapter 5, the implausibly expansive reading of the DMCA safe harbor means that digital platforms are largely immune from liability for engaging in activities that facilitate mass infringement, so long as those platforms conform to a checklist of relatively modest precautions (such as maintaining a notice and takedown mechanism) that have limited deterrent effect against the unlicensed usage of proprietary content. Hence a massive "shadow" pool of pirated content continues to distort pricing in the market for licensed content. The similarly expansive—and similarly contestable—application of the fair use doctrine, through the vehicle of the transformative use concept, not only places at risk the derivative right (as now recognized by the Supreme Court), but also enables mass infringement by institutional users that have no shortage of resources with which to remunerate content originators. The fair use doctrine is now being deployed as a legal defense by some developers and users of generative AI technologies, which copy, aggregate, and make use of textual, visual, and video content, typically without payment to content originators.

At the onset of the digital economy in creative works, this lax approach to copyright enforcement reflected in part the view that more robust enforcement levels could stifle the growth of the internet through costly disputes between rights holders, platforms, and end-users. That technological assumption is challenging to defend today. The emergence of licensed streaming services for audio and video content, such as iTunes and Spotify in the music industry and Netflix and Amazon in the video industry, which can track and price the use of proprietary content through subscription or ad-based models to billions of users around the world, rebut the proposition that the functioning of digital content platforms would be impeded by the "burden" of having to make payments to copyright owners and, in the case of subscription models, collect payments from users. Even in market segments where courts have explicitly exempted certain limited uses of proprietary content, such as the Google Books project, platforms have negotiated agreements with copyright holders to secure consent for more extensive uses, such as the extended previews of books that the Google Books website now shows through the Google Publishers program (which requires the consent of the copyright owner). As discussed in Chapter 15, existing services for licensing digital images similarly support micro-licensing transactions involving visual content, and the long-standing existence of collective licensing entities for public performance rights in musical works, demonstrate the feasibility of mass licensing of copyright-protected works. These old and new licensing models show that the meaningful implementation of copyright protections poses no appreciable burden to content dissemination and user access through digital platforms.

The evolution of the digital content landscape and, in particular, the development of feasible technologies for securing consent from copyright owners, tracking usage, and securing payment from end-users demonstrate that a key factual assumption behind courts' generous interpretations of these two key exemptions from copyright liability is now out of date. Put differently, there is no longer any persuasive case that robust enforcement of copyright in digital content environments would raise transaction costs that would stifle the digital economy. In fact, just the opposite might now be true. If copyright were enforced *more* robustly, then it would bolster the formation of more complete markets and more extensive transactions in digital content assets and, specifically, would enable content creators to secure appropriate remuneration on uses of their content.

There are emergent developments suggesting that the market is already moving in the direction of restoring the functional equivalent of property rights in certain creative segments.

As discussed previously in Chapter 16, certain digital content platforms provide remuneration to individuals who produce and distribute original content on those platforms. These individual creators exert a functional property right by virtue of the fact that they can elect the platforms on which to post their content (or can elect to do so on a single platform exclusively). However, individual creators can only fully capture the value embedded in their content assets in a secure copyright environment (or theoretically, a technological equivalent) in which their content is not exposed to unauthorized copying and distribution once it is posted online.

The function of copyright in the digital environment of the 21st century tracks the core purpose of copyright in its original literary context in the 18th century, as set forth in the Statute of Anne: namely, to provide a property right that enables originators to bargain for a share of the commercial value embedded in a creative asset, whether a text, image, musical work, or other form of expression. In 1710, the Statute of Anne provided authors with a property right that enabled them to bargain on a more level playing field with publishers who had previously enjoyed a collective monopoly over book publishing in England. Today, a narrower understanding of the fair use and DMCA Section 512(c) exemptions from infringement liability would enable rights holders to bargain on a more level playing field with leading digital platforms (including the developers of generative AI technologies) that are in the best position to institute mechanisms to deter mass infringement.

Given current technological capacities to track and therefore price the use of digital content at highly granular levels, existing copyright jurisprudence concerning the scope of the fair use exemption and Section 512(c) safe harbor turns the copyright system on its head by implicitly transferring wealth from individuals and entities that specialize in the origination of content assets to individuals and entities that specialize in the use and consumption of those assets. This is not a plausible infrastructure for a robust and self-sustaining content ecosystem.

17.1.1. Fair Use Defense

In the case of the fair use defense, there are already cases in which courts have rejected attempts by infringers to make use of the defense for obviously self-serving commercial purposes. In a case brought by seven major book publishers against Amazon, the plaintiffs claimed that Amazon's display of proprietary literary content, for purposes of showing captions to accompany the audio narration in its Audible service, constituted copyright infringement. Amazon claimed that the caption feature was protected by fair use, principally on the grounds that it did not divert revenues from the copyright owners' sales of the original work. This argument conveniently ignores the fact that Amazon's use *did* divert licensing income from the rights holder. While the court did not issue a ruling, the settlement resulted in an effective win for the copyright owners since Amazon agreed to pay undisclosed amounts to the plaintiff publishers, and the court issued an injunction barring Amazon from using copyright-protected works in the Audible caption feature without the consent of the rights holder.[1] The terms of the settlement indicate a lack of confidence on the part of Amazon that it would be able to prevail in a fully adjudicated review of its fair use defense.

Amazon's lack of confidence was probably well-founded. In recent cases, courts have rejected attempts by for-profit entities to deploy the fair use defense to protect business models that are predicated on the use of content produced by others. As discussed previously, in *Fox News Network v. TVEyes*, a 2018 decision, the Second Circuit rejected a fair use defense brought by a service that maintained a database consisting of copyright-protected televised news broadcasts, which paying subscribers could then search and view clips lasting up to 10 minutes.[2] In *Dr. Seuss Enterprises v. ComicMix LLC*, a 2021 decision, the Ninth Circuit rejected a fair use defense concerning a "mashup" of material from a Dr. Seuss book and the Star Trek franchise, on the ground that the use was neither transformative nor parodic (as the defense had claimed).[3] In *McGucken v. Pub Ocean Ltd.*, a 2022 decision, the Ninth Circuit rejected a fair use defense brought by a book publisher that had reproduced nature photographs without seeking a license, principally on the grounds that the use was insufficiently transformative and constituted extensive copying of the original work.[4] Also, as discussed previously, in *Warhol Foundation v. Goldsmith*, the Supreme Court in 2023 rejected a fair use defense brought by the Warhol Foundation in a suit alleging infringement of a photograph that was reproduced as part of an illustration by Andy Warhol, principally on the grounds that the use was insufficiently transformative and deprived the artist of licensing income.[5] Clearly there is a growing trend among courts to limit the near-reflexive acceptance of fair use defenses that has characterized much of copyright jurisprudence.

17.1.2. DMCA Safe Harbor

In the case of the Section 512(c) safe harbor, there are no indications at present that courts or legislators are rethinking the prevailing infringer-friendly interpretation of the statutory conditions that must be met to qualify for this liability exemption. However, the Copyright Office has recognized that change is necessary to reinstate a balance between the interests of copyright owners, on the one hand, and the interests of digital platforms, on the other hand. In a study prepared over the course of five years and published in 2020,[6] the Copyright Office gave significant weight to the view that certain prevailing judicial applications of the safe harbor do not conform to congressional intent and do not provide adequate protection for copyright owners against mass infringement. In particular, the report concluded that the operation of Section 512's notice-and-takedown mechanism is "unbalanced" and departs from Congress's intent to achieve a trade-off between the interests of content owners and those of digital intermediaries.[7] In strong language that would be unlikely to appear in most contemporary court opinions (and most law review articles) relating to copyright, the Office stated: "[D]espite the advances in legitimate content options and delivery systems, and despite the millions of takedown notices submitted on a daily basis, the scale of online copyright infringement and the lack of effectiveness of section 512 notices to address that situation remain significant problems."[8]

The report also drew a connection between pervasive user infringement on digital platforms and excessively broad judicial interpretations of certain elements of the safe harbor. Using diplomatic language, the report expressed the view that "current interpretations of the section 512 knowledge requirements for online service providers (OSPs) may be narrower than Congress initially intended,"[9] obviously referring to court decisions that had, as discussed previously, conflated red-flag knowledge with actual knowledge (which in turn makes it difficult for an intermediary to fail the red-flag test).[10] Clearly rejecting the position expressed by some courts that the DMCA absolved intermediaries of any affirmative enforcement burden, the Office's report stated that "Congress' intent [in the DMCA] was to set up a system whereby an OSP *must* act upon any red flag knowledge or actual knowledge that it obtains."[11] To rectify these deficiencies, the report both recommended that courts revisit current interpretations of certain elements of the DMCA safe harbor and discussed (without endorsing) various modifications to the current regime. Those modifications include a "notice and stay down" mechanism that would address the "whack-a-mole" problem in which infringing content repeatedly appears on a platform even if, as required by the DMCA safe harbor, the content owner diligently sends takedown notices and the platform responds expeditiously to those notices. A stay-down obligation (which was adopted by the European Union in 2019[12]) would require intermediaries to take reasonable efforts to deter repeated uploads of infringing materials after receiving the initial notice from the copyright owner.[13]

If policymakers wish to restore a level playing field in interactions between content owners and digital intermediaries, it would be necessary to make changes legislatively to narrow the scope of the DMCA safe harbor as a counterweight to courts' tendencies to adopt an especially broad understanding of this exemption. This type of legislative intervention would help to restore the legal baseline of secure property rights that can support the development of a more complete transactional infrastructure for efficiently financing, distributing, and pricing digital content assets.

17.2. Patents: Restoring the Injunction Backstop

In any recognizable form of a market economy grounded in secure property rights, the injunction remedy is of critical importance since it provides the legal basis for the pricing mechanism that allocates resources based on the competitive forces of supply and demand. If the holder of an asset cannot credibly threaten to stop unauthorized use through legal or technological means, then the asset's pricing will be discounted to reflect the effective lack of exclusivity. In turn, distorted asset prices suppress efficient transactions and discourage investors from placing capital at risk. This common-sense relationship between the security of property-rights and the supply of investment capital implies that any IP system that does not provide injunctive relief against adjudicated infringers will discourage investment in innovation projects, unless the innovator has technological or other mechanisms to adequately deter unauthorized usage or otherwise extract positive returns.

This is the current state of affairs in the U.S. patent system in significant segments of the innovation economy since the Supreme Court's 2006 decision in *eBay Inc. v. MercExchange LLC*, or at least the accumulation of post-*eBay* case law that has interpreted the decision as having granted courts authority to deny injunctions in a broad range of circumstances. The effective withdrawal of injunctive relief now impacts infringement litigation brought by patent licensing entities (the original target of the *eBay* decision), the holders of standard-essential patents in electronics markets, and, in many courts, the holder of a patent that covers a single component in a multi-component product or system.

It is often objected that the *eBay* decision does not adversely impact the innovation ecosystem because patent owners can still collect damages from adjudicated infringers. This objection is unpersuasive for three reasons.

First, this objection ignores the fact that the patent owner must endure a lengthy and costly litigation to secure damages and, in many if not most cases, will not recover its legal fees. For patent owners that lack sufficient litigation resources, the theoretical possibility of securing damages in lieu of an injunction has little practical meaning, although this predicament can sometimes be mitigated by the availability of third-party litigation funding. Second, this objection ignores the fact that, in a legal regime in which infringers do not fear being subject to a "shutdown" injunction, well-resourced infringers often have no rational incentive to take a license from, or settle with, the patentee. So long as the likelihood of being found liable for willful infringement (which can trigger up to treble damages) is sufficiently low, an infringer may determine that its preferred strategy is to incur legal fees in exchange for the opportunity to invalidate the patent or secure a below-market royalty if the patent owner is willing to settle to avoid further costs and delay. Third, in a legal regime in which injunctive relief is chronically denied, the accuracy of courts' reasonable royalty damages determinations would be impacted adversely since those determinations often rely on evidence of royalties negotiated in comparable licenses. Yet, in a world in which injunctive relief is generally not granted, all such royalties would be discounted to reflect the fact that the patent owner, especially if it is not especially well-resourced, may lack a credible threat to litigate and may therefore agree to a royalty that understates the intrinsic value of the patented technology.

The low likelihood of injunctive relief for significant categories of patent owners under the *eBay* regime has ramifications for every licensing or set-tlement negotiation between those patent owners and actual or potential infringers. Under that regime, infringers have no meaningful risk of being subject to injunctive relief so long as they refrain from actions that could be deemed to constitute willful infringement (which requires meeting a de-manding standard of "intentional and willful infringement"[14]) and therefore face a worst-case scenario of having to pay reasonable royalty damages that are designed to mimic the royalty that would have been paid in the event of a voluntary transaction between licensor and license. As discussed previously in the context of standard-essential patents in Chapter 10, if the infringer has ample resources to fund a protracted litigation and there is a sufficiently low likelihood of injunctive relief, then its preferred strategy is to make use of the patented technology and prompt the patent owner to seek remuneration through the costly and delayed process of litigation. The incentive to infringe is even stronger if the patent owner is a smaller entity that lacks resources to support a protracted litigation, or the patent covers a technology that is rap-idly depreciating due to a fast pace of technological advance in the relevant industry. This implicit license to infringe runs counter to the fundamental purpose of the patent system.

Assuming the Supreme Court is unwilling to reverse *eBay* or to clarify that the decision was not intended to upset the historical presumption in favor of injunctive relief (as had been communicated in the concurrence to *eBay* by Chief Justice Roberts and Justice Ginsburg[15]), the simplest step to restore an undistorted playing field between patent owners and infringers would be a legislative amendment providing that, in the event a patent owner defends the presumption of patent validity and demonstrates infringement, a court must assume that irreparable harm would be caused by continuing infringement. That presumption would satisfy the predicate conditions in most cases for issuing an injunction under the existing four-factor test set forth in *eBay*. In fact, Congress made just such a change in a 2021 amendment to the federal trademark statute, providing that plaintiffs are "entitled to a presumption of irreparable injury" upon a finding of likelihood of success on the merits of a trademark infringement claim.[16] The amendment was made to overrule court decisions that had applied *eBay* to trademark cases and upended trademark owners' traditional expectations that adjudicated infringers would be subject to injunctive relief.

This change is unlikely to unleash a wave of patent trolls that abuse the patent system for opportunistic purposes. As in other areas of civil litigation, courts already have at their disposal multiple tools (including fee-shifting and other penalties) to mitigate the incidence of such behavior. It would be expected that courts would make vigorous use of those tools to deter opportunistic patent litigation even under a regime in which the presumption of injunctive relief had been restored. Moreover, courts would retain the ability (as they had prior to the *eBay* decision) to delay issuance of an injunction when demanded by the "public interest" in exceptional circumstances involving matters such as public health or national security. This is the case in Germany: while courts have discretion to deny injunctions in certain cases of hardship (and were given expanded discretion under a legislative amendment in 2021), courts do not typically make use of that exception and injunctions typically follow a finding of validity and infringement.[17]

17.3. Concluding Thoughts

It is widely understood that private interests seek economic and other advantages by securing and expanding legal entitlements from the state. Academic commentators and policy advocates have applied this standard presumption to IP rights, which has translated into a widely held presumption that the pursuit of broader IP rights reflects the pursuit of monopoly rents at the expense of the public interest. The successful effort to narrow IP rights in the U.S. innovation economy over the past two decades presents an unconventional case in which competitive advantages have been secured by efforts to *weaken* a legal entitlement—specifically, the legal exclusivity associated with a patent or copyright. Specifically, aggregators, distributors, and other net-IP users have sought (mostly successfully) to erode IP protections as a means to reduce the costs incurred to acquire technology inputs, which in turn can raise entry barriers to innovation specialists that rely on IP rights to capture returns on R&D investments and artists that rely on IP rights to capture returns on creative investments. If that is the case, then the public interest demands taking action to restore the security of IP rights in content and technology environments, which will expand the market's ability to design the most efficient transactional structures to fund and sustain the innovation and commercialization process. In this chapter, I have identified policy changes to rectify some of the most glaring departures from a reasonable baseline of IP protection. It is hoped that this book will provide the basis for serious consideration of these proposals and other steps that can restore a robust property-rights foundation for today's knowledge-based economy.

Conclusion

As a matter of political economy, the critical question in IP policy is whether the influence exerted by private interests over the trajectory of IP rights—as implemented by the legislature, courts, intellectual property offices, and antitrust agencies—intersects with the public interest in enabling the market to efficiently allocate resources to innovation activities. Almost inevitably, depending on the balance of power between innovators and implementers— that is, between entities that mostly develop and entities that mostly use innovations—in influencing the strength of IP protections made available by the state, we can expect periodic divergence toward either inefficiently weak or strong levels of IP coverage. This book has provided an account of a dramatic swing of the pendulum in this balance of power during a critical turning point in U.S. intellectual property history, running approximately from the early 1980s through the present.

This period is unique because it exhibited a legal response to technological "shocks" in both content and technology markets that provided new opportunities for technological and creative innovation, while raising challenges to the enforcement of IP rights that support a well-functioning market in financing, producing, and distributing intangible assets. In both patent and copyright law, the judiciary initially responded to the emergence of these new technologies by bolstering IP rights as preferred by innovators and the holders of innovation assets. In the life sciences, the judiciary responded to the emergence of biotechnological innovations in the 1982 *Chakrabarty* decision, which extended patent protection to those innovations and, as a result, enabled innovators and investors to cultivate this transformative technology through licensing, joint ventures, and other transactions involving differently specialized firms, institutions, and individuals. This decision was reinforced by concurrent policy actions that ended a multi-decade period during which patents had faced a hostile enforcement climate, including enactment of the Bayh-Dole Act in 1980, establishment of the Federal Circuit in 1982, and a shift in antitrust case law and agency guidelines that substantially expanded IP owners' freedom of action in licensing transactions. In

The Big Steal. Jonathan M. Barnett, Oxford University Press. © Oxford University Press 2024.
DOI: 10.1093/oso/9780197629529.003.0019

content markets, the judiciary responded to the emergence of peer-to-peer file-sharing sites, and the rapid explosion of mass infringement, in the 1998 *Napster* decision and the 2005 *Grokster* decision, which bolstered copyright protections for content assets in the face of technological changes that dramatically weakened the ability to enforce those rights.

These decisions elicited a vigorous critique from scholarly commentators, advocacy groups, and substantial segments of the tech business community. According to this critique, the judiciary's actions had disserved the public interest by favoring private business interests—principally, "Big Pharma" in patent law and "Big Media" in copyright law—through "excessive" levels of IP protection that purportedly enabled those interests to extract monopoly profits at the expense of consumers and to impose litigation and licensing burdens on subsequent innovators.

This critique of robust enforcement of patent and copyright law still prevails as conventional wisdom in much of scholarly and other commentary on IP policy. In copyright law, this critique has resulted in a body of case law that, since approximately the mid-2000s, has dramatically expanded the scope of the fair use exemption and adopted a broad understanding of the DMCA safe harbor that is difficult to reconcile with statutory intent. In patent law, this critique has resulted in substantial limitations on the availability of injunctive relief since the Supreme Court's *eBay* decision in 2006, establishment of the PTAB in 2012 and expanded opportunities to challenge the validity of issued patents, an antitrust campaign to limit the enforcement and licensing of standard-essential patents in wireless communications, and an ongoing initiative to cut back on the effective scope of the Bayh-Dole Act in the pharmaceutical sector.

In hindsight, it should not be surprising that the academic and ideological critique of patent and copyright law was so readily adopted by the courts, legislators, and agencies. For policymakers, that widely asserted critique sent a powerful signal concerning the perceived dominant policy preference among policymakers' constituencies, especially concerning copyright protections in digital content markets and patent protections in pharmaceutical markets that are disfavored by consumers. Only a policymaker with a strong ideological or intellectual commitment to robust IP rights would have rationally forfeited political goodwill to resist this apparent consensus across the academy and much of the public.

The result today is a truncated IP infrastructure that impedes monetization by individuals and entities (encompassing businesses and research institutions) that specialize in innovation but lack capacities independently to convert innovations into commercially viable products and services. In wireless communications markets, barriers to patent enforcement endanger licensing structures that efficiently disseminate foundational technologies among device producers, while advantaging a handful of large integrated producers that are net-technology users or can extract returns on innovation through end-to-end technological ecosystems. In the biopharmaceutical markets, which raise not only economic but also public-health implications, threats to patent protections and other IP rights pose the most serious potential risks to innovation incentives since even large integrated firms rely on legal exclusivity to attract the capital required to support the costly and lengthy process of drug development, testing, and production. If left unmitigated by legal action or technological controls, mass infringement will continue to endanger the economic viability of content market segments that require significant capital investment. While some digital content markets have made significant progress in constructing synthetic property rights through technological mechanisms, significant levels of mass infringement persist and cast a shadow over licensed content markets. This gap in property-rights coverage (whether construed in legal or technological terms) in content markets will expand as generative AI models are deployed more widely in creative media.

Conventional wisdom has advanced the view that the IP rights infrastructure in U.S. content and technology markets was strengthened excessively under the influence of business interests that sought to extract monopoly rents from individual consumers and to raise entry barriers to the competitive threats posed by subsequent innovators. As this book has shown in detail, just the opposite has occurred. A weakened property-rights infrastructure, challenged by technological developments that facilitated infringement and policy actions that impeded enforcement, has produced an institutional environment in which the enforcement of IP rights is a challenging and often futile endeavor, especially for patent owners with limited resources or copyright owners facing mass infringement. This effective devaluation of IP-protected assets distorts innovation markets by advantaging digital intermediaries and other entities that operate under integrated business models that integrate content and technology assets into a complex products and services ecosystem. Far from promoting the public interest, this strategic erosion of the property-rights infrastructure behind the knowledge economy threatens to displace the innovators that stand at the heart of a robust technology and creative ecosystem.

Notes

Introduction

1. Pareles 2002.
2. For the most well-known contemporary example, see Boldrin and Levine 2008.
3. 138 S. Ct. 1365, 1375 (2018). The Court qualified this conclusion by stating that its "decision should not be misconstrued as suggesting that patents are not property for purposes of the Due Process Clause or the Takings Clause," id. at 1379.
4. 547 U.S. 388 (2006).
5. Barlow 1994.
6. Brand can be viewed using the phrase at a hackers' conference in 1984, at https://www.gettyima ges.com/detail/video/at-the-first-hackers-conference-in-1984-steve-wozniak-and-news-foot age/146496695.
7. Schiff 1971.
8. Plant 1934.
9. Breyer 1970.
10. Khan 2004; 2005, 280–83.
11. For examples of this opinion as expressed by legal academics, see Benkler 2006; Boyle 2008; Lessig 2001, 2004; Litman 2001; Patry 2009; Samuelson 1996; Vaidhyanathan 2001.
12. For the initial presentation of this argument, see Barnett 2018.
13. Sources: SEC filings or annual company reports.
14. Solow 1957.

Chapter 1

1. For classic sources, see Buchanan and Tullock 1962; Downs 1957; Olson 1971; Tullock 2005.
2. A similar term in the political science literature is "expediency point," which denotes the policy position "most likely to optimize future reelection chances"; see Stimson, Mackuen, and Erikson 1995, 544.
3. For the classic analysis, see Olson 1971.
4. Usselman 1991, 1047–75; 1999, 76–80; 2002, 170, 174–75, 186–89.
5. Allison, Dunn, and Mann 2007, 1583–86; Barnett 2021a, 142–44.
6. *eBay Inc. v. MercExchange LLC*, 547 U.S. 388, 396 (2006) (injunction); *Bilski v. Kappos*, 561 U.S. 593 (2010) (patentable subject matter); *Mayo Collaborative Services v. Prometheus Labs, Inc.*, 566 U.S. 66 (2012); *Association for Molecular Pathology v. Myriad Genetics, Inc.*, 569 U.S. 589 (2013) (patentable subject matter); *Alice Corp. Pty. Ltd. v. CLS Bank International*, 573 U.S. 208 (2014) (patentable subject matter).
7. DiMasi, Grabowski, and Hansen 2016.
8. Landau 2000, 35–36, U.S. Copyright Office n.d.
9. U.S. Copyright Office 2011, 5.
10. Sonny Bono Copyright Term Extension Act, Pub. L. No. 105-298, 112 Stat. 2827 (1998).
11. See Gray 2020; Levine 2011; Taplin 2017, who recognize to varying degrees that weakening copyright protections favor the interests of digital platforms or other content aggregators.
12. For widely cited works that express these views, see Boyle 2008; Benkler 2006; Lessig 2001; Litman 2001; Vaidhyanathan 2001.
13. Stop Online Piracy Act, H.R. 3261, 112th Cong. (2011).
14. PROTECT IP Act of 2011, S. 968, 112th Cong. (2011).
15. Kane 2012.
16. Bayh-Dole Act, 35 U.S.C. §§ 200–212, Pub. L. No. 96-517, 94 Stat. 3015.
17. Federal Courts Improvement Act of 1982, Pub. L. No. 97-164, 96 Stat. 25.
18. On this period, see Barnett 2021a, 2021b.

19. Sources: company annual reports.
20. I thank Erika Lietzan for observations on this point.

Chapter 2

1. This paragraph is informed by the facts as found in *U.S. v. Microsoft Corp.*, 84 F.Supp.2d 9 (D.D.C. 1999).
2. Complaint, *U.S. v. Microsoft, Inc.*, Civil Action No. 98-1232, at 5 (D.D.C. May 18, 1998) (stating that Microsoft spent "hundreds of millions of dollars to develop, test, and promote Internet Explorer").
3. Klein 2001, 49. See also Quain 1996 (reporting a price of $49 for the Navigator browser as of 1996).
4. Windrum 2004.
5. Wallack 1998.
6. Corcoran 1998.
7. Laplante 2015, 186.
8. Eadicicco 2015; Levy 2011, 215–16.
9. This paragraph relies on Barnett 2011, 1917–18.
10. Statista, Global market share held by mobile operating systems from 2009 to 2023, by quarter.
11. Hoffman 2015, 31–36; Sturgeon and Kawakami 2011, 142.
12. Gannes 2015.
13. Gu et al 2020; Wortham and Helft 2009.
14. Gibbs 2015.
15. Complaint, *U.S. v. Microsoft, Inc.*, Civil Action No. 98-1232 (D.D.C. May 18, 1998).
16. Klein 2001, 48.
17. Lohr 1998.
18. Rosoff 2011.
19. This point is often attributed to Arrow 1962.
20. In the video recording of Brand's remarks (available at https://www.gettyimages.com/detail/video/at-the-first-hackers-conference-in-1984-steve-wozniak-and-news-footage/146496695), he states: "On the one hand, information wants to be expensive, because it's so valuable.... On the other hand, information wants to be free, because the cost of getting it out is lower and lower all the time. So you have these two fighting against each other."
21. For a discussion of various open-source licenses, see Fink 2003; Rosen 2005.
22. See, e.g., Benkler 2006; Lessig 2001; Raymond 1999.
23. For a review of this literature, see Barnett 2010, 1785–86.
24. The following discussion relies in part on Barnett 2010, 1804–13; 2016, 26–27.
25. CNET 2002.
26. Kroah-Hartman, Corbet, and McPherson 2009.
27. Capek et al. 2005, 257 n.4.
28. Red Hat 2019.
29. For detailed discussion, see Barnett 2011, 1905–6.
30. Ibid., 1905.
31. Lobbying Disclosure Act of 1995, as amended by the Honest Leadership and Open Government Act of 2007, Pub. L. No. 104-65, 109 Stat. 69.
32. Information sourced from organization website or IRS Form 990.
33. Levine 2016; Roberts 2016.
34. Letter from Ralph Oman and Marybeth Peters 2016.
35. Pallante 2011.
36. Pallante 2013, 327–28.
37. Pub. L. No. 116-260, Div. Q, Title II, § 212, 134 Stat. 2176, codified at U.S.C. §§ 1501-1511.
38. Pallante 2014.
39. Pallante 2016.
40. Kafka 2017.
41. For discussion, see Dippon 2016.
42. Levine 2011, 157.
43. Cleland 2016; Levine 2011, 157–58.
44. Letter from Institute for Policy Innovation 2016.
45. Public Knowledge 2016.
46. Levine 2016.

Chapter 3

1. Sound Recording Act of 1971, Pub. L. No. 92-140, 85 Stat. 39 (Oct. 15, 1971).
2. 17 U.S.C. § 504 (c)(2).
3. Complaint, *A&M Records Inc. v. Napster, Inc.*,114 F. Supp. 2d 896 (No. 3:99-cv-05183-MHP) (N.D. Cal. 2000).
4. *A&M Records, Inc. v. Napster, Inc.*, 114 F.Supp. 2d 896, 927 (N.D. Cal. 2000); *A&M Records, Inc. v. Napster, Inc.*, 239 F.3d 1004, 1029 (9th Cir. 2001).
5. CNNMoney 2000, n.p.
6. *A&M Records, Inc. et al. v. Napster, Inc.*, 284 F.3d 1091 (9th Cir. 2002).
7. Borland 2002, n.p.
8. *UMG Recordings, Inc. v. MP3.com, Inc.*, 92 F.Supp.2d 349, 352 (S.D.N.Y. 2000).
9. 545 U.S. 913 (2005).
10. 464 U.S. 417 (1984).
11. 508 F.3d 1136 (9th Cir. 2007).
12. Bayot 2005.
13. Lessig 2001, 2004.
14. For a leading proponent of this view, see Benkler 2006.
15. Boyle 1988; Woodmansee 1984.
16. Patry 2007–2021. Patry had previously acted as the editor of the Latman copyright treatise; see Latman 1986.
17. Patry 2009, 74.
18. For examples, see Benkler 2006; Ku 2002; Zimmerman 2011.
19. Waldfogel 2011, 1.
20. For a review of these models, see Liebowitz 2005.
21. Hui and Png 2003; Pietz and Waelbroeck 2004.
22. Oberholzer-Gee and Strumpf 2004, 2007.
23. Child 2007.
24. Oberholzer-Gee and Strumpf 2004.
25. Oberholzer-Gee and Strumpf 2005.
26. *Metro-Goldwyn-Mayer Studios, Inc. v. Grokster, Ltd.*, 545 U.S. 913, 962 (2005).
27. For critiques of the OGS study, see Liebowitz 2007, 2010, 2016a, 2016b, 2017; Yager 2010. For a response, see Oberholzer-Gee and Strumpf 2016.
28. The study (Anderson and Frenz 2008) claimed to find that file-sharing had positive (or, in a later published version [Anderson and Frenz 2010], neutral aggregate) effects on purchases of recorded music. However, subsequent researchers (Barker and Maloney 2012) used the same survey data and, once certain omitted portions of the survey data were integrated into the analysis, found that file-sharing had significant adverse effects on music purchases.
29. Liebowitz 2016b.
30. Danaher, Smith, and Telang 2014, 34.
31. Ibid., 43.
32. Oberholzer-Gee and Strumpf 2010, 2016.
33. Smith and Telang 2009. As the authors note, movies are shown on broadcast television at a later stage in a movie's "product lifecycle" and therefore these results do not necessarily indicate the effects of piracy on sales in periods closer to a movie's initial release.
34. Adermon and Liang 2014; Danaher et al. 2013, 2019.
35. See, e.g., Allen and Qian 2009, 144 n.16; Park 2007, 87–90; Travis 2016, 120–21.
36. The original study is Anderson and Frenz 2010; the replication study is Barker and Maloney 2012.
37. See, e.g., Raustiala and Sprigman 2006.
38. 464 U.S. 417 (1984).
39. Litman 2006, 358.
40. Diehl 2012, 153–65.
41. *RealNetworks, Inc. v. DVD Copy Control Association, Inc.*, 641 F.Supp.2d 913, 931–32 (2009).
42. For the classic account, see Levy 2010.
43. This discussion is principally based on Battelle 2005, 75.
44. Brin and Page 1998; Page et al. 1999.
45. Battelle 2005, 123–24.
46. Brin and Page 1998.
47. Battelle 2005, 125.

48. On this point, see Levine 2011, 101.
49. Sorkin and Peters 2006.
50. 676 F.3d 19, 32–33 (2nd Cir. 2012).
51. Healey 2001.
52. Jones 2008, 131–33; Levine 2011, 59; Patry 2009, 8–10.
53. Charny 2006.
54. Sources: Statista, Number of paying YouTube Music and YouTube Premium subscribers worldwide, from 2020 to 2022; Statista, Number of YouTube users worldwide from 2019 to 2028.
55. For the relevant statute, see 17 U.S.C. § 106(4).
56. *Viacom International, Inc. et al. v. YouTube, Inc. et al.*, 940 F.Supp.2d 110, 112–20 (S.D.N.Y. 2013).
57. Levine 2011, 94.
58. Borland 2002.
59. *Metro-Goldwyn-Mayer Studios Inc. et al. v. Grokster, Ltd., et al.*, 545 U.S. 913, 923 (2005).
60. Cuban 2006, n.p.
61. Allison and Van Duyn 2006, n.p.
62. *Viacom Int'l Inc. et al. v. YouTube Inc.*, 940 F.Supp.2d 110, 117 n.3 (S.D.N.Y. 2013).

Chapter 4

1. *Andy Warhol Foundation for Visual Arts, Inc. v. Goldsmith* (S. Ct., May 18, 2023).
2. *Folsom v. Marsh*, 9 F. Cas. 342 (C.C.D. Mass. 1841).
3. Id.
4. 17 U.S.C. § 107 (1982).
5. Id.
6. *Harper & Row v. Nation Enterprises*, 471 U.S. 539 (1984).
7. Id., 545.
8. Id., 562.
9. Id., 566.
10. Netanel 2011, 734.
11. *American Geophysical Union v. Texaco, Inc.*, 60 F.3d 913 (2d Cir. 1992).
12. *Compaq Computer Corp. v. Procone Tech., Inc.*, 908 F.Supp. 1409 (S.D. Tex. 1995).
13. *Lamb v. Starks*, 949 F.Supp. 753 (N.D. Cal. 1996).
14. *Ringgold v. Black Entertainment Television, Inc.*, 126 F.3d 70 (2d Cir. 1997).
15. *Campbell, aka Skyywalker, et al. v. Acuff-Rose Inc.*, 510 U.S. 569 (1994).
16. See, e.g., *Bloom & Hamlin v. Nixon*, 125 F. 977, 978 (C.C. E.D. Pa. 1903); *Jerome H. Remick & Co. v. American Automobile Accessories Co.*, 298 F. 628, 632 (S.D. Ohio 1924), rev'd, 5 F.2d 411 (6th Cir. 1925); *Green v. Minzensheimer*, 177 F. 286 (C.C. S.D.N.Y. 1909).
17. *Campbell, aka Skyywalker, et al. v. Acuff-Rose Inc.*, 510 U.S. 569, 591–92 (1994).
18. See, e.g., Hung 1994; Myers 1996.
19. *Campbell, aka Skyywalker, et al. v. Acuff-Rose Inc.*, 510 U.S. 569, 584, 594 (1994).
20. 471 U.S. 539, 562 (1985).
21. *Campbell, aka Skyywalker, et al. v. Acuff-Rose Inc.*, 510 U.S. 569, 579 (1994).
22. Leval 1990, 1105, 1110, n.29.
23. *Cary v. Kearsley*, [1802] 170 Eng. Rep. 679 (K.B.) 681–82.
24. Leval 1990, 1111.
25. Ibid.
26. Ibid.
27. *Campbell, aka Skyywalker, et al. v. Acuff-Rose Inc.*, 510 U.S. 569, 574 (1994).
28. See, e.g, Loren 1997, 31. For further discussion of these views, see Tushnet 2015, 871–72.
29. Leval 1990, 1112–13 (criticizing *Salinger v. Random House, Inc.*, 650 F. Supp. 413 (S.D.N.Y. 1986) and partially agreeing with *Salinger v. Random House, Inc.*, 811 F.2d 90 (2d Cir. 1987), which had reversed the district court's finding of fair use).
30. Lemley 1997, 1077; Loren 1997, 29.
31. *Harper & Row v. Nation Enterprises*, 471 U.S. 539, 566 (1984).
32. Beebe 2008, 618–20.
33. Netanel 2011, 734, 743–44.
34. Ibid., 742.
35. *Harper & Row v. Nation Enterprises*, 471 U.S. 539, 566 (1984).
36. *Cariou v. Prince*, 714 F.3d 694 (2d Cir. 2013).
37. Id., 707–8.
38. Id., 709.

39. *Cariou v. Prince*, 784 F.Supp.2d 337, 344 (S.D.N.Y. 2011)
40. *Harper & Row v. Nation Enterprises*, 471 U.S. 539, 568 (quoting *Sony Corp. of America v. Universal City Studios*, 464 U.S. 417, 451 (1984)) (my emphasis).
41. Elkin-Koren and Netanel 2020, 17–18.
42. For a comprehensive account, see Gray 2020, 50–54.
43. Elkin-Koren and Netanel 2020, 4–6.
44. Cooke 2017, n.p.
45. Electronic Frontier Foundation n.d.; Hughes 2015, 45.
46. Max Planck Inst. for Innovation & Competition 2014.
47. Berne Convention for the Protection of Literary and Artistic Works, Sept. 28, 1979, 331 U.N.T.S. 21.
48. Copyright Modernization Act of 2012, S.C. 2012, c. 20 (Can.).
49. Anderson 2017, 2021.
50. PWC 2015, 62.
51. Anderson 2021. For the decision, see *York University v. Canadian Copyright Licensing Agency (Access Copyright)*, 2021 SCC 32.
52. *Perfect 10, Inc. v. Amazon.com, Inc. et al.*, 508 F.3d 1146, 1172 (9th Cir. 2007).
53. Cooke 2017, n.p.
54. *Kelly v. Arriba Soft Corp.*, 280 F.3d 934 (9th Cir. 2002), *withdrawn, re-filed at* 336 F.3d 811 (9th Cir. 2003).
55. Hughes 2015, 46–47.
56. Epstein, Landes, and Posner 2013, 1–14.
57. Jeffrey 1995.
58. 464 U.S. 417, 454 (1984).
59. *Universal City Studios v. Sony Corporation of America*, 659 F.2d 963, 967 (9th Cir. 1981).
60. Litman 2006, 366.
61. Ibid., 367–68.
62. Ibid., 366.
63. Ibid., 382.
64. *Harper & Row Publishers Inc. v. Nation Enterprises*, 471 U.S. 539, 566 (1985).
65. For previous discussion of Google's efforts to influence copyright policy, see Gray 2020.
66. *Kelly v. Arriba Soft Corp.*, 336 F.3d 811 (9th Cir. 2003).
67. *Perfect 10, Inc. v. Amazon.com, Inc. et al.*, 508 F.3d 1146 (9th Cir. 2007).
68. *Kelly v. Arriba Soft Corp.*, 336 F.3d 811, 821–22 (9th Cir. 2003).
69. *Perfect 10, Inc. v. Amazon.com, Inc. et al.*, 508 F.3d 1146, 1171–72 (9th Cir. 2007).
70. *Metro Goldwyn Mayer Studios, Inc. v. Grokster, Ltd.*, 545 U.S. 913 (2005).
71. *Perfect 10, Inc. v. Amazon, Inc. et al.*, 508 F.3d 1146, 1172 (9th Cir. 2007).
72. *Authors Guild, Inc. et al. v. HathiTrust et al.*, 755 F.3d 87 (2nd Cir. 2014); *Authors Guild, Inc. et al. v. Google, Inc.*, 804 F.3d 202 (2nd Cir. 2015).
73. Leetaru 2008.
74. Xie and Matusiak 2015, 1–35.
75. Leetaru 2008.
76. *Authors Guild, Inc. et al. v. Google, Inc.*, 770 F.Supp.2d 666, 680–82 (S.D.N.Y. 2011).
77. *Authors Guild, Inc. et al. v. Google, Inc.*, 954 F.Supp.2d 282 (S.D.N.Y. 2013); *Authors Guild, Inc. et al. v. Google, Inc.*, 804 F.3d 202 (2d Cir. 2015).
78. *Authors Guild, Inc. et al. v. Google, Inc.*, 804 F.3d 202, 214–18 (2nd Cir. 2015).
79. *Authors Guild Inc. et al. v. HathiTrust et al.*, 755 F.3d 87, 97–98 (2nd Cir. 2014)
80. *Authors Guild, Inc. et al. v. Google, Inc.*, 804 F.3d 202, 209–10 (2nd Cir. 2015); *Authors Guild, Inc. et al. v. HathiTrust et al.*, 755 F.3d 87, 99–100 (2nd Cir. 2014).
81. See, e.g., American Library Association 2013; Meyer 2015.
82. Brief of Digital Humanities and Law Scholars as Amici Curiae in Partial Support of Defendants' Motion for Summary Judgment, *Authors Guild, Inc. v. HathiTrust*, 902 F. Supp. 2d 445 (2012) (No. 11 Civ 06351 (HB)), 2012 WL 3966152.
83. Eadicicco 2015; Levy 2011, 215–16.
84. Gartner 2018.
85. European Commission 2018, 48–49.
86. Competition & Markets Authority 2022, App. E; Edelman 2014; European Commission 2018, 40, 45–49. For an example of a MADA contract, see Mobile Application Distribution Agreement 2009.
87. European Commission 2018, 40–42.

88. Ibid.
89. *Oracle America, Inc. v. Google Inc.*, 750 F.3d 1339, 1350 (Fed. Cir. 2014).
90. Id.
91. On the distinction between declaring and implementing code, see Oman 2018, 648–51.
92. *Oracle America, Inc. v. Google Inc.*, 750 F.3d 1339 (Fed. Cir. 2014).
93. *Google LLC v. Oracle America, Inc.*, 141 S. Ct. 1183, 1202–4 (2021).
94. *Harper & Row, Publishers, Inc. et al. v. Nation Enterprises et al.*, 471 U.S. 539, 566 (1984).
95. *Google LLC v. Oracle America, Inc.*, 141 S. Ct. 1183, 1206 (2021).
96. Id., 1203–4, 1208.
97. Id., 1203.
98. Id., 1190–91.
99. Competition & Markets Authority 2022, App. E; Edelman 2014; European Commission 2018, 40, 45–49. For an example of a MADA contract, see Mobile Application Distribution Agreement 2009.
100. Amadeo 2018.
101. Open Handset Alliance ("Members"), https://www.openhandsetalliance.com/oha_memb ers.html.
102. Amadeo 2018.
103. Stohr 2021.
104. See, e.g., Carlisle 2021.

Chapter 5

1. Goodman 2012.
2. Kerr 2012.
3. CNN Wire Staff 2012.
4. *Viacom Int'l Inc. et al. v. YouTube, Inc.*, 676 F.3d 19 (2d Cir. 2012); *Viacom Int'l Inc. et al. v. YouTube, Inc.*, 940 F.Supp.2d 110 (S.D.N.Y. 2013).
5. *Authors Guild, Inc. et al. v. Hathitrust* et al., 755 F.3d 87 (2nd Cir. 2014); *Authors Guild, Inc. et al. v. Google, Inc.*, 804 F.3d 202 (2015).
6. Digital Millennium Copyright Act, Pub. L. No. 105-304, 112 Stat. 2860 (codified at 17 U.S.C. §§ 1201–1205 (Supp. IV 1998)).
7. For classic works, see Peltzman 1976; Stigler 1971.
8. For the classic work, see Buchanan and Tullock 1962. For other leading works on rent-seeking, see Ekelund and Tollison 1997; Krueger 1974; Posner 1975.
9. For an extensive (although somewhat one-sided) historical discussion of the negotiation process that resulted in the DMCA, see Litman 2006, 122–51. For a more balanced account, see Levine 2011, 28–34.
10. See, e.g., *Playboy Enterprises, Inc. v. Frena*, 839 F.Supp. 1552, 1559 (M.D. Fla. 1993) (finding operator of dial-up electronic bulletin board liable for infringing Playboy's copyrights in photos that users had uploaded to the site and rejecting fair use defense); *Marobie-FL, Inc. v. National Association of Fire Equipment Distributors and Northwest Nexus*, 983 F.Supp. 1167, 1178–79 (N.D. Ill. 1997) (holding that provider of "host computer" for purposes of online transmission could only have liability if it satisfied the necessary elements of vicarious or contributory theories of indirect infringement).
11. Lehman 1995, 117.
12. Ibid., 122.
13. Levine 2011, 63; U.S. Copyright Office 2020, 17.
14. Levine 2011, 22–24, 29–30.
15. U.S. Congress, House of Representatives 1998, at Part 2, 21.
16. U.S. Copyright Office, "Section 512 Study," https://www.copyright.gov/policy/section512/.
17. U.S. Copyright Office 2020, 1.
18. 17 U.S.C. § 512(c)(1).
19. U.S. Congress, Senate 1998, 40; U.S. Congress, House of Representatives 1998, at Part 2, 48–49.
20. See, e.g., *Columbia Pictures Indus. v. Fung*, 710 F.3d 1020 (9th Cir. 2013).
21. U.S. Department of Commerce 2013, 3.
22. U.S. Copyright Office 2020, 29.
23. U.S. Department of Commerce 2013, 3.
24. Hansell 2000.
25. Ionescu 2009.

26. Trendacosta 2020.
27. See, e.g., Seltzer 2010; Urban and Quilter 2006.
28. 718 F.Supp.2d 514 (S.D.N.Y. 2010)
29. *Viacom Int'l Inc. et al. v. YouTube, Inc. et al.*, 676 F.3d 19 (2nd Cir. 2012).
30. *Viacom Int'l Inc. et al. v. YouTube, Inc. et al.*, 940 F.Supp.2d 110 (S.D.N.Y. 2013).
31. *Viacom Int'l Inc. et al. v. YouTube, Inc., et al.*, 718 F.Supp. 514, 518 (S.D.N.Y. 2010) (quoting Viacom Br., Dkt. No. 186, at 1).
32. Id., 518.
33. Id., 519.
34. Federal Rules of Civil Procedure, Rule 56: Summary Judgment, Fed. R. Civ. P. 56.
35. *Viacom Int'l Inc. et al. v. YouTube, Inc., et al.*, 940 F.Supp.2d 110, 118, 120 (S.D.N.Y. 2013).
36. *Viacom Int'l Inc. et al. v. YouTube, Inc.*, 718 F.Supp. 514, 518 (S.D.N.Y. 2010)
37. Id., 524.
38. 17 U.S.C. § 512(c)(1)(A). Emphasis added.
39. 17 U.S.C. § 512(m)(1).
40. U.S. Copyright Office 2020, 111 n.591.
41. 17 U.S.C. § 512(m)(1), referring to 17 U.S.C. § 512(i)
42. U.S. Congress, House of Representatives 1998, at Part 1, 26.
43. Id., at Part 2, 57. Emphasis added.
44. *Viacom Int'l Inc. et al. v. YouTube, Inc.*, 676 F.3d 19, 31 (2d Cir. 2012).
45. Nimmer & Nimmer § 12B.04(A)(1)(b)(iii) (20220.
46. *UMG Recordings, Inc. v. Veoh Networks, Inc.*, 665 F.Supp.2d 1099, 1108 (C.D. Cal. 2009); *UMG Recordings, Inc. v. Shelter Capital Partners LLC*, 667 F.3d 1022, 1038–37 (9th Cir. 2011).
47. *Viacom Int'l Inc. et al. v. YouTube, Inc.*, 718 F.Supp. 514, 527 (S.D.N.Y. 2010)
48. Nimmer & Nimmer § 12B.04(A)(1)(b)(v)(I) (2022).
49. *Viacom Int'l Inc. et al. v. YouTube, Inc.*, 676 F.3d 19, 35 (2d Cir. 2012).
50. Id.
51. U.S. Copyright Office 2020, 126. Emphasis added.
52. 17 U.S.C. § 512(c)(1)(B).
53. *Viacom Int'l Inc. et al. v. YouTube, Inc.*, 718 F. Supp. 2d 514, 516 (S.D.N.Y. 2010).
54. Report of the House Committee on the Judiciary 1998, pt. 1.
55. *Viacom Int'l Inc. et al. v. YouTube, Inc.*, 676 F.3d 19, 38 (2d Cir. 2012).
56. See, e.g., *UMG Recordings, Inc. v. Shelter Capital Partners LLC*, 667 F.3d 1022, 1029 (9th Cir. 2011).
57. *Viacom Int'l Inc. et al. v. YouTube, Inc.*, 940 F.Supp.2d 110, 117–22 (S.D.N.Y. 2013).
58. *Viacom Int'l Inc. et al. v. YouTube, Inc.*, 718 F.Supp.2d 514, 528 (S.D.N.Y. 2010).
59. See, e.g., *UMG Recording, Inc. v. Shelter Capital Partners LLC*, 718 F.3d 1006, 1030–31 (9th Cir. 2013) (upholding grant of summary judgment under DMCA safe harbor because defendant did not have the "right and ability to control infringing activity" and further holding that the mere ability to remove copyright-protected content is not enough to fall outside this qualifying condition); *Wolk v. Photobucket.com*, 569 Fed. Appx. 51, 52 (2d Cir. 2014) (upholding grant of summary judgment based on DMCA safe harbor because defendant maintained repeat infringer policy, responded to take-down notices, and did not have "right and ability to control infringing activity"); *Capitol Records, LLC et al. v. Vimeo, LLC et al.*, 826 F.3d 78, 99 (2d Cir. 2016) (holding that burden of showing facts to support "red flag" knowledge shifts to plaintiff after defendant claims 512(c) safe harbor and finding that district court used test that would unduly restrict access to the safe harbor); *Capitol Records, LLC et al. v. Vimeo, LLC* et al., 972 F.Supp.2d 500, 522–23 (S.D.N.Y. 2018) (holding that the mere fact that defendant's employees interacted with videos on the defendant's site containing "recognizable copyrighted songs" did not constitute "red flag" knowledge).
60. 844 F.3d 79 (2nd Cir. 2016).
61. Weiss 2000.
62. *EMI Christian Music Group, Inc. v. MP3 Tunes, LLC*, 844 F.3d 79 (2nd Cir. 2016).
63. Id., 93–94.
64. Google n.d.
65. Washenko 2015.
66. 464 U.S. 417 (1984).
67. 545 U.S. 913 (2005).
68. 710 F.3d 1020 (9th Cir. 2013).

69. BBC News 2012.
70. Associated Press 2022.
71. YouTube 2021, 10.
72. Abbott et al. 2017, 6.
73. U.S. Copyright Office 2020, 83.
74. *Perfect 10, Inc. v. CCBill LLC*, 488 F.3d 1102, 1114 (9th Cir. 2007).
75. U.S. Congress, Senate 1998, 48.
76. U.S. Copyright Office 2020, 136.
77. *Metro-Goldwyn-Mayer Studios Inc. et al. v. Grokster, Ltd., et al.*, 545 U.S. 913 (2005).
78. *Viacom Int'l Inc. et al. v. YouTube, Inc.*, 676 F.3d 19 (2d Cir. 2012).
79. *Campbell, aka Skyywalker, et al. v. Acuff-Rose Inc.*, 510 U.S. 569 (1994).

Chapter 6

1. *Kiennitz v. Sconnie Nation*, 766 F.3d 756 (2d Cir. 2014).
2. 17 U.S.C. §§ 101, 106(2).
3. Barnett 2013.
4. *Kiennitz v. Sconnie Nation*, 766 F.3d 756, 758 (7th Cir. 2014).
5. Nimmer & Nimmer § 13.05(B)(6) (2022).
6. 883 F.3d 169 (2d Cir. 2018).
7. Id., 139, citing *Harper & Row Publishers Inc. v. Nation Enterprises*, 471 U.S. 539, 566 (1985).
8. *Authors Guild, Inc. et al. v. HathiTrust et al.*, 755 F.3d 87 (2nd Cir. 2014).
9. This paragraph relies on facts set forth in *American Broadcasting Companies, Inc. et al. v. Goodfriend and Sports Fan Coalition NY, Inc.*, No. 19-cv-7136, 2021 U.S. Dist. LEXIS 164978 (S.D.N.Y. Aug. 14, 2021).
10. 17 U.S.C. § 111(a)(5).
11. *American Broadcasting Companies, Inc. et al. v. Goodfriend and Sports Fan Coalition NY, Inc.*, No. 19-cv-7136, 2021 U.S. Dist. LEXIS 164978 (S.D.N.Y. Aug. 14, 2021).
12. Joint Motion for Entry of Consent Judgment and Permanent Injunction, *American Broadcasting Companies, Inc. et al. v. Goodfriend and Sports Fan Coalition NY, Inc.*, No. 19-cv-7136-LLS (S.D.N.Y. Oct. 28, 2021).
13. Editorial Board 2022.
14. *Cariou v. Prince*, 714 F.3d 694 (2d Cir. 2013).
15. *Andy Warhol Foundation for Visual Arts, Inc. v. Goldsmith*, 11 F.4th 26, 38–39 (2d Cir. 2021).
16. *Andy Warhol Foundation for Visual Arts, Inc. v. Goldsmith*, at 16 (S. Ct., May 18, 2023).
17. Id., 28.
18. Maryland House Bill 518 (SB 432).
19. Id.
20. N.Y. Assemb. 5837B, 2021 Leg., Reg. Sess. (N.Y. 2021); State of New York, Executive Chamber, Veto #72 (Dec. 29, 2021), https://www.authorsguild.org/wp-content/uploads/2021/12/Govern orHochulVetoMessage.pdf.
21. H.R. 4120, 192nd Gen. CT., Reg. Sess. (Mass. 2021); H.R. 2210, 101st Gen. Assemb., 2nd Reg. Sess. (Mo. 2022); H.R. 4470, 102nd Gen. Assemb., Reg. Sess. (Ill. 2022); S. 1955, 112th Gen. Assemb., Reg. Sess. (Tenn. 2022); S. 131, 2022 Gen. Assemb., Reg. Sess. (Conn. 2022); H.B. 1412, 32nd Leg., Reg. Sess. (Haw. 2023).
22. 17 U.S.C. §301.
23. Brittain 2022.
24. Dwyer 2020; Roberts 2020.
25. Martin 2020.
26. Complaint, *Hachette Book Group Inc. v. Internet Archive*, No. 1:20-cv-04160 (S.D.N.Y. June 1, 2020).
27. Amici Curiae Brief of 17 Copyright Scholars in Support of Defendants' Motion for Summary Judgment, *Hachette Book Group, Inc. v. Internet Archive*, No. 1:20-cv-04160 (S.D.N.Y., filed July 14, 2022); Amicus Curiae Brief of Intellectual Property Law Professors as Amici Curiae in Support of Defendants' Motion for Summary Judgment, *Hachette Book Group Inc. v. Internet Archive*, No. 1:20-cv-04160 (S.D.N.Y. July 14, 2022).
28. Amicus Brief of Kenneth D. Crews and Kevin L. Smith in Support of Defendant Internet Archive's Motion for Summary Judgment and in Opposition to Plaintiffs' Cross-Motion for Summary Judgment, *Hachette Book Group, Inc., v. Internet Archive*, No. 1:20-cv-04160 (S.D.N.Y. July 14, 2022).

29. Publishers' Memorandum of Law in Support of Their Motion for Summary Judgment, *Hachette Book Group, Inc., et al. v. Internet Archive et al.*, Case No. 20-cv-4160-JGK), at 12–13 (S.D.N.Y., July 7, 2022).

30. Id., at 17–18.

31. Id., at 13; Enis 2019 (stating that, through Better World Books, "selected titles will now be directed into IA's [Internet Archive's] massive book digitization program").

32. Publishers' Memorandum of Law in Support of Their Motion for Summary Judgment, *Hachette Book Group, Inc., et al. v. Internet Archive et al.*, Case No. 1:20-cv-04160-JGK, at 13 (S.D.N.Y. July 7, 2022); see also Enis 2019 (describing acquisition).

33. Publishers' Memorandum of Law in Support of Their Motion for Summary Judgment, *Hachette Book Group, Inc., et al. v. Internet Archive et al.*, Case No. 1:20-cv-04160-JGK, at 4, 14, 28 (S.D.N.Y. July 7, 2022); *Hachette Book Group, Inc., et al. v. Internet Archive et al.*, Case No. 1:20-cv-04160-JGK, at 27 (Koeltl, J., S.D.N.Y. Mar. 24, 2023).

34. Publishers' Memorandum of Law in Support of Their Motion for Summary Judgment, *Hachette Book Group, Inc., et al. v. Internet Archive et al.*, Case No. 1:20-cv-04160-JGK, at 13–14, 28 (S.D.N.Y., July 7, 2022); *Hachette Book Group, Inc., et al. v. Internet Archive et al.*, Case No. 1:20-cv-04160-JGK, at 8–9, 26–27 (Koeltl, J., S.D.N.Y. Mar. 24, 2023)

35. Id., 16–18.

36. Id., 31–32.

37. Id., 34, 39–40.

38. Id., 38–39.

39. Pallante 2013, 340.

Chapter 7

1. Nordhaus 2004.

2. Anderson and Moris 2023.

3. Author's calculations, based on data from U.S. Patent & Trademark Office and U.S. Census Bureau.

4. On the electronics industry, see Chandler 2001, 31–34; on the automotive industry, see Statement of William J. Abernathy 1981, 154–56, 158–59.

5. Allvine and Tarpley 1976, 46.

6. Abramson 2007, 5.

7. Barnett 2021a, 78–79.

8. Ibid., 80–81.

9. Bayh-Dole Act, 35 U.S.C. §§ 200-212, Pub. L. No. 96-517, 94 Stat. 3015 (1980).

10. Federal Courts Improvement Act of 1982, P.L. No. 97-164, 96 Stat. 25.

11. *Diamond v. Chakrabarty*, 447 U.S. 303 (1980) (upholding the patentability of a genetically engineered microorganism); *Diamond v. Diehr*, 450 U.S. 175 (1981) (upholding the patentability of a computer program that controlled certain functions in a manufacturing apparatus).

12. See, e.g., *Carter-Wallace, Inc. v. Davis-Edwards Pharmacal Corp.*, 443 F.2d 867, 871 (2d Cir. 1971).

13. *H. H. Robertson, Co. v. United Steel Deck, Inc.*, 820 F.2d 384, 390 (1987).

14. *W. L. Gore & Associates, Inc. v. Garlock, Inc.*, 842 F.2d 1275, 1281 (Fed. Cir. 1988).

15. *Richardson v. Suzuki Motor Co.*, 868 F.2d 1226, 1246-47 (Fed. Cir. 1989).

16. Id.

17. *Polaroid Corp. v. Eastman Kodak Co.*, 641 F.Supp. 828 (D. Mass. 1986). The decision was upheld on appeal, see *Polaroid Corp. v. Eastman Kodak Co.*, 789 F.2d 1556 (Fed. Cir. 1986).

18. *News & Record* 1990.

19. Jaffe and Lerner 2004.

20. Bessen and Meurer 2008.

21. Boldrin and Levine 2008.

22. Ibid., 228.

23. Dosi and Stiglitz 2014, 20; Dreyfuss 2010, 796.

24. Dosi and Stiglitz 2014, 20.

25. Barnett 2021a, 139–50.

26. See, e.g., Heller and Eisenberg 1998.

27. Barnett 2021a, 109–11.

28. Ibid.

29. 547 U.S. 388 (2006).

30. 138 S. Ct. 1365 (2018).

Chapter 8

1. Jaffe and Lerner 2004, 12.
2. Ibid., 11–12.
3. Ibid., 11–12.
4. Ibid., 11–12.
5. Barnett 2021a, 68.
6. Ibid., 72–74.
7. Ibid., 86–87.
8. *Diamond v. Chakrabarty*, 447 U.S. 303 (1980).
9. Barnett 2021a, 80–81; Barnett 2021b, 221–24, 227–28.
10. Heller and Eisenberg 1998.
11. For similar evaluations of the literature, see Adelman 2005, 985–96; Egan and Teece 2015; Epstein and Kuhlik 2004; Kitch 2003; McManis and Yagi 2014; Shiu 2009, 414–15; Teece 2017, 1508–10.
12. Cohen and Walsh 2007; Walsh, Cho, and Cohen 2005; Walsh, Cohen, and Cho 2007.
13. Caulfield et al. 2006, 1992.
14. Seymore 2021, 180.
15. Murray et al. 2009.
16. Cockburn, Stern, and Zausner 2011, 119.
17. Eisenberg 2008, 1098–99.
18. Heller 2013, 22.
19. Barnett 2015, 147.
20. Egan and Teece 2015.
21. Murray and Stern 2007.
22. Shapiro 2001.
23. Caulfield et al. 2006, 1094.
24. Barnett 2021a, 80–81; Barnett 2021b, 227–28.
25. For similar views and supporting evidence, see Thursby and Thursby 2011, 1083.
26. Kaplan and Murray 2010, 116 (describing evidence).
27. Haeussler, Harhoff, and Mueller 2014.
28. Adelman and DeAngelis 2007, 1678. On the connection between biotech start-ups and research universities, see Blumenthal et al. 1996.
29. Barnett 2021a, 115–19.
30. This discussion relies on Barnett 2021a, 120–22.
31. See, e.g., Jaffe and Lerner 2004, 25–26, 32–35.
32. Petherbridge and Wagner 1007, 2054, stating that the "scholarly and popular literature is replete with the assertions that the standards for patentability (especially obviousness) have been dramatically weakened by the Federal Circuit."
33. Federal Trade Commission 2003, 7.
34. Merrill, Levin, and Myers 2004, 54.
35. Noveck 2010, 64.
36. Frakes and Wasserman 2015, 621. In a subsequent review of the empirical literature, the authors conclude that "[t]here is widespread agreement that the . . . PTO . . . allows too many invalid patents to issue that unnecessarily drains consumer welfare"; see Frakes and Wasserman 2019.
37. Frakes and Wasserman 2015, 621.
38. Patent No. 6368227B1, Method of swinging on a swing (Steven Olson, filed Nov. 17, 2000).
39. Patent No. 5443036A, Method of exercising a cat (Kevin T. Amiss and Martin H. Abbot, filed Nov. 2, 1993).
40. Patent No. 6004596A, Sealed crustless sandwich (Len C. Kretchman and David Geske, filed Dec. 8, 1997).
41. Quillen and Webster 2001, 3.
42. Quillen, Webster, and Eichmann 2002, 38. In Quillen and Webster 2006, the authors published an updated study, finding grant rates of approximately 85% for the 2002 study and 80%–87% from 1986 to 2005.
43. Federal Trade Commission 2003, 6.
44. Merrill, Levin, and Myers 2004, 52–53.
45. Lemley and Sampat 2008, 101.
46. Clarke 2003, 340, 343. For a similar critique, see Ebert 2004.
47. Katznelson 2007.

48. Carley, Hegde, and Marco 2015.
49. Frakes and Wasserman 2015.
50. Lemley and Sampat 2008.
51. Jensen, Palangkaraya, and Webster, 2006; Martinez and Guellec 2004; OECD 2004.
52. On both points, see Chien 2018, 85–88; Katznelson 2007, 16–20.
53. Katznelson 2007, 27–28.
54. Ibid., 4.
55. For an extensive review of the empirical literature on this point, see Frakes and Wasserman 2019.
56. Beauchamp 2016, 850.
57. Davis 2023.
58. Jaffe and Lerner 2004, 13.
59. Bessen and Meurer 2008, 127–29.
60. Executive Office of the President 2013, 5.
61. Doody 2012, 111–13.
62. Katznelson 2014.
63. Cotropia, Kesan, and Schwartz 2014; Katznelson 2014.
64. Beauchamp 2016.
65. Leahy-Smith America Invents Act, Pub. L. No. 112-29, 125 Stat. 284 (2011).
66. Matal 2012, 438, 441.
67. Ibid., 439 n.22.
68. Doody 2012, 1.
69. 35 U.S.C. §§ 311–319.
70. 35 U.S.C. § 311
71. European Patent Convention (amended Nov. 29, 2000), Art. 99 (1).
72. U.S. Patent & Trademark Office 2022b.
73. American Intellectual Property Law Association 2019, 52.
74. U.S. Patent & Trademark Office 2020, 12.
75. U.S. Patent & Trademark Office 2021, 6; U.S. Patent & Trademark Office 2022a, 6.
76. U.S. Patent Trademark Office 2022a, 9.
77. Id., 16.
78. Source: https://www.unifiedpatents.com/members.
79. Unified Patents 2023, Fig. 11.
80. Author's calculations based on data in Unified Patents 2023, Fig. 18.
81. Id.
82. *NHK Spring Co. Ltd. v. Intri-Plex Technologies, Inc.*, No. IPR2018-00752, 2018 WL 4373643 (P.T.A.B. Sept. 12, 2018); *Apple Inc. v. Fintiv, Inc.*, No. IPR2020-0019, 2020 WL 2126495 (P.T.A.B. Mar. 20, 2020).
83. Wolfe 2020.
84. Letter to The Honorable Lindsey Graham 2020.
85. Order Granting Motion to Dismiss, *Apple Inc. et al. v. Iancu*, Case No. 5-20-cv-06128-EJD (N.D. Cal. Nov. 10, 2021).
86. Rodkey 2022.
87. Vidal 2022, 2.
88. U.S. Patent & Trademark Office 2022b, 23.

Chapter 9

1. Barnett 2020.
2. Ibid.
3. Federal Trade Commission 2003, 38.
4. *eBay Inc. v. MercExchange LLC*, 547 U.S. 388, 396 (2006) (Kennedy, J., et al., concurring).
5. Executive Office of the President 2013, 12.
6. White House 2013.
7. *Commil USA, LLC v. Cisco Systems, Inc.*, 135 S. Ct. 1920, 1930 (2015).
8. Federal Trade Commission 2016, 9.
9. Bessen and Meurer 2008.
10. Ibid., 16–17.
11. Bessen, Ford, and Meurer 2011, 31.
12. Id., 31.
13. Ibid., 33.

14. Bessen and Meurer 2014.
15. On references to the 2011 paper in the trade press, see Schwartz and Kesan 2014, 432. For a trade press reference to the $83 billion estimate (and, over five years, approximately $500 billion), see Goldman 2011.
16. Federal Trade Commission 2016, 25 n.94, 31.
17. Ziedonis 2008.
18. Schwartz and Kesan 2014.
19. Lunney 2008.
20. Katznelson 2016.
21. Lunney 2008, 41–44.
22. Ziedonis 2008.
23. Executive Office of the President 2013, 5 (citing Chien 2013).
24. Kamdar, Nazer, and Ranieri 2015, 1.
25. Unified Patents 2024.
26. Government Accountability Office 2013, 17.
27. Mazzeo, Ashtor, and Zyontz 2013.
28. Government Accountability Office 2013, 14–19.
29. Beauchamp 2016.
30. Cotropia, Kesan, and Schwartz 2014. Allison, Lemley, and Walker 2009 and Allison, Lemley, and Schwartz 2017 construct similarly fine-grained taxonomies of the NPE universe, using somewhat different entity categories.
31. Cotropia, Kesan, and Schwartz 2014, 656–60.
32. Ibid., 694.
33. Abrams et al. 2019.
34. 547 U.S. 388 (2006).
35. 210 U.S. 405, 424 (1908).
36. 547 U.S. 388, 395 (2006) (Roberts, C. J., concurring).
37. Barnett 2021a, 72.
38. Simler and McClleland 2011.
39. 547 U.S. 388, 391 (2006) (Roberts, C. J., concurring), citing *Weinberger v. Romelo-Barcero*, 456 U.S. 305, 320 (1982).
40. 547 U.S. 388, 396 (2006) (Kennedy, J., concurring).
41. Id., 393.
42. Holte 2018, 140–41; Lee 2015, 127–33.
43. Seaman 2016, 1988.
44. Ibid., 1990.
45. *Apple, Inc. v. Samsung Electronics Co., Ltd.*, 2014 WL 7496140, at *14 (N.D. Cal., Koh, J., Aug. 27, 2014).
46. *Apple, Inc. v. Samsung Electronics Co., Ltd.*, 809 F.3d 633, 640–44 (9th Cir. 2015).

Chapter 10

1. The remainder of this paragraph relies on Barnett 2019, 228–30.
2. Lemley 2007; Lemley and Shapiro 2007.
3. Federal Trade Commission and U.S. Department of Justice 2007, 8 n.11, 35 n.42.
4. Federal Trade Commission 2011, 235.
5. Hesse 2012.
6. U.S. Department of Justice and U.S. Patent & Trademark Office 2013.
7. Kuhn, Scott-Morton, and Shelanski 2013.
8. Armstrong, Mueller, and Syrett, 2014, 2.
9. Ibid.
10. Cohen 2019.
11. *Apple, Inc. v. Motorola, Inc.*, 869 F.Supp.2d 901, 913–14 (N.D. Ill. 2012) (Posner, J.) (stating that "I don't see how, given FRAND, I would be justified in enjoining Apple from infringing the '898 [patent] unless Apple refuses to pay a royalty that meets the FRAND requirement").
12. Case AT.39985 Motorola—Enforcement of GPRS standard essential patents, Apr. 29, 2014, http://ec.europa.eu/competition/antitrust/cases/dec_docs/39985/39985_928_16.pdf; Case AT.39939 – Samsung – Enforcement of UMTS standard essential patents, Apr. 29, 2014, http://ec.europa.eu/competition/antitrust/cases/dec_docs/39939/39939_1501_5.pdf.
13. *Apple Inc. v. Motorola Inc.*, 757 F.3d 1286, 1331–32 (Fed. Cir. 2014).

14. *Huawei Technologies Co. Ltd. v. ZTE Corp. and ZTE Deutschland GmbH*, Court of Justice of the European Union, judgment dated July 16, 2015, Case No. C-170/13.
15. *Unwired Planet International Ltd. et al. v. Huawei Technologies (UK) Co. Ltd. et al.*, [2017] EWHC 2988 (Pat); *Unwired Planet International Ltd. et al. v. Huawei Technologies (UK) Co. Ltd. et al.*, [2020] UKSC 37.
16. *Tagivan (MPEG LA) v. Huawei*, District Court of Dusseldorf, Case No. 4a O 17/17 (Nov. 15, 2018); *TQ Delta v. ZyXEL Communications*, Case No. HP-2017-000045-[2019] EWHC 745 (Pat); *Koninklijke Philips N.V. v. Asustek Computers Inc.*, Court of Appeal of The Hague, Case No. 200.221.250/01 (May 7, 2019); *Conversant v Daimler*, Regional Court (Landgericht) of Munich I, Case No. 21 O 11384/19 (Oct. 30, 2020). This is a list of selected cases and not intended to be comprehensive.
17. Bartz 2017.
18. Barnett and Kappos 2023.
19. *Apple, Inc. v. Motorola Mobility, Inc.*, No. 11-cv-178-bbc, slip op. at 5 (W.D. Wis. Nov. 8, 2012).
20. Inv. 337-TA-794, In re Certain Electronic Devices, including Wireless Communication Devices, Portable Music and Data Processing Devices and Tablet Computers 62–63 (July 5, 2013).
21. Michael Froman, Disapproval of the U.S. International Trade Commission's Determination in the Matter of Certain Electronic Devices, Including Wireless Communication Devices, Portable Music and Data Processing Devices, and Tablet Computers, Investigation No. 337-TA-794 (Aug. 3, 2013).
22. *Federal Trade Commission v. Qualcomm Inc.*, 411 F.Supp.3d 658 (N.D. Cal. 2019).
23. Lemley and Shapiro 2007.
24. Tibken 2019a.
25. *Federal Trade Commission v. Qualcomm Inc.*, 411 F.Supp.3d 658 (N.D. Cal. 2019).
26. *Federal Trade Commission v. Qualcomm Inc.*, 969 F.3d 974 (9th Cir. 2020).
27. Galetovic and Gupta 2020; Galetovic, Haber and Levine 2015.
28. Galetovic and Gupta 2020.
29. Galetovic, Haber, and Zaretzki, 2018; Galetovic, Haber, and Levine 2015; Mallinson 2016; Sidak 2016.
30. Galetovic, Haber, and Zaretzki 2018.
31. Dedrick, Kraemer, and Linden 2010, 19–20.
32. Kraemer, Linden, and Dedrick 2011, 4–5.
33. Dedrick and Kraemer 2017, 102.
34. See, e.g., Melamed and Shapiro 2018, 2117–18; Shapiro and Lemley 2020, 2040–41.
35. Morton and Shapiro 2016, 124.
36. Federico, Morton, and Shapiro 2020, 156.
37. U.S. Department of Justice 2017.
38. U.S. Department of Justice 2019.
39. U.S. Department of Justice 2020.
40. Remaly 2019.
41. U.S. Department of Justice 2017, 2019, 2020.
42. White House 2021.
43. U.S. Department of Justice 2021.
44. Comments of Former Administration Officials 2022; Comments of Former U.S. International Trade Commissioner 2022.
45. U.S. Department of Justice 2022.
46. European Commission 2023.
47. This paragraph relies on information in Barnett 2017; Mock 2005.
48. Cave, Genakos, and Valleti 2019.

Chapter 11

1. As noted in the Acknowledgments, portions of this chapter appeared previously in Barnett 2023.
2. Cohen 2016, n.p.
3. Jinping 2021a, n.p.; first published as Jinping 2021b.
4. Central Commission for Cybersecurity and Informatization 2021.
5. See sources indicated under Figure 11.1. Value for Taiwan calculated based on OECD, Balanced International Trade in Services (2005–2021) (charges for the use of intellectual property n.i.e.), https://stats.oecd.org/Index.aspx?DataSetCode=BATIS_EBOPS2010.
6. On this topic, see Suchodolski, Harrison, and Heiden 2020.

7. Barnett 2019, 234–35; Ezell and Atkinson 2014, 13–22; Sokol and Zheng 2013, 80–81; U.S. International Trade Commission 2011, 2-21 to 2-22.
8. Tabeta 2024.
9. On the TD-CDMA standard, see U.S. International Trade Commission 2011, 5–24. On the WAPI standard, see Gao 2008. On the failure of Chinese attempts to mandate indigenous technology standards in wireless communications, see Ezell and Atkinson 2014, 16–17.
10. Sokol and Zheng 2013, 78–79.
11. On the 2017 guidelines, see Ginsburg, Kobayashi, and Wright, 2017; Wong-Ervin 2017. On the 2012 draft guidelines, see Wenjing 2022, 272–73.
12. Barnett 2023.
13. Sokol and Zheng 2013, 78.
14. Wenjing 2022, 272–74.
15. Barnett 2023.
16. *Aspen Skiing Co. v. Aspen Highlands Skiing Corp.*, 472 U.S. 585 (1985).
17. Barnett 2023.
18. Huang et al. 2022. For related discussion, see Barnett 2023.
19. Randewich and Miller 2015.
20. Cohen 2013; Gao 2020, 455–57. The cases are *Huawei v. InterDigital Communications*, Shenzhen Intermediate People's Court, Decision of Feb. 2013, No. 2011 858; *Huawei v. InterDigital Communications*, Guangdong Higher People's Court No. 2013.
21. Eversheds Sutherland 2013.
22. Gao 2020, 467.
23. Ibid., 457.
24. Barnett 2023.
25. Anti-Monopoly Guidelines on Abuse of Intellectual Property Rights (Exposure Draft) § 3 (Anti-Monopoly Commission of the State Council, Dec. 31, 2015), https://web.archive.org/web/20160914225143/http://uschinatradewar.com/files/2016/01/IPR-Guideline-draft-20151231-EN.pdf (unofficial English translation).
26. Contreras et al. 2019, 187, citing Interpretation (II) of the Supreme People's Court on Several Issues concerning the Application of Law in the Trial of Patent Infringement Dispute Cases, art. 24 (effective Apr. 1, 2016).
27. On the guidelines issued by the courts, see Gao 2020, 473–75. On the guidelines issued by the competition regulator, see State Administration for Market Regulation, State Council Anti-Monopoly Committee Anti-Monopoly Guidelines in the Field of Intellectual Property Rights, Art. 15 (published Sept. 18, 2020, promulgated Jan. 4, 2019), partial unofficial English translation available at Wininger 2020.
28. For the European decision, see Case C-170/13, *Huawei Technologies Co. Ltd. v. ZTE Corp., ZTE Deutschland GmbH* 2014 E.C.R. 477 ¶¶ 61–67; for the UK decision, see *Unwired Planet Int'l Ltd. v. Huawei Techs. Co.*, [2017] EWHC (Pat.) 711; for the U.S. decision, see *Apple, Inc. v. Motorola, Inc.*, 757 F.3d 1286, 1331-32 (Fed. Cir. 2014).
29. Gao 2020, 467–69, 471. On the 2018 litigation involving Huawei and Samsung, see Yiu and Vary 2018.
30. Gao 2020, 466–67; Sokol and Zheng 2013, 86.
31. Gao 2020, 479; Sokol and Zheng 2013, 84–85, citing Provisions on the Administration of Formulating and Revising National Standards Involving Patents (Interim) (Draft for Public Comments), art. 9 (Standardization Admin. China, Nov. 2, 2009).
32. Sokol and Zheng 2013, 84.
33. Gao 2020, 479, citing Administration Regulations for the National Standards Relating to Patents, Bulletin of the National Standards Administration Committee and State Intellectual Property Office of China 2013, art. 9.
34. Gao 2020, 455, citing Working Guidelines on the Trial of Standard Essential Patent Dispute Cases (for Trial Implementation) (Guangdong High People's Court, Apr. 26, 2018).
35. Lemley and Shapiro 2013, 1148 (arguing that the "reasonable royalty" for a SEP should not include any "value attaching to the creation and adoption of the standard").
36. Gao 2020, 477.
37. Wong 2014.
38. Gao 2020, 462.
39. Cohen and Clark 2018, 51–57; U.S. Chamber of Commerce 2014, 63 n.257 (citing Jinbiao 2013).
40. Woo and Michaels 2023, n.p.

41. Cohen 2021.
42. Cohen 2023, at 230 (citing Xuewen and Ming 2021).
43. Cheng 2022; Wininger 2021, citing *Sharp Corp. and ScienBizip Japan Corp. v. OPPO Guangdong Mobile Telecommunications Co. Ltd. and Shenzhen Branch of OPPO Guangdong Mobile Telecommunications Co. Ltd.*, Supreme People's Court of the People's Republic of China, Civil Ruling (2020) Zui Gao Fa Zhi Min Xia Zhong No. 517. For unofficial English translation, see https://chinaipr.com/wp-content/uploads/2021/10/spcs-ruling-on-jurisdiction-objection-appeal-in-oppo-v.-sharp-case-1.pdf.
44. Cohen 2021.
45. Wininger 2021.
46. European Union 2022, 4.
47. Cohen 2021, n.p.
48. For discussion, see Cohen 2023; Contreras 2019, 2020. The specific cases in which ASIs have been issued in the United States are: *Microsoft Corp. v. Motorola Inc.*, 871 F.Supp.2d 1089 (W.D. Wash. 2012), in which the court issued an order precluding enforcement of an injunction secured by Motorola in a German court; *TCL Commc'n Tech. Holdings et al. v. Ericsson Inc. et al.*, Docket No. 279-1, at 5–11 (C.D. Cal. June 29, 2015), in which the court issued an order barring the patent holder from pursuing infringement claims against the defendant in several other countries, on the ground that both parties sought a global resolution of the dispute in the U.S. federal court; and *Huawei Technologies Co. Ltd. v. Samsung Electronics Co.*, 340 F.Supp.3d 934 (N.D. Cal. 2018), in which the court issued an injunction barring Huawei from enforcing an injunction it had secured from a Chinese court against Samsung.
49. *Animal Science Products, Inc. v. Hebei Welcome Pharma Co. Ltd.*, No. 13-4791-CV, 2021 WL 3502632 (2d Cir. Aug. 10, 2021).
50. Cohen 2022a, 13.
51. Cohen 2023.
52. Cohen 2022b. n.p.
53. Ibid. (referring to *Lenovo v. Nokia* decision by Chinese Supreme People's Court).
54. Ibid. (citing China's IPR Abuse Rules, Art. 16).
55. Ibid. (citing China's IPR Abuse Rules, Arts. 21–22).
56. Ibid. (citing China Anti-Monopoly Law, Art. 2).
57. Cohen 2022a, 17.
58. Gao 2020, 477.
59. Ibid.
60. *TCL Commc'n Tech. Holdings Ltd., et al. v. Ericsson Inc.*, 2018 WL 4488286, at *52 (C.D. Cal. Sept. 14, 2018).
61. European Union 2022, 7–8.
62. This paragraph relies on the account of the decision in Treacy and Gobac 2021.
63. Statista, Revenue of Apple by geographical region from the first quarter of 2012 to the 4th quarter of 2023.
64. Jie 2022.
65. Bartz 2017.
66. Bartz and Nellis 2017.
67. Pinsent Masons 2017.
68. Qualcomm, Opening Statement, *Apple Inc. v. Qualcomm Inc.*, Case No. 3:17-cv-0108-GPC-MDD (S.D. Cal. Apr. 16, 2019). Available through Scribd, https://www.scribd.com/document/407463620/Qualcomm-opening-statement.
69. For similar analysis of these documents, see Ginsburg and Wright 2019.
70. Id., at 6, 16, and 37.
71. Id., at 7.
72. Id., at 11.
73. Id., at 7.
74. *Federal Trade Commission v. Qualcomm Inc.*, 969 F.3d 974 (9th Cir. 2020).

Chapter 12

1. I developed the model for this argument most fully in Barnett 2021a.
2. Anderson and Moris 2023.
3. Barnett 2021a, 24–27.
4. Barnett 2015, 156–57.

5. Barnett 2014, 32.
6. For more detailed discussion of some of these issues, see Barnett 2018.
7. *Viacom Int'l Inc. et al. v. YouTube, Inc. et al.*, 676 F.3d 19 (2nd Cir. 2012); *Viacom Int'l Inc. et al. v. YouTube, Inc. et al.*, 940 F.Supp.2d 110 (S.D.N.Y. 2013).
8. In the pharmaceutical sector, drug producers enjoy a period of exclusivity following FDA approval, which protects against generic entry for a certain period and therefore can supplement the exclusivity protections provided by the patent system.
9. DiMasi, Grabowski, and Hansen 2016.
10. 447 U.S. 303 (1980).
11. U.S. Patent No. 4237224A, Process for producing biologically functional molecular chimeras (filed Jan. 4, 1979).
12. Genentech 2016.
13. This paragraph is informed by Barnett 2021a, 142–45.
14. Con Diaz 2019.
15. Computer Software Copyright Act of 1980, Pub. L. No. 96-517, § 10; 94 Stat. 3015, 3018 (1980).
16. *Diamond v. Diehr,* 450 U.S. 175 (1981).
17. Nvidia 2020.
18. Tiernan 2017.
19. McGrath 2018.
20. Hollister and Byford 2022.
21. Ibid., 1807.
22. West and Dedrick 2001, at 100, 104.
23. Barnett 2010, 1806–13.
24. Statista, Global server share by operating system 2018–19.
25. Barnett 2021a, 89–114.
26. 547 U.S. 388 (2006).
27. Ozden and Khashabi 2023. Following Levin et al. (1987), discrete technologies refer to innovations that comprise a small number of components (more prevalent in the life sciences), as distinguished from complex technologies that comprise a bundle of multiple complementary components (more prevalent in information technology sectors).
28. Schultz 2020.
29. Barnett 2021b, 219–28.
30. Ibid., 232–40.
31. Arrow 1962.
32. Barnett 2021a.
33. Baumol 2005, 5 (emphasis in original).
34. Barnett 2024.
35. Barnett 2021a.

Chapter 13

1. Cohen, Nelson, and Walsh 2000; Levin et al. 1987; Mansfield 1986.
2. Graham et al. 2009.
3. This discussion is informed by Li 2022; Mossoff 2022; *U.S. v. International Trade Commission* 2022
4. *Sonos v. International Trade Commission,* Case 22-1421 (Fed. Cir. Apr. 8, 2024).
5. Patel 2022, n.p..
6. U.S. International Trade Commission 2022.
7. Thurott 2022.
8. Yasiejko 2023.
9. *Sonos v. International Trade Commission,* Case 22-1421 (Fed. Cir. Apr. 8, 2024).
10. Gilbert 2023.
11. Tilley 2023.
12. Brittain 2024.
13. Yasieko 2024.
14. Netflix earnings call, Oct. 19, 2021, https://s22.q4cdn.com/959853165/files/doc_financials/2021/q3/Netflix,-Inc.,-Q3-2021-Earnings-Call,-Oct-19,-2021.pdf.
15. Amazon.com Inc. Form 10-K (2021), 48. Amount for Amazon Video "includes licensing and production costs associated with content offered within Amazon Prime memberships, and costs associated with digital subscriptions and sold or rented content"; see ibid.

16. Statista, Forecast of the number of YouTube users in the World from 2017 to 2025.
17. Nickinson 2023. Values are estimates as of December 2023.
18. This paragraph is informed by Barnett 2011, 1872–74; Evans, Hagiu, and Schmalensee 95–107; and findings of fact in *U.S. v. Microsoft, Inc.*, 87 F.Supp.2d 30 (D.D.C. 2000).
19. Baldwin 2021, 22.
20. Evans, Hagiu, and Schmalensee 2006, 98–101.
21. Ibid.
22. Barnett 2021a, 42–44.
23. Sherman 2018.
24. Conley, Bican, and Ernst 2013, 111.
25. Ibid., 111.
26. Williams, Isom, and Smith-Peaches 2003, 85.
27. Goldscheider 1996, 181.
28. Sherman 2018, n.p.
29. Barnett 2017, 2022.
30. Barnett 2017, 2021a.

Chapter 14

1. DiMasi, Grabowski, and Hansen 2016 (based on data current as of 2013).
2. Barbiarz and Pisano 2008.
3. Pammolli, Magazzini, and Riccaboni 2011.
4. Drug Price Competition and Patent Term Restoration Act, Pub. L. 98-417, 98 Stat. 1285, codified at 21 U.S.C. ch. 9 § 301; 21 U.S.C. ch. 9 subch. V §§ 355 & 360cc.
5. Cohen, Nelson, and Walsh 2000; Graham et al. 2009; Levin et al. 1987.
6. Barnett 2021a, 146–48.
7. Brown, Martinsson, and Petersen 2017; Ginarte and Park 1997; Kyle and McGahan 2009; Qian 2007.
8. For examples from the academic literature, see Boldrin and Levine 2008; Stiglitz 2007.
9. Agreement on Trade-Related Aspects of Intellectual Property Rights, Apr. 15, 1994, Marrakesh Agreement Establishing the World Trade Organization, Annex 1C, 1869 U.N.T.S. 299, 33 I.L.M. 1197 (1994).
10. World Trade Organization 2020.
11. Report of the United Nations Secretary-General 2016, 7.
12. Office of the U.S. Trade Representative 2021.
13. Akhtar 2022, n.p.
14. Office of the U.S. Trade Representative 2022, n.p.
15. U.S. International Trade Commission 2023.
16. Plotkin et al. 2017.
17. Congressional Budget Office 2021.
18. U.S. International Trade Commission 2023, 16.
19. Dolgin 2021.
20. Reuters 2021.
21. Kaplan and Wehrwein 2021.
22. Mueller 2020.
23. BioNTech Group Form 20-F (2021), 156. For additional discussion, see Gaviria and Kilic 2021.
24. BioNTech Group Form 20-F (2021), 157–58.
25. Reuters 2022.
26. France24 2021.
27. Sanjai 2022.
28. Nebehay and Miller 2021.
29. Saul 2022.
30. Bayh-Dole Act, 35 U.S.C. § 203.
31. Id., § 203(a).
32. Kersten and Athanasia 2022.
33. U.S. Department of Health and Human Services 2021, 22.
34. U.S. Department of Health and Human Services 2023, n.p.
35. National Institute of Standards and Technology 2024, at 85598.
36. Bayh-Dole Act, 35 U.S.C. § 201(f).
37. Bayh and Dole 2002.

38. Thomas 2016, at 10, citing National Institutes of Health 1997.
39. The remainder of this paragraph is informed by Barnett 2021a, 80–81; Barnett 2021b, 219–28.
40. Barnett 2021a, 80–81.
41. This paragraph is based on Ezell 2022, which refers in various places to findings in Umemura 2008.
42. Ezell 2022, 12–13.
43. Inflation Reduction Act of 2022, Pub. L. 117-169, 136 Stat. 1818, §§ 11001–2 (Subtitle B—Prescription Drug Pricing Reform, Parts 1 and 2).
44. Shah et al. 2023.

Chapter 15

1. Locke 1690, § 222.
2. Ibid.
3. Madison 1787–88, No. 43.
4. Madison 1787–88, No. 10.
5. U.S. Constitution, Art. I, Sec. 8, Cl. 8.
6. Benkler 2011.
7. Future of Journalism 2009.
8. Fletcher and Nielsen 2016, 1175–76.
9. Ibid., 1176.
10. Simon and Graves 2019.
11. Leurdijk, Slot, and Nieuwenhuis 2012, 65.
12. Kafka 2023; Mullin and Robertson 2023.
13. Flynn 2021.
14. Leurdijk, Slot, and Nieuwenhuis 2012, 24.
15. Mitchelstein, Siles, and Boczkowski 2015, 2; Radcliffe 2021.
16. Faulconbridge 2019; Fletcher and Nielsen 2016; Mitchelstein, Siles, and Boczkowski 2015.
17. Radcliffe 2021, 21–22.
18. Newman et al. 2019, 10.
19. PwC 2016.
20. Pew Research 2021.
21. Scherer and Cho 2022, 6.
22. Newman et al. 2019, 117.
23. Nel and Milburn-Curtis 2020–21 (citing Pew Research Center analysis of U.S. Bureau of Labor statistics).
24. Flynn 2021.
25. On these concerns, see Cairncross Review 2019; Newman et al. 2022.
26. Pew Research Center 2010; Waldman 2011, 10–12.
27. Breiner 2016; Karr and Aaron 2019.
28. Scherer and Cho 2022, 11.
29. Leurdijk, Slot, and Nieuwenhuis 2012, 8.
30. Ibid.; Mitchelstein, Siles, and Boczkowski 2015, 2.
31. Slot and Nieuwenhuis 2012, 36, Fig. 8 (citing data from WAN-IFRA).
32. Nel and Milburn-Curtis 2020–2021.
33. Fanta and Dachwitz 2020, 14.
34. Scherer and Cho 2022, 17.
35. Investigation of Competition in Digital Markets 2020, 59.
36. Pew Research 2014, 6.
37. Scherer and Cho 2022, 1.
38. Newman et al. 2019, 9.
39. Newman et al. 2022, 24.
40. See, e.g., *Bell v. Willmott Storage Services, LLC*, 12 F.4th 1065 (9th Cir. 2021)
41. *Ringgold v. Black Entertainment Television, Inc.*, 126 F.3d 70 (2nd Cir. 1997) (upholding finding of copyright infringement concerning display of quilt in television show for up to four seconds).
42. Directive (EU) 2019/790 of the European Parliament and of the Council of 17 April 2019 on copyright and related rights in the Digital Single Market and amending Directives 96/9/EC and 2001/29/EC.
43. European Parliament 2019.

44. AP News 2022.
45. Treasury Laws Amendment (News Media and Digital Platforms Mandatory Bargaining Code) Act 2021.
46. Kaye 2021; Turvill 2022.
47. Ghaffary, Starr, and Ford, 2024; O'Brien 2023.
48. Peers 2023.
49. Newman et al. 2019, 9–10; Newman et al. 2023, 10.
50. Leurdijk, Slot, and Nieuwenhuis 2012, 10–11.
51. Scherer and Cho 2022, 15–16.
52. Ibid., 3–4.
53. Newman et al. 2022, 11.
54. Ibid.
55. Glaser 2021.
56. Breiner 2016.
57. Radcliffe 2021, 44.
58. For an effort to document grants from these initiatives, see Miller 2023.
59. Fanta and Dachwitz 2020, 44–51, 63.
60. Ibid., 33; Tech Transparency Project 2019.
61. Meta 2020.
62. Ringer 1974, 19.

Chapter 16

1. For the pioneering work, see Barzel 1997.
2. This paragraph is informed by Barnett 2021a, 39–40, 121–22.
3. See, e.g., Benkler 2004, 353.
4. Barnett 2013.
5. Krueger 2005.
6. Recording Industry Association of America, https://www.riaa.com/u-s-sales-database/ (last visited July 28, 2023).
7. Barker 2018; IFPI 2022, 24; Stassen 2022.
8. Google n.d. "Learn about Content ID claims," https://support.google.com/youtube/answer/6013276?hl=en#zippy=%2Cshare-revenue%2Cremove-the-claimed-content.
9. Statement of Katherine Oyama 2014, 49.
10. Google n.d.
11. YouTube 2022, 1.
12. U.S. Copyright Office 2020, 43–44.
13. Newman 2024.
14. Clark 2023.
15. Ibid.
16. Rieder, Coromina, and Matamoros-Fernandez 2020.
17. Ibid.

Chapter 17

1. Albanese 2020.
2. *Fox News Network, LLC v. TVEyes, Inc.*, 883 F.3d 169 (2d Cir. 2018).
3. *Dr. Seuss Enterprises, LP v. ComicMix LLC*, 983 F.3d 443, 452–55, 458–61 (9th Cir. 2020).
4. *McGucken v. Pub Ocean Ltd.*, 42 F.4th 1149, 1158–64 (9th Cir. 2022).
5. *Andy Warhol Foundation for Visual Arts v. Goldsmith* (S. Ct. May 18, 2023), upholding *Andy Warhol Foundation for Visual Arts v. Goldsmith*, 11 F.4th 26 (2d Cir. 2021).
6. U.S. Copyright Office 2020.
7. Ibid., 72.
8. Ibid., 197.
9. Ibid., 3.
10. Ibid., 3–4.
11. Ibid., 111 (my emphasis).
12. Directive (EU) 2019/790 of the European Parliament and of the Council of 17 April 2019 on copyright and related rights in the Digital Single Market and amending Directives 96/9/EC and 2001/29/EC.

13. U.S. Copyright Office 2020, 186–93.
14. *Halo Electronics, Inc. v. Pulse Electronics, Inc.*, 136 S. Ct. 1923 (2016).
15. *eBay Inc. v. MercExchange LLC*, 547 U.S. 388, 394-397 (2006).
16. Trademark Modernization Act of 2020, Pub. L. 116-260, 134 Stat. 2200.
17. Klos 2022.

References

Judicial opinions, statutes, regulations, securities filings, and treaties are not listed because the complete citation information for those sources appears in the Notes. URLs are only included for digital sources that cannot be readily located through an online search query.

Abbott, Alden, Adam Mossoff, Kristen Osenga, Brian O'Shaughnessy, and Mark Schultz. 2017. *Creativity and Innovation Unchained: Why Copyright Law Must Be Updated for the Digital Age by Simplifying It.* Regulatory Transparency Project.

Abrams, David S., Ufuk Akcigit, Gokhan Oz, and Jeremy G. Pearce. 2019. "The Patent Troll: Benign Middleman or Stick-Up Artist?" National Bureau of Economic Research Working Paper No. 25713.

Abramson, Bruce D. 2007. *The Secret Circuit: The Little-Known Court Where the Rules of the Information Age Unfold.* Rowman & Littlefield.

Adelman, David E. 2005. "A Fallacy of the Commons in Biotech Patent Policy." *Berkeley Technology Law Journal* 20: 985–1030.

Adelman, David E., and Kathryn L. DeAngelis. 2007. "Patent Metrics: The Mismeasure of Innovation in the Biotech Patent Debate." *Texas Law Review* 85: 1677–744.

Adermon, Adrian, and Che-Yuan Liang. 2014. "Piracy and Music Sales: The Effects of an Anti-Piracy Law." *Journal of Economic Behavior and Organization* 105: 90–106.

Akhtar, Shayerah. 2022. "World Trade Organization: 'TRIPS Waiver' for COVID-19 Vaccines." *Congressional Research Service.* Aug. 31.

Albanese, Andrew. 2020. "Settlement Terms Revealed (Mostly) in Audible Captions Litigation." *Publishers Weekly.* Mar. 5.

Allen, Franklin, and Jun "QJ" Qian. 2009. "Comparing Legal and Alternative Institutions in Finance and Commerce." In *Global Perspectives on the Rule of Law,* ed. James J. Heckman, Robert L. Nelson, and Lee Cabatingan, 118–44. Routledge.

Allison, John R., Abe Dunn, and Ronald J. Mann. 2007. "Software Patents, Incumbents, and Entry." *Texas Law Review* 85: 1579–625.

Allison, John R., Mark A. Lemley, and David L. Schwartz. 2017. "How Often Do Non-Practicing Entities Win Patent Suits?" *Berkeley Technology Law Journal* 32: 235–308.

Allison, John R., Mark A. Lemley, and Joshua Walker. 2009. "Extreme Value or Trolls on Top? The Characteristics of the Most-Litigated Patents." *University of Pennsylvania Law Review* 158: 1–37.

Allison, Kevin, and Aline van Duyn. 2006. "Google to Buy YouTube for $1.65bn." *Financial Times.* Oct. 9.

Allvine, Fred C., and Fred A. Tarpley, Jr. 1976. "The New State of the Economy: The Challenging Prospect." In *U.S. Economic Growth from 1976 to 1986: Prospects, Problems, and Patterns,* Vol. 7: *The Limits to Growth.* Studies Prepared for the Joint Economic Committee, Congress of the United States. U.S. Government Printing Office.

Amadeo, Ron. 2018. "Google's Iron Grip on Android: Controlling Open Source by Any Means Necessary." *ars technica.* July 21.

Amazon.com Inc. 2022. *2022 U.S. Political Engagement Policy and Statement.* https://ir.aboutamazon.com/corporate-governance/Political-Engagement/default.aspx.

Amazon.com Inc. 2017–2021. *Political Engagement Archive.* https://ir.aboutamazon.com/corporate-governance/Political-Engagement/Political-Engagement-Archive/default.aspx.

American Association for the Advancement of Science. 2007. *International Intellectual Property Experiences: A Report of Four Countries.*

American Intellectual Property Law Association. 2019. *Report of the Economic Survey.* https://www.aipla.org/home/news-publications/economic-survey/2019-report-of-the-economic-survey.

American Library Association. 2013. *Libraries Applaud Dismissal of Google Books Search Case.* Nov. 14. https://www.ala.org/news/node/9704.

Anderson, Birgitte, and Marion Frenz. 2008. *The Impact of Music Downloads and P2P File-Sharing on the Purchase of Music: A Study for Industry Canada.* Industry Canada. https://publications.gc.ca/collections/collection_2022/isde-ised/iu64/lu64-132-2007-eng-.pdf.

Anderson, Birgitte, and Marion Frenz. 2010. "Don't Blame the P2P File-sharers: The Impact of Free Music Downloads on the Purchase of Music CDs in Canada." *Journal of Evolutionary Economics* 20: 715–40.

Anderson, Gary, and Francisco Moris. 2023. *Federally Funded R&D Declines as a Share of GDP and Total R&D.* NSF 23-339. National Science Foundation, National Center for Science and Engineering Statistics. https://ncses.gov/pubs/nsf23339/.

Anderson, Porter. 2017. "On Copyright and Copies in Canada: A Federal Court Ruling Backs Publishers." *Publishing Perspectives.* Aug. 2.

Anderson, Porter. 2021. "Canadian Publishers: Supreme Copyright Ruling Is 'Discouraging.'" *Publishing Perspectives.* Aug. 3.

Apple Inc. 2020. Environmental Progress Report. https://www.apple.com/environment/pdf/Apple_Environmental_Progress_Report_2020.pdf.

Apple Inc. n.d. Public Policy Advocacy. https://www.apple.com/public-policy-advocacy/.

Armstrong, Ann, Joseph Mueller, and Tim Syrett. 2014. "The Smartphone Royalty Stack: Surveying Royalty Demands for the Components within Modern Smartphones." May 29. https://www.ssrn.com/sol3/papers.cfm?abstract_id=2443848.

Arrow, Kenneth. 1962. "Economic Welfare and the Allocation of Resources for Inventions." In *The Rate and Direction of Inventive Activity: Economic and Social Factors*, 609–26. National Bureau of Economic Research.

Associated Press. 2013. "Google Sets Up £52m Fund to Settle French Publishing Row." *The Guardian.* Feb. 1.

Associated Press. 2022. "To Avoid U.S. Extradition, Megaupload Pair Plead Guilty in NZ." *Courthouse News Service.* June 22.

Bai, Jie, and Joel Waldfogel. 2012. "Movie Piracy and Sales Displacement in Two Samples of Chinese Consumers." *Information Economics and Policy* 24: 187–96.

Baldwin, Carliss Y. 2021. "The IBM PC." In *Design Rules*, Vol. 2: *How Technology Shapes Organizations.* https://www.ssrn.com/abstract=3320532.

Barbiarz, Josephe C., and Douglas J. Pisano. 2008. "Overview of FDA and drug development." In *FDA Regulatory Affairs: A Guide for Prescription Drugs, Medical Devices and Biologics*, ed. Douglas J. Pisano and David S. Mantus, 1–32. Routledge.

Barker, George R. 2018. "Global Music Revenues, Music Streaming and the Global Music Value Gap." December 10. https://papers.ssrn.com/sol3/papers.cfm?abstract_id=3340040.

Barker, George R., and Tim Maloney. 2012. "The Impact of Free Music Downloads on the Purchase of Music CDs in Canada." *Review of Economic Research on Copyright Issues* 9: 55–78.

Barlow, John Perry. 1994. "The Economy of Ideas." *Wired.* Mar. 1.

Barnett, Jonathan M. 2010. "The Illusion of the Commons." *Berkeley Technology Law Journal* 25: 1751–1816.

Barnett, Jonathan M. 2011. "The Host's Dilemma: Strategic Forfeiture in Platform Markets for Informational Goods." *Harvard Law Review* 124: 1861–938.

Barnett, Jonathan M. 2013. "Copyright without Creators." *Review of Law & Economics* 9: 389–438.

Barnett, Jonathan M. 2014. "From Patent Thickets to Patent Networks: The Legal Infrastructure of the Digital Economy." *Jurimetrics Journal* 55: 1–53.

Barnett, Jonathan M. 2015. "The Anti-Commons Revisited." *Harvard Journal of Law & Technology* 29: 127–203.

Barnett, Jonathan M. 2016. "Three Quasi-Fallacies in the Conventional Understanding of Intellectual Property." *Journal of Law, Economics & Policy* 12: 1–45.

Barnett, Jonathan M. 2017. "Why Is Everyone Afraid of IP Licensing?" *Harvard Journal of Law & Technology* 30: 123–45.

Barnett, Jonathan M. 2018. "The Costs of Free: Commoditization, Bundling and Concentration." *Journal of Institutional Economics* 14: 1097–120.

Barnett, Jonathan M. 2019. "Antitrust Overreach: Undoing Cooperative Standardization in the Digital Economy." *Michigan Technology Law Review* 25: 163–238.

Barnett, Jonathan M. 2020. "The Long Shadow of the Blackberry Shutdown That Wasn't." Center for the Protection of Intellectual Property. https://cip2.gmu.edu/wp-content/uploads/sites/31/2020/07/Barnett-Long-Shadow-of-the-Blackberry-Shutdown.pdf.

Barnett, Jonathan M. 2021a. *Innovators, Firms, and Markets: The Organizational Logic of Intellectual Property.* Oxford University Press.

Barnett, Jonathan M. 2021b. "The Great Patent Grab." In *The Battle over Patents: History and the Politics of Innovation,* ed. Stephen H. Haber and Naomi Lamoreaux, 208–77. Oxford University Press.

Barnett, Jonathan M. 2022. "The 'License as Tax' Fallacy." *Michigan Technology Law Review* 28: 197–256.

Barnett, Jonathan M. 2023. "Antitrust Mercantilism: The Strategic Devaluation of Intellectual Property Rights in Wireless Markets." *Berkeley Technology Law Journal* 38 (Special Issue): 259–312.

Barnett, Jonathan M. 2024. "'Killer Acquisitions' Reexamined: Economic Hyperbole in the Age of Populist Antitrust." *University of Chicago Business Law Review* 3: 39–108.

Barnett, Jonathan M., and David Kappos. 2023. "Restoring Deterrence: The Case for Enhanced Damages in a No-Injunction Patent System." In *5G and Beyond: Intellectual Property and Competition Policy in the Internet of Things,* ed. Jonathan M. Barnett and Sean M. O'Connor. Cambridge University Press.

Bartz, Diane. 2017. "Apple Sues Qualcomm in Beijing Seeking 1 Billion Yuan." *Reuters.* Jan. 25.

Bartz, Diane, and Stephen Nellis. 2017. "Apple Files $1 Billion Lawsuit against Chip Supplier Qualcomm." *Reuters.* Jan. 20.

Barzel, Yoram. 1997. *Economic Analysis of Property Rights.* 2nd ed. Cambridge University Press.

Battelle, John. 2005. *The Search: How Google and Its Rivals Rewrote the Rules of Business and Transformed Our Culture.* Portfolio.

Baumol, William J. 2005. "Education for Innovation: Entrepreneurial Breakthroughs vs. Corporate Incremental Improvements." National Bureau of Economic Research Working Paper No. 10578.

Bayh, Birch, and Robert Dole. 2002. "Our Law Helps Patients Get New Drugs Sooner." *Washington Post,* Apr. 11.

Bayot, Jennifer. 2005. "Grokster File-Sharing Service Shuts Down in Settlement." *New York Times.* Nov. 7.

Beauchamp, Christopher. 2016. "The First Patent Litigation Explosion." *Yale Law Journal* 125: 848–944.

BBC News. 2012. "Megaupload File-Sharing Site Shut Down." *BBC News.* Mar. 8.

Beebe, Barton. 2008. "An Empirical Study of U.S. Copyright Fair Use Opinions, 1978–2005." *University of Pennsylvania Law Review* 156: 549–624.

Benkler, Yochai. 2004. "Sharing Nicely: On Shareable Goods and the Emergence of Sharing as a Modality of Economic Production." *Yale Law Journal* 114: 273–358.

Benkler, Yochai. 2006. *The Wealth of Networks: How Social Production Transforms Markets and Freedom.* Yale University Press.

Benkler, Yochai. 2011. "Voluntary Payment Models." In *Berkman Center for Internet and Society, Rethinking Music: A Briefing Book,* 27–32. Berkman Center for Internet and Society.

Bessen, James, Jennifer Ford, and Michael J. Meurer. 2011. "The Private and Social Costs of Patent Trolls." *Regulation* 34: 26–35.

Bessen, James, and Michael J. Meurer. 2008. *Patent Failure: How Judges, Bureaucrats, and Lawyers Put Innovators at Risk*. Princeton University Press.

Bessen, James, and Michael J. Meurer. 2014. "The Direct Costs from NPE Disputes." *Cornell Law Review* 99: 387–424.

Bhattacharjee, Sudip, Ram D. Gopal, Kaveepan Lertwachara, and James R. Marsden. 2006. "Impact of Legal Threats on Online Music Sharing Activity: An Analysis of Music Industry Legal Actions." *Journal of Law and Economics* 49: 91–114.

Blumenthal, David, Nancyanne Causino, Eric Campbell, and Karen Seashore Louis. 1996. "Relationships between Academic Institutions and Industry in the Life Sciences: An Industry Survey." *New England Journal of Medicine* 334: 368–734.

Boldrin, Michele, and David K. Levine. 2008. *Against Intellectual Monopoly*. Cambridge University Press.

Bounie, David, Marc Bourreau, and Patrick Waelbroeck. 2006. "Piracy and the Demand for Films: Analysis of Piracy Behavior in French Universities." *Review of Economic Research on Copyright Issues* 3: 15–27.

Borland, John. 2002. "Judge Issues Injunction against Napster." *CNET*. Jan. 2.

Boyle, James D. A. 1988. "The Search for an Author: Shakespeare and the Framers." *American University Law Review* 37: 625–43.

Boyle, James. 2003. "The Second Enclosure Movement and the Construction of the Public Domain." *Law & Contemporary Problems* 66: 33–74.

Boyle, James. 2008. *The Public Domain: Enclosing the Commons of the Mind*. Yale University Press.

Breiner, James. 2016. "The Economics of Accountability Journalism: What Price Is Right?" *International Symposium on Online Journalism*. Apr. 17.

Breyer, Stephen. 1970. "The Uneasy Case for Copyright: A Study of Copyright in Books, Photocopies, and Computer Programs." *Harvard Law Review* 84: 281–351.

Brin, Sergey, and Lawrence Page. 1998. "The Anatomy of a Large-Scale Hypertextual Web Search Engine." *Computer Networks* 30: 107–17.

Brittain, Blake. 2022. "Maryland Ebook Licensing Law Is Unconstitutional, U.S. Court Rules." *Reuters*. June 14.

Brittain, Blake. 2024. "Apple Asks U.S. Appeals Court to Reverse Apple Watch Import Ban." *Reuters*. Apr. 6.

Brown, Campbell. 2019. "Facebook Is Doing More to Support to Local News." *Meta for Media*. Jan. 15. https://www.facebook.com/formedia/blog/facebook-supports-local-news.

Brown, Campbell. 2020. "Facebook Invests Additional $100 Million to Support News Industry during the Coronavirus Crisis." *Meta for Media*. March 30. https://www.facebook.com/journalismproject/coronavirus-update-news-industry-support.

Brown, James R., Gustav Martinsson, and Bruce C. Petersen. 2017. "What Promotes R&D? Comparative Evidence from Around the World." *Research Policy* 46: 447–62.

Buchanan, James M., and Gordon Tullock. 1962. *The Calculus of Consent: Logical Foundations of Constitutional Democracy*. University of Michigan Press.

Burk, Dan L., and Mark A. Lemley. 2009. *The Patent Crisis and How the Courts Can Solve It*. University of Chicago Press.

Cairncross Review: A Sustainable Future for Journalism. 2019. Feb. 12. https://assets.publishing.service.gov.uk/media/5c6bfcd4e5274a72b933311d/021919_DCMS_Cairncross_Review_.pdf.

Capek, Peter G., Steven P. Frank, Steve Gerdt, and David Shields. 2005. "A History of IBM's Open-Source Involvement and Strategy." *IBM Systems Journal* 44: 249–57.

Carley, Michael, Deepak Hegde, and Alan Marco. 2015. "What Is the Probability of Receiving a U.S. Patent?" *Yale Journal of Law & Technology* 17: 203–23.

Carlisle, Madeleine. 2021. "How Google's Big Supreme Court Victory Could Change Software Forever." *Time*. Apr. 6.

Cass, Ronald A., and Keith N. Hylton. 2013. *Laws of Creation: Property Rights in the World of Ideas*. Harvard University Press.

Caulfield, Timothy, Robert M. Cook-Deegan, F. Scott Kieff, and John P. Walsh. 2006. "Evidence and Anecdotes: An Analysis of Human Gene Patenting Controversies." *Nature Biotechnology* 24: 1091–94.

Cave, Martin, Christos Genakos, and Tommaso Valleti. 2019. "The European Framework for Regulating Telecommunications: A 25-Year Appraisal." *Review of Industrial Organization* 55: 47–62.

Central Commission for Cybersecurity and Informatization. 2021. *14th Five-Year Plan for National Informatization*. Dec. 28. Translated in DigiChina. https://digichina.stanford.edu/work/translation-14th-five-year-plan-for-national-informatization-dec-2021/.

Chandler, Alfred D., Jr. 2001. *Inventing the Electronic Century: The Epic Story of the Consumer Electronics and Computer Industries*. Harvard University Press.

Charny, Ben. 2006. "MySpace Starts Rooting Out Pirates." *MarketWatch*. Oct. 30.

Chen, Wenjing. 2022. "The Royalty Rate Is FRAND or Excessive? The Practice in the EU, China, and the Applicability of Selected Economic Models." *U.S.-China Law Review* 19: 267–80.

Cheng, Zhongren. 2022. "The Chinese Supreme Court Affirms Chinese Courts' Jurisdiction over Global Royalty Rates of Standard-Essential Patents: *Sharp v. Oppo*." *Berkeley Technology Law Journal Blog*. Jan. 3.

Chien, Colleen V. 2009. "Of Trolls, Davids, Goliaths, and Kings: Narratives and Evidence in the Litigation of High-Tech Patents." *North Carolina Law Review* 87: 1571–615.

Chien, Colleen V. 2013. "Patent Trolls by the Numbers." Santa Clara University Legal Studies Research Paper No. 08-13. https://papers.ssrn.com/sol3/papers.cfm?abstract_id=2233041.

Chien, Colleen V. 2018. "Comparative Patent Quality." *Arizona State Law Journal* 50: 71–140.

Chien, Colleen V., and Mark A. Lemley. 2012. "Patent Holdup, the ITC, and the Public Interest." *Cornell Law Review* 98: 101–44.

Child, Maxwell L. 2007. "Harvard Professor Argues That Piracy Does Not Effect Sales." *New York Times*. Apr. 5.

Clark, Brian. 2023. "How Much Do Spotify and Other Streaming Services Pay per Stream?" *MusicianWave*. July 26.

Clarke, Robert A. 2003. "U.S. Continuity Law and Its Impact on the Comparative Patenting Rates of the U.S., Japan and the European Patent Office." *Journal of the Patent & Trademark Office Society* 85: 335–49.

Cleland, Scott. 2016. "FCC's AllVid Proposal Is Really the Great Google Ad Grab." *Precursor Blog*. Jan. 29. https://precursorblog.com/?q=content/fcc's-allvid-proposal-really-great-google-ad-grab.

CNET. 2002. "IBM to Spend $1 Billion on Linux in 2001." *CNET*. Jan. 2.

CNNMoney. 2000. "Judge Nixes Napster." *CNNMoney*. July 26.

CNN Wire Staff. 2012. "Lawmakers Withdraw Support of Anti-Piracy Bills after Online Protest." *CNN*. Jan. 19.

Cockburn, Iain M., Scott Stern, and Jack Zausner. 2011. "Finding the Endless Frontier: Lessons from the Life Sciences Innovation System for Energy R&D." In *Accelerating Energy Innovation: Insights from Multiple Sectors*, ed. Rebecca M. Henderson and Richard G. Newell, 113–57. University of Chicago Press, National Bureau of Economic Research.

Cohen, David L. 2019. "The SEP Royalty Stacking Myth—Apple Calls Its Own Bluff." *Kidon IP*. July 22. https://www.kidonip.com/standard-essential-patents/the-sep-royalty-stacking-myth-apple-calls-its-own-bluff/.

Cohen, David L., and Douglas Clark. 2018. "China's Anti-Monopoly Law as a Weapon against Foreigners." *IAM* 51–57. Nov./Dec.

Cohen, Mark. 2013. "Huawei/InterDigital Appeal Affirms Shenzhen Lower Court on Standards Essential Patents." *China IPR*. Oct. 29. https://chinaipr.com/2013/10/29/huaweiinterdigital-appeal-affirms-shenzhen-lower-court-on-standards-essential-patent/.

Cohen, Mark. 2016. "New State Council Decision on Intellectual Property Strategy for China as a Strong IP Economy." *China IPR*. July 24. https://chinaipr.com/2016/07/24/new-state-council-decision-on-intellectual-property-strategy-for-china-as-a-strong-ip-country/.

Cohen, Mark. 2021. "Three SPC Reports Document China's Drive to Increase Its Global Role on IP Adjudication." *China IPR*. May 5. https://www.chinaipr.com/2021/05/05/three-spc-reports-document-chinas-drive-to-increase-its-global-role-on-ip-adjudicatio.

Cohen, Mark. 2022a. Comment on Draft Policy Statement on Licensing Negotiations and Remedies for Standard-Essential Patents Subject to Voluntary F/RAND Commitments. Feb. 3. https://www.regulations.gov/comment/ATR-2021-0001-0118.

Cohen, Mark. 2022b. "The Pushmi-Pullyu of Chinese Anti-Suit Injunctions and Antitrust in SEP Licensing." *China IPR*. July 31. https://www.chinaipr.com/2022/07/31/the-pushmi-pullyu-of-chinese-anti-suit-injunctions-and-antitrust-in-sep-licensing/

Cohen, Mark. 2023. "China's Practice of Anti-Suit Injunctions in SEP Litigation: Transplant or False Friend?" In *5G and Beyond: Intellectual Property and Competition Policy in the Internet of Things*, ed. Jonathan M. Barnett and Sean M. O'Connor, 215–41. Cambridge University Press.

Cohen, Wesley M., Richard R. Nelson, and John P. Walsh. 2000. "Protecting Their Intellectual Assets: Appropriability Conditions and Why U.S. Manufacturing Firms Patent (or Not)." National Bureau of Economic Research Working Paper No. 7552.

Cohen, Wesley M., and John P. Walsh. 2007. "Real Impediments to Academic Biomedical Research." *Innovation Policy and the Economy* 8: 1–30.

Colangelo, Guiseppe, and Valerio Torti. 2023. "Anti-Suit Injunctions and Geopolitics in Transnational SEP Litigation." *European Journal of Legal Studies* 14: 45–84.

Comments of Former Administration Officials on December 6, 2021. "Draft Policy Statement on Licensing Negotiations and Remedies for Standards-Essential Patents Subject to Voluntary F/RAND Commitments." 2022. https://www.ipwatchdog.com/wp-content/uploads/2022/02/Comments-on-Draft-SEP-Policy-Statement-by-Former-Administration-Officials.pdf.

Comments of Former U.S. International Trade Commissioner and Chair Deanna Tanner Okun on the December 6, 2021 Draft Policy Statement on Licensing Negotiations and Remedies for Standards-Essential Patents Subject to Voluntary F/RAND Commitments. 2022. Feb. 7. https://www.regulations.gov/comment/ATR-2021-0001-0149.

Competition & Markets Authority. 2022. *Mobile Ecosystems Market Study*. https://www.gov.uk/cma-cases/mobile-ecosystems-market-study.

Con Díaz, Gerardo. 2019. *Software Rights: How Patent Law Transformed Software Development in America*. Yale University Press.

Congressional Budget Office. 2021. *Research and Development in the Pharmaceutical Industry*. CBO.

Conley, James G., Peter M. Bican, and Holger Ernst. 2013. "Value Articulation: A Framework for the Strategic Management of Intellectual Property." *California Management Review* 55: 102–20.

Contreras, Jorge L. 2019. "The New Extraterritoriality: FRAND Royalties, Anti-Suit Injunctions and the Global Race to the Bottom in Disputes over Standards-Essential Patents." *Boston University Journal of Science & Technology Law* 25: 251–90.

Contreras, Jorge L. 2020. "It's Anti-Suit Injunctions All the Way Down—The Strange New Realities of International Litigation over Standard Essential Patents." *IP Litigator* 26: 1–7 (July/Aug).

Contreras, Jorge L., Thomas F. Cotter, Sang Jo Jong, Brian J. Love, Nicholas Petit, Peter George Picht, Norman V. Siebrasse, Rafal Sikorski, Masabumi Suzuki, and Jacques de Werra. 2019. "The Effect of FRAND Commitments on Patent Remedies." In *Patent Remedies and Complex Products: Toward a Global Consensus*, ed. C. Bradford Biddle, Jorge L. Contreras, Brian J. Love, and Norman V. Siebrasse, 160–201. Cambridge University Press.

Cooke, Chris. 2017. "Google Says We Need More 'Fair Use,' But Ex-RIAA Man Isn't So Sure." *CMU*. Feb. 24.

Corcoran, Elizabeth. 1998. "AOL Closes Deal to Buy Netscape for $4.2 Billion." *Washington Post*, Nov. 25.

Cotropia, Christopher A., Jay P. Kesan, and David L. Schwartz. 2014. "Unpacking Patent Assertion Entities." *Minnesota Law Review* 99: 649–703.

Cotropia, Christopher A., Cecil Quillen, Jr., and Ogden H. Webster. 2013. "Patent Applications and the Performance of the U.S. Patent and Trademark Office." *Federal Circuit Bar Journal* 23: 179–91.

Cotter, Thomas F., Erik Hovenkamp, and Norman Siebrasse. 2019. "Demistifying Patent Holdup." *Washington & Lee Law Review* 76: 1501–65.

Cuban, Mark. 2006. "I Still Think Google Is Crazy:)." *BLOG MAVERICK*. Oct. 9. https://blogm averick.com/2006/10/09/i-still-think-google-is-crazy/.

Danaher, Brett, Samuel Hersh, Michael D. Smith, and Rahul Telang. 2019. "The Effect of Piracy Website Blocking on Consumer Behavior." https://www.ssrn.com/sol3/papers.cfm?abstract _id=2612063.

Danaher, Brett, and Michael D. Smith. 2014. "Gone in 60 Seconds: The Impact of the Megaupload Shutdown on Movie Sales." *International Journal of Industrial Organization* 33: 1–8.

Danaher, Brett, Michael D. Smith, and Rahul Telang. 2014. "Piracy and Copyright Enforcement Mechanisms." In *Innovation Policy and the Economy*, ed. Josh Lerner and Scott Stern, 25–61. Vol. 14. National Bureau of Economic Research. University of Chicago Press.

Davis, Ryan. 2023. "Patent Suits Mostly Stayed Level in 2022, Yet Appeals Fell." *Law360*. Feb. 15.

De Vany, Arthur S., and W. David Walls. 2007. "Estimating the Effects of Movie Piracy on Box-Office Revenue." *Review of Industrial Organization* 30: 291–301.

Dechert LLP. 2015. "A Case Study: How the Record Breaking Antitrust Penalty against Qualcomm Transforms the Landscape of SEPs Licensing in China." Mar. 27. https://www. dechert.com/knowledge/onpoint/2015/3/a-case-study-how-the-record-breaking-antitr ust-penalty-against.html.

Dedrick, Jason, and Kenneth L. Kraemer. 2017. "Intangible Assets and Value Capture in Global Value Chains: The Smartphone Industry." World Intellectual Property Organization. Economic Research Working Paper No. 41.

Dedrick, Jason, Kenneth L. Kraemer, and Greg Linden. 2010. "Who Profits from Innovation in Global Value Chains?: A Study of the iPod and Notebook PCs." *Industrial & Corporate Change* 19: 81–116.

Diehl, Eric. 2012. *Securing Digital Video: Techniques for DRM and Content Protection*. Springer.

DiMasi, Joseph A., Henry G. Grabowski, and Ronald W. Hansen. 2016. "Innovation in the Pharmaceutical Industry: New Estimates of R&D Costs." *Journal of Health Economics* 47: 20–33.

Dippon, Christian M. 2016. "The FCC's Latest Attempt to Promulgate More Regulation in the Multichannel Video Distribution Market Will Ultimately Hinder Innovation, Increase Prices, and Be Detrimental to Consumer Welfare." *NERA Economic Consulting*. https:// www.nera.com/content/dam/nera/publications/2016/PUB_FCC_Regulation_0516.pdf.

Dolgin, Elie. 2021. "The Tangled History of mRNA Vaccines." *Nature* 597: 318–24.

Doody, Patrick A., ed. 2012. "Comprehensive Legislative History of the Leahy-Smith America Invents Act." *Pillsbury Law*. https://www.pillsburylaw.com/images/content/4/0/v2/4067/ AIA-LegislativeHistory-final.pdf.

Dosi, Giovanni, and Joseph Stiglitz. 2014. "The Role of Intellectual Property Rights in the Development Process, with Some Lessons from Developed Countries: An Introduction." In *Intellectual Property Rights: Legal and Economic Challenges for Development*, ed. Mario Cimoli, Giovanni Dosi, Keith E. Maskus, Ruth L. Okediji, Jerome H. Reichman, and Joseph Stiglitz, 1–53. Oxford University Press.

Downs, Anthony. 1957. *An Economic Theory of Democracy*. Cambridge University Press.

Dreyfuss, Rochelle C. 2010. "What the Federal Circuit Can Learn from the Supreme Court-and Vice Versa." *American University Law Review* 59: 787–807.

Dwyer, Colin. 2020. "Publishers Sue Internet Archive for 'Mass Copyright Infringement.'" *NPR*. June 3. https://www.npr.org/2020/06/03/868861704/publishers-sue-internet-arch ive-for-mass-copyright-infringement.

Eadicicco, Lisa. 2015. "The Rise of Android: How a Flailing Startup Became the World's Biggest Computing Platform." *Business Insider*. Mar. 27.

Ebert, Lawrence B. 2004. "Patent Grant Rates at the United States Patent and Trademark Office." *Chicago-Kent Journal of Intellectual Property* 4: 108–16.

Edelman, Ben. 2014. "Secret Ties in Google's 'Open' Android." February 13. https://www.ben edelman.org/news-021314/.

Editorial Board. 2022. "Gigi Sohn's Business Model." *Wall Street Journal*. Jan. 28.

Egan, Edward J., and David J. Teece. 2015. "Untangling the Patent Thicket Literature." Tusher Center for Management of Intellectual Capital Working Paper No. 7.

Eisenberg, Rebecca S. 2008. "Noncompliance, Nonenforcement, Nonproblem? Rethinking the Anticommons in Biomedical Research." *Houston Law Review* 45: 1059–99.

Ekelund, Robert B, Jr., and Robert D. Tollison. 1997. *Politicized Economies: Monarchy, Monopoly, and Mercantilism*. Texas A&M University Press.

Electronic Frontier Foundation. n.d. "The Three-Step Test." https://www.eff.org/files/filen ode/three-step_test_fnl.pdf.

Electronic Frontier Foundation. 2017. *Annual Report*. https://www.eff.org/files/annual-rep ort/2017/index.html.

Elkin-Koren, Niva, and Neil Weinstock Netanel. 2020. "Transplanting Fair Use across the Globe: A Case Study Testing the Credibility of U.S. Opposition." *Hastings Law Journal* 72: 1121–82.

Enis, Matt. 2019. "Better World Libraries, Internet Archive Partner, Acquires Better World Books." *Library Journal*. Dec. 2.

Epstein, Lee, William M. Landes, and Richard A. Posner. 2013. *The Behavior of Federal Judges: A Theoretical and Empirical Study of Rational Choice*. Harvard University Press.

Epstein, Richard A., and Bruce N. Kuhlik. 2004. "Is There a Biomedical Anticommons?" *Regulation* 27: 54–58.

European Commission. 2023. Proposal for a Regulation of the European Parliament and of the Council on Standard-Essential Patents and Amending Regulation (EU)2017/1001. Apr. 27. https://single-market-economy.ec.europa.eu/system/files/2023-04/COM_2023_232_1_E N_ACT_part1_v13.pdf.

European Commission, Competition DG. 2018. Case AT.40099: Google Android. Antitrust Procedure Council Regulation (EC) 1/2003. July 18.

European Parliament. 2019. Questions and Answers on Issues about the Digital Copyright Directive. Mar. 27. https://www.europarl.europa.eu/news/en/press-room/20190111IPR23 225/questions-and-answers-on-issues-about-the-digital-copyright-directive.

European Union. 2022. EU Challenges China at the WTO to Defend Its High-Tech Sector. Feb. 18. https://ec.europa.eu/commission/presscorner/detail/en/ip_22_1103.

Evans, David, Andrei Hagiu, and Richard Schmalensee. 2006. *Invisible Engines: How Software Platforms Drive Innovation and Transform Industries*. MIT Press.

Executive Office of the President. 2013. *Patent Assertion and U.S. Innovation*. June 4. https:// obamawhitehousearchives.gov/sites/default/ files/docs/patent_report.pdf.

Ezell, Stephen J. 2022. "How Japan Squandered Its Biopharmaceutical Competitiveness; A Cautionary Tale." *Information Technology & Innovation Foundation*.

Ezell, Stephen J., and Robert D. Atkinson. 2014. "The Middle Kingdom Galapagos Island Syndrome: The Cul-De-Sac of Chinese Technology Standards." *Information Technology & Innovation Foundation*.

Faulconbridge, Guy. 2019. "The Media Has a Big Problem, Reuters Institute Says: Who Will Pay for the News?" *Reuters*. June 11.

Federal Trade Commission. 2003. *To Promote Innovation: The Proper Balance of Competition and Patent Law and Policy*.

Federal Trade Commission and U.S. Department of Justice. 2007. *Antitrust Enforcement and Intellectual Property Rights: Promoting Innovation and Competition.*

Federal Trade Commission. 2011. *The Evolving IP Marketplace: Aligning Patent Notice and Remedies with Competition.*

Federal Trade Commission. 2016. *Patent Assertion Entity Activity: An FTC Study.*

Federico, Giulio, Fiona Scott Morton, and Carl Shapiro. 2020. "Antitrust and Innovation: Welcoming and Protecting Disruption." In *Innovation Policy and the Economy*, Vol. 20, ed. Josh Lerner and Scott Stern, 125–90. National Bureau of Economic Research.

Feldman, Robin, Thomas Ewing, and Sara Jeruss. 2013. "The AIA 500 Expanded: The Effects of Patent Monetization Entities." *UCLA Journal of Law & Technology* 17: 1–107.

Fink, Martin. 2003. *The Business and Economics of Linux and Open Source.* Prentice Hall PTR.

Fletcher, Richard, and Rasmus Klein Nielsen. 2016. "Paying for Online News: A Comparative Analysis of Six Countries." *Digital Journalism* 5: 1173–91.

Flynn, Kerry. 2021. "BuzzFeed Lays off 70 HuffPost Staffers in Massive 'Restructure' Less than a Month after Acquisition." *CNN.* Mar. 9.

Frakes, Michael D., and Melissa F. Wasserman. 2015. "Does the U.S. Patent and Trademark Office Grant Too Many Bad Patents? Evidence from a Quasi-Experiment." *Stanford Law Review* 67: 613–76.

Frakes, Michael D., and Melissa F. Wasserman. 2019. "Empirical Scholarship on the Prosecution Process at the USPTO." In *Research Handbook on the Economics of Intellectual Property Law*, ed. Ben Depoorter, Peter Menell, and David Schwartz, 77–91. Edward Elgar.

France24. 2021. "Covid-19 Vaccine Firms Pledge 3.5 Billion Doses for Poorer Nations." *France24.* May 21.

Future of Journalism: Hearing before the Senate Comm. of Commerce, Science, and Transportation, Subcommittee on Communications, Technology, and the Internet. 2009. 111th Cong., 1st Sess. May 6.

Galetovic, Alexander, and Kirti Gupta. 2020. "The Case of the Missing Royalty Stack in the World Mobile Wireless Industry." *Industrial and Corporate Change* 29: 827–53.

Galetovic, Alexander, Stephen Haber, and Ross Levine. 2015. "An Empirical Examination of Patent Holdup." *Journal of Competition Law & Economics* 11: 549–78.

Galetovic, Alexander, Stephen Haber, and Lew Zaretzki. 2017. "Is There an Anticommons Tragedy in the World Smartphone Industry?" *Berkeley Technology Law Journal* 32: 1527–58.

Galetovic, Alexander, Stephen Haber, and Lew Zaretzki. 2018. "An Estimate of the Average Cumulative Royalty Yield in the World Mobile Phone Industry: Theory, Measurement, and Results." *Telecommunications Policy* 42: 263–76.

Gannes, Liz. 2015. "Ten Years of Google Maps, from Slashdot to Ground Truth." *Vox.* Feb. 8.

Gao, Jie. 2020. "Development of the FRAND Jurisprudence in China." *Columbia Science & Technology Law Review* 21: 446–88.

Gao, Ping. 2008. "WAPI: A Chinese Attempt to Establish Wireless Standards and the International Coalition that Resisted." *Communication of the Association for Information Systems* 23: 151–62.

Gartner. 2018. "Gartner Says Annual Smartphone Sales Surpassed Sales of Feature Phones for the First Time in 2013." Feb. 13. https://www.gartner.com/en/newsroom/press-relea ses/2014-02-13-gartner-says-annual-smartphone-sales-surpassed-sales-of-feature-pho nes-for-the-first-time-in-2013.

Gaviria, Mario, and Burcu Kilic. 2021. "A Network Analysis of COVID-19 mRNA Vaccine Patents." *Nature Biotechnology* 39: 546–48.

Genentech. 2016. "Cloning Insulin." Apr. 7. https://www.gene.com/stories/cloning-insulin.

Ghaffary, Shirin, Graham Starr, and Brody Ford. 2024. "OpenAI in Talks with CNN, Fox and Time to License Content." *Bloomberg.* Jan. 11.

Gilbert, Annelise. 2023. "Judge Slams Sonos, Rules Patents Invalid in Google Speaker Case." *Bloomberg Law.* Oct. 9.

Ginarte, Juan C., and Walter G. Park. 1997. "Determinants of Patent Rights: A Cross-National Study." *Research Policy* 26: 283–301.

Ginsburg, Douglas, Bruce Kobayashi, and Joshua Wright. 2017. "Comment of the Global Antitrust Institute, Antonin Scalia Law School, George Mason University, on the Anti-Monopoly Commission of the State Council's Anti-Monopoly Guidelines against Abuse of Intellectual Property Rights." George Mason Law & Economics Research Paper No. 17–19.

Ginsburg, Douglas H., and Joshua D. Wright. 2019. "A Bargaining Model v. Reality in *FTC v. Qualcomm*: A Reply to Kattan & Muris." https://papers.ssrn.com/sol3/papers.cfm?abstract_id=3389476.

Glaser, Mark. 2021. "How Philanthropy Became a Growing Revenue Stream for Local News." *Knight Foundation*. Aug. 19. https://knightfoundation.org/articles/how-philanthropy-became-a-growing-revenue-stream-for-local-news/.

Goldman, David. 2011. "Patent Trolls Cost Inventors Half a Trillion Dollars." *CNNMoney*. Sept. 21.

Goldscheider, Robert. 1996. "The Employment of Licensing Expertise in the Arena of Intellectual Property Litigation." *IDEA: The Journal of Law & Technology* 36: 159–201.

Goodman, Amy. 2012. "The Sopa Blackout Protest Makes History." *The Guardian*. Jan. 18.

Google. n.d. "Content Delistings Due to Copyright." *Google Transparency Report*. https://transparencyreport.google.com/copyright/overview?hl=en (last accessed Dec. 31, 2023).

Google. 2010–2021. *U.S. Public Policy: Transparency*. https://www.google.com/publicpolicy/transparency.

Google News Initiative. 2020. *Digital News Innovation Fund Impact Report*. https://newsinitiative.withgoogle.com/dnifund/report/.

Google News Initiative. 2021. *Digital News Innovation Fund Impact Report*. https://newsinitiative.withgoogle.com/dnifund/report/.

Google Transparency Project. 2019. *Google's Media Takeover*. https://www.techtransparencyproject.org/sites/default/files/GTP-Media-Takeover.pdf.

Government Accountability Office. 2013. *Intellectual Property: Assessing Factors That Affect Patent Infringement Litigation Could Help Improve Patent Quality*. https://www.gao.gov/assets/gao-13-465.pdf.

Graham, Stuart J. H., Robert P. Merges, Pamela Samuelson, and Ted M. Sichelman. 2009. "High Technology Entrepreneurs and the Patent System: Results of the 2008 Berkeley Patent Survey." *Berkeley Technology Law Journal* 24: 255–327.

Gray, Joanne E. 2020. *Google Rules: The History and Future of Copyright under the Influence of Google*. Oxford University Press.

Gu, Samuel, Junho Song, Hoil Shin, Jaeho Shin, and Hongsuk Yang. 2020. "Corporate Strategies in the Smartphone Era: The Case of Garmin Ltd." *Journal of Information and Operations Management* 30: 11–19.

Haeussler, Carolin, Dietmar Harhoff, and Elisabeth Mueller. 2014. "How Patenting Informs VC Investors: The Case of Biotechnology." *Research Policy* 43: 1286–98.

Hansell, Saul. 2000. "Not-So-Subtle Engine Drives AOL Profit Forecasts." *New York Times*. Jan. 31.

Healey, Jon. 2001. "Music Subscription Services Singing Different Tunes." *Los Angeles Times*. Dec. 13.

Heller, Michael. 2013. "The Tragedy of the Anticommons: A Concise Introduction and Lexicon." *Modern Law Review* 76: 6–25.

Heller, Michael, and Rebecca S. Eisenberg. 1998. "Can Patents Deter Innovation? The Anticommons in Biomedical Research." *Science* 280: 698–701.

Hennig-Thurau, Thorsten, Victor Henning, and Henrik Sattler. 2007. "Consumer File Sharing of Motion Pictures." *Journal of Marketing* 71: 1–18.

Herman, Bill D. 2012. "A Political History of DRM and Related Copyright Debates, 1987–2012." *Yale Journal of Law & Technology* 14: 162–225.

Herz, Benedikt, and Kamil Kiljanski. 2018. "Movie Piracy and Displaced Sales in Europe: Evidence from Six Countries." *Information Economics and Policy* 43: 12–22.

Hesse, Renata B. 2012. "Remarks as Prepared for the ITU-T Patent Roundtable: Six 'Small' Proposals for SSOs before Lunch." Oct. 10. https://www.justice.gov/atr/file/518951/download.

Hiller, R. Scott. 2016. "Sales Displacement and Streaming Music: Evidence from YouTube." *Information Economics and Policy* 34: 16–26.

Hoffman, Alan N. 2015. "TomTom: New Competition Everywhere!" In *Strategic Management and Business Policy: Globalization, Innovation and Sustainability*, 15th ed., ed. Thomas L. Wheelan, J. David Hunger, Alan N. Hoffman, and Charles E. Bamford, 31-1 to 31-15. Pearson Education.

Hollister, Sean, and Sam Byford. 2022. "Nvidia's Huge Arm Deal Has Just Been Scrapped." *The Verge*. Feb.7. https://www.theverge.com/2022/2/7/22922731/nvidia-no-longer-buying-acquiring-arm-reportedly.

Holte, Ryan T. 2018. "Clarity in Remedies for Patent Cases." *George Mason Law Review* 26: 128–67.

Hong, Seung-Hyun. 2011. "Measuring the Effect of Napster on Recorded Music Sales: Difference-in-Differences Estimates under Compositional Changes." *Journal of Applied Econometrics* 28: 297–324.

Hu, Jim. 2002. "Record Label Signs Deal with Napster." *CNET*. Jan. 11.

Huang, Wei, Fan Zhu, Bei Yin, and Xiumin Ruan. 2022. "A Review of the Development of SEP-Related Disputes in China and Outlook for the Future Trend." *CPI Columns Asia*. Nov. 15.

Hughes, Justin. 2015. "Fair Use and Its Politics—At Home and Abroad." In *Copyright Law in the Age of Exceptions and Limitations*, ed. Ruth L. Okediji, 234–74. Cambridge University Press.

Hui, Kai-Lung, and Ivan Png. 2003. "Piracy and the Legitimate Demand for Recorded Music." *Contributions to Economic Analysis and Policy* 2: art. 11.

Hung, Lisan. 1994. "Supreme Court Holds that Parody May Be a Fair Use under Section 107 of the 1976 Copyright Act." *Santa Clara High Technology Law Journal* 10: 507–18.

IFPI. 2022. *Engaging with Music*. https://www.ifpi.org/wp-content/uploads/2022/11/Engaging-with-Music-2022_full-report-1.pdf.

Ionescu, Daniel. 2009. "Evolution of the MP3 Player." *PCWorld*. Oct. 29.

Jaffe, Adam B., and Josh Lerner. 2004. *Innovation and Its Discontents: How Our Broken Patent System Is Endangering Innovation and Progress, and What to Do about It*. Princeton University Press.

Jeffrey, Don. 1995. "Music-Spending Growth Seen Slowing." *Billboard*. Aug. 26.

Jensen, Paul H., Alfons Palangkaraya, and Elizabeth Webster. 2006. "Disharmony in International Patent Office Decisions." *Federal Circuit Bar Journal* 15: 679–704.

Jeruss, Sara, Robin Feldman, and Joshua Walker. 2012. "The America Invents Act 500: Effects of Patent Monetization Entities on U.S. Litigation." *Duke Law & Technology Review* 11: 357–89.

Jie, Yang. 2022. "Apple Looks to Boost Production Outside China." *Wall Street Journal*. May 21.

Jinbiao, Lin. 2013. "A Battle across the Pacific Ocean: Conclusion of Trial by the Higher People's Court of Guangdong Province of the Case of Anti-Monopoly Dispute between Huawei and IDC Regarding Abuse of Market Dominance." *People's Court News*. Oct. 29.

Jinping, Xi. 2021a. "Stepping Up Intellectual Property Rights Protection to Stimulate Innovative Vigor for Fostering a New Development Dynamic." *Qiushi Journal*. Mar.–Apr. http://en.qstheory.cn/2021-04/30/c_617533.htm.

Jinping, Xi. 2021b. "Comprehensively Strengthen the Protection of Intellectual Property Rights, Stimulate Innovation Vitality, and Promote the Construction of a New Development Pattern." Jan. 31. http://politics.people.com.cn/n1/2021/0131/c1024-32018021.html.

Jones, Dylan. 2008. *iPOD, Therefore I Am*. Bloomsbury.

Kafka, Peter. 2017. "The FCC Won't Force Cable Companies to Unlock Their Set-Top Boxes after All." *Vox*. Jan. 31.

Kafka, Peter. 2023. "RIP, BuzzFeed News. Who's Next?" *Vox.* Apr. 20.

Kamdar, Adi, Daniel Nazer, and Vera Ranieri. 2015. *Defend Innovation: How to Fix Our Broken Patent System.* Electronic Frontier Foundation. https://www.eff.org/files/2015/02/24/eff-defend-innovation_0.pdf.

Kane, Paul. 2012. "SOPA, PIPA Votes to be Delayed in House and Senate." *Washington Post.* Jan. 20.

Kaplan, Deborah Abrams, and Peter Wehrwein. 2021. "The Price Tags on the COVID-19 Vaccines." *Managed Healthcare Executive.* Mar. 15.

Kaplan, Sarah, and Fiona Murray. 2010. "Entrepreneurship and the Construction of Value in Biotechnology." In *Technology and Organization: Essays in Honour of Joan Woodward*, ed. Nelson Phillips, Graham Sewell, and Dorothy Griffiths, 107–47. Emerald Group.

Katznelson, Ron D. 2007. "Bad Science in Search of 'Bad' Patents." *Federal Circuit Bar Journal* 17: 1–30.

Katznelson, Ron D. 2014. "A Century of Patent Litigation in Perspective." https://www.ssrn.com/abstract=2503140.

Katznelson, Ron D. 2016. "The $83 Billion Patent Litigation Fallacy." *Regulation* 39: 14–18.

Kerr, Dara. 2012. "Millions Sign Google's Anti-SOPA Petition." *CNET.* Jan. 18.

Kersten, Alexander, and Gabrielle Athanasia. 2022. "March-In Rights and U.S. Global Competitiveness." Center for Strategic and International Studies. Mar. 24.

Khan, B. Zorina. 2004. "Does Copyright Piracy Pay? The Effects of U.S. International Copyright Laws on the Market for Books, 1790–1920." National Bureau of Economic Research Working Paper No. 10271.

Khan, B. Zorina. 2005. *The Democratization of Invention: Patents and Copyrights in American Economic Development, 1790–1920.* Cambridge University Press.

Kitch, Edmund W. 2003. "Comments on the Tragedy of the Anticommons in Biomedical Research." *Advances in Genetics* 50: 271–73.

Klein, Benjamin. 2001. "The Microsoft Case: What Can a Dominant Firm Do to Defend Its Market Position?" *Journal of Economic Perspectives* 15: 45–62.

Klos, Mathieu. 2022. "One Year since the New German Patent Law, the Injunction Remains the Same." Juve Patent. Aug. 17. https://www.juve-patent.com/legal-commentary/one-year-since-the-new-german-patent-law-the-injunction-remains-the-same/.

Koh, Byungwan, Il-Horn Hann, and Srinivasan Raghunathan. 2019. "Digitization of Music: Consumer Adoption amidst Piracy, Unbundling, and Rebundling." *MIS Quarterly* 43: 25–45.

Kraemer, Kenneth L., Greg Linden, and Jason Dedrick. 2011. "Capturing Value in Global Networks: Apple's iPad and iPhone." https://citeseerx.ist.psu.edu/document?repid=rep1&type=pdf&doi=9cb5262a46e7c9131de43433b7c5f9b65386f8e2.

Kroah-Hartman, Greg, Jonathan Corbet, and Amanda McPherson. 2009. *Linux Kernel Development: How Fast It Is Going, Who Is Doing It, What They Are Doing, and Who Is Sponsoring It: An August 2009 Update.* Linux Foundation.

Krueger, Alan. 2005. "The Economics of Real Superstars: The Market for Rock Concerts in the Material World." *Journal of Labor Economics* 23: 1–30.

Krueger, Anne O. 1974. "The Political Economy of the Rent-Seeking Society." *American Economic Review* 64: 291–303.

Ku, Raymond Shih Ray. 2002. "The Creative Destruction of Copyright: Napster and the New Economics of Digital Technology." *University of Chicago Law Review* 69: 263–324.

Kuhn, Kai-Uwe, Fiona Scott Morton, and Howard Shelanski. 2013. "Standard Setting Organizations Can Help Solve the Standard Essential Patents Licensing Problem." *CPI Antitrust Chronicle.* Mar. 5.

Kyle, Margaret, and Anita McGahan. 2009. "Investments in Pharmaceuticals before and after TRIPS." National Bureau of Economic Research Working Paper No. 15468.

Landau, Michael B. 2000. "Publication, Musical Compositions and the Copyright Act of 1909: Still Crazy after All These Years." *Vanderbilt Journal of Entertainment & Technology Law* 2: 29–51.

Laplante, Phillip A., ed. 2015. *Encyclopedia of Information Systems and Technology.* Vol. I. CRC Press.

Latman, Alan. 1986. *Latman's The Copyright Law*, ed. William E. Patry. 6th ed. Bureau of National Affairs.

Lee, Edward. 2015. "Patent Trolls: Moral Panics, Motions in Limine, and Patent Reform." *Stanford Technology Law Review* 19: 113–49.

Lee, Yimou, and Stephen Nellis. 2018. "Qualcomm Settles Anti-Trust Case with Taiwan Regulator for $93 Million." *Reuters.* Aug. 10.

Leetaru, Kalev. 2008. "Mass Book Digitization: The Deeper Story of Google Books and the Open Content Alliance." *First Monday* 13. https://firstmonday.org/ojs/index.php/fm/article/view/2101.

Lehman, Bruce A. 1995. *Intellectual Property and the National Information Infrastructure: The Report of the Working Group on Intellectual Property Rights.* U.S. Information Infrastructure Task Force.

Lemley, Mark A. 1997. "The Economics of Improvement in Intellectual Property Law." *Texas Las Review* 75: 989–1084.

Lemley, Mark A. 2003. "Patenting Nanotechnology." *Stanford Law Review* 58: 601–30.

Lemley, Mark A. 2007. "Ten Things to Do about Patent Holdup of Standards (and One Not to)." *Boston College Law Review* 48: 149–68.

Lemley, Mark A., and Bhaven Sampat. 2008. "Is the Patent Office a Rubber Stamp?" *Emory Law Journal* 58: 101–28.

Lemley, Mark A., and Carl Shapiro. 2007. "Patent Holdup and Royalty Stacking." *Texas Law Review* 85: 1991–2049.

Lemley, Mark A., and Carl Shapiro. 2013. "A Simple Approach to Setting Reasonable Royalties for Standard-Essential Patents." *Berkeley Technology Law Journal* 28: 1135–66.

Lemley, Mark A., and Carl Shapiro. 2020. "The Role of Antitrust in Preventing Patent Holdup." *University of Pennsylvania Law Review* 168: 2019–60.

Lessig, Lawrence. 2001. *The Future of Ideas: The Fate of the Commons in a Connected World.* Random House.

Lessig, Lawrence. 2004. *Free Culture: How Big Media Uses Technology and the Law to Lock Down Culture and Control Creativity.* Penguin Press.

Letter from Institute for Policy Innovation to Rep. Fred Upton, Chair, Committee on Energy and Commerce. 2016. Mar. 21. https://www.ipi.org/ipi_issues/detail/letter-to-house-committee-leaders-on-the-fccs-allvid-set-top-box-mandate.

Letter from Makan Delrahim, Assistant Attorney General, U.S. Department of Justice, to Sophia A. Muirhead, General Counsel & Chief Compliance Officer. Sept. 10, 2020. https://www.justice.gov/atr/page/file/1315291/download.

Letter from Ralph Oman and Marybeth Peters to The Honorable Chuck Grassley, The Honorable Patrick Leahy, The Honorable Bob Goodlatte, and The Honorable John Conyers. 2016. Nov. 28. https://www.copyrightalliance.org/wp-content/uploads/2016/11/Copyright-Office-letter-and-Enclosure-2.pdf.

Letter from Renata B. Hesse, Acting Assistant Attorney General, U.S. Department of Justice, to Michael A. Lindsay, Esq., Dorsey & Whitney LLP. 2015. Feb. 2. https://www.justice.gov/atr/response-institute-electrical-and-electronics-engineers-incorporated.

Leurdijk, Andra, Mijke Slot, and Ottilie Nieuwenhuis. 2012. *Statistical, Ecosystems and Competitiveness Analysis of the Media and Content Industries: The Newspaper Publishing Industry.* European Commission, JRC Technical Reports.

Leval, Pierre N. 1990. "Toward a Fair Use Standard." *Harvard Law Review* 103: 1105–36.

Levin, Richard C., Alvin K. Klevorick, Richard R. Nelson, and Sidney G. Winter. 1987. "Appropriating the Returns from Industrial Research and Development." *Brookings Papers on Economic Activity: Special Issue on Microeconomics* 3: 783–831.

Levine, Robert. 2011. *Free Ride: How Digital Parasites Are Destroying the Culture Business, and How the Culture Business Can Fight Back.* Doubleday.

Levine, Robert. 2016. "Maria Pallante's Departure from the Copyright Office: What It Means and Why It Matters." *Billboard*. Oct. 25.

Levy, Steven. 2010. *Hackers: Heroes of the Computer Revolution*. O'Reilly Media.

Levy, Steven. 2011. *In the Plex: How Google Thinks, Works, and Shapes Our Lives*. Simon and Schuster.

Li, Abner. 2022. "Final U.S. ITC Ruling Finds That Google Infringed on Sonos Patents, Import Ban Not Likely." *9to5Google*. Jan. 6. https://www.9to5google.com/2022/01/06/google-sonos-itc-final-ruling/.

Liebowitz, Stan J. 2005. "Economists' Topsy-Turvy View of Piracy." *Review of Economic Research on Copyright Issues* 2: 5–17.

Liebowitz, Stan J. 2007. "How Reliable Is the Oberholzer-Gee and Strumpf Paper on File-Sharing?" University of Texas at Dallas Working Paper. http://papers.ssrn.com/sol3/papers.cfm?abstract_id=1014399.

Liebowitz, Stan J. 2008. "Testing File-Sharing's Impact by Examining Record Sales in Cities." *Management Science* 54: 852–59.

Liebowitz, Stan J. 2010. "The Oberholzer-Gee/Strumpf File-Sharing Instrument Fails the Laugh Test." University of Texas at Dallas Working Paper. https://papers.ssrn.com/sol3/papers.cfm?abstract_id=1598037.

Liebowitz, Stan J. 2016a. "Why the Oberholzer-Gee/Strumpf Article on File-Sharing Is Not Credible." *Econ Journal Watch* 13: 373–96.

Liebowitz, Stan J. 2016b. "How Much of the Decline in Sound Recording Sales Is Due to File Sharing?" *Journal of Cultural Economics* 40: 13–28.

Liebowitz, Stan. 2017. "A Replication of Four Quasi-Experiments and Three Facts from 'The Effect of File-Sharing on Record Sales: An Empirical Analysis.'" *Economics: The Open-Access, Open-Assessment E-Journal* 11: 1–21. http//dx.doi.org/10.5018/economics-ejournal.ja.2017-13.

Litman, Jessica D. 2001. *Digital Copyright*. Prometheus Books.

Litman, Jessica. 2006. "The Story of *Sony v. Universal Studios:* Mary Poppins Meets the Boston Strangler." In *Intellectual Property Stories*, ed. Jane C. Ginsburg and Rochelle C. Dreyfuss, 358–94. Foundation Press.

Locke, John. 1690. *Second Treatise of Government*. https://www.gutenberg.org/files/7370/7370-h/7370-h.htm.

Lohr, Steve. 1998. "Spyglass, a Pioneer, Learns Hard Lessons about Microsoft." *New York Times*. Mar. 2.

Loren, Lydia Pallas. 1997. "Redefining the Market Failure Approach to Fair Use in an Era of Copyright Permission Systems." *Journal of Intellectual Property Law* 5: 1–58.

Lunney, Glynn S., Jr. 2008. "On the Continuing Misuse of Event Studies: The Example of Bessen and Meurer." *Journal of Intellectual Property Law* 16: 35–56.

Ma, Liye, Alan L. Montgomery, Param Vir Singh, and Michael D. Smith. 2014. "An Empirical Analysis of the Effect of Pre-Release Movie Piracy on Box Office Revenue." *Information Systems Research* 25: 590–603.

Madison, James. *Federalist Papers,* Nos. 10, 43. 1787–88. In Alexander Hamilton, John Jay, and James Madison, *The Federalist Papers*. https://guides.loc.gov/federalist-papers/full-text.

Mallinson, Keith. 2016. "Don't Fix What Isn't Broken: The Extraordinary Record of Innovation and Success in the Cellular Industry under Existing Licensing Practices." *George Mason Law Review* 23: 967–1006.

Mann, Ronald. 2005. "Do Patents Facilitate Financing in the Software Industry?" *Texas Law Review* 83: 961–1030.

Mansfield, Edwin. 1986. "Patents and Innovation: An Empirical Study." *Management Science* 32: 173–81.

Martin, Carolyn Wimbly. 2020. "Internet Archive's Open Library and Copyright Law: Second Addendum." *Lutzker & Lutzker LLP*. Nov. 19. https://www.lutzker.com/internet-archives-open-library-and-copyright-law-second-addendum.

Martinez, Catalina, and Dominique Guellec. 2004. "Overview of Recent Changes and Comparison of Patent Regimes in the United States, Japan, and Europe." In *Patents, Innovations and Economic Performance: OECD Conference Proceedings*, 125–62.

Matal, Joseph. 2012. "A Guide to the Legislative History of the America Invents Act: Part I of II." *Federal Circuit Bar Journal* 21: 435–513.

Max Planck Inst. For Innovation & Competition, Declaration on Patent Protection: Regulatory Sovereignty under TRIPS. 2014. https://www.mpg.de/8132986/Patent-Declaration.pdf.

Mazzeo, Michael J., Jonathan H. Ashtor, and Samantha Zyontz. 2013. "Do NPEs Matter? Non-Practicing Entities and Patent Litigation Outcomes." *Journal of Competition Law & Economics* 9: 879–904.

McGrath, Dylan. 2018. "Qualcomm Rejects Revised Broadcom Offer." *EETimes*. Feb. 8. https://www.eetimes.com/qualcomm-rejects-revised-broadcom-offer.

McKenzie, Jordi, and W. David Walls. 2016. "File Sharing and Film Revenues: Estimates of Sales Displacement at the Box Office." *B.E. Journal of Economic Analysis and Policy* 16: 25–57.

McManis, Charles R., and Brian Yagi. 2014. "The Bayh-Dole Act and the Anticommons Hypothesis: Round Three." *George Mason Law Review* 21: 1049–91.

Melamed, A. Douglas, and Carl Shapiro. 2018. "How Antitrust Law Can Make FRAND Commitments More Effective." *Yale Law Journal* 127: 2110–41.

Merges, Robert P. 2011. *Justifying Intellectual Property*. Harvard University Press.

Merrill, Stephen A., Richard C. Levin, and Mark B. Myers, eds. 2004. *A Patent System for the 21st Century*. Committee on Intellectual Property Rights in the Knowledge-Based Economy, Board on Science, Technology and Economic Policy, Policy and Global Affairs Division. National Academies Press.

Meta. n.d. *Meta Political Engagement*. https://about.meta.com/facebook-political-engagement/.

Meta. 2020. "Facebook Invests $100 Million to Support News Industry during Coronavirus." *Meta for Media*. Mar. 30. https://www.facebook.com/journalismproject/coronavirus-upd ate-news-industry-support.

Meyer, Robinson. 2015. "After 10 Years, Google Books Is Legal." *The Atlantic*. Oct. 20.

Michel, Norbert J. 2006. "The Impact of Digital File Sharing on the Music Industry: An Empirical Analysis." *Topics in Economic Analysis and Policy* 6 (1): 1–22.

Miller, Gabby. 2023. "Where Did Facebook's Funding for Journalism Really Go?" *Columbia Journalism Review*. Feb. 27 (updated Mar. 10).

Miller, Shawn, et al. 2018. "Who's Suing Us? Decoding Patent Plaintiffs since 2000 with the Stanford NPE Litigation Dataset." *Stanford Technology Law Review* 21: 235–75.

Mitchelstein, Eugenia, Ignacio Siles, and Pablo Boczkowski. 2015. "Online Newspapers." In *The International Encyclopedia of Digital Communications and Society*, ed. R. Mansell et al. John Wiley & Sons.

Mobile Application Distribution Agreement between Motorola, Inc. and Google Inc. 2009. Filed with the Securities & Exchange Commission. May 1. https://www.sec.gov/Archives/ edgar/containers/fix380/1495569/000119312510271362/dex1012.htm.

Mock, Dave. 2005. *The Qualcomm Equation: How a Fledgling Telecom Company Forged a New Path to Big Profits and Market Dominance*. AMACOM.

Morris, Emily Michiko. 2016. "The Irrelevance of Nanotechnology Patents." *Connecticut Law Review* 49: 499–551.

Morton, Fiona Scott, and Carl Shapiro. 2016. "Patent Assertions: Are We Any Closer to Aligning Reward to Contribution?" *Innovation Policy and the Economy* 16: 89–133.

Mossoff, Adam. 2022. "Google's Loss to Sonos Settles It: Big Tech Has an IP Piracy Problem." *TechCrunch*. Jan. 13.

Mueller, Benjamin. 2020. "U.K. Approves Pfizer Coronavirus Vaccine, a First in the West." *New York Times*. Dec. 2.

Mullin, Benjamin, and Katie Robertson. 2023. "BuzzFeed News, Which Dragged Media into the Digital Age, Shuts Down." *New York Times*. Apr. 20.

Murray, Fiona E., Philippe Aghion, Mathias Dewatripont, Julian Kolev, and Scott Stern. 2009. "Of Mice and Academics: Examining the Effect of Openness on Innovation." National Bureau of Economic Research Working Paper No. 14819.

Murray, Fiona, and Scott Stern. 2007. "Do Formal Intellectual Property Rights Hinder the Free Flow of Scientific Knowledge? An Empirical Test of the Anti-Commons Hypothesis." *Journal of Economic Behavior &Organization* 63: 648–87.

Myers, Gary. 1996. *"Trademark Parody: Lessons from the Copyright Decision in* Campbell v. Acuff-Rose Music, Inc." *Law & Contemporary Problems* 59: 181–211.

National Institute of Standards and Technology. 2024. Request for Information Regarding the Draft Interagency Guidance Framework for Considering the Exercise of March-In Rights.

National Institutes of Health, Office of the Director. 1997. Determination in the Case of Petition of CellPro, Inc. Aug. 1. http://web.archive.org/web/20070102183356/http://www.nih.gov/icd/od/foia/cellpro/pdfs/foia_cellpro39.pdf.

National Research Council. 2006. *Reaping the Benefits of Genomic and Proteomic Research: Intellectual Property Rights, Innovation, and Public Health*, ed. Stephen A. Merrill and Anne-Marie Mazza. National Academies Press.

Nebehay, Stephanie, and John Miller. 2021. "Covid-19 Vaccine Makers Should License Technology to Overcome 'Grotesque' Inequity—WHO." *Reuters*. Mar. 22.

Nel, Francois, and Coral Milburn-Curtis. 2020–2021. *World Press Trends*. WAN-IFRA, World Association of News Publishers.

Netanel, Neil Weinstock. 2011. "Making Sense of Fair Use." *Lewis and Clark Law Review* 15: 715–71.

Newman, Nic with Richard Fletcher, Antonis Kalogeropoulos, and Rasmus Kleis Nielsen. 2019. *Reuters Institute Digital News Report 2019*. Reuters Institute, University of Oxford.

Newman, Nic with Richard Fletcher, Craig T. Robertson, Kirsten Eddy, and Rasmus Kleis Nielsen. 2022. *Reuters Institute Digital News Report 2022*. Reuters Institute, University of Oxford.

Newman, Tom. 2024. *How Much Music Streaming Services Pay per Stream in 2023*. RouteNote Blog. May 2. https://routenote.com/blog/how-much-music-streaming-services-pay/.

News & Record. 1990. "Kodak to Pay Polaroid $900 M in Patent Case." *News & Record*. Oct. 13. https://greensboro.com/kodak-to-pay-polaroid-900-m-in-patent-case/article_486b3887-a504-5535-97fa-c52c4db179ed.html.

Nickinson, Phil. 2023. "The 10 Most Popular Streaming Services, Ranked by Subscriber Count." *Digital Trends*. Dec. 13.

Nikolic, Igor. 2022. "Global Standard Essential Patent Litigation: Anti-Suit and Anti-Anti-Suit Injunctions." Working Paper (Robert Schumann Centre for Advanced Studies RSC 2022/10, Florence School of Regulation).

Nimmer, Melville B., and David Nimmer. 2022. *Nimmer on Copyright* (rev. ed.). LexisNexis.

Nordhaus, William. 2004. "Retrospective on the 1970s Productivity Slowdown." National Bureau of Economic Research Working Paper No. 10950.

Noveck, Beth Simone. 2010. *Wiki Government: How Technology Can Make Government Better, Democracy Stronger, and Citizens More Powerful*. Brookings Institution Press.

Nvidia. 2020. *NVIDIA to Acquire Arm for $40 Billion, Creating World's Premier Computing Company for the Age of AI*. Sept. 13. https://nvidianews.nvidia.com/news/nvidia-to-acquire-arm-for-40-billion-creating-worlds-premier-computing-company-for-the-age-of-ai.

O'Brien, Matt. 2023. "ChatGPT-Maker OpenAI Signs Deal to License News Stories." *AP*. July 13.

Oberholzer-Gee, Felix, and Koleman Strumpf. 2004. "The Effect of File-Sharing on Record Sales: An Empirical Analysis." Working Paper. March. https://web.archive.org/web/20080613031108/http://www.unc.edu/~cigar/papers/FileSharing_March2004.pdf.

Oberholzer-Gee, Felix, and Koleman Strumpf. 2005. Brief *Amici Curiae* of Felix Oberholzer-Gee and Koleman Strumpf in Support of Respondents. *Metro-Goldwyn-Mayer Studios, Inc. et al. v. Grokster, Ltd. et al.*, Supreme Court of the United States, No. 04-480. Mar. 1.

Oberholzer-Gee, Felix, and Koleman Strumpf. 2007. "The Effect of File-Sharing on Record Sales: An Empirical Analysis." *Journal of Political Economy* 115: 1–42.

Oberholzer-Gee, Felix, and Koleman Strumpf. 2010. "File Sharing and Copyright." In *Innovation Policy and the Economy*, Vol. 10, ed. Josh Lerner and Scott Stern, 19–55. National Bureau of Economic Research.

Oberholzer-Gee, Felix, and Koleman Strumpf. 2016. "The Effect of File Sharing on Record Sales, Revisited." *Information Economics and Policy* 37: 61–66.

Office of the U.S. Trade Representative. 2021. *Statement from Ambassador Katherine Tai on the COVID-19 TRIPS Waiver.* May 5.

Office of the U.S. Trade Representative. 2022. *Ambassador Tai Requests USITC Investigation of COVID-19 Diagnostics and Therapeutics.* Dec. 16.

Olson, Mancur. 1971. *The Logic of Collective Action: Public Goods and the Theory of Groups.* Harvard University Press.

Oman, Ralph. 2018. "Copyright Software as Copyright Subject Matter: *Oracle v. Google*, Legislative Intent, and the Scope of Rights in Digital Works." *Harvard Journal of Law & Technology* 31: 639–52.

Organisation for Economic Co-operation and Development (OECD). 2004. *Patents and Innovation: Trends and Policy Challenges.*

Ozden, Senem Aydin, and Pooyan Khashabi. 2023. "Patent Remedies and Technology Licensing: Evidence from a Supreme Court Decision." *Strategic Management Journal* 44: 2311–88.

Page, Lawrence, Sergey Brin, Rajeev Motwani, and Terry Winograd. 1999. "The PageRank Citation Ranking: Bringing Order to the Web." Jan. 29. https://web.mit.edu/6.033/2004/wwwdocs/papers/page98pagerank.pdf.

Pallante, Maria A. 2011. "Keynote: Register of Copyrights Maria Pallante @ Summit11." *YouTube*, Dec. 15. https://www.youtube.com/watch?v=KaG3ffkUb8A.

Pallante, Maria A. 2013. "The Next Great Copyright Act." *Columbia Journal of Law and the Arts* 36: 315–44.

Pallante, Maria A. 2014. "Copyright and the Digital Economy: Where to From Here?" *Copyright Reporter: Journal of the Copyright Society of Australia* 32: 6–13.

Pallante, Maria A. 2016. Letter from the Register of Copyrights of the United States to Representatives Blackburn, Butterfield, Collins, and Deutch. Aug. 3. https://www.copyright.gov/laws/hearings/fcc-set-top-box-proposal.pdf.

Pammolli, Fabio, Laura Magazzini, and Massimo Riccaboni. 2011. "The Productivity Crisis in Pharmaceutical R&D." *Nature* 10 (June): 428–38.

Pareles, Jon. 2002. "David Bowie, 21st-Century Entrepreneur." *New York Times.* June 9.

Park, David J. 2007. *Conglomerate Rock: The Music Industry's Quest to Divide Music and Conquer Wallets.* Lexington Books.

Patel, Nilay. 2022. "Inside Sonos' Decision to Sue Google—and How it Won." *The Verge.* Mar. 1.

Patry, William F. 2007–2021. *Patry on Copyright.* Thomson Reuters.

Patry, William F. 2009. *Moral Panics and the Copyright Wars.* Oxford University Press.

Peers, Martin. 2023. "Apple in Talks to License News Content for AI." *The Information.* Dec. 22.

Peltzman, Sam. 1976. "Toward a More General Theory of Regulation." *Journal of Law and Economics* 19: 211–40.

Petherbridge, Lee, and R. Polk Wagner. 2007. "The Federal Circuit and Patentability: An Empirical Assessment of the Law of Obviousness." *Texas Law Review* 85: 2051–110.

Peukert, Christian, Jorg Claussen, and Tobias Kretschmer. 2017. "Piracy and Box Office Movie Revenue: Evidence from Megaupload." *International Journal of Industrial Organization* 52: 188–215.

Pew Research Center. 2014. "Key Indicators in Media & News." *Pew Research Center*, March 26.

Pietz, Martin, and Patrick Waelbroeck. 2004. "The Effect of Internet Piracy on Music Sales: Cross-Section Evidence." *Review of Economic Research on Copyright Issues* 1: 71–79.

Pinsent Masons. 2017. "Apple Files Complaints against Qualcomm in China." Jan. 27. https://www.pinsentmasons.com/out-law/news/apple-files-complaints-against-qualcomm-in-china.

Pisani, Joseph. 2023. "Apple Appeals U.S. Ban That Halted Watch Sales." *Wall Street Journal.* Dec. 26.

Plant, Arnold. 1934. "The Economic Aspects of Copyright in Books." *Economica* 1: 167–95.

Plotkin, Stanley, et al. 2017. "The Complexity and Cost of Vaccine Manufacturing: An Overview." *Vaccine* 35: 4064–71.

Posner, Richard A. 1975. "The Social Costs of Monopoly and Regulation." *Journal of Political Economy* 83: 807–28.

Public Knowledge. 2021. *Annual Giving from Major Supporters & Sponsors.* https://publickn owledge.org/wp-content/uploads/2023/04/2021-Annual-Giving-From-Major-Support ers-and-Sponsors.pdf.

Public Knowledge. 2022. *Funding Sources.* https://publicknowledge.org/sources-of-funding-for-public-knowledge/.

PwC. 2015. "Economic Impacts of the Canadian Educational Sector's Fair Dealing Guidelines." https://www.accesscopyright.ca/media/1106/access_copyright_report.pdf.

PwC. 2016. "Understanding the Costs and Benefits of Introducing a 'Fair Use' Exception." https:// www.screenrights.org/wp-content/uploads/2017/10/PwC_Fair_Dealing_CBA_Final.pdf.

Qian, Yi. 2007. "Do National Patent Laws Stimulate Domestic Innovation in a Global Patenting Environment? A Cross-Country Analysis of Pharmaceutical Patent Protection, 1978–2002." *Review of Economics and Statistics* 89: 436–53.

Quain, John R. 1996. "Nothing but Netscape." *Fast Company.* Oct. 31.

Quillen, Cecil D., Jr., and Ogden H. Webster. 2001. "Continuing Patent Applications and Performance of the U.S. Patent and Trademark Office." *Federal Circuit Bar Journal* 11: 1–21.

Quillen, Cecil D., Jr., and Ogden H. Webster. 2006. "Continuing Patent Applications and Performance of the U.S. Patent and Trademark Office—Updated." *Federal Circuit Bar Journal* 15: 635–77.

Quillen, Cecil D., Jr., Ogden H. Webster, and Richard J. Eichmann. 2002. "Continuing Patent Applications and Performance of the U.S. Patent and Trademark Office—Extended." *Federal Circuit Bar Journal* 12: 35–55.

Radcliffe, Damian. 2021. *50 Ways to Make Media Pay. What's New in Publishing Insight Report.* https://mediamakersmeet.com//50-ways-to-make-media-pay-fully-updated-report-download/.

Rai, Arti K., and Rebecca S. Eisenberg. 2003. "Bayh-Dole Reform and the Progress of Biomedicine." *Law & Contemporary Problems* 66: 289–314.

Randewich, Noel, and Matthew Miller. 2015. "Qualcomm to Pay $975 Million to Resolve China Antitrust Dispute." *Reuters.* Feb. 9.

Raustiala, Kal, and Christopher Sprigman. 2006. "The Piracy Paradox: Innovation and Intellectual Property in Fashion Design." *Virginia Law Review* 92: 1687–777.

Raymond, Eric S. 1999. *The Cathedral & the Bazaar: Musings on Linux and Open Source by an Accidental Revolutionary.* O'Reilly Media.

Red Hat. 2019. "IBM Closes Landmark Acquisition of Red Hat for $34 Billion; Defines Open, Hybrid Cloud Future." *Red Hat.* July 9. https://www.redhat.com/en/about/press-releases/ ibm-closes-landmark-acquisition-red-hat-34-billion-defines-open-hybrid-cloud-future.

Remaly, Ben. 2019. "DOJ Submits Unusual Intervention in FTC's Qualcomm Suit." *Global Competition Review.* July 18.

Report of the United Nations Secretary-General's High-Level Panel on Access to Medicines: Promoting Innovation and Access to Health Technologies. 2016. Sept. 14. https://www.uns gaccessmeds.org/final-report.

Reuters. 2021. "Early Backers of Vaccine Maker BioNTech in $719 Million Payday." *Reuters.* Feb. 4.

Reuters. 2022. "Vaccines Delivered under COVAX Sharing Scheme for Poorer Countries." *Reuters.* Nov. 25.

Rieder, Bernhard, Oscar Coromina, and Ariadna Matamoros-Fernandez. 2020. "Mapping YouTube: A Quantitative Exploration of a Platformed Media System." *First Monday.* https:// www.firstmonday.org/ojs/index.php/fm/article/download/10667/9575.

Ringer, Barbara A. 1974. *The Demonology of Copyright*. R. R. Bowker.

Rob, Rafael, and Joel Waldfogel. 2006. "Piracy on the High Cs: Music Downloading, Sales Displacement, and Social Welfare in a Sample of College Students." *Journal of Law and Economics* 49: 29–62.

Rob, Rafael, and Joel Waldfogel. 2007. "Piracy on the Silver Screen." *Journal of Industrial Economics* 55: 379–95.

Roberts, Jeff John. 2016. "U.S. Copyright Office Is in Turmoil amid a Firing and Lobbying Controversy." *Fortune*. Oct. 27.

Roberts, Jeff John. 2020. "As Libraries Fight for Access to E-books, a New Copyright Champion Emerges." *Fortune*. Nov. 28.

Rosen, Lawrence. 2004. *Open Source Licensing: Software Freedom and Intellectual Property Law*. Prentice Hall PTR.

Rosoff, Matt. 2011. "Worst Miss Ever? Microsoft Tried to Buy Netscape in 1994." *Business Insider*. Oct. 28.

Samuelson, Pamela. 1996. "The Copyright Grab." *Wired*. Jan. 1.

Sanjai, P. R. 2022. "World's Biggest Vaccine Maker Serum Halts Production over Millions of Unused Doses." *Bloomberg*. Apr. 22.

Saul, Derek. 2022. "35 Manufacturers Granted Licenses to Produce Generic Version of Pfizer's COVID Antiviral Pill for Developing Countries." *Forbes*. Mar. 17.

Scherer, Dana A., and Clare Y. Cho. 2022. "Stop the Presses? Newspapers in the Digital Age." *Congressional Research Service*. Jan. 27.

Schiff, Eric. 1971. *Industrialization without National Patents: The Netherlands, 1869–1912; Switzerland, 1850–1907*. Princeton University Press.

Schultz, Mark F. 2020. *The Importance of an Effective and Reliable Patent System to Investment in Critical Technologies*. Alliance for U.S. Startups & Inventors for Jobs.

Schwartz, David L., and Jay P. Kesan. 2014. "Analyzing the Role of Non-Practicing Entities in the Patent System." *Cornell Law Review* 99: 425–56.

Schwartz, John. 2004. "A Heretical View of File Sharing." *New York Times*. Apr. 5.

Seaman, Christopher B. 2016. "Permanent Injunctions in Patent Litigation after eBay: An Empirical Study." *Iowa Law Review* 101: 1949–2019.

Seltzer, Wendy. 2010. "Free Speech Unmoored in Copyright's Safe Harbor: Chilling Effects of the DMCA on the First Amendment." *Harvard Journal of Law & Technology* 24: 171–232.

Seymore, Sean B. 2021. "The Research Patent." *Vanderbilt Law Review* 74: 143–86.

Shah, Suchita, Jim Meyers, Mitch Kirby, and Lu Chen. 2023. *Navigating the Inflation Reduction Act's Impact on Drug Pricing and Innovation*. Boston Consulting Group. Sept. 14.

Shapiro, Carl. 2001. "Navigating the Patent Thicket: Cross Licenses, Patent Pools, and Standard Setting." In *Innovation Policy and the Economy*, ed. Adam B. Jaffe, Josh Lerner, and Scott Stern, 119–50. MIT Press.

Shapiro, Carl, and Mark A. Lemley. 2020. "The Role of Antitrust in Preventing Patent Holdup." *University of Pennsylvania Law Review* 168: 2019–60.

Sherman, Andy. 2018. "Doing Intellectual Property the Dolby Way." *IAM*. Nov. 30.

Shiu, Chester J. 2009. "Of Mice and Men: Why an Anticommons Has Not Emerged in the Biotechnology Realm." *Texas Intellectual Property Law Journal* 71: 413–56.

Sidak, J. Gregory. 2016. "What Aggregate Royalty Do Manufacturers of Mobile Phones Pay to License Standard-Essential Patents?" *Criterion Journal on Innovation* 1: 701–19.

Simler, Benjamin N., and Scott McClelland. 2011. "A Model for Predicting Permanent Injunctions after eBay v. MercExchange." *Bloomberg Law Reports*. https://www.hollandhart.com/files/model_for_predicting_permanent_injunctions_after_eba.pdf.

Simon, Felix M., and Lucas Graves. 2019. "Pay Models for Online News in the U.S. and Europe: 2019 Update." *Reuters Institute for the Study of Journalism*.

Smith, Michael D., and Rahul Telang. 2009. "Competing with Free: The Impact of Movie Broadcasts on DVD Sales and Internet Piracy." *Management Information Systems Quarterly* 33: 321–38.

Sokol, D. Daniel, and Wenton Zheng. 2013. "FRAND in China." *Texas Intellectual Property Law Journal* 22: 71–93.

Solow, Robert M. 1957. "Technological Change and the Aggregate Production Function." *Review of Economics and Statistics* 39: 312–20.

Sorkin, Andrew Ross, and Jeremy W. Peters. 2006. "Google to Acquire YouTube for $1.65 Billion." *New York Times.* Oct. 9.

Stassen, Murray. 2022. "Music Piracy Has Plummeted in the Past 5 Years. But in 2021, It Slowly Started Growing Again." *MusicBusiness Worldwide.* Feb. 3.

Statement of Katherine Oyama, Senior Copyright Policy Counsel, Google Inc. 2014. Section 512 of Title 17: Hearing before the Subcommittee on Courts, Intellectual Property, and the Internet of the House Committee on the Judiciary, 113th Cong., 2d Sess. Mar. 13.

Statement of William J. Abernathy, Prof. of Business Administration, Harvard Univ. Business School. 1981. *Hearings before the Senate Committee on the Budget, Subcommittee on Industrial Growth and Productivity.* 97th Cong., 1st Sess. Jan. 27.

Stigler, George J. 1971. "The Theory of Economic Regulation." *Bell Journal of Economics and Management Science* 2: 3–21.

Stigler, George J. 1980. "Economics or Ethics?" *The Tanner Lectures on Human Values.* Delivered at Harvard University, Apr. 24, 25, and 28. https://tannerlectures.utah.edu/_re sources/documents/a-to-z/s/stigler81.pdf.

Stiglitz, Joseph E. 2007. "Prizes, Not Patents." *Project Syndicate.* Mar. 6.

Stimson, James A., Michael B. Mackuen, and Robert S. Erikson. 1995. "Dynamic Representation." *American Political Science Review* 89: 543–65.

Stohr, Greg. 2021. "Google Wins Oracle Copyright Row at Top Court, Ending Battle (1)." *Bloomberg Law.* Apr. 5.

Sturgeon, Timothy J., and Momoko Kawakami. 2011. "Global Value Chains in the Electronics Industry: Characteristics, Crisis, and Upgrading Opportunities for Firms from Developing Countries." *International Journal of Technological Learning, Innovation and Development* 4: 120–47.

Suchodolski, Jeanne, Suzanne Harrison, and Bowman Heiden. 2020. "Innovation Warfare." *North Carolina Journal of Law & Technology* 22: 175–258.

Tabeta, Shunsuke. 2024. "EV Powerhouse China to Set Own Standards for Automotive Semiconductors." *Nikkei Asia.* Jan. 22.

Taplin, Jonathan. 2017. *Move Fast and Break Things: How Facebook, Google, and Amazon Cornered Culture and Undermined Democracy.* Little Brown.

Tech Transparency Project. 2018. "FTC Tech Hearings Stacked with Google-Funded Speakers." *Tech Transparency Project,* Sept. 12. https://www.techtransparencyproject.org/ articles/ftc-tech-hearings-heavily-feature-google-funded-speakers.

Tech Transparency Project. 2019. "Google's Media Takeover." *Tech Transparency Project,* October 9. https://www.techtransparencyproject.org/articles/googles-media-takeover.

Tech+IP Advisory, LLC. 2022. *4G-5G SEP Landscape—Patents Declared through Dec 31, 2021.* https://www.techip.cc/news/2021-4g-5g-sep-landscape-update.

Teece, David J. 2017. "The 'Tragedy of the Anticommons' Fallacy: A Law and Economics Analysis of Patent Thickets and FRAND Licensing." *Berkeley Technology Law Journal* 32: 1489–525.

Thomas, John R. 2016. "March-In Rights under the Bayh-Dole Act." *Congressional Research Service.* Aug. 22.

Thurrott, Paul. 2022. "Google Is Violating the Sonos ITC Import Ban." *Thurrott.* June 28. https://www.thurrott.com/music-videos/sonos/269432/google-is-violating-the-sonos-itc-import-ban.

Thursby, Jerry G., and Marie C. Thursby. 2011. "Has the Bayh-Dole Act Compromised Basic Research?" *Research Policy* 40: 1077–83.

Tibken, Shara. 2019a. "Qualcomm Wraps up Defense after Expert Rebuts FTC Witness." *CNET.* Jan. 25.

Tibken, Shara. 2019b. "Qualcomm's Not a Monopoly, Japan Decides after Decadelong Investigation." *CNET*. Mar. 15.

Tiernan, Ray. 2017. "Qualcomm: Broadcom Would Throw Licensing to the Wolves, Says Bernstein." *Barron's*, Nov. 17.

Tilley, Aaron. 2023. "When Apple Comes Calling, 'It's the Kiss of Death.'" *Wall Street Journal*. Apr. 20.

Travis, Hannibal. 2016. "The Economics of Book Digitization and the Google Books Litigation." In *Research Handbook on Electronic Commerce Law*, ed. John A. Rothschild, 117–36. Edward Elgar.

Treacy, Pat, and Iva Gobac. 2021. *"Ketian v. Hitachi*: China's First Compulsory License?" *Bristows*, Nov. 25. https://www.bristows.com/news/ketian-v-hitachi-chinas-first-compuls ory-licence/.

Trendacosta, Katharine. 2020. "Reevaluating the DMCA 22 Years Later: Let's Think of the Users." *Electronic Frontier Foundation*. Feb. 12.

Tullock, Gordon. 2005. *The Rent-Seeking Society: The Selected Works of Gordon Tullock*, Vol. 5, ed. Charles Kershaw Rowley. Liberty Fund.

Tushnet, Rebecca. 2015. "Content, Purpose, or Both?" *Washington Law Review* 90: 869–92.

U.S. Chamber of Commerce, International Affairs. 2014. *Competing Interests in China's Competition Law Enforcement: China's Anti-Monopoly Law Application and the Role of Industrial Policy*.

U.S. Congress, House of Representatives. 1998. Report 105-551: *Digital Millennium Copyright Act of 1998*. July 22. 105th Cong., 2d Sess. https://www.congress.gov/105/crpt/hrpt551/ CRPT-105hrpt551.pdf.

U.S. Congress, Senate. 1998. Report 105-190: *Digital Millennium Copyright Act of 1998*. May 11. 105th Cong., 2d Sess. https://www.congress.gov/105/crpt/srpt190/CRPT-105srpt190.pdf.

U.S. Copyright Office. n.d. *A Brief History of Copyright in the United States*. https://copyright. gov/circs/circ1a.html.

U.S. Copyright Office. 2011. *Federal Copyright Protection for Pre-1972 Sound Recordings: A Report of the Register of Copyrights*. Dec.

U.S. Copyright Office. 2020. *Section 512 of Title 17: A Report of the Register of Copyrights*. May.

U.S. Department of Commerce, National Telecommunications and Information Administration and Economics and Statistics Administration. 2013. *Exploring the Digital Nation: Embracing the Mobile Internet*. June.

U.S. Department of Health and Human Services. 2021. *Comprehensive Plan for Addressing High Drug Prices: A Report in Response to the Executive Order on Competition in the American Economy*.

U.S. Department of Health and Human Services. 2023. "HHS and DOC Announce Plan to Review March-In Authority." Mar. 21.

U.S. Department of Justice. 2017. "Assistant Attorney General Makan Delrahim Delivers Remarks at the USC Gould School of Law's Center for Transnational Law and Business Conference." Nov. 10.

U.S. Department of Justice. 2019. "Department of Justice, United States Patent and Trademark Office, and National Institute of Standards and Technology Announce Joint Policy Statement on Remedies for Standard-Essential Patents." Dec. 19.

U.S. Department of Justice. 2020. "Assistant Attorney General Makan Delrahim Delivers Remarks at the LeadershIP Virtual Series." Sept. 10.

U.S. Department of Justice. 2021. "Public Comments Welcome on Draft Policy Statement on Licensing Negotiations and Remedies for Standards-Essential Patents Subject to F/RAND Commitments." Dec. 6.

U.S. Department of Justice. 2022. "Justice Department, U.S. Patent and Trademark Office and National Institute of Standards and Technology Withdraw 2019 Standards-Essential Patents (SEP) Policy Statement." June 8. https://www.justice.gov/opa/pr/justice-department-us-pat ent-and-trademark-office-and-national-institute-standards-and.

U.S. Department of Justice and U.S. Patent & Trademark Office. 2013. *Policy Statement on Remedies for Standard-Essential Patents Subject to Voluntary F/RAND Commitments.* Jan. 8. https://www.justice.gov/atr/page/file/1118381/download.

U.S. International Trade Commission. 2011. *China: Effects of Intellectual Property Infringement and Indigenous Innovation Policies on the U.S. Economy.* Inv. No. 332–519, USITC Pub. 4266.

U.S. International Trade Commission. 2022. Notice of Issuance of a Final Determination Finding a Violation of Section 337. In the Matter of Certain Audio Players and Controllers, Components Thereof, and Products Containing the Same. Investigation No. 337-TA-1191. Jan. 6.

U.S. International Trade Commission. 2023. COVID-19 Diagnostics and Therapeutics: Supply, Demand, and TRIPS Agreement Flexibilities. Publication No. 5469. Investigation No. 332–596. Oct.

U.S. Patent and Trademark Office. 2016. "Intellectual Property and the U.S. Economy: 2016 Update."

U.S. Patent and Trademark Office. 2017. "Chat with the Chief: An Analysis of Multiple Petitions in AIA Trials." Oct. 24.

U.S. Patent and Trademark Office. 2020. "Boardside Chat: New Developments." June 11.

U.S. Patent and Trademark Office. 2021. "PTAB Trial Statistics FY21 Q1 Outcome Roundup IPR, PGR, CBM: Patent Trial and Appeal Board Fiscal Year 2021."

U.S. Patent and Trademark Office. 2022a. "PTAB Trial Statistics: FY22 End of Year Outcome Roundup IPR, PGR."

U.S. Patent and Trademark Office. 2022b. "Patent Trial and Appeals Board Parallel Litigation Study."

Umemura, Maki. 2008. "Unrealised Potential: Japan's Post-War Pharmaceutical Industry, 1945–2005." Thesis submitted to the Dept. of Econ. History, London School of Economics. https://etheses.lse.ac.uk/2172/1/U613404.pdf.

Unified Patents. 2013–2023. *Patent Dispute Report.* Annual reports available at https://www.unifiedpatents.com.

Unified Patents. 2024. *Patent Dispute Report: 2023 in Review.* Jan. 8. https://www.unifiedpatents.com/insights/2024/1/8/patent-dispute-report-2023-in-review.

Urban, Jennifer M., and Laura Quilter. 2006. "Efficient Process or Chilling Effects: Takedown Notices under Section 512 of the Digital Millennium Copyright Act." *Santa Clara High Technology Law Journal* 22: 621–93.

Usselman, Steven W. 1991. "Patents Purloined: Railroads, Inventors, and the Diffusion of Innovation in Nineteenth-Century America." *Technology and Culture* 32: 1047–75.

Usselman, Steven W. 1999. "Patents, Engineering Professionals, and the Pipelines of Innovation: The Internalization of Technical Discovery by Nineteenth-Century American Railroads." In *Learning by Doing in Markets, Firms, and Countries,* ed. Naomi R. Lamoreaux, Daniel M. G. Raff, and Peter Temin, 61–102. University of Chicago Press.

Usselman, Steven W. 2002. *Regulating Railroad Innovation: Business, Technology, and Politics in America, 1840–1920.* Cambridge University Press.

Vaidhyanathan, Siva. 2001. *Copyrights and Copywrongs: The Rise of Intellectual Property and How It Threatens Creativity.* New York University Press.

Vidal, Katherine K. 2022. Memorandum: Interim Procedure for Discretionary Denials in AIA Post-Grant Proceedings with Parallel District Court Litigation. U.S. Patent & Trademark Office. June 21. https://s3-us-west-1.amazonaws.com/ptab-filings%2FIPR2022-01293%2F1019.

Waldfogel, Joel. 2010. "Music File Sharing and Sales Displacement in the iTunes Era." *Information Economics and Policy* 22: 306–14.

Waldfogel, Joel. 2011. "Bye, Bye, Miss American Pie? The Supply of New Recorded Music Since Napster." National Bureau of Economic Research Working Paper No. 16882.

Wallack, Todd. 1998. "Netscape Taken Down a Peg." *Network World.* Apr. 20.

Walsh, John P., Ashish Arora, and Wesley M. Cohen. 2003. "Effects of Research Tools Patents and Licensing on Biomedical Innovation." In *Patents in the Knowledge-Based Economy*, ed. Wesley M. Cohen and Stephen A. Merrill, 285–340. National Research Council.

Walsh, John P., Charlene Cho, and Wesley M. Cohen. 2005. "View from the Bench: Patents and Material Transfers." *Science* 309: 2002–3.

Walsh, John P., Wesley M. Cohen, and Charlene Cho. 2007. "Where Excludability Matters: Material Versus Intellectual Property in Academic Biomedical Research." *Research Policy* 36: 1184–203.

Washenko, Anna. 2015. "RIAA and BPI Have Submitted 200 Million URLs for Google Takedowns." *Rain News*. May 11. https://rainnews.com/riaa-and-bpi-have-submitted-200-million-urls-for-google-takedowns/.

Weiss, Todd R. 2000. "MP3.com Ordered to Pay $53.4 Million in Digital Copyright Case." *Computerworld*. Nov. 15.

West, Joel, and Jason Dedrick. 2001 (Summer). "Open Source Standardization: The Rise of Linux in the Network Era." *Knowledge, Technology & Policy* 14: 88–112.

White House. 2013. "White House Task Force on High-Tech Patent Issues." June 4. https://www.obamawhitehouse.archives.gov/the-press-office/2013/06/04/fact-sheet-white-house-task-force-high-tech-patent-issues.

White House. 2021. Executive Order on Promoting Competition in the American Economy. July 9. https://www.whitehouse.gov/briefing-room/presidential-actions/2021/07/09/ executive-order-on-promoting-competition-in-the-american-economy/.

Williams, Pamela Hawkins, Dotcy Isom, III, and Tiffini D. Smith-Peaches. 2003. "A Profile of Dolby Laboratories: An Effective Model for Leveraging Intellectual Property." *Northwestern Journal of Technology and Intellectual Property* 2: 81–98.

Windrum, Paul. 2004. "Leveraging Technological Externalities in Complex Technologies: Microsoft's Exploitation of Standards in the Browser Wars." *Research Policy* 33: 385–94.

Wingrove, Patrick. 2022. "PTAB Top Petitioners, Patent Owners and Law Firms in 2021." *Managing IP*. Feb. 28.

Wininger, Aaron. 2020. "China Releases Antitrust Guidelines for Intellectual Property." *China IP Law Update*. Sept. 28.

Wininger, Aaron. 2021. "China's Supreme People's Court Affirms Right to Set Royalty Rates Worldwide in OPPO/Sharp Standard Essential Patent Case." *China IP Law Update*. Sept. 5.

Wolfe, Jan. 2020. "Apple, Google Team Up to Sue Patent Office over 'Invalid' Policy Change." *Reuters*. Aug. 31.

Wong-Ervin, Koren W. 2014. "Standard-Essential Patents: The International Landscape." *ABA Section of Antitrust Law, Intellectual Property Committee*.

Wong-Ervin, Koren W. 2017. "An Update on the Most Recent Version of China's Anti-Monopoly Guidelines on the Abuse of Intellectual Property Rights." *CPI Asia Column*. May.

Woo, Stu, and Daniel Michaels. 2023. "China's Newest Weapon to Nab Western Technology—Its Courts." *Wall Street Journal*. Feb. 20.

Woodmansee, Martha. 1984. "The Genius and the Copyright: Economic and Legal Conditions of the Emergence of the 'Author.'" *Eighteenth-Century Studies* 17: 425–48.

World Trade Organization. 2020. *Waiver from Certain Provisions of the TRIPS Agreement for the Prevention, Containment and Treatment of COVID-19: Communication from India and South Africa*. Council for Trade-Related Aspects of Intellectual Property Rights. Oct. 2.

Wortham, Jenna, and Miguel Helft. 2009. "Hurting Rivals, Google Unveils Free Phone GPS." *New York Times*. Oct. 28.

Xie, Iris, and Krystyna K. Matusiak. 2015. *Discover Digital Libraries: Theory and Practice*. Elsevier.

Xuewen, Ke, and Lu Ming, eds. 2021. "By the Establishment of Intellectual Property Courts and Quick Trial of Technical Cases Involving 'Bottlenecks,' the Hubei Courts Have Organized an Intellectual Property Network." *Hubei Daily*. Oct. 27.

Yager, Loren. 2010. *Intellectual Property: Observations on Efforts to Quantify the Economic Effects of Counterfeit and Pirated Goods.* U.S. Government Accountability Office.

Yang, Heekyong. 2019. "Qualcomm to Appeal Record South Korean Anti-Trust Fine." *Reuters.* Dec. 3.

Yasiejko, Christopher. 2023. "Sonos Beats Google Attempt to Block U.S. Imports of Smart Speakers." *Bloomberg Law.* Dec. 14.

Yasiejko, Christopher. 2024. "Apple Fights to Block Masimo's New Watch on Heels of Import Ban." *Bloomberg Law.* Jan. 23.

Yiu, Christine, and Richard Vary. 2018. "Shenzhen Court Issues Written Judgment in Huawei v. Samsung Case." *Bird & Bird.* Mar. 25. https://www.twobirds.com/en/insights/2018/global/shenzhen-court-issues-written-judgment-in-huawei-v-samsung-case.

YouTube. 2021. Copyright Transparency Report (July 1, 2021–Dec. 31, 2021). Available at https://transparencyreport.google.com/report-downloads.

YouTube. 2022. Copyright Transparency Report (July 1, 2022–Dec. 31, 2022). Available at https://transparencyreport.google.com/report-downloads.

Yu, Peter K., Jorge L. Contreras, and Yu Yang. 2022. "Transplanting Anti-Suit Injunctions." *American University Law Review* 71: 1537–1618.

Zentner, Alejandro. 2006. "Measuring the Effect of File Sharing on Music Purchases." *Journal of Law and Economics* 49: 63–90.

Ziedonis, Rosemarie H. 2008. "On the Apparent Failure of Patents: A Response to Bessen and Meurer." *Academy of Management Perspectives* 22: 21–29.

Zimmerman, Diane Leenheer. 2011. "Copyrights as Incentives: Did We Just Imagine That?" *Theoretical Inquiries in Law* 12: 29–58.

Zingg, Raphael, and Marius Fischer. 2018. "The Nanotechnology Patent Thicket." *Journal of Nanoparticle Research* 20: 1–6.

Index

For the benefit of digital users, indexed terms that span two pages (e.g., 52–53) may, on occasion, appear on only one of those pages.

Tables are indicated by an italic *t* following the page number.

Singular terms are understood to include use of the plural and other derivative forms.